DEVELOPING HELPING SKILLS

DEVELOPING HELPING SKILLS

A Step-by-Step Approach to Competency

SECOND EDITION

Valerie Nash Chang
Indiana University

Sheryn T. Scott
Azusa Pacific University

Carol L. Decker
Indiana University

BROOKS/COLE
CENGAGE Learning·

Australia • Brazil • Japan • Korea • Mexico • Singapore • Spain • United Kingdom • United States

BROOKS/COLE
CENGAGE Learning·

Developing Helping Skills:
A Step-by-Step Approach to Competency,
Second Edition
Valerie Chang, Sheryn Scott, Carol Decker

Acquisitions Editor: Seth Dobrin

Assistant Editor: Naomi Dreyer

Editorial Assistant: Suzanna Kincaid

Media Editor: Elizabeth Momb

Marketing Program Manager: Tami Strang

Design and Production Services: PreMediaGlobal

Manufacturing Planner: Judy Inouye

Rights Acquisition Specialist: Thomas McDonough

Cover Image: © Dariusz Gudowicz/ Shutterstock

Compositor: PreMediaGlobal

For product information and technology assistance, contact us at **Cengage Learning Customer & Sales Support, 1-800-354-9706.**

For permission to use material from this text or product, submit all requests online at **www.cengage.com/permissions**. Further permissions questions can be emailed to **permissionrequest@cengage.com**.

Library of Congress Control Number: 2011941995

ISBN-13: 978-0-8400-2867-9

ISBN-10: 0-8400-2867-9

Brooks/Cole
20 Davis Drive
Belmont, CA 94002-3098
USA

Cengage Learning is a leading provider of customized learning solutions with office locations around the globe, including Singapore, the United Kingdom, Australia, Mexico, Brazil, and Japan. Locate your local office at **www.cengage.com/global**.

Cengage Learning products are represented in Canada by Nelson Education, Ltd.

To learn more about Brooks/Cole visit **www.cengage.com/brookscole**.

Purchase any of our products at your local college store or at our preferred online store **www.cengagebrain.com**.

Printed in the United States of America
3 4 5 6 7 16 15 14

To our clients, our students, our colleagues, our families, and our friends;
we have learned so much from each of you.

CONTENTS

CONTRIBUTING AUTHORS

Chapter 1, Importance of Self-Understanding

Influence of Culture, Race, and Ethnicity — Alice Fok-Trela

Influence of Gender — Co-written by Kathy Lay

Influence of Sexual Orientation — Kathy Lay

Influence of Socioeconomic Status — Carolyn Gentle-Genitty

Influence of Spirituality and Religion — Sabrina Williamson Sullenberger

Influence of Family of Origin — Co-written by Kathy Lay

Influence of Life Stages — Carolyn Gentle-Genitty

Influence of Disability and Ability — Stephan Viehweg

Chapter 2, Ways of Understanding and Perceiving Self and Others

Case Study: Hector and His Family — Thomas L. Moore

The Resilience Perspective — Mulunesh Abebe Alebachew

The Dual Perspective — Carol Hostetter

Chapter 3, Values, Ethics, and Legal Obligations

Legal Obligations — Heather A. McCabe

Cases in the Instructor's Manual

Bill: Are you saying she's going to die?	Susan Charlesworth
John: Where do I fit in?	Phyllis Shea
Buddy comes home.	Sabrina Williamson
The 10th Street community comes together.	Carolyn Gentle-Genitty
Tony: I want to live at home.	Sabrina Williamson

PREFACE

Considerable information is available regarding techniques for working with specific systems such as individuals, organizations, families, or groups. Few texts explore the overarching skills, knowledge, and processes that are essential to working with any of these systems. This text is designed to fill that gap by focusing on skills that are used in working with systems of all sizes. Our premise is that beginning practitioners need to develop self-understanding, knowledge of ethical principles and professional relationships, and mastery of foundational practice information. Competency in the use of self and basic professional tasks and skills is essential before moving to advanced approaches or system-specific knowledge and skills. This book focuses on the practice behaviors and competencies that have been identified as important in the major helping professions.

The book is organized into five sections: I. Foundation; II. Building Relationships; III. Exploring and Assessing with Clients; IV. Defining the Focus; and V. Doing, Evaluating, and Ending the Work. Each section includes several chapters. Each chapter is an essential building block in the development of competent beginning level practice.

- The Foundation section includes chapters covering the information and tasks that must be mastered before beginning to see clients. These building blocks include the importance of self-understanding, major ways of perceiving self and others, values, ethics and legal obligations, and professional relationships and roles.
- The chapters in Sections II through V describe skills and qualities used by practitioners and strengths and resources contributed by clients. Each of these chapters provides ample opportunities for students to use practice skills.
  - Section II, Building Professional Relationships, includes chapters on developing working relationships, basic interpersonal skills, opening and closing a meeting, and expressing understanding.

- Section III, Exploring and Assessing with Clients, includes chapters on gaining further information, developing deeper understanding, and assessing readiness and motivation.
- Section IV, Defining the Focus, includes chapters on identifying challenges and establishing goals.
- Section V, Doing, Evaluating, and Ending the Work, includes chapters on taking action, evaluating progress, and ending.

NEW IN THIS EDITION

- In each chapter
  - New, revised, and updated information
  - A focus on competencies from the educational standards is included in each chapter
  - Key terms are highlighted, defined, and included in the new Glossary
- Additions
  - A chapter on Values, Ethics, and Legal Obligations
  - A chapter on Professionalism and Professional Relationships
  - New sections on the influence of socio-economic status, life stages, and disability in Chapter 1
  - A case with questions related to each of the perspectives in Chapter 2
  - A new section on the family systems perspective in Chapter 2
  - A new modified problem-based case in Chapters 7 through 15
  - References to specific parts of the DVD that provide examples of using the skills discussed in the chapters and questions related to each section of the DVD
  - A discussion of assessing readiness to change using social cognitive theory in Chapter 11
  - Discussion of ways to monitor the client–practitioner relationship and progress on goals in Chapter 13
  - An expanded Instructor's Manual and Student Website

COMPETENCIES FROM THE EDUCATIONAL STANDARDS IN THE TEXTBOOK

Major competencies covered in the book	Social work	Professional psychology at the begin practicum level	Counseling	Human services	Location in book by chapter
Professional identity	2.1.1	Professional demeanor & professional relationships	Professional orientation and ethical practice	Values & attitudes #18	4
Self-development	Not specifically listed in social work	Knowledge of self-boundaries & affect in developing relationships		Self-development #19	1

COMPETENCIES FROM THE EDUCATIONAL STANDARDS IN THE TEXTBOOK (CONTINUED)

Major competencies covered in the book	Social work	Professional psychology at the begin practicum level	Counseling	Human services	Location in book by chapter
Ethics	2.1.2	Ethics	Professional orientation and ethical practice	Values & attitudes #18	3
Apply critical thinking	2.1.3	Implicit in applying theory & interventions			7, 10 & 11, 13–15
Diversity	2.1.4	Diversity & cultural adaptability	Social & cultural diversity		1 & throughout in examples & in cases
Advance human rights, social & economic justice	2.1.5	Professional orientation and ethical practice			1–4
Research informed practice	2.1.6	Knowledge of the sources & utility of scientific literature			15
Apply human behavior & social environment knowledge	2.1.7	Human growth & development	Human growth & development	Knowledge & theories of human systems of all sizes # 12	2 & 6–15
Conditions that promote or inhibit human growth		Importance of relational skills in clinical relationship		Conditions that promote or inhibit human growth #13	1 & 2
Policy practice	2.1.8	Advocacy training			Not covered
Respond to context	2.1.9	Knowledge of how different worldviews impact relationships			Not covered
Engage, assess, intervene, & evaluate	2.1.10	Interviewing & relationships; Interpersonal communication	Counseling, prevention, & intervention	Direct practice & appropriate intervention # 16 Interpersonal communication #17	6–15
Helping relationships	Not specifically listed in social work	Assumed in interventions & relationships	Helping relationships		4 & 5

(continued)

COMPETENCIES FROM THE EDUCATIONAL STANDARDS IN THE TEXTBOOK (*CONTINUED*)

Major competencies covered in the book	Social work	Professional psychology at the begin practicum level	Counseling	Human services	Location in book by chapter
Engagement	2.1.10a	Intervention planning & developing relationships	See general item above	See general item above	6–8 & 13
Assessment	2.1.10b	Assessment	See general item above	See general item above	12, 13, & 14
Interventions	2.1.10c	Intervention implementation	See general item above	See general item above	14 & 15
Evaluation	2.1.10d	Intervention evaluation	See general item above	See general item above	15
Group work	Not specifically listed in social work	Not specifically listed in psychology	Group work		6–15
Research & program evaluation	Not specifically listed in social work	Under research competency	Research & program evaluation		Not covered
Information management	Not specifically listed in social work	Not specifically listed in psychology		Information management #14	Not covered

STUDENT WEBSITE

Cengage Learning's CourseMate brings course concepts to life with interactive learning, study, and exam preparation tools that support the printed textbook. Access an integrated eBook and learning tools including expected competencies, quizzes, videos and case studies with related questions, and more in your CourseMate, accessed through CengageBrain.com.

INSTRUCTOR'S MANUAL

The *Instructor's Manual* includes additional suggestions for enhancing student learning, tips for creating effective student groups, information related to the DVD, and test question for each chapter. For each chapter there are resources including: an overview, outline, power point presentation, list of key terms, practice exercise guidelines, appropriate case section and questions, related DVD sections with transcripts and discussion questions. Access the *Instructor's Manual* by going to login.cengage.com and either signing in to your account or creating a new account. To create a new account select "Create a new Faculty Account" and follow the prompts.

A FEW WORDS ABOUT LANGUAGE

Although we believe that there are no right ways to deal with the challenges of language, we value clarity. Therefore, we will explain the language decisions that we have made. We have chosen to use the word *practitioner* to refer to helping professionals from all backgrounds (e.g., counseling, psychology, social work, pastoral care, nursing, marriage and family therapy, and so on). We use gender-specific pronouns when appropriate, but otherwise use *he/she* or *his/her*. When referring to clients who may be individuals, families, groups, or organizations, we specify a particular system size if that designation is needed; otherwise we use the word *client* to refer to the many system sizes. We use the word *group* to refer to a task group (people working on a project), a support group (people whose goal is to support and encourage each other), and a counseling group (people who are helping each other to make life changes). We use the word *meeting* to refer to any engagement between a practitioner and client, including individual, family, couple sessions, group meetings, and meetings with organizations. Finally, we have chosen to use the word *counseling* when referring to the many activities engaged in by practitioners when working to facilitate change with individuals, families, and groups.

ACKNOWLEDGMENTS

We want to thank all of those who have contributed to our work: clients, students, teachers, and colleagues at Indiana University School of Social Work and Azusa Pacific University, Department of Graduate Psychology, our families, our friends, the reviewers, editors, and all of the many other people who have contributed to this project.

We are grateful to all of the staff at Cengage Learning who helped and encouraged us at each step of the process related to the first edition. Lisa Gebo, our first editor, suggested that we write a practice book that would meet the needs of several disciplines. Her suggestions and ideas helped us through the beginning phases of creating the plans for the book. Alma Dea Michelena, the next editor, met with us and facilitated thinking through the plans for the DVD. Our last editor was Seth Dobrin. His high standards, patience, good ideas, and wonderful support were essential to the completion of the book. Tangelique Williams, Development Editor, certainly deserves her title. She helped us develop every part of the book. There have been many others at Cengage who have provided support along the way, including Tracy Stuart, Senior Custom Editor, who has been very patient and helpful in creating custom editions of the book; Marcus Boggs, Publisher; Julie Aquilar, Technology Project Manager; and Stephanie Rue, Assistant Editor. Aaron Downey, Project Editor at Matrix Productions, was terrific to work with during the production phase of this project. Janet Tilden, Copy Editor, has done a wonderful job of improving every page of this text.

We appreciate the work of all the people who helped with the production of the DVD. Our Production Director, Steve Stiles, and his production staff were wonderful. Thanks to Bob Decker who provided the "settings" for our DVD.

Of course, the film could not have been made without the participation of the volunteers who were in the film, including Misha Bennett, Karen Butterworth, Rochelle Cohen, Barbara Furlow, Carolyn Gentle-Genitty, Eddie Johnson, Jeremy Johnson, Joseph Johnson, Nicholas Johnson, Gina Kammerer, Lisa Lewis, Christy Meyer, and Justine Sherwood. For reasons of confidentiality, actual clients were not used; however, the individuals in the DVD were playing the roles of real clients that we know. None of the roles were scripted. The practitioners were responding to the challenges presented.

We have been fortunate to have many other Cengage professionals helping us with this second edition. Seth Dobrin is, in our opinion, the very best and easiest to work with editor. He has helped us through each step of the process of creating this edition. His ideas related to all the major decisions have been invaluable. We are fortunate to have been guided and helped by Mia Dreyer, Project Manager, who was involved with all aspects of this project; Alicia McLaughlin, Assistant Editor, who was particularly helpful with the Student Workbook; Elizabeth Momb, Associate Media Editor, who made putting a student website together easy; Lisa Thomas, Copy Editor, who did an excellent and very thorough review of the text-book; and Katy Gabel, Content Project Manager, who has been very patient and supportive as we have worked through the final aspects of this project. The many reviewers of this edition have been excellent. They read the material carefully and gave us excellent, thoughtful, detailed suggestions about ways to improve the book.

This book would not have been written if we had not had the opportunity to work with many clients and students. From our clients we learned about what really is effective. From our students we learned what methods of teaching they find most helpful in their journey to becoming competent practitioners.

We have been fortunate to have the assistance of many contributing authors, including Alice Fok-Trela, Kathy Lay, Carolyn Gentle-Genitty, Sabrina Williamson Sullenberger, Mulunesh Abebe Alebachew, Heather A. McCabe, Carol Hostetter, Stephan Viehweg, Thomas L. Moore, Lynne Fisher, Susan Charlesworth, and Phyllis Shea. In addition, Alice Folk, Diane Puchbauer, Lauren Adelchanow, and Jennifer Costillo offered editorial expertise that helped to make the text and the test bank questions more readable for the first edition. Brigette Worthen, Gisette Alvarado and Joshua Ziebel provided similar assistance for this edition.

From Valerie Chang

I want to particularly thank my family: Jeff, Amy, James, Matthew, Laura, Rachael, and Stan. Their loving support makes everything I do possible and adds joy to my life. I am blessed with many, very dear friends who have been encouraging, understanding, and very patient through the challenges of writing this second edition. I will always be grateful to my parents, Ava and Howard Nash, who told me "you can do it" and believed that I could do whatever I decided to do. A special thanks to the faculty and students who used and liked the first edition and gave us suggestions for enhancing it in the second edition.

From Sheryn Scott

There are many students, friends, and family members who sacrificed time so that I could work on this text. I particularly want to thank my daughters, Ali Borden, who, having gone through the process of writing a book, was always encouraging me that there was an end point to the work, and Kara Russ, who provided wonderful grandchildren as a necessary distraction to the hard complexities of writing a book. No part of my participation in the project could have happened without the patient support of my husband, Larry Hixon, who put up with my absences and helped to see that the household ran when I was immersed in meeting one deadline or another. Lastly I want to recognize the many supervisors and teachers who taught me the knowledge, skills, and attitudes that we hope to teach others with this book.

From Carol Decker

I want to thank my husband for his support throughout the writing and rewriting process, and all of the patient "teachers" I have had over the years of my life, beginning with my mother, Phyllis Linzer. As my first teacher, she instilled a love of learning that has remained constant throughout my life. I especially want to thank the many families at Riley Hospital for Children who enhanced my life in ways they will never know. It has been a privilege to work with each and every one. I also want to thank my co-authors, who have been a delight and pleasure to work with, even through our most hectic times.

INTRODUCTION: THE TEACHING-LEARNING SYSTEM

This book is written with four main goals in mind. *The first goal* is to provide fundamental knowledge necessary for students preparing for careers in the fields of social work, psychology, educational counseling, counseling, marriage and family therapy, pastoral counseling, human services, and related helping professions. *The second goal* is to explain and give multiple examples of how basic practice skills are used when working with individuals, families, different types of groups, and organizations. *The third goal* is to give students enough opportunities to reflect on and apply the knowledge so the new information can be integrated and used in many situations throughout their career. *The fourth goal* is to provide students with opportunities to demonstrate their competency in the use of the basic practice skills necessary to work effectively with clients. In order to achieve these goals, the following teaching-learning system is recommended.

Becoming a competent practitioner requires learning how to apply practice knowledge, how to think about clients in the ways used by experienced practitioners, and how to appropriately and effectively use the skills and tasks necessary to work effectively with clients. This book's learning system provides information and practice exercises that will help you become a competent, self-reflective professional, so that you are able to evaluate your practice and identify your strengths and areas for growth.

This learning system can be used in a variety of ways. Instructors may select the parts of the learning system that best suit their course objectives, teaching philosophy, and style. Detailed suggestions and additional information related to each aspect of the teaching-learning system are provided in the *Instructor's Manual* available on the Cengage website.

Achieving competency requires multiple methods of learning. Although each person learns in his/her own unique way, active learning methods are proven effective and popular with undergraduate and graduate students. This teaching-learning system involves the following learning methods:

- *Reading* about information related to professional practice and the skills and tasks needed to work effectively with clients
- *Thinking and writing* about ideas related to the concepts that are discussed
- *Watching and discussing* a DVD demonstration of use of the skills
- *Applying* knowledge and skills to a specific client situation
- *Working in task groups* on cases
- *Practicing* skills in a simulated interview
- *Evaluating* the use of the skills immediately after practicing them

Reading

Each chapter begins with questions for students to consider as they are reading the chapter, and a list of learning objectives related to the chapter and also to educational standards. Either the chapter learning objectives or the competencies can be used as learning objectives for classes. As each new concept, skill, or task is introduced, students read about how the knowledge or skill is applied with different system sizes, including individuals, families, groups, and larger systems. The chapter ends with a list of key terms introduced and defined in the chapter and a review of the specific competencies the students should be able to demonstrate.

Thinking and Writing

Homework exercises are provided following the introduction of new concepts. The purpose of the homework exercises is to enhance learning by inviting students to think about the concepts and skills and to write about and actively use the concepts. In many homework exercises, students are encouraged to reflect on how the concept is related to their own life experiences. If homework exercises are completed by the class period when the chapter is being discussed, students begin active learning before coming to class. At the beginning of class, further active learning can be stimulated by asking students to discuss specific homework exercises with a partner or in small groups.

Watching and Discussing

The text is accompanied by a DVD which demonstrates the use of the skills discussed in the book with an individual, a family, and a psycho-educational support group. Following the introduction of a group of new skills, students can see how three experienced practitioners use these skills in conjunction with their own unique, personal way of relating to clients. Seeing skills used with different clients helps students understand how to apply these skills.

There are various ways to use the DVD to enhance learning and evaluate competency. For example, many instructors give students basic information about the client and ask the students to answer questions before seeing the DVD. Such questions include:

- How would you prepare for a meeting with this client?
- What do you need to learn about before meeting with this client?
- What are your hunches about what the client might be thinking, feeling, and expecting?
- What are your concerns about working with this client?
- What, if any, personal issues would working with this client bring up for you?

Exercises for each section of the DVD include asking students to name the skills being used, to identify other skills that might be used, to evaluate the practitioner's use of the skills, and to discuss the quality of the relationship between the practitioner and the client. Transcripts for each section of the DVD and possible discussion questions are included in the *Instructor's Manual* and the *Student Website*. Using the transcripts, students can discuss specific transactions or sets of transactions and/or identify the skills used by the practitioner.

Basic DVD Client Information

- **Individual:** This older Jewish woman's husband died after a long illness. She was referred to the practitioner by the hospital social worker after she had surgery for cancer.
- **Family:** This African American-Caucasian family includes three boys ranging in age from 7 to 13 years old. The family was referred by the school counselor, who is concerned about the low grades of the oldest boy.
- **Psycho-educational support group:** This group of women lives in a low-income area of an urban community. Responding to an identified need, the local neighborhood community center announced a group for mothers who wanted to talk about issues such as parenting, stress, and family life.

Length of Time of Each Segment

	Individual	Family	Group
Beginning	4:23	6:49	21:20
Exploring	15:19	13:44	11:17
Exploring & Goal Setting	23:17	18:31	20:14
Action	23:35	19:06	17:05
Evaluation & Ending	7:19	10:44	12:39

Working with Cases

For many students, information and skills learned in class do not transfer to real-world practice (Koerin, Harrigan, & Reeves, 1990; Lombardi, 2007; Vayda & Bogo, 1991). One way to help students transfer knowledge and skills is by providing opportunities for them to work on real-life cases and to learn how professionals think about case information (Middendorf & Pace, 2005). Using the case provided in the text and the 5 additional cases in the *Instructor's Manual*, students can apply knowledge and skills to real world situations and begin thinking like professionals who must take into account facts, impressions, knowledge, values, ethics, and laws as they decide on appropriate action and use their practice skills (Brooks, Harris, & Clayton, 2010; Lynn, 1999).

Thinking through the complexity of working with cases based on actual practice situations helps students learn to think like professionals (Lynn, 1999; Wolfer & Scales, 2005). Students learn that there is no "right" answer to problems, and that appropriate responses are relative and situation specific. Working with cases fosters an understanding of and a respect for the uniqueness of each client's situation, needs, and resources. By using cases, students learn both subject matter and skills such as critical thinking, communication, group collaboration, and self-assessment. Cases also provide an opportunity for students to develop the problem-solving, diagnostic, and clinical reasoning skills that are vital to the counseling process.

Case-based learning involves interactive, student-centered exploration of realistic and specific situations. The specific type of case-based learning used in the book is problem-based learning (PBL), a learning system that replicates practice by giving students one section of a case at time. Research shows that PBL makes learning more exciting and interesting to students (Albanese & Mitchell, 1993; Barrows & Tamblyn, 1980; Searight & Searight, 2009; Vasconez, Donnelly, Mayo, & Schwartz, 1993; Vernon & Blake, 1993). By using this interactive, student-driven approach to learning, retention and reinforcement of information is enhanced (Bennett-Levy, 2006; Bernstein, Tipping, Bercovitz, & Skinner, 1995). Problem-based learning involves engaging in active learning, setting learning goals, discovering gaps in knowledge, and sharing responsibility for completing assignments. Using problem-based learning, your instructor serves as an advisor or guide, not the expert.

One case is included in the book. Starting in Chapter 7, sections of a case are presented; each new section adds information. In our modified problem-based learning (MPBL), general questions for students to consider and discuss are added at the end of each case section. The questions have been developed to help students learn the basic ways that practitioners approach thinking about case situations. The questions require students to differentiate between impressions and facts, and to identify and seek out needed information. Students report that using the MPBL method required them to think about how to apply theory to practice, prepared them to work with clients, and helped them to feel confident about their readiness to work with clients (Chang & Sullenberger, 2009). The *Instructor's Manual* includes additional information about using the modified problem-based learning method and suggests other ways to use the cases to enhance student learning.

The book case can be used in class to demonstrate how to work with cases. To maximize student participation and learning, we suggest having students form groups to work on the cases. Students answer all the questions individually prior to coming together with their group to discuss the answers. The final step is for the group to present and/or write their answers to each question.

Working in Task Groups

Current research on teaching identifies that learning is enhanced when students work together in groups. Working in a group gives students the opportunity to learn about the viewpoints and experiences of other people, and to move from passive learner to active, self-directed learner. By discussing cases in a small group, each group member has the opportunity to share experiences, thoughts, and perspectives. Just as practitioners discuss case-related dilemmas with their team or colleagues, each member of your group will serve as a resource. Group members can share in leading the discussion and recording the group's progress. Group work is more effective when groups establish ground rules, such as the way members will report their information and what should happen when a member is absent or doesn't complete the assignment. For students planning to enter the helping professions, learning to work effectively in a group is essential as they will often be working on teams.

As they work in groups, students develop skills in assessment, planning, and evaluating, as well as gain an appreciation for the benefits of collaboration. As a group, students identify their learning goals and determine the resources needed to accomplish their goals. Using this book, groups can be used to discuss homework assignments, the DVD, and either the book case or the cases in the *Instructor's Manual*. Group collaboration is very helpful when dealing with the complexity of each case. The *Instructor's Manual* includes tips and assignments that can be used to help students work effectively in groups.

Practicing

The practice exercises give students opportunities to apply their practice skills and demonstrate their competency. Starting in Chapter 6, practice exercises invite students to demonstrate their level of competency. In the practice exercises, students work in a group of three people and take turns playing the roles of practitioner, client, and peer supervisor. Each practice exercise includes specific directions for these three roles. Students who have used this system reported learning a great deal in each role.

Using this learning system, students focus on one group of skills at a time. After mastering one group of skills, students move on to the next discrete group of skills. With each practice session, students repeat the previously practiced skills and add new skills. As students improve their ability to use skills, they receive positive feedback and experience increasing confidence in their ability to use the practiced skills. The practice exercises simulate work with an individual client because this is easiest for students. As students gain confidence using the skills with individuals, they can move on to using the skills with families, groups, communities, and organizations.

After developing an adequate repertoire of basic skills, students can learn more advanced skills and ways to use skills effectively with a wide variety of clients in many different situations. As their mastery of these skills improves, their ability to be empathic, warm, respectful, and genuine will increase as will their ability to be attuned with their clients. Over time most practitioners develop a personal style or ways to more fully include their unique ways of relating in the helping process. Using this book and education system, students gain competency in the use of the basic knowledge and skills necessary to effectively facilitate the change process.

Evaluating

As students practice new skills, it is important for them to evaluate their competency (Bennett-Levy & Beedie, 2007). This book includes an evaluation system that has been tested and shown to be valid (Pike, Bennett, & Chang, 2004). Undergraduate and graduate students, as well as agency supervisors, have been able to quickly learn and use this system. After teaching the students about the importance of immediate, honest feedback, instructors can demonstrate how to use this simple system.

The evaluation system provides students with immediate feedback about their use of skills and their demonstration of the core interpersonal qualities (warmth, empathy, respect, and genuineness). Immediate feedback is a central part of this learning system. After each practice session, the student's work is evaluated: the person in the client role gives feedback about whether or not he/she felt understood and thought there was a respectful connection with the practitioner, the practitioner identifies his/her perceived strengths and weaknesses, and the peer supervisor gives the practitioner feedback on the use of skills. In the role of peer supervisor, students learn to constructively evaluate both the use of skills and the demonstration of core interpersonal qualities. Guidelines for making these judgments are provided so that beginning practitioners can learn to accurately evaluate skills and recognize strengths and limitations. Having clear, behavioral descriptors helps beginning practitioners become aware of their strengths and their mistakes (Kruger & Dunning, 1999; Tsai, Callaghan, Kohlenberg, Follette, & Darrow, 2009). Additional directions related to doing the practice exercises and evaluating each exercise are included before the first practice exercise in Chapter 6.

Many instructors rotate among student groups and offer feedback to the students in the role of peer supervisor and practitioner. Some instructors ask students to do a beginning video interview. As students gain skills, they can evaluate this beginning interview. Later in the course, instructors may require students to do a final video interview demonstrating their use of all of the skills and evaluated by the student and instructor using this evaluation system. Additional information on using the evaluation system is available in the *Instructor's Manual*.

When the students move on to practicum or internship placements, they can assess the quality of their work with clients using this evaluation system. If their supervisors have been trained to use this evaluation system, students and their supervisors can use this system to move from beginning evaluations of practice skills to setting specific goals for improvement. Using this evaluation system in class and/or in field settings is an excellent way to measure and demonstrate skill competency. Ultimately, our goal is that each student becomes an effective, reflective practitioner who uses self-evaluation, learns from mistakes and successes, and is continuously improving.

FOUNDATION

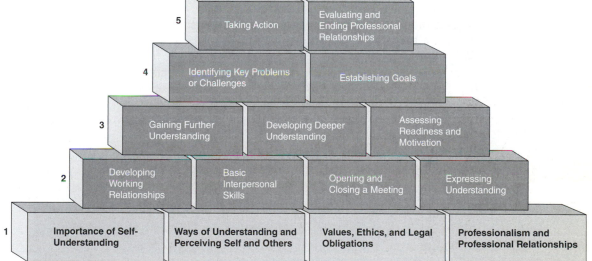

5 — Taking Action | Evaluating and Ending Professional Relationships

4 — Identifying Key Problems or Challenges | Establishing Goals

3 — Gaining Further Understanding | Developing Deeper Understanding | Assessing Readiness and Motivation

2 — Developing Working Relationships | Basic Interpersonal Skills | Opening and Closing a Meeting | Expressing Understanding

1 — Importance of Self-Understanding | Ways of Understanding and Perceiving Self and Others | Values, Ethics, and Legal Obligations | Professionalism and Professional Relationships

© Cengage Learning 2013

As is true in any profession, becoming a skilled practitioner takes energy, perseverance, dedication, and time. Your efforts to enhance your ability to work effectively and collaboratively with clients will bring many rewards. There is satisfaction in seeing individuals develop self-esteem, families work together, communities find a renewed sense of purpose, and organizations build a culture of acceptance and encouragement.

To become a competent and effective practitioner, you'll need to acquire an array of new skills and knowledge. Developing this knowledge base can be compared to building a wall. Beginning with the foundational information covered in Chapters 1 through 4, each chapter is an essential building block that adds to your development as a practitioner. Chapter 1, Importance of Self-Understanding, provides information and exercises that will help you understand influences of personal development; culture, race, and ethnicity; gender, sexual orientation, socio-economic status, spirituality and religion; life stages; family of origin; disability and ability; and stress and demands on each person. Because all practitioners use themselves to help others, self-understanding is vital. Chapter 2, Ways of Understanding and Perceiving Self and Others, includes discussion of the following perspectives constructivist, family systems, ecological, strengths, resilience, empowerment, and dual. Each of these perspectives influences our perceptions of and actions toward ourselves and others. Chapter 3, Values, Ethics, and Legal Obligations, gives an overview of ethical, legal, and professional standards that apply to practice behavior with clients and provides a decision making model to use when dealing with ethical dilemmas. Chapter 4, Professionalism and Professional Relationships, deals with developing a professional identity, maintaining professional relationships, using supervision and consultation effectively, engaging in career long learning, advocating for change and understanding the unique nature of practitioner relationships with clients.

IMPORTANCE OF SELF-UNDERSTANDING

5 Taking Action	Evaluating and Ending Professional Relationships		
4 Identifying Key Problems or Challenges	Establishing Goals		
3 Gaining Further Understanding	Developing Deeper Understanding	Assessing Readiness and Motivation	
2 Developing Working Relationships	Basic Interpersonal Skills	Opening and Closing a Meeting	Expressing Understanding
1 **Importance of Self-Understanding**	Ways of Understanding and Perceiving Self and Others	Values, Ethics, and Legal Obligations	Professionalism and Professional Relationships

© Cengage Learning 2013

Questions to consider as you read this chapter:

1. What influences on my personal development are important to consider as I begin to learn to work with clients as a helping professional?
2. Why is it important to learn more about myself as I develop as a helping professional?

This chapter covers practice behaviors related to self-understanding and understanding others. *You will learn the importance of:*

*   Understanding the influence on yourself and others of culture, race, and ethnicity; gender; sexual orientation; socioeconomic status; religion and spirituality; family of origin; life stage; ability and disability; and stress and demands
*   Gaining sufficient self-understanding to recognize the influence of personal biases & values in working with diverse groups of people
*   Recognizing the importance of difference in shaping life experiences
*   Recognizing the extent to which a culture's structures and values may oppress, marginalize, alienate, or create or enhance privilege and power
*   Understanding the need to consider all aspects of diversity issues in your work with clients

INFLUENCES ON PERSONAL DEVELOPMENT

Personal experiences, capacities, physical abilities, privileges, and limitations influence development. As we grow and develop our self-concept, we absorb and are influenced by culture, race and ethnicity, gender and sexual orientation, socioeconomic status, life stage, ability and disability, family, and spiritual beliefs and norms. A task of practitioners is to understand that their personal beliefs and views of "truth" are only one way of looking at a situation. Some viewpoints may be ingrained so deeply that other perspectives can seem not only different, but wrong. For example, in one therapeutic group, a client who experienced a difficult childhood believed that the world was a dangerous place. She often felt scared that something frightening might happen in her neighborhood. Other members of her group told her they experienced her neighborhood as a very safe place to live, but she wasn't able to see it that way herself. Our perception of what is true depends on the beliefs we hold.

As a practitioner, understanding and accepting yourself is an essential step toward understanding others (Hill & Lent, 2006). Developing self-understanding and an awareness of personal biases is a particularly important process in the journey to becoming a competent practitioner (Bennett-Levy, 2006; Williams, Hurley, O'Brien, & DeGregorio, 2003). Self-understanding can be gained by reading and taking classes, receiving competent supervision, being in personal therapy, and setting aside time for self-reflection. When working with a client, your life experiences can influence how you perceive your client. In this chapter, basic information related to understanding yourself and others will be covered. Pay particular attention to areas you may not have considered before.

The way you see the world has been influenced by the family you grew up in, the culture you inhabit, and the way you interpreted the events of your life. Your beliefs affect how you think about yourself, others, and the world. For example, a woman who was teased a lot during childhood learned to perceive herself as inadequate. As an adult, she believed she was only capable of obtaining a low-level job despite her college degree. She believed others would not take her seriously and would see her as inadequate.

Before doing this first Homework Exercise, remember from the Introduction that the purpose of each Homework Exercise is to augment your learning and understanding of concepts by giving you an opportunity to reflect on and use the material. Since the material in this book is essential to your work as a professional, you need to learn it in a deep, meaningful way so the concepts will be available for you to use in your career.

HOMEWORK EXERCISE 1.1 | UNDERSTANDING YOUR PERSONAL BELIEF SYSTEM

It is important to recognize the beliefs that have established your views of yourself, others, and the world. A cultural belief that was once common was "A penny saved is a penny earned." What truisms about money did you learn in your family? Perhaps you received messages about how to behave, such as: "If you don't go to church, you'll go to hell," "Cleanliness is next to Godliness," "The early bird catches the worm," and "We don't associate with those kind of people." Recall other adages you learned as a child? You may have absorbed beliefs about human nature such as "Being beholden to others is wrong," "You can't trust men, they just want one thing," "Working hard is the way to succeed," "Poor people are just lazy," "Beggars can't be choosers," or "It is best to be cautious around others because you can't count on them." Write one belief related to each of the following: success, money, and relationships. These beliefs will influence your values, your reactions to life experiences, your culture, and other factors.

INFLUENCE OF CULTURE, RACE, AND ETHNICITY
Written by Alice Fok-Trela

The minority and immigrant populations in the United States have increased over the past 30 years and are projected to continue to grow over the next 40 years (U.S. Census Bureau, 2008). As these populations continue to grow, practitioners are likely to see an increasing number of clients from various ethnicities, races, and culture. Of course, practitioners will be from various ethnicities, races, and cultures.

Research suggests that multicultural competence seems to be a significant predictor of satisfaction in counseling for both practitioners and clients. In fact, Fuertes et al. (2006) found that cultural awareness affected the practitioner's satisfaction with his/her own work and increased the client's perception of the practitioner's empathy and the client's satisfaction with treatment. Conversely, difficulties in counseling arise from unacknowledged differences in the perceptions between the practitioner and the client. Therefore, it is critical for practitioners to understand their own cultural beliefs and to be aware of the ways in which these beliefs influence their behavior and expectations of others (Cartwright, Daniels & Zhang, 2008; Roysircar, 2004).

Although the terms *race, culture*, and *ethnicity* are often used interchangeably, they are defined differently. **Race** refers to a group of people with specific physical characteristics that differentiate them from other groups of people (Tseng, 2001). **Ethnicity** refers to a group of people distinguished by a shared history, culture, beliefs, values, and behaviors (Tseng, 2001). In contrast, **culture** is defined as the customary beliefs, social forms, and behavior patterns of a racial, religious, or social group. In this section, we will be discussing how culture affects our beliefs and values.

Culture's Influence on the Practitioner

As practitioners, our culture, race, and ethnicity shape our identity and our worldview. They offer us unique life experiences that teach us our language, behaviors, rules, and ways of understanding others. Culture provides us with a framework of assumptions or premises for understanding the world and communicating that understanding to others. Our culture, race, ethnicity, and worldview influence our values and beliefs about what behaviors are considered normal, appropriate, or healthy (Fuertes, 2006). In Western culture, a common assumption is that healthy individuals are constantly striving to achieve success and upward social mobility (Liu et al., 2007). This is known as the *upward mobility bias*. This bias affects how we judge others. For example, how would you view a man with a PhD, who has chosen to be a full-time parent to his children, ages 8 and 10?

Because of the invisible influence culture has on our perceptions, it is critical for practitioners to examine their beliefs, assumptions, and biases. As a practitioner, you should be on a journey of self-discovery. Accepting that how you see the world is only one way out of many equally valid ways of viewing the world will allow you to accept and appreciate the worldviews of others (Jernigan, Green, Helms, Perez-Gualdron, & Henze, 2010). According to Saltzburg (2008), during our self-reflection we should ask ourselves:

- What is our cultural identity and what are the values surrounding this identity?
- What are the origins of our beliefs and assumptions?
- How does the notion of privilege influence our formation of personal biases?

HOMEWORK EXERCISE 1.2 | CULTURE, RACE, ETHNICITY, AND VALUES

1. How do you identify yourself culturally, racially, and/or ethnically?
2. List three values you learned growing up.
3. How does your culture describe a successful adult?

As you become aware of your belief system, you begin to see similarities and differences among diverse cultures and recognize how these beliefs can influence your reaction to the behavior of others. Increased awareness of your culture and other cultures is vital to your development as a practitioner. How does a practitioner develop an understanding and appreciation for culture, race, and ethnicity issues in counseling? Multicultural knowledge can be partially achieved through the following tasks:

1. Reading about other races, cultures, and ethnic groups;
2. Recognizing strengths and weaknesses of dominant and minority racial groups;

3. Developing meaningful relationships with people from various racial and cultural groups;

4. Developing relationships with colleagues and mentors who are open to discussions on cultural or racial issues;

5. Watching films about other cultures and races; and

6. Participating in cultural activities or visiting other countries. (Jernigan et al., 2010)

HOMEWORK EXERCISE 1.3 | YOUR CULTURAL BELIEFS

- When did you first realize that your family belonged to a certain group of people (e.g., African-American, Caucasian-American, Mexican-American, Asian-American, Irish-American, Euro-American, etc.)?

- What were you taught in your family about people from other ethnic or racial groups? How were differences dealt with in your family?

Culture's Influence on Clients

Although it is important to understand your cultural belief system, it is equally important to develop an understanding of the cultures of your clients (Carter, 2003; Cartwright, Daniels & Zhang, 2008; Daniel, Roysircar, & Abeles, 2004). We need to become familiar with the culture and political history of clients who differ from ourselves. Cultural influences occur at many levels including such areas as ways of coping with stress and adversity (Ponterotto, Casas, Suzuki, & Alexander, 2010; Tseng, 2001). For example, when coping with illness, pain, and other life challenges, what does your culture think is appropriate: crying, complaining, gritting your teeth, being strong, sharing with supportive others, or seeking immediate help?

Culture has a strong influence on the roles that are seen as appropriate. These may be age-related roles, such as beliefs about the proper behavior of children toward parents, teachers, and society. As you watch children and parents interact, how do your beliefs about the role of children affect your opinion of the behavior you see? Practitioners need to become particularly aware of cultural differences in attitudes regarding independence and autonomy, patterns of communication (verbal and nonverbal), family boundaries and responsibilities, and the expression of emotions (Kim, Ng, & Ahn, 2005). When thinking about the cultural background of a family, you need to consider the ways that culture has influenced values about work, education, health care, religion, and family structure and responsibilities (Congress, 2002). For example, in many Asian societies, adult children are expected to provide shelter and care for their elderly parents. In some cultures, parents and other family members expect to be involved in decisions made by adult children, such as choice of marriage partner and how money is spent.

The level of acculturation of immigrants and their ability to communicate in the local language is also important. People who are the first generation in a new country tend to be greatly influenced by their culture of origin. The children of these first-generation immigrants have grown up in the new country and often feel torn between the culture of their parents and the culture of their friends. Some clients have come to your community as refugees, or perhaps their parents were refugees. Many minority individuals are expected to present themselves as representative of all members of that culture (Tummala-Narra, 2010). Practitioners must recognize both the shared cultural experiences and the unique differences in cultural groups.

Chang and Berk (2009) found that clients working with practitioners who were of a different race or culture had different expectations of the practitioner and used different standards for evaluating expertise, credibility, and competence. For example, the researchers (Chang & Berk, 2009) found that Asian participants, while valuing insight and personal growth, tended to prefer expert guidance, advice, explicit instruction, and structured, problem-focused suggestions. Practitioners who were more directive were rated more favorably and were seen as being more helpful. Chang and Berk's (2009) study suggests that effective practitioners need to demonstrate culture-specific knowledge.

Communication patterns include the appropriateness and timing of eye contact, the directness with which a person comes to the point of a discussion, personal space when one converses, and even facial expressions. For example, in Western society, direct eye contact is considered polite and appropriate. However, in some cultural groups, this is considered rude. In some societies, business is discussed only after a period of social exchanges unrelated to the purpose of the meeting. In addition, smiling may represent feelings of discomfort, distress, sadness, or anger, rather than happiness (Ansfield, 2007; Tseng, 2001). These communication patterns come into play in counseling and may create problems if the practitioner and the client are operating on different patterns of communication.

Although it is important to understand the differences between you and your clients, there will be times when you work with clients who have problems or backgrounds that are similar to yours. You may have a greater intuitive understanding about what their life has been like or the pressures they may be experiencing. You may make assumptions that their life is just like yours, and that they feel and think as you do. However, these assumptions may be incorrect and can lead to misunderstandings.

Cultural knowledge helps us understand the individual in the context of their cultural, racial, or ethnic values and beliefs. Although becoming a culturally competent practitioner is a lifetime task, you should become knowledgeable about the cultures of your clients. As practitioners, we need to become aware of the "beauty, depth, and complexity of cultures and ways of being in the world other than [our] own" (Blitz, 2006, p. 246).

Influences of the Dominant Culture

Members of the dominant culture may have difficulty identifying the influence of their own culture because it is accepted as the norm. A person who benefits from privilege is unaware of it while accepting and using it as a natural right (Liu et al., 2007). Privilege may be awarded based on race, gender, class, physical ability, sexual orientation, or age. **White privilege** is an institutionalized set of benefits granted to those who resemble the people in power in a culture's institutions (Kendall, 2001) where the majority of the population is Caucasian. For example, you may have heard of the term the "old boy's club." Those belonging to this club (albeit non-official) are white, male, upper class individuals, and they have access to elite social and business connections not available to others. People of color (a description that includes those who perceives themselves as non-white) do not receive these privileges. These benefits include greater access to power and resources, the ability to make decisions that affect everyone without taking others into account, and the ability to discount the experiences of individuals of color (Kendall, 2001). Moreover, the underlying power structures in society allow for the persistence of covert racial oppression (Branscombe, Schmitt, & Schiffhauer, 2006, Pewewardy, 2004).

The beliefs related to white privilege influence our perceptions of our clients and their experiences. Being aware of the privileges granted to members of the dominant group and the related disadvantages of members of minority groups can help you understand the experiences of both the dominant and minority groups. Some practitioners might feel shame, guilt, and/or denial in response to the idea of white privilege. As a practitioner you need to be aware of the potential effects of white privilege or institutionalized biases on your client's life and situation. By increasing your awareness and sensitivity to white privileges, you will be better able to empathically join with your client and to appreciate your client's worldview.

HOMEWORK EXERCISE 1.4 | BENEFITS FOR DOMINANT GROUPS

Make a list of at least five benefits that members of the dominant group have simply because of their race.

INFLUENCE OF GENDER
Co-written by Kathy Lay

A number of factors influence who and what we are. One of the most important in our society is gender. From the first moment that a woman knows she is pregnant the question she will ponder and be asked is about the baby's sex. This knowledge of the baby's sex influences interpretations of movements in utero, how the future child is addressed, and how others treat the baby from moment of birth. For example, at birth, the baby is wrapped in either pink for girls or blue for boys. The social context of the parents will inform what is considered male or female.

A person's sex is determined based on genitals. "Gender is present in our lives from the time our genitals are first discernible—often in utero" (Burdge, 2007, p. 245) and has broad consequences on the future of the child. Growing out of a social context, **gender** pertains to what our culture teaches is true or will be true of someone who is biologically female or male. Gender includes societal beliefs, stereotypes, and ingrained views about what is assumed to be the fundamental nature of boys and girls, women and men. Everything from appropriate toys to clothes, schooling, and behaviors are understood and planned based on gender.

Gender stereotypes prescribe roles, how a person should respond to life circumstances, and whether a behavior is considered pathological or adaptive. Anger, sadness, fear, and happiness are all human responses, but some may be more acceptable based on the gender of the individual expressing the emotion. The social construction of gender continues throughout our lives and influences choices, access to resources, and ultimately, quality of life.

Some individuals feel uncomfortable with their assigned sex. **Transgender** refers to individuals who do not identify with or conform to the gender roles assigned to their sex. Some individuals who are transgendered become **transsexual**, meaning they choose to change their body surgically and/or with hormones in order to align their body with their chosen gender. Understanding these descriptions of gender is crucial to self-understanding and doing effective work with clients.

Gender bias in counseling comes through the use of unexamined stereotypes. The use of gender stereotypes as the standard for defining adaptive or healthy behavior and good psychological functioning may lead the practitioner to define dependency in men as bad and sadness in women as more acceptable than anger (Gilbert & Scher, 1999; Plant, Hyde, Keltner, & Devine, 2000; Seelau & Seelau, 2005). Practitioners who believe in the importance of equal relationships between men and women might be inclined to encourage female clients to be more assertive or independent with their partners than they might choose to be, or feel that they are allowed to be by their culture.

HOMEWORK EXERCISE 1.5 | GENDER INFLUENCES

Reflect and examine your perception of your own gender. Do you see yourself as strong, weak, emotional, thoughtful, adventurous, empathic, careful, fearful, curious, skillful, or independent? Identify the characteristics commonly associated with male and female gender. In what ways has your gender limited or restricted your options and in what ways has it enhanced your options? What were the different expectations for the men and women in your family related to moving away from the family, going to college, going to graduate school, staying home with children, and caring for elderly parents? Name three ways your life might have been different if you were a member of the other gender.

INFLUENCE OF SEXUAL ORIENTATION
Written by Kathy Lay

Sexual orientation is another powerful determinate of who we are and how we respond to others. **Sexual orientation** is the direction or directions of one's sexual, affectionate, or loving attraction on a continuum from only same-sex attraction to only opposite sex attraction. **Bisexual** people are attracted to both sexes. Individual sexual activity does not confirm sexual orientation. For example, in some Middle Eastern countries there is a practice involving using young boys who are dressed as girls as entertainment and sexual partners for men in the military. These men may prefer opposite sex partners.

Embedded in our sexual orientation are societal beliefs, stereotypes, and views about relational and sexual expression. Recent research indicates sexual orientation is determined by psychobiological influences (Friedman & Downey, 2008, Rahman & Wilson, 2003). Many experience their sexual orientation as a natural developmental process in which they are encouraged and supported throughout their psycho-social–sexual development regardless of whether they are heterosexual, lesbian, or gay. Others identify their sexual orientation, or "come out," later in life due to a variety of factors including family, religious, and/or cultural prohibitions about recognizing or acknowledging homosexual feelings.

The coming out process is complicated by social and cultural constraints experienced due to heterosexism and/or homophobia. Heterosexism is a belief that male-female sexuality is the only natural, normal, or moral mode of sexual behavior (Mohr, 2003). **Heterosexism** legitimizes only traditional assumptions and stereotypes about male/female relationships (Harris, 2010). **Homophobia** is an individualized fear and hatred of homosexuals (Madureira, 2007). Behaviors associated with homophobia have manifested in a broad range of oppressive acts from covert activities to verbal aggression and violence (Tomsen, 2006; Tully, 2000). Regardless of the orientation of the practitioner, heterosexism and homophobia may be operational in his/her worldview. It is institutionalized in most systems and manifests in cultural behaviors and norms (Morrow & Messinger, 2006). Effective practitioners have both awareness and knowledge of the impact of heterosexism and homophobia on themselves and others.

The helping professions are not immune to the influence of heterosexism and homophobia. Examples of heterosexism and homophobia include forms constructed for intake purposes that reflect only heterosexual relationships, exclusive definitions of family, and agency policies that do not honor alternative partnership/family constructions. Gays and lesbians are often the brunt of jokes that reinforce stereotypes and bias. Awareness of our own heterosexism and homophobia will lead to deconstruction of bias and to respectful practices with others from diverse backgrounds. Attendance to our bias is a life-long learning process that will result in skillful and respectful interactions with clients.

HOMEWORK EXERCISE 1.6 | SEXUAL ORIENTATION INFLUENCES

When were you first aware of someone with a sexual orientation different from your own orientation? What was your reaction to this awareness? What experiences did you have in high school related to sexual orientation biases?

INFLUENCE OF SOCIOECONOMIC STATUS
Written by Carolyn Gentle-Genitty

The idea of sorting people and their resources into categories has been a concept long understood by many people in many cultures. It is more evident in a capitalist country where wealth, or lack thereof, structures and dictates the grouping to which one is placed and how resources are distributed. For example, people qualify for public assistance and/or certain benefits if their income is below an established poverty line. Those living below the poverty line have limited access to healthcare, education, and housing in the United States. Those with higher socioeconomic status have more power and access to resources.

Socioeconomic status is the position in the social hierarchy that is attributed to individuals, families, and groups, based on such variables as income, occupation, and education. "Socioeconomic status is used as a way to think about economic, social, and political relationships involved in the production, control, and distribution of wealth" (Mahoney, 2003, p. 803).

The concept of socio-economic status refers to standards and measurements of economic wealth and structures such as low, middle, and upper class. The influence of socioeconomic class is not merely individual but generational. In most instances if your family has a history of wealth, you and others in that family will be in the same class. On the contrary, if your family has been poor, it is often quite difficult to move from the lower class into the middle or upper class.

Your socioeconomic status influences many aspects of your life. Researchers point to the fact that socioeconomic class greatly impacts quality health care, obesity, education, housing, child care and development, and behaviors (Dodge, Pettit, & Bates, 1994; Fryer & Levitt, 2004; Goodman, 1999; Hoff, 2003; Kington & Smith, 1997; Sirin, 2005; Walsh & Kosson, 2007; Williams, 2004). In fact most of the studies on socioeconomic status point to the disparity in access to health care. Poverty and lower socioeconomic status affect access to education, community resources, social services, employment, and housing especially in regards to people of color (Everson, Maty, Lynch, & Kaplan, 2002; Starfield, 2006). Specifically, Everson and colleagues (2002) reported that "data from the studies demonstrate that the effects of economic disadvantage are cumulative with the greatest risk of poor mental and physical health among those who experienced sustained hardship" (p. 891). Research has shown that people with higher socioeconomic status have better health and live longer due, at least in part, to better access to health care, healthier diets, and lifestyles (Kington & Smith, 1997; Shavers, 2007).

The socioeconomic status of each of us and all of our clients influences our lives in many significant ways. Dodge and colleagues (1994) argue that socioeconomic class is ingrained and impacts how we socialize and evaluate our experiences. We tend to relate more comfortably with people from the same socioeconomic class. As a practitioner, it is imperative that you understand the impact of the invisible but powerful socioeconomic status boundary lines. Socioeconomic class influences our view of ourselves, the resources we have, and our perceptions of others. Your view of your family and of yourself has been influenced by the socioeconomic status of your family. Think about the ways that your self-concept has been affected by your socioeconomic status. Take a minute and remember when you first realized that some of your friends had much more money or much less money than you had. What impact did that have on your view of those friends? In U.S. society we tend to see those with more wealth and higher socioeconomic status as somehow better and more powerful. It is important that you acknowledge your thoughts and judgments related to socioeconomic status so that as a practitioner you will be able to set these learned judgments aside and not use them to create conclusions about your clients.

Effective practitioners must be self-aware, open to continual self-growth and self-assessment, and willing to understand each client's particular situation. As practitioners we must not view all African Americans, persons of African decent, and Hispanics as living in poverty. Biases like these harm rapport building and personal relationships with clients (Johnson, Bastien, & Hirschel, 2009; Mahoney, 2003; Williams, 2004).

HOMEWORK EXERCISE 1.7 | SOCIOECONOMIC CLASS

Spend 15 minutes in a discussion with a person you don't know very well. Talk to this person without using any labels you would normally share when you introduce yourself to someone. For instance, don't discuss your job, family background, school history, income, home address/neighborhood, etc. as you describe who you are. After the discussion, consider how much of your life is influenced by the various aspects that make up your socioeconomic status. Make a list of at least 10 specific factors that are related to your socioeconomic status. Rank each factor with number 1 being most important in shaping who you are today.

INFLUENCE OF SPIRITUALITY AND RELIGION
Written by Sabrina Williamson Sullenberger

Although you may or may not consider yourself to be a spiritual or religious person, many of your clients will be influenced by spiritual or religious beliefs and training. Just as humans are physical creatures with psychological and social dimensions, many people believe we also have a spiritual aspect to our being. Because there will be clients for whom these topics are important, it is essential for practitioners to have at least a beginning understanding of the influence of religion and spirituality on themselves and on the helping process.

Religion can be understood to be communal behaviors (prayer, fasting, celebration of certain holy days, etc.) that are the result of people with similar beliefs coming together to practice those beliefs in a shared setting, such as a church, synagogue, or mosque (Heyman, Buchanan, Marlowe & Sealy, 2006; Hodge, 2005). In the past, people from different religions were often isolated from each other. We are now in era when interaction between people of the major religions is common. There is conflict between religious totalitarians who believe their religion is the only legitimate religion and religious pluralists who believe that each religion has unique contributions (Patel, 2007). Many people with totalitarian views believe their religion should be dominant and/or exclusive. This belief can lead to war.

Spirituality can be understood as an individual's relationship with God or any Ultimate Power (including nature, sacred texts, etc.) that influences his/her mission or purpose in life (Hodge, 2005). Fundamentally, spirituality is how each of us makes meaning out of the events that occur in our lives (Canda & Furman, 1999; Prest & Keller, 2007). Our spirituality also shapes how we see ourselves and how we participate in the lives of others and in the world around us. Someone can correctly consider him/herself to be a "spiritual person" but not necessarily a "religious person."

Just as gender, culture, age, ethnicity, and other factors can influence the counseling relationship, so can spiritual or religious beliefs held by either party. Practitioners have the responsibility to be aware of how their experiences with religion and spirituality shape their view of self, others, the world, and their work with clients. If you have had negative, unpleasant, or little personal experiences with religion or spirituality, you have to set aside those experiences to work effectively with a person who is positively influenced by their religion. On the other hand, if your religious or spiritual experience is a positive, supportive, and important aspect of your life, working with a client who is not religious might be challenging. As a competent and self-aware practitioner, you are expected to be able to work effectively with a wide range of diverse clients. Diversity extends to working competently with clients of different religious backgrounds ranging from religious totalitarians to religious pluralists, as well as clients who do not engage in any religious or spiritual practices (Abrams & Moio, 2009).

HOMEWORK EXERCISE 1.8 | THE INFLUENCE OF RELIGION OR SPIRITUALITY

If you were involved with organized religion as a child, have your ideas about religion changed? If so, how have your ideas of religion changed? What factors led to the changes that you have made in your religious beliefs? If you consider yourself a spiritual or religious person, in what ways is that helpful, supportive, or limiting to you? If you were or are religious, what are some of the values that you have learned from your religion? Has your religious background influenced your desire to become a practitioner? If you do not consider yourself religious and do not have a spiritual practice, how do you imagine that might impact you if you are working with a client who has a strong faith background?

You probably have some awareness of the ways in which your religious or spiritual beliefs may affect your work with clients (Gilligan & Furness, 2006; Prest, Russel, & D'sousa, 1999). For example, your beliefs may shape your understanding about when life begins, and this understanding will influence your views on abortion and birth control. Similarly, your beliefs may shape your understanding about end of life issues and these beliefs will influence your thoughts about euthanasia, suicide, and the death penalty. When practitioners work with a pregnant teen or a person dying of cancer, their beliefs may influence the way they relate to the client. Depending on the client and the setting in which help is being provided, these beliefs may help in building and maintaining rapport with a client. They can also be a barrier to the work with clients.

Your client's spiritual beliefs influence his/her behavior and may affect the helping process (Carlson, Kirkpatrick, & Hecker, 2002; Hagedorn, 2005; Passalacqua & Cervantes 2008). For example, a woman who believes that the institution of marriage is an everlasting commitment may not be willing to leave an abusive partner. Parents who believe in God or a Higher Power as the ultimate healer may not seek traditional medical care for a child who is seriously ill. You will have clients who, in the midst of a crisis, cope very well. These clients may believe that their ability to cope is an extension of their spiritual faith that teaches they will not be tested beyond what they can bear. As with other cultural norms, clients' religious beliefs and practices may influence how they communicate about their problems and view the helping process (Walsh, 2010), shape their gender preference for a professional helper (Ayonrinde, 2003; Passalacqua & Cervantes 2008), and influence the way they view family issues (child rearing, roles of women and men). All of these topics may be discussed in the helping process (Hodge, 2005b; Nash, 2006; Whitney, Tajima, Herrenkohl, & Huang, 2006).

Just as a practitioner's beliefs can be an asset or barrier in his/her work with clients, spirituality or religion can be a source of strength for some clients in making meaning out of their struggles and achieving their goals. For other clients, it may hinder progress toward goals. For example, a woman with two children may have a goal related to starting a career or going back to school. If she or her husband practices a religion that forbids the use of birth control, additional pregnancies may limit her ability to achieve her goal.

Honoring diverse spiritual and religious beliefs is as important as respecting other types of diversity (Constantine, Lewis, Conner, & Sanchez, 2000; Marterella & Brock, 2008). Practitioners should explore the influence of religion and spirituality on their clients and themselves. As competent practitioners, we must recognize the value of our personal religious and spiritual beliefs, but these personal beliefs should not be brought into the helping process in any way that could possibly influence or infringe upon the rights of clients to make their own decisions.

INFLUENCE OF LIFE STAGES
Written by Carolyn Gentle-Genitty

From birth on you move through life stages that are influenced by your biological development. Erikson identified eight developmental/psychosocial stages of life: trust vs. mistrust (infant); autonomy vs. shame and doubt (toddler); initiative vs. guilt (preschooler); industry vs. inferiority (school-age child); identify vs. role confusion (adolescent); intimacy vs. isolation (young adult); generativity vs. stagnation (middle-age adult), and integrity vs. despair (older adult) (Schriver, 2010). Current researchers have added a ninth stage, emerging adulthood (Henig, 2010; Tanner & Arnett, 2009). This stage between adolescence and young adulthood (age 18–25 years old) is characterized by identity explorations, feeling "in between," instability, self-focus, and possibilities (Tanner & Arnett, 2009, p. 39). This stage delays activities associated with independent adulthood such as moving away from home, getting married, and starting a career. As the research on this stage emerges, there will be shifts in what is considered developmentally appropriate (Cunha, Heckman, Lochner, & Masterov, 2005; Fox, 2005; Tanner & Arnett, 2009).

You may have criticized yourself or others for not following the life stages as defined. For example, if you are an adult returning to school to pursue a degree, you may believe that you are way behind and you should have gotten a degree years ago. If you are young and acquired a degree and became independent, you may believe you are successful. We often judge our success by the accomplishment of life stage milestones. Stop for a minute and consider some of the circumstances that might have kept the person in the first example from going to college when she was younger. Now consider some of the circumstances that helped the person in the second example finish college at a younger age.

Different rates of physical development and social pressures influence life stage related decisions. For example, look at a group of 16 year olds and notice the obvious differences in the maturity of their bodies and social skills. A decision that one 16 year old may be ready to handle another 16 year old may not be ready to handle. Of course, even those who are physically and mentally ready to deal with a life stage challenge may be negatively influenced by others. You probably can think of more than one example of an adolescent who made a negative decision based on peer pressure. As teenagers, many young people try hard to fit in with their peers. This need to go along with peers can lead to damaging life decisions. Feeling the need to compete or fit in, adults may make decisions they later regret. As you develop self-understanding, you may accept that past decisions you now regret were probably the best decision you could make at the time given your life stage, level of maturity, and the forces influencing you. You will meet clients who were taken advantage of when they were younger and blame themselves for the problems, not realizing they were coerced by an adult. As a practitioner who understands the challenges of various life stages, you will be able to help your clients realize the many influences on past decisions including life stage, mental capacity, and influential others.

As you move into your practice you will often be helping clients deal with challenges each life stage presents. You need to understand the challenges your clients face as they go through life stages and accept that their way of facing these challenges may be quite different than your way. Sometimes we think that other people should be able to accomplish what we have accomplished. For example, if you graduated from high school at age 18, everyone should be able to do that. Just as there are diverse populations, there is diversity in the way people go through the stages of life. Judging clients based on your own experience is not acceptable. Consider how you would view the following people: a never-married 40 year old man living at home with his parents who has no contact with his three children or their mother, a 25 year old unmarried woman with four children who has never been employed, a 75 year old couple raising four grandchildren, and a 30 year old moving back home. In order to understand how these people are coping with life stages, we need much more information.

HOMEWORK EXERCISE 1.9 | LIFE STAGES

If possible find pictures of yourself in three different life stages. If you don't have pictures available, identify a significant event you remember from three life stages. Think about each life stage. Identify one significant decision you made during each life stage. What factors influenced those decisions? Looking back you may think you would have made a different or better decision now. Given what you know about yourself in that life stage, was that the best decision you could have made at the time? Write a brief summary of your thoughts about this exercise.

INFLUENCE OF FAMILY OF ORIGIN
Co-written by Kathy Lay

Family experiences have an important and sustained influence on our worldview. Understanding how we have been affected by our own family helps us recognize these experiences as personal and not assume the same meanings and experiences are true for those we serve (Nichols & Schwartz, 2006). Understanding the meaning of family is challenging. There is no commonly agreed upon definition of family. Family is defined differently within cultures and from one culture to another. A possible definition of **family** is two or more people who define themselves as a family based on ties of affection, co-residence, biology, or tradition. Even this very general definition does not work for some people because it doesn't include pets. Some definitions of family only include blood relatives while others extend the definition to include significant friends and neighbors. As a competent practitioner, you need to understand your definition and view of family and how that has influenced your life. After understanding how you define family, critically think about the inclusive or exclusive nature of your definition.

There are a number of groups of people who are called "family" beyond the Euro-American traditional family consisting of a father, a mother, and two children, preferably one of each sex. Today a family may be two gay parents and their adopted or biological children. It could include step-parents, grandparents, aunts, uncles, or other extended family members. Some families have only one parent in the home, with the other parent being completely absent from the children's lives. Other children are being raised by two different families formed when their parents divorced and re-married (Conley & Glauber, 2008; Goldenberg & Goldenberg, 1998; Jones, 2003). Family also can be a couple without children or adults living with their siblings. Depending on the practitioner's family of origin and the client's family of origin, expectations for what a family is or should be will vary greatly and influence how the client and practitioner see one another.

HOMEWORK EXERCISE 1.10 | INFLUENCES OF YOUR FAMILY BACKGROUND

Interview a member of your extended family. Ask for information about your father's and mother's family going back two generations. Learn dates of births and deaths, marriages and divorces, children, and significant health issues. Think about how the family's relationship patterns, ethnicity, struggles, and illnesses have affected you. Write a paragraph description of the influences of your family background on you.

In addition to recognizing different types of families, practitioners should understand the developmental stages of families (Carter & McGoldrick, 1999; O'Brien, 2005). A nuclear family is formed when two people join together in a committed relationship with or without a legal agreement. At this life stage, the couple set up their patterns and ways of living that will influence their future. Stressors may include pressure from their parents, decisions related to money management, and finding ways to mesh views of "how things should be done."

With the addition of children, the family enters a new stage of development with new stressors. These stressors include such things as making childcare arrangements, dealing with illness, dividing household chores, deciding where the family will live, financial strains, and new role definitions to be negotiated. In a single-parent family, concerns related to finances, childcare, and self-care issues can be even greater. Raising children is often a stressful period. Couples who cannot have children or choose not to have children often experience societal pressure to defend or explain their childlessness. As children grow through adolescence, they challenge the family's way of functioning. As adolescents more clearly define their own personalities, the family must make a number of adjustments. These adjustments can be difficult, depending on the amount of support the parent(s) have from others and the flexibility of the family. An additional stressor at this time or later may be caring for aging parents. When children leave home (a stage that varies from one culture to another), parents may experience the loneliness of an "empty nest" along with greater freedom and increased opportunities for personal growth.

With many adults today living well into their 80s in good health, many families experience an extended-retirement phase. The manner in which families experience this life stage depends on the status of family members' health, finances, and relationships. If good health, stable finances, and supportive relationships are present, the aging process is likely to go more smoothly. For some, the adjustment to retirement can be difficult if it is forced or undesired. For others, it may be a time of fulfillment. At each life stage, the family experiences multiple changes. How well they adapt to each stage depends on the resources of each family.

Practitioners are influenced not only by the patterns of their family of origin, but also by their family's developmental stage. If practitioners have young children to care for, are approaching retirement, or are dealing with aging parents, these stressors will affect their own functioning. Awareness of your own stage in the life cycle and that of your family is essential.

The concept of family has faced changes and challenges over the last decades. Social and economic struggles such as changing gender roles, diversity of families, and longer life span are a few of the trends that influence the family (Walsh, 2006). Challenges experienced by the family can lead to family and individuals developing strengths (Walsh, 2006) or can sometimes lead to the dissolution of the family unit. Think of families you have known that have experienced the death or serious illness of a child or parent and how this has affected them.

In families we learn how to behave appropriately with our social groups and culture (Becvar & Becvar, 2006). Family also teaches coping strategies for and adaptation to stressors. For example, families choose different ways to cope with the illness and death of a family member. When dealing with the illness of an older family member, some families believe the aging person should be cared for at home while others think that nursing home care is appropriate. It is important to understand how you have been affected by your family in order to differentiate these experiences as personal and not ascribe particular meaning or truth to those experiences as truths for those we serve.

HOMEWORK EXERCISE 1.11 | YOUR FAMILY'S WAYS OF COPING

Identify some of your family of origin's ways of coping. Think about how family members are treated when they are sick, have lost a job, flunk out of school, or have a relationship that is viewed as unacceptable.

INFLUENCE OF DISABILITY AND ABILITY
Written by Stephan Viehweg

A major influence on how you see and think about yourself is your abilities and disabilities. As students you may feel good about your intellectual abilities. What other abilities are you particularly glad you have? You may not have thought of abilities you take for granted such as being able to hear in class and see the Power-Point presentation. Many of you probably have some disabilities that are pretty easily corrected. For example, vision problems that can be corrected with contact lenses or glasses. Think about the challenges you would face if you became blind or deaf. Think for a minute about how your life would be different if you were born with limited intellectual abilities. Consider issues related to mobility. Some of you enjoy sports or dancing. How would you cope if something happened and you weren't able to get around as you do now? People who haven't been challenged with disabilities may not consider the challenges other individuals face every day. Many people that have disabilities that cannot be corrected have found ways to do what is important to them in spite of the challenges.

It is estimated that as many as 20 percent of people will experience some form of disability in their lifetime (National Association of Social Workers, 2009). Mackelprang and Salsgiver (2009) define **disability** as being unable or without ability. People who are disabled live in communities and belong to families. The likelihood that you either have or will personally experience a loved one who has a disability is extremely high. The likelihood that as a practitioner you will work with someone who has a disability is certain. What characteristics do you have that will help you understand the challenges of someone with a serious disability?

It is important to consider issues related to disabilities and to how you view people with disabilities. Disabilities come in all shapes and sizes and affect everyone regardless of age, sex, gender, economic status, geographic location, etc. Disabilities include physical, sensory, and cognitive impairments as well as mental, physical, and chronic illness. Some disabilities are temporary and some last a lifetime. Some are visible to all and others are not readily seen. Many studies confirm that people with disabilities overall have an inferior status in society and lack access to employment, transportation, educational, and recreational opportunities (National Association of Social Workers, 2009).

Developmental disabilities can be particularly challenging to individuals and families. Children with developmental disabilities often lack adequate support and services and are segregated from others in school and work. Here is a current legal description of developmental disability.

> **Developmental disabilities** are a severe, chronic disability of an individual that are: 1) attributable to a mental or physical impairment or combination of mental and physical impairments; 2) manifested before the individual attains age 22; 3) likely to continue indefinitely; 4) results in substantial functional limitations in self-care, language, learning, mobility, self-direction, independent living, and/or economic self-sufficiency; and 5) reflect the individual's need for a combination and sequence of special, interdisciplinary, or generic services, individualized supports, or other forms of assistance that are of lifelong or extended duration and are individually planned and coordinated. (114 STAT. 1684 PUBLIC LAW 106-402-OCT. 30, 2000)

In the past, many people with all types of disabilities were kept isolated and away from the mainstream community. At one time, parents of children born with disabilities or who developed disabilities as children were told to put them in long term institutions. However, many parents decided to keep their families together and advocated for their children to be included in school and other community activities. They pushed for legislation and programs to provide the education, skills, supports, and services necessary for their children with disabilities to live full, complete lives in their own communities with jobs and homes of their own (http://museumofdisability.org).

Our country has had an awareness of people with disabilities and their needs dating back to the American Revolutionary War in 1776 when there were services to support veterans who suffered from physical wounds. Since the 1960's, there have been many efforts to enact legislation and to address the needs of people with disabilities. Significant pieces of legislation include the Americans with Disabilities Act (ADA), the Individuals with Disabilities Education Act (IDEA), the Civil Rights Act, the Fair Housing Act, the Rehabilitation Act, and most recently the America's Affordable Health Choices Act. As a practitioner it is important to know about relevant legislation and how it affects clients, families, and communities.

One outcome of the advocacy efforts by people with disabilities and their families is an appreciation for "people first language." **People first language** is a form of language aiming to avoid perceived and subconscious dehumanization when discussing people with disabilities. This type of language involves reframing the language we use when referring to people with disabilities. Instead of putting the description of the disability first such as in "autistic boy," the recommendation is to say "boy with autism." Instead of saying "handicapped woman confined to a wheelchair," say "person with a disability who uses a wheelchair." What other examples can you think of in your everyday language that reflects people first language?

Most recently there has been an effort to remove the word "retarded" from our common language because the word retarded has many negative connotations. Instead, people with cognitive challenges are referred to as having "Intellectual Disabilities." **Intellectual disabilities** are disabilities characterized by significant limitations both in intellectual functioning and in adaptive behaviors that cover many everyday social and practical skills. This disability originates before the age of 18 (American Association on Intellectual and Developmental Disabilities, 2010). The language we use is powerful. Framing how we refer to all people, including people with disabilities, is important. The positive language you use can be a model to others.

HOMEWORK EXERCISE 1.12 | YOUR VIEW OF DISABILITIES

Draw a picture of your earliest recollection of disability. It could be your own, a family member, or friend. Use words if you prefer to describe the scenario. Who is in the picture? What are the circumstances? What are the associated feelings? How old were you in the scene? How did this experience influence your perceptions of disabilities? How did your perceptions change over time? How did this experience influence your life as a young person?

Share your picture with another student or colleague and talk about the answers to these questions. Explore with your colleague your insights about your perceptions of disability and how this will influence your work as a practitioner.

INFLUENCE OF STRESS AND DEMANDS

Because the stress and demands on professional practitioners are continuous and numerous, taking care of yourself is essential. Responsible self-care is interdependent with good practice (Cozolino, 2004; Shapiro, Biegel, & Warren, 2007). Self-care involves awareness of the stressors in your private life as well as those in your professional life. Maintaining a sense of perspective is another important aspect of self-care. This involves noticing whether you are living vicariously through your clients, are getting enough support outside your work, are following your passions, and are doing what you want to be doing (Cozolino, 2004; Shapiro, Biegel, & Warren, 2007). Helping others can be tedious, grueling, and demanding. You are constantly forced to face your own problems and differentiate them from those of your clients. To manage the stress involved in your professional life, it is important to take every opportunity to understand yourself as thoroughly as possible. As you become aware of problems in your life that you can't resolve on your own, you should consider seeking help from professional practitioners.

Remember that in the helping relationship, you are the instrument. Just as a musical instrument must be cared for and kept in tune, so you must keep yourself in top form in order to be the best helper you can be. The factors that influenced your decision to become a practitioner will often affect how you take care of yourself. Many people who choose the helping professions learned early in life to work hard, to keep peace in the family, or to take care of a parent or sibling. They may have learned to put their needs on hold while attending to the needs of others. By the time they are adults they may not even be fully aware of what they need. This *other-centeredness* can eventually lead to burnout unless you learn to attend to your own needs.

Burnout has been defined as a syndrome involving "increasing discouragement and emotional and physical exhaustion" (Dewees, 2006, p. 316). Burnout is not uncommon for practitioners who must handle large caseloads and/or deal with difficulties related to managed care, who have little external support, and/or who are working with involuntary clients or with emotionally charged situations such as abused children and elders (Dewees, 2006; Rupert & Morgan, 2005). Some ways to avoid burnout are to ensure that you have a life outside of the office, to monitor your stress level, to periodically evaluate your goals and priorities, to attend professional conferences, to develop hobbies, and/or to attend to your spiritual growth. Learning to take good care of yourself is essential (Skovholt, 2001; Shapiro, Biegel, & Warren, 2007).

Start now to build a healthy lifestyle. Many students think that they need to put off self-care until they graduate because they erroneously believe that they will be less busy then. This is rarely the case. Life keeps on being busy. How you handle the stress of school will likely be the same pattern you will follow after you graduate. Learn to relax, breathe, eat well, participate in physical activities, and set aside time for recreation with your family and friends.

Another stress that many practitioners experience is secondary traumatic stress. This stress occurs when practitioners are working with clients who are in a great deal of emotional or physical pain. For example, when practitioners work with a community group where many children have been killed as a result of gang violence or with a person whose marital partner died as a result of an automobile accident in which the client was driving, they may experience being overwhelmed. Dealing with loss of this magnitude can make practitioners feel as if they have been traumatized themselves. Secondary traumatic stress is an even greater risk for practitioners if the traumatic events experienced by their clients are in some way similar to their own life experiences. If your client's traumas or problems are similar to your own, it is important to carefully evaluate with your supervisor whether it will be in the client's best interest for you to be the practitioner. For example, if you have been raped, working with a rape victim may be too emotionally difficult. Even when you believe you have fully worked through the issues or trauma, you may still discover unresolved wounds as you work with the client. Another challenge is thinking that you understand your client because his/her trauma seems so similar to what you experienced. Your experience may help you to understand your client's situation, but it is important to remember that your client's experiences and feelings will be unique.

HOMEWORK EXERCISE 1.13 | INFLUENCE OF STRESS AND DEMANDS

Make a list of all the stressful events in your life in the last year. Remember that positive events such as going on vacation, moving to a nicer apartment, or getting married may be as stressful as negative events such as being in a car accident, getting sick, receiving a low grade, or not having enough money to pay your bills. Positive and negative events add extra demands to your life. Now put a number between 1 and 10 after each stressful event. A 10 would be something very stressful that had a big impact on your life, such as the death of a family member, and a 1 would be something not very stressful, such as a minor illness. Add up your stress points. Now think about how you react when there is too much stress in your life. Some people become more accident prone, some are more irritable, some withdraw, and some are more likely to get sick. Finally, in what ways have you successfully reduced the effects of stress in your life?

INFLUENCE OF YOUR VIEW OF SELF AND OTHERS

All the areas that we have discussed in this chapter influence your view of yourself and others. It is important for you to consider each of these influences and to know yourself well. As a professional practitioner, knowing who you are will help you to clearly differentiate what is true for you from what is true for your clients. Self-knowledge tends to grow over time. As you work with clients, you will learn more about your uniqueness and become aware of beliefs and values that you did not know you had. One of the joys and challenges of professional practitioners is to always be developing and changing.

Lastly, developing the character strengths and virtues recommended by Peterson and Seligman (2004) will stand you in good stead for the entirety of your career. These strengths and virtues are wisdom and knowledge (creativity, curiosity, open-mindedness, love of learning, perspective); courage (bravery, persistence, integrity, vitality); humanity (love, kindness, social intelligence); justice (citizenship, fairness, leadership); temperance (forgiveness and mercy, modesty and humility, prudence, self-regulation); and transcendence (appreciation of beauty and excellence, gratitude, hope, humor, spirituality).

HOMEWORK EXERCISE 1.14 | SELF-UNDERSTANDING

Make a list of strengths you value most in others. Who are the people you have admired most? Have they had the virtues and strengths proposed by Peterson and Seligman? Which strengths are you in the process of developing?

EXPECTED COMPETENCIES

In this chapter you have learned about several aspects vital to thinking and acting as a practitioner.

You should be able to define the following terms (listed in the order that they were covered): race, ethnicity, culture, white privilege, identity achievement, gender, transgender, transsexual, sexual orientation, bisexual, heterosexism, homophobia, socioeconomic status, religion, spirituality, family, disability, developmental disabilities, intellectual disabilities, people first language, and burnout. All terms are listed and defined in the glossary.

You should now be able to:

- Identify some of the influences of your culture, race, ethnicity, gender, sexual orientation, socioeconomic status, religion and spirituality, life stage, family of origin, abilities and disability, and stress and demands on your attitudes and behavior and identify how these influences may impact your clients.
- Identify several risks of burnout for practitioners and ways to minimize these risks.

WAYS OF UNDERSTANDING AND PERCEIVING SELF AND OTHERS

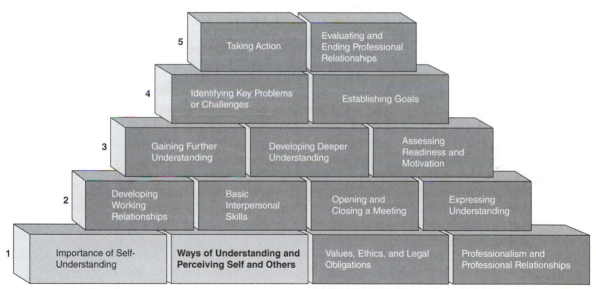

CHAPTER 2

5   Taking Action   Evaluating and Ending Professional Relationships

4   Identifying Key Problems or Challenges   Establishing Goals

3   Gaining Further Understanding   Developing Deeper Understanding   Assessing Readiness and Motivation

2   Developing Working Relationships   Basic Interpersonal Skills   Opening and Closing a Meeting   Expressing Understanding

1   Importance of Self-Understanding   **Ways of Understanding and Perceiving Self and Others**   Values, Ethics, and Legal Obligations   Professionalism and Professional Relationships

Questions to consider as you read this chapter:

- How will the way I view the world affect my work with clients?
- What are some new ways of thinking about clients that might enhance our work together?

This chapter covers practice behaviors related to understanding seven ways of perceiving reality. *You will learn the importance of:*

- Realizing that each person constructs reality in their own unique way (constructivism)
- Seeing families as systems in which each person impacts the others and the whole system (family systems)
- Knowing the many effects of the environment on individuals, family, and groups (ecological)
- Identifying the strengths in individuals, families, groups, and organizations (strengths)
- Seeing the capacity that individuals, families, and groups use to cope in difficult situations (resilience)
- Encouraging people to deal with and learn from challenges (empowerment)
- Seeing that many people need to constantly adapt to living in more than one culture (dual perspective)

In the first chapter you learned about the importance of self-understanding and that your worldview is determined by many factors. Your views are even influenced by how you are feeling at any given moment. If you aren't feeling well, have a headache, or are tired, you might not notice positive things like flowers blooming or the sun shining.

In this chapter you will focus on a second important task in building a foundation for competent practice, which is developing an understanding of seven major perspectives. These perspectives provide a variety of ways of viewing and understanding clients. Your view of other people is determined in part by the lens or perspective you use. In the past, helping professionals often viewed the world through a problem-solving lens. Although using this lens is important for professionals as they try to understand the difficulties their clients are experiencing, it should be only one of several perspectives practitioners use to view a situation. If you are looking at your clients using only a problem-solving perspective, you might not see their strengths and abilities to successfully cope with difficult situation. As a competent helping professional you need to identify the perspective you usually use and learn to use other perspectives that will help you more fully understand and successfully work with your clients.

In this chapter we will discuss seven perspectives that are used by helping professionals: constructivist, ecological, resilience, systems, strengths, empowerment, and the dual perspective. At the end of the chapter, Table 2.2 summarizes practitioner strategies, concepts, and the assumptions of each perspective. Throughout the book we will refer back to these perspectives as we discuss ways of working with clients.

Throughout the chapter you will be asked to refer back to the following case study and answer questions about how you would view this situation from each of the perspectives.

CASE STUDY: HECTOR AND HIS FAMILY
Written by Thomas L. Moore

Hector, age 19, is a student at Mid-city Community College (MCC), the largest community college in the state. He is there on a scholarship for soccer. Hector has been referred by the counseling center at MCC. He was initially seeing a counselor at the school because of adjustment and academic problems. Hector also tested positive for cannabis in a required drug screen by the athletic department. The soccer coach considers Hector a star player. The coach wants him "fixed" and to receive passing grades in his classes so he is eligible to play.

Hector considers himself of multi-racial background; his father is Mexican-American and his mother is Caucasian. They met while serving in the first Gulf War. Hector's father, Julian, has struggled since the war due to Gulf War Illness, experiencing fatigue, headaches, skin rashes, etc. Because of his medical issues, employment has been unsteady, contributing to financial difficulties for the family. Carol, Hector's mother, returned to school after her military service, received a degree in education and works as an elementary school teacher. She would best be described as a "helicopter mom." Even before Calvin, the outpatient center counselor, met with Hector or completed confidentiality releases, Carol called and left three messages. Carol is overwhelmed with the care of her husband and their four children. Hector is the oldest. Hector's only opportunity for a college education is to maintain his athletic scholarship. His high school grades were slightly below average. He was diagnosed with ADHD in elementary school; however, Hector states that he does not like how he feels on Ritalin. He says that marijuana is the only thing that calms him down. He is anxious to get Calvin to state that there is no substance problem and to return to playing soccer and living the rest of his life.

THE CONSTRUCTIVIST PERSPECTIVE
Defining the Constructivist Perspective

Constructivism, as explained in the pioneering work of George Kelly (1955/1991), is a perspective that identifies how individuals describe their experience in terms of personal constructs. A **personal construct** is an explanation of an event or series of events that becomes the lens through which the individual sees the world. These constructs are developed as individuals interpret and give meaning to their experiences. Constructs are not consciously developed. They develop and change over time based on the individual's total life experience and view of self. In any situation each person pays attention to and gives importance, value, and meaning to certain elements and ignores and devalues other elements. You are probably aware that if you ask a group of people to describe a situation each person will describe the scene differently. Those people in a similar age group and from a similar cultural background are more likely to have descriptions that are more similar than those from a different age group and background.

A personal construct can include decisions about life ("It's hard"), other people ("They are helpful"), how to behave ("You should be responsible"), and self ("I am not very smart"). These constructs might be broad, such as "Work before play" or more specific, such as "My mother is a safe person."

People test their personal constructs by noting how well the constructs predict life circumstances. Constructs may be changed based on new experiences. For example, if your construct was "I am not very intelligent" and you did well in college coursework, you might revise your construct about yourself ("I am really smart after all!") or you might revise your construct about college ("College isn't really as difficult as I was led to believe. Anyone can succeed in college if they work hard enough, even if they aren't smart"). Most of us know someone who appears to be thin or at least is not overweight, but who is always on a diet because his or her construct is "I am fat." According to constructivism, each individual is continually testing his or her constructs.

Personal and Social Constructs

Gergen (2006) and Stam (1998) emphasize the importance of social and cultural factors in the construction of individual reality. Gergen contended that there are as many realities as there are cultures, contexts, and ways of communicating. **Social constructivists** focus on how relationships, language, and context influence an individual's or a group's interpretation of self, others, and the world.

Personality is a socially constructed idea (Burr, 1995; Gergen, 2006; Hosking, 2005; Stular, 1998; Thompson, 2006; Williams & Thornton, 1998). **Personality** includes the qualities, traits, characteristics, and behavior patterns that distinguish each individual. The ways in which people are identified, talked about, and treated all have an influence on their personality. As each child grows, his/her personality is constructed based first on experiences in the family and later on experiences in the world (neighborhood, school, culture) (Burr, Vutt, & Epting, 1997; Thompson, 2006). Some of the firmest constructs are developed in childhood. These constructs are often difficult to change because individuals experience these ideas as *truth* about themselves. For example, if your mother said that you were intelligent, handsome, or funny, you probably accepted those qualities as true. Some constructs are quite limiting, such as "I am no good at sports." These constructs might have developed in early childhood based on the mother or father repeatedly telling the child he was awkward and would never be good at sports or maybe the child was encouraged to try many sports and never found a sport in which he excelled. Other personal constructs can be harmful in relationships such as, "no one will love me unless I am (thin, beautiful, charming, muscular, etc.)." Childhood experiences also lead to the development of constructs about others and the world such as: "People who aren't like us can't be trusted" and "The world is a dangerous place."

Culture strongly influences whether the words used to describe someone's personality are seen as positive or negative. The advantaged or dominant cultural group names their preferred characteristics and uses negative terms to describe people in minority groups. For example, *assertive, strong,* and *independent* generally are viewed as positive descriptions of women today in the U.S. culture, but in the past and in other cultures, these descriptions would have been considered negative descriptions of women. Members of minority groups often accept the dominant view as true and evaluate themselves against this standard.

Language is an important factor in the process of making meaning of experiences, since the ways that people talk about themselves and their world influence

HOMEWORK EXERCISE 2.1 | SOCIAL CONSTRUCTIONIST

List five descriptive words related to personality that the dominant cultural group identifies as positive. List five descriptive words related to personality the dominant culture group identifies as negative. Discuss how one of these positive words and one of these negative words could be limiting to someone in a minority group or be advantageous to the dominant group. For example, "To be beautiful women must be thin." How has this construct affected women? How has this construct advantaged wealthy white men who are marketing products to women?

their perceptions. In English there is one word for snow, but the Aleuts of Alaska have a number of different words for snow. Those who speak English may not even notice aspects of snow that an Aleut would see as significant. Even though constructivists acknowledge that social factors play an important part in shaping people's views of themselves and the world, the individual person is still seen as the prime source of his or her own constructs (Raskin, 2001). Constructivists do not believe people are programmed by parents, society, or others. Rather, individuals decide who they are and how they will make sense of their world. The individual interprets every event and experience that happens to him or her, and it is this interpretation or construct that influences the person's beliefs and behavior. For example, if a mother has serious problems and cannot be counted on to be nurturing or supportive, her daughter might grow up believing that "The only person you can really count on is yourself." Another person might put a completely different meaning on those childhood experiences and grow up believing that "I am unlovable." In many cases people are not aware of their personal constructs and believe that their understanding of themselves, others, and the world is the only correct interpretation.

All people are constructivists in the sense that they give meaning to the events and experiences they have. If you grow up in a neighborhood where violence is the way to solve problems, then you may decide that trying to resolve disagreements peacefully would be a waste of time. People live within a web of meaning that they have woven (Mahoney, 2003).

HOMEWORK EXERCISE 2.2 | YOUR CONSTRUCTS OF SELF, OTHERS, AND THE WORLD

Think of a time when your life was going well or you were satisfied. Reflect on that time and write down the ideas you held about yourself. Complete the sentence "I am …" with several descriptive words. Based on your view of others at that same time, complete the sentence "They are …" with several words describing your perceptions of other people. Finally, complete the sentence "The world is …" with several descriptive words. That is one set of constructs or beliefs that you have about yourself, others, and the world.

Now remember a time when you felt depressed, discouraged, sick, exhausted, and/or basically miserable. Think about that time and do the same exercise, completing the sentences, "I am …" " They are …" and "The world is …." These statements are another set of constructs or beliefs that you have about yourself, others, and the world.

The constructs you just recorded are true for you. Someone else might perceive you, others, or the world quite differently. Who would be right? If you answered that both perceptions would be right, you are correct. Each person's construction of reality is true for that person.

Applying the Constructivist Perspective

Using a constructivist perspective helps practitioners remember that their view of the world may be different from their client's view. Practitioners may think a problem is caused by physical illness, stress and demands, oppressive cultural factors, etc., but their clients may have a completely different view. For example, a client may attribute his alcoholism to his lack of willpower and the practitioner may see alcoholism as a disease that is inherited.

As practitioners work with clients, they will see constructs such as "They won't treat you fairly" that may be based on past experiences (e.g., people of color may have had negative encounters in the dominant culture). Groups may develop constructs such as "We can't make a difference in our community."

As a practitioner you need to figure out, understand, accept, and work within your client's view of reality. It is not your job to change another person's view of reality. If your clients see problems with their constructs, they may decide to change them. Constructivists propose that change happens when constricting personal constructs are challenged and constructs that embrace new ideas and behavioral possibilities are developed (Newton, 2006; Sexton & Griffin, 1997).

When an individual, family, or group becomes aware of a construct that is unsatisfying or limiting, the individual can develop another meaning for events or experiences. Practitioners using a constructivist perspective work with clients to help them become aware of existing constructs. Once the clients are aware of negative constructs that are causing them problems, practitioners help them change these constructs by identifying exceptions to their negative constructs. If your client's construct is "I'll never get a good job," what might you say to invite the client to think of exceptions? First you would express your understanding. "It sounds like you are feeling hopeless about the job situation." You could then say, "What are the strengths you have that an employer would value?" or "Tell me about how you have gotten jobs in the past. Let's start with your very first job." Positive constructs can be used to challenge limiting constructs.

Problems arise when individual constructs for two people in a relationship are very different. For example, a couple seeking help to improve their relationship may need to recognize that each partner conceptualizes the issues differently depending on his or her own personal constructs. Think about a relationship in which the husband's construct is "As a man I should support the family. Women should stay home and take care of the children." What if his wife's construct is "Women can have whatever career they want." The practitioner might encourage the husband to understand the wife's interest in her career as a sign of her intelligence and willingness to contribute financially to the family rather than as a belief that he isn't a good provider. The practitioner might encourage the wife to see the husband's desire to be the family provider as an indication of his love for her and their children and his sense of responsibility towards them. The constructivist perspective is useful to practitioners as they work to understand the worldviews or constructs of individuals, groups, and community organizations. The constructivist perspective encourages active involvement, hope, and belief in the possibility of making changes, and participation of individuals and communities in their own unfolding (Snyder & Lopez, 2001). When people recognize that they construct their own reality and can have a positive influence in their lives, they may realize they can make changes and have an impact on their world. Clients and practitioners collaborate to create new meanings and possibilities for the future. These new constructs contribute to differences in their lives and the lives of those with whom they are connected.

HOMEWORK EXERCISE 2.3 | IDENTIFYING CONSTRUCTS

As you listen to others this week, see if you can identify their personal constructs. For example, when a man mentions how slowly the woman in front of him was driving, what are your guesses about his construct of women driver? What do they believe about the world, themselves, and others? How do you think these constructs might enhance or inhibit their lives? Reflect on how your personal constructs have led you to where you are today.

HOMEWORK EXERCISE 2.4 | CASE EXAMPLE

Using a constructivist perspective, what are your hunches about the personal constructs (helpful and limiting) influencing Julian, Carol, and Hector?

FAMILY SYSTEMS

Systems theory takes into account the entire "system" with which an individual interacts. A **system** is seen as a complex entity within which interactions are as important as the individuals (Breunlin, Schwartz, & MacKune-Karrer, 1997). Any group of people can be a system as long as they have some relation to one another and are contained by a boundary or understanding of which people are part of the system. For example, in some families there is an understanding that Jane (mother's good friend who lives with the family and may be called Aunt Jane) is a member of the family even though she is not biologically related to the family. Families form repetitive patterns, or systems, over time.

Family systems are organized by a set of rules or patterns that enable each person to learn what is expected or permitted of him or her as well as others in family interactions. These rules, often unstated, help regulate and stabilize how families function as a unit. Family rules demonstrate their values, set up family roles consistent with these values, function to provide stability to relationships within the family system, are often carried over from previous generations, and are influenced by culture. Rules include roles of females and males, husbands and wives, and parents and children. Rules define who can say what to whom and how individuals make decisions. Some rules are negotiable, while others are not.

Changing one part of the family system will result in changes to other parts. For example, if one of the parents begins working full time, in order for the family to function well, some of that parent's roles will need to be assumed by other family members. Families change over time and individuals assume different roles in response to these changes. Think back to the family developmental stages discussed in Chapter 1. In each stage, individuals may assume different roles.

There are a number of different types of family systems or ways that members of a family interact with each other (Goldenberg & Goldenberg, 1998; O'Brien, 2005). Families form repetitive patterns, or systems, over time. A family system may be open or closed in various degrees. A **closed family system** is described as a system that tends to exist in relative isolation, with communication taking place primarily between members. Family members are suspicious of outsiders and dependent on each other. Families within a closed system avoid change and hold onto their established traditions and values.

In contrast, an **open family system** is a system characterized by the willingness to assimilate new information and to engage in ongoing interactions with their environment. Members are free to move in and out of transactions with each other and with people outside the family. The family has no single correct way of doing things. As the family matures, changes are tolerated, supported, and celebrated.

Most families have characteristics of both closed and open systems. If the closed aspects of the system become rigid, then the family will become increasingly stressed. For example, an adolescent might want to radically change his hairstyle or hair color, but to do so would violate the way a family thinks individuals ought to look. Such a violation might cause considerable tension and fighting in a family with a rigid system. If, after a death or divorce, the members of an open family system do not bond together without the missing family member, the family system may be too open. If the mother who was the central figure that tied the family together dies, the feeling of being a family may be lost leaving the father and children unsure how to function in her absence.

HOMEWORK EXERCISE 2.5 | FAMILY SYSTEMS

Consider your own family of origin. Rules related to family interaction govern how much open communication is allowed. How much openness was allowed in your family? Families define what is involved in the roles of each partner, parent and children. Describe three characteristics of the following roles in your family: such as each partner, parent, and child. Now think of another family you have spent time with. Describe how the roles such as each partner, parent, and child are different in that family. Do you consider your family a mostly closed or open system? List a few observations about your family to support your view.

Applying the Family Systems Perspective

Using a systems perspective, practitioners begin by gaining an understanding of how interactions within systems affect clients. Practitioners assist clients in identifying reciprocal relationships between their behavior and influences of the systems within which they interact. Clients may see how someone else's behavior is influencing them and be less clear about how their behavior is influencing others. Using a family systems perspective, practitioners focus on interactions within the family. For example, a couple brings in a teenager, complaining about the constant arguments with the step-parent. As the practitioner explores the situation, the parents describe a pattern where the biological parent steps in to defend the teen as the argument escalates. Everyone in the family, including the teen, is aware that the teen's behavior invites anger from the step-parent and leads to arguments. Despite the unhappiness of all family members, the pattern continues with the teen continuing to defy and provoke the step-parent. What the family members may not recognize is that when the biological parent defends the teen, an alliance is created between the biological parent and the teen against the step-parent. The family may also not notice that the arguing between the teenager and step-parent takes the focus off of the other problems between the parents. The practitioner helps the clients see the patterns in the family system and begin to change those patterns that are destructive.

HOMEWORK EXERCISE 2.6 | Case Example

Changes in one part of a family system leads to changes in another part of the family system.

- Describe a change in this family system.
  - How might this change have affected roles of mother and father?

- How might this change affect how individuals in this family make decisions?
- How might changes in this system have encouraged Carol to take the role of "helicopter mom?"

THE ECOLOGICAL PERSPECTIVE

Defining the Ecological Perspective

The **ecological perspective** views people and their environment as evolving, adapting, and continuously interacting (Brower, 1988; Dishion & Stormshak, 2007; Germain & Gitterman, 1995; Ungar, 2002). Derived from concepts of biological ecology, this framework enables practitioners and clients to think about the reciprocal relationships between people and their environment. Practitioners seek to understand the interconnected personal, environmental, and cultural factors involved in clients' situations. While cause-and-effect linear thinking can be used to explain simple phenomena, it is inadequate to explain the complex human behavior seen by practitioners (Ungar, 2002). An ecological perspective is less concerned with cause and effect and more concerned with the transactions that occur between people and their environments. These **transactions** are defined as interactions that are reciprocal processes used by people to shape their environments while they are in turn being shaped by their environments over time (Dishion & Stormshak, 2007; Germain & Gitterman, 1995). For example, cause and effect might predict that a mother who applies new techniques in disciplining her little girl might see fewer tantrums. In contrast, the ecological perspective would also consider the changes in the mother's sense of competency and willingness to learn new skills. The child in turn might now see her mother as more confident and respond with adaptive behavior.

Ecological Perspective Concepts

The ecological perspective (Germain and Gitterman, 1995; Wolski, 2004) has three important components: person-environment fit, adaptations, and life stressors. **Person-environment fit** refers to how well a person's (or group's) needs, goals, and rights mesh with the traits and functioning of their physical and social environment, since the environment includes their culture (Miley O'Melia, & De Bois, 2004; Wolski, 2004). In the following example, identify possible problems in the person-environment. A first generation Mexican-American young woman from a poor family might be pushed to go to work to help support the family rather than follow her dreams and continue her education. If the interactions are generally negative, both the individual and the environment are likely to experience detrimental effects. For example, when a homosexual teen experiences negative feedback from his environment (i.e., the family, the neighborhood, the school, or the community), this poor person-environment fit is likely to impact abilities to meet their needs and achieve their goals. In contrast, if the homosexual teen's environment is positive, he is more likely to develop self-acceptance.

Adaptations are the processes people use to sustain or increase the level of fit between themselves and their environment. These adaptations are ongoing and include cognitive, behavioral, and sensory-perceptual changes. Adaptations can be actions to change the environment (such as leaving an abusive relationship), changes within the individual (such as learning new parenting skills), or both. Think about the previous Mexican-American family. If a Mexican-American teacher or the family's priest talked to the family about the long term importance of a higher education, the family might become more accepting of their daughter's goals. The daughter in turn might feel more confident about pursuing her dreams. As you can see from the example, one change can start a continuous cycle of adaptation.

Life stressors are issues that are perceived as exceeding personal and environmental resources available to manage them. These stressors can include social or developmental transitions, traumatic events, or anything that changes the existing person-environment fit. While a stressor might be seen as presenting the possibility of serious harm, loss, or danger for some, the same stressor may be viewed as an opportunity for growth (Lazarus & Folkman, 1984; Perkins, Crim, Silberman, & Brown, 2004). For example, a house fire is a serious environment stressor. An individual's reactions to such an event are tempered by his or her characteristics and resources to deal with the problems that result from the event. It is natural to have a feeling of loss in such a situation; yet some individuals also see it as an opportunity to make changes in their environment. This is only possible when sufficient resources are available. If a family is unable to re-create an adequate home environment due to lack of resources, they may not be able to move beyond their feelings of loss and disruption, resulting in high levels of stress.

When high levels of stress continue over a period of time, this may cause emotional and/or psychological disturbances such as feelings of guilt, anxiety, depression, anger, fear, or helplessness. Over time these feelings may lead to diminished self-esteem, and sense of competence (DeLongis & Holtzman, 2005; Sassaroli & Ruggiero, 2005). Coping strategies are behaviors that are used to manage stress.

Coping strategies may be positive such as seeing a counselor, using problem-solving strategies, or seeking support from friends and family. Negative strategies include such things as substance abuse, violence, and withdrawal. Successful coping serves to decrease the misfit between people and their environments.

Applying the Ecological Perspective

Using an ecological perspective, behaviors are not seen as dysfunctional or mal-adaptive. Since behaviors are viewed as adaptations that adapt to improve the goodness of fit between the individual and their environment, how can these behaviors be considered maladaptive? There are behaviors that are unacceptable and have negative consequences, but all behaviors make sense in context. For example, a teenager who carries a gun around the neighborhood may be engaging in unde-sirable behavior, but if that teenager's friend was recently killed in a gun violence incident, his decision to have a gun would be understandable.

All behavior must be viewed in environmental context. A behavior that is appropriate in one situation, such as a boy playfully pushing and shoving other children at the local park, is not at all appropriate in another situation such as a classroom setting. Such behavior on the playground may increase the boy's status among his peers, but the same behavior in the classroom may cause him to be labeled *antisocial* and a *behavior problem*. Problems arise when challenges occur in unresponsive environments. Returning to the boy who pushes and shoves in the classroom, a teacher who understands the child's need for attention from his peers could help him meet that need in a different way. In contrast, if the teacher pun-ishes and humiliates him, his behavior may become more hostile and unacceptable and have an impact on all his interactions in the school environment, causing him to harbor a negative attitude toward school.

How we work with people and their situations is based on our perception of human behavior. Viewing clients from an ecological perspective helps us under-stand how they have developed their strengths and vulnerabilities and influences what we do to support growth and change in clients. The ecological perspective emphasizes a focus on the strengths people demonstrate in response to a difficult situation or environment. Practitioners work to help clients build on the strengths they possess. The ecological perspective and strengths perspective (described later in this chapter) work well together.

HOMEWORK EXERCISE 2.7 | ECOLOGICAL PERSPECTIVE

Reflect on your life experiences using an ecological perspective. What are some ways that you have adapted to your environment? For example, if you had to drive in rush hour traffic today, that might have caused you to feel stressed, to think negative thoughts about the other drivers, and to act in more aggressive or competitive ways than usual.

Identify at least five ways you adapt to your family of origin, to your friends, and to the challenges in your life.

Identify the five to ten most stressful events that have happened to you in the last year. What coping strategies did you use as you dealt with those stresses?

The ecological perspective is useful when working with groups as well as individuals (Conyne & Bemak, 2004). Kurt Lewin (1952) suggested using the force field perspective to figure out possible barriers to the achievement of group goals and to gain a better understanding of how these goals might be achieved. Lewin defined a **force field** as the total psychological environment existing for an individual or group at a certain point in time. He saw the force field as dynamic and changing with time and experience. Lewin posited that groups are more than the sum of the members. Instead, the group is an integration of the members with a unique structure, goals, and relation to other groups. Each group has needs that are linked to individual goals. For example, in a class task group, one member of the group may have a goal related to getting an A on a group project. Similar to the poor fit between a person and his/her environment, small or large groups are committed to working to achieve a better fit with its environment. An example of this quest for a better fit is the battle for women's right to vote during the early twentieth century. As women began to see themselves as a disenfranchised group, they fought for their right to be recognized as valued, contributing, voting members of society. In a similar fashion, the civil rights movements of the 1960's came about from the inequity of the "rules" for African-Americans, such as different restrooms, drinking fountains, areas of public transportation, obtaining service in restaurants, and many others. In both examples the poor fit between the group and environment led to group action and resulting environmental changes. Extending Lewin's (1952) force field perspective, Brueggemann (2001) described the barriers and benefits groups face in achieving their goals. Barriers to achieving goals, called **restraining forces**, are the disadvantages and costs involved with each action taken to fulfill the identified need. Examples of restraining forces include limited time, money, and manpower. **Compelling forces**, the advantages or benefits of taking action, include an increased quantity and quality of services and greater effectiveness in meeting the group's needs. For example, a group from a poor community might consider building a park in an area of substandard housing. To achieve this goal, the group would need to obtain permission to use or purchase land for the park (restraining force). Compelling forces include having a safe place for children to play and improving the appeal of the neighborhood. When the restraining forces and the compelling forces are identified, the group can move on to finding people, groups, and/or organizations to help them overcome the restraining forces and achieve the goal. Recalling the example of women's right to vote, there were many restraining forces (threats to those in power) as well as compelling forces (expansion of human rights and potential benefits of the important input women have to offer) that led to the passage of laws granting women the right to vote.

HOMEWORK EXERCISE 2.8 | CASE EXAMPLE

Using the ecological perspective discuss Julian, Carol, and Hector.

- What life stressors are Julian, Carol, and Hector facing?

- What behaviors are they using to cope with these stressors?
- How well are they coping with these stressors?
- Describe the person-environment fit for Hector. What is a positive aspect of the fit?

THE STRENGTHS PERSPECTIVE

Defining the Strengths Perspective

The **strengths perspective** is a perspective that views all people as having strengths. The strengths perspective focuses on assets clients have developed throughout their life (Saleebey, 1992). Using the strength perspective, practitioners work with clients to identify their talents, strengths, interests, dreams, and goals. A strength is "any psychological process that consistently enables a person to think and act so as to yield benefits to himself or herself and society" (McCullough & Snyder, 2000, p. 3). Strengths are sometimes developed as people struggle to overcome difficulties, traumas, oppression, disappointments, and adversity. Strengths are also related to personal qualities or virtues that are admired, such as intelligence, common sense, patience, loyalty, sense of humor, commitment, responsibility, warmth, flexibility, friendliness, generosity, and many other qualities. Developed and under-developed talents are strengths. These include such things as being a musician, a writer, a poet, a good cook, a car mechanic, a carpenter, a vocalist, or a painter (Saleebey, 2002c). Every person has untouched "mental, physical, emotional, social, and spiritual abilities" (Weick, Rapp, Sullivan, & Kisthardt, 1989, p. 352). These undeveloped capacities can be a source of power and hope (Weick & Chamberlain, 1996).

Families also have strengths. For example, a family's major strength may be an ability to stay together and support each other through challenges and trauma. Other family strengths include encouraging each other, helping each other, loving and caring for each other, accepting each other, and standing up for each other. Even very troubled families can identify good times when they were supportive to each other and had fun together.

Communities, groups, and organizations have strengths. Organizations identified as being *family-friendly* places to work have strengths such as on-site child care, opportunities to work from home, time off for family emergencies, and other supportive services that make it easier for parents to be effective on the job and at home. Groups may have strengths such as being effective, efficient, supportive, cooperative, focused, accepting, and/or fun. Communities or neighborhood strengths may include helping each other out, watching out for each other, sharing resources with each other, and working together to achieve goals.

Saleebey (2002a) stated that "focusing and building on client strengths is an imperative" in order to demonstrate values related to "equality, respect for the dignity of the individual, inclusiveness and diversity and the search for maximum autonomy" (p. 264). Whether we are working with individuals, couples, families, groups, or organizations, it is valuable to look for their strengths, to identify their resources (such as money, social support, adequate housing, education, past experiences, etc.), and to invite them to focus on possibilities for the future.

Applying the Strengths Perspective

Using a strengths perspective, practitioners begin by gaining an understanding of the challenges and struggles their clients are experiencing. As the practitioner listens to clients discuss problems, he/she also pays attention to the strengths and abilities clients have used in dealing with the problems. Instead of focusing exclusively on deficits, problems, and weaknesses in clients, strengths-perspective practitioners also focus on their clients' strengths, capacity, and potential (Wong, 2006). Focusing exclusively on problems tends to invite people to feel hopeless and discouraged. When clients are feeling discouraged, it is helpful to invite them to identify past successes, however small, and to look at the qualities and strengths that helped them achieve those successes. Using a strengths perspective, practitioners focus on what is right with clients instead of what is wrong with them. They openly acknowledge and show respect for the strengths of their clients.

Appreciative Inquiry is another variation on the strengths perspective that is useful in working with groups, neighborhoods, or organizations. Practitioners using Appreciative Inquiry ask about, focus on, and recognize or appreciate the strengths in the teams or groups with whom they work (Hammond, 1998). The practitioner might talk about a time when "the team/group performed really well," "went beyond what was expected," and/or "put forth extra effort" (Hammond, 1998, p. 34). The practitioner might ask about positive behavior or outcomes.

- What did each of you do in order to produce such a thorough report?
- What are your ideas about what your team is doing in order to work so effectively and cooperatively together?
- This organization seems to be very concerned about the well-being of employees. I wonder how this level of concern developed.

HOMEWORK EXERCISE 2.9 | STRENGTHS

Find a partner and discuss accomplishments in your life before you were five years old. For each accomplishment allow some time to explore the strengths necessary to achieve that accomplishment. For example, during your first five years of life you probably learned to walk, talk, and perhaps tie your shoes. What capacities do you believe made these successes possible? Move to the next five years of your life when you may have mastered skills such as riding a bicycle, reading, writing, and doing arithmetic. List some of the strengths necessary to master each of these very complex skills.

Now discuss an experience you have had in which someone saw and identified a strength in you that previously had been outside of your awareness. How did that experience affect you? As you were growing up, was it more common for people to identify your strengths or your weaknesses? What impact do you believe that positive or negative emphasis has had on your life?

Since language so powerfully affects our thinking, some authors suggest that using the language of challenges is more positive than talking about problems (Bennet, Wolin, & Reiss, 1987; Hubble & Miller, 2004; Wolin, 1999, 2003). The authors of this text agree that using the word *challenges* is better than using the word *problems*. Challenges are usually experienced as something that can be overcome and may represent an opportunity for growth. Problems, on the other hand, may be experienced as negative and more difficult to change.

Incorporated into the strengths perspective is the belief that everyone has the capacity to develop new resources, to make positive changes, and to use his/her competencies to solve problems. Using the strengths perspective, it is the practitioner's job to invite clients to discover, think about, and figure out how to use their strengths. The past and present are explored to identify strengths and capacities. When clients talk about problems and difficulties from the past, practitioners can help them focus on how they coped with the challenges. Working from a strengths perspective, practitioners often ask clients what they learned from past challenges. Research has shown a significant correlation between a strengths-based approach and client improvement (Lopez & Magyar-Moe, 2006; Rapp, Siegal, Li, & Saha, 1998; Wolin, 2003).

Using a strengths perspective, practitioners explore client competencies, capacities, abilities, and resources and then focus on future possibilities. Practitioners might ask clients to talk about what they do well, what they have taught another person, what they would like to accomplish in the next year, and/or what their wishes or dreams are. By expressing interest in clients' hopes, dreams, and goals, and by focusing on competence and future possibilities, the practitioner heightens clients' belief in the possibility of change (Cheavens, Feldman, Woodward, & Snyder, 2006; Saleebey, 2002b; Wolin, 1999).

HOMEWORK EXERCISE 2.10 | STRENGTHS AND CHALLENGES

Think of a challenging time in your life or the life of your family. What strengths did you or members of your family develop as you coped with the challenge?

What did you learn about yourself, others, and the world from that experience?

HOMEWORK EXERCISE 2.11 | CASE EXAMPLE

Make a list of strengths, talents, and capacities of Julian, Carol, Hector, and their family.

How is Carol's tendency to be a "helicopter mom" a strength?

THE RESILIENCE PERSPECTIVE
Written by Mulunesh Abebe Alebachew

Resilience is another useful perspective. **Resilience** is the ability to survive and thrive in the face of overwhelming life challenges (Early & GlenMaye, 2000; Humphreys, 2003; Jenson, 2007; Lamond et al., 2009; Waller, 2001). Resilience is a dynamic process that is the outcome of positive adaption in the face of significant adversity, stress, or risk (Aisenberg & Herrenkohl, 2008; Gilligan, 2004; Leadbeater, Dodgen, & Solarz, 2005; Levy & Wall, 2000; Lietz, 2006, 2007; Peters, Leadbeater, & McMahon, 2005; Schoon & Bynner, 2003; Werner, 2005).

Resilience is not a fixed personality trait or an inborn characteristic found in some lucky individuals and absent in others. No one is either vulnerable or resilient all of the time. Resilience is a set of learned behaviors and a pattern of adaptation that may or may not be present from one time to another time. Resilience depends on the availability of protective factors (Gilligan, 2004; Olsson, Bond, Burns, Vella-Brodrick, & Sawyer, 2003; Riley & Masten, 2005; Tremblay, 2005; Waller, 2001). Resilience is developed from the dynamic interaction of risk and protective processes involving individual, family, community, and societal factors in a certain context (Rink & Tricker, 2005; Walsh, 2002).

Risk factors are any influencing factors that can bring or predict negative outcomes on the functioning and overall development of the individual. These factors include biological and social influences found at individual, family, community, and societal levels. Risk factors include such things as: genetic disorders, low birth weight, disability, harsh parenting, homelessness, dangerous neighborhoods, poverty or poor socioeconomic conditions, losing significant family members, community violence, maltreatment, divorce, chronic family discord, ethnic minority, and catastrophic life events (Greeff & Merwe, 2003; Humphreys, 2003; Hyman & Williams, 2001; Lam & Grossman, 1997; Lietz, 2006, 2007; McClure, Chavez, Agars, Peacock, & Matosian, 2008; Riley & Masten, 2005; Seccombe, 2002; Werner, 2005; Williams & Mickelson, 2004). Some risk factors are avoidable and some are inevitable. Risk factors often come together. For instance, a child who belongs to a minority racial group is more likely to experience economic disadvantages, poor schools, family discord, and other related conditions. When practitioners identify a risk factor in a client, they should look for other risk factors.

Protective factors include strengths, capabilities, talents, coping skills, resources and assets. **Protective factors** are any factors that can exert either direct or indirect influences to buffer, mediate, lessen, or alter the negative effects of risk factors. Like risk factors, these protective factors are within the individual, family, community, and larger socio-cultural contexts. An individual's resiliency is a product of the interaction between risk and protective factors at the individual, family, community, and socio-cultural levels (Doyle, 2001; Gilligan, 2004; Olsson et al., 2003; Peters et al., 2005; Riley & Masten, 2005; Rink & Tricker, 2005; Schoon & Bynner, 2003; Waller, 2001; Walsh, 2002; Werner, 2005; Wolkow & Ferguson, 2001; Worthington & Scherer, 2007). The following table summarizes the most common protective factors.

All of these protective factors tend to coexist, interact, aggregate, and have a positive chain or synergy leading to a favorable developmental outcome. The same is true for risk factors (Olsson et al., 2003; Riley & Masten, 2005; Rink & Tricker, 2005; Schoon & Bynner, 2003). For instance, a positive temperament increases the likelihood of eliciting positive responses from parents and caregivers. This positive response in turn will enhance children's social skills and their responsiveness to others (Olsson et al., 2003).

Protective factors can reduce some effects of negative experience (Gilligan, 2004). For instance, intimate partner violence (IPV) against women is a significant risk factor that affects a woman's overall well-being. There may be protective factors within the woman, her family, community, and society that buffer, moderate, and/or modify the adverse and devastating effects of IPV.

Resilience represents both a *process* and the *outcome* of competent functioning. When resilience is seen as a process, it involves the interplay of risk and protective

TABLE 2.1 | LIST OF PROTECTIVE FACTORS ACROSS FOUR ECOSYSTEM LEVELS

Individual Factors	Family Factors	Community Factors	Socio-cultural Factors
• Positive temperament	• Competent parents	• Adequate resources for child care	• Positive ethnic identity
• Responsiveness to others	• Parental warmth, encouragement, and assistance	• Good schools	• Resistance to oppression
• Pro-social attitudes	• Model competent behavior	• Clear rules	• Identification with traditional beliefs or values
• Attachment to others	• Authoritative parenting style	• Effective curricula/ teaching/ counseling	• Participation in traditional practices
• Competence on normative roles	• Close relationship with a caring adult or positive attachment	• Focus on instilling self-esteem, goal setting, clear communication, problem solving	• Ethnic socialization
• Trust in people as resources	• Access to knowledge	• Collaboration between family and school	• Positive peers
• Communication skills	• Belief in the child	• Access to material resources	• Access to resources, education, employment opportunities, and transportation
• Social skills	• High but realistic expectations	• Mentoring initiatives	
• Problem-solving skills	• Value children's accomplishments	• Community well-being, stability, cohesiveness	
• Emotional regulation	• Reading to children	• Rites of passage programs	
• Hopefulness	• Connection to other competent adults	• Availability of pro-social role models, norms and values	
• Sense of humor	• Socioeconomic advantages	• Supportive friends, neighbors, teachers	
• Strategies to deal with stress/coping skills	• Partner harmony	• Opportunity for belonging and meaningful involvement in pro-social school, sports, religious, community activities	
• Balanced perspectives on experience	• Religious/affiliation/participation	• Well-delineated community	
• Realistic appraisal of the environment	• Children have family/household duties		
• Tolerance of negative affect	• Cohesion and care within the family		
• Willingness to forgive	• Marital support		
• Enduring set of values	• Family resilience		
• Internal locus of control	• Family self-efficacy		
• Self-confidence			
• Self-esteem			
• Empathy			

(continued)

TABLE 2.1 | LIST OF PROTECTIVE FACTORS ACROSS FOUR ECOSYSTEM LEVELS (*CONTINUED*)

Individual Factors	Family Factors	Community Factors	Socio-cultural Factors
• Faith/religious affiliation • Talents and accomplishments • Sense of direction or purpose • Planning and decision making • Academic skills/aspirations • Good health	• Non-blaming or non-critical • Family educational attainment • Family talents or hobby recognized by others • Affectionate bonds with alternative care givers		

factors. Resilience as an outcome refers to the resultant positive functioning or competence developed when facing adversity. In other words, in order to say resilient behavior is evident there must be dynamics present. First there must be significant risk that can cause a negative impact. Second, there should be protective factors that mediate to alter the negative impacts of the risk factors. Third, there should be patterns of competent behavior or successful coping by the individual. Resilience is a characteristic inferred from the observable competent behaviors of the individual who has experienced overwhelming adversities or risk factors (Lietz, 2006, 2007; Peters et al., 2005; Riley & Masten, 2005).

HOMEWORK EXERCISE 2.12 | YOUR RESPONSE TO A LIFE CHALLENGE

Think of a time when you successfully faced adversity. Answer the following questions:

• What were three significant risk factors related to this challenge?

• What were three protective factors that helped you deal with the risk factors?

• Describe the observable competent behaviors developed or enhanced as a result of dealing with this challenge.

Applying the Resilience Perspective

Practitioners using the resilience perspective start with an assessment of the relevant factors and then focus on helping clients build on the resilience they have developed. There are many factors to explore when assessing resilience including:

• Protective and risk factors
• Life challenges
• Relationships to family, community, church, society, etc. (Leadbeater et al., 2005).

When working with clients using the resilience perspective, practitioners' tasks include helping clients:

- Develop a positive outlook on life and self-confidence by increasing their awareness of their strengths and competencies
- Learn to maintain, promote, and enhance protective factors
- Recall successful events in their life and identify what they learned from these events
- Identify resources within themselves, their family, friends, neighborhoods, school, and work place. Trust others and establish close and secure relationships with them
- View a mistake as a window of learning and failure as an event that does not mean they failed
- Focus on the present and future rather than dwelling on their past failures

It is important for practitioners to be aware that people of color may turn to sources of support in times of stress that are different from those of the majority culture. Although much of the research historically has focused on individual traits (Davis, 2001; Gordon, 1995), more recent research has noted that culture, ethnicity, and environment play key protective roles in the manifestation of resilience in individuals and communities, particularly among people of color (Clauss-Ehlers, 2004). Experiences involving racism, trauma, oppression, immigration, and poverty have led members of minority groups to develop a heightened sense of connectivity, including social ties and community supports (Dudley-Grant, Mendez, & Zinn, 2000). When a group or individuals feel attacked or persecuted, they turn to people like themselves for support. On occasion this may be isolating, but often it is helpful in both surviving and developing more powerful and effective ways to fight oppression. The Civil Rights Movement and the Montgomery Bus Boycott are well-known examples of members of a persecuted group working closely together to bring about change.

HOMEWORK EXERCISE 2.13 | CASE EXAMPLE

Using the case example, identify risk factors and protective factors related to Hector's family. What behaviors in each family member do you think demonstrate resilience?

THE EMPOWERMENT PERSPECTIVE

Defining the Empowerment Perspective

Empowerment is "the means by which individuals, groups and/or communities become able to take control of their circumstances and achieve their own goals, thereby being able to work towards helping themselves and others to maximize the quality of their lives" (Adams, 2003, p. 8). Empowerment has internal and external components. The *internal component,* or **psychological empowerment,** involves a sense of control over our motivations, cognition, and personality and a belief that we can competently make decisions, solve problems, achieve goals, and have a significant impact on our environment (Rappaport, 1985; Siegall & Gardner, 2000). For members of oppressed groups, empowerment has been described as the development of the aptitudes, strengths, and sense of power or competence necessary to be recognized as equal (Littrell & Beck, 1999; Miller, 2004; Nash, 2005; Rose, 2005). The **external component** of empowerment includes the tangible knowledge, competencies, skills, information, opportunities, and resources that allow a person to take action and to actively advocate change (Cheung et al., 2005).

Empowerment is a process as well as an outcome (Hardina, 2005; Miley, O'Melia, & DuBois, 2004). When new abilities are learned through life experiences, the process of using the new abilities or competencies results in an increased sense of personal empowerment (Lyons, Smuts, & Stephens, 2001; Rappaport, 1981). Research shows a direct correlation between levels of participation and empowerment (Cheung et al., 2005; Zimmerman, 1990; Zimmerman & Rappaport, 1988). For example, the more involved or active a person is in a challenging project, the more likely it is that he/she will experience an increased sense of empowerment. Think of a group in which you have participated. Those who actively participated in this group gained more of a sense of empowerment or competency than those who remained passive and uninvolved. As a sense of empowerment increases, individuals take more responsibility for actively improving the quality of their lives and of the environment (Miley et al., 2004). The outcome of this process is a sense of competency, personal power (psychological empowerment), and life satisfaction that is supported by having the skills, knowledge, and competencies necessary to actively solve problems and advocate for change (Cheung et al., 2005).

HOMEWORK EXERCISE 2.14 | UNDERSTANDING EMPOWERMENT

Identify at least one experience that has been empowering to you. This might be an experience in which you took on some task, problem, or challenge that initially seemed very difficult, demanding, and/or complicated to you. It might be something you had never done before or maybe something that you feared you could not do. This experience might be something you did alone or with other people. In what ways did dealing with this situation enhance your sense of personal competence? What competencies and/or strengths did you acquire as you dealt with this situation? In retrospect, would you have been better off if someone had intervened and just fixed it for you?

Applying the Empowerment Perspective

No matter what system size the practitioner is working with (individuals through whole organizations), using an empowerment perspective allows clients to develop a sense of power and competency as they experience using their skills and knowledge in new and challenging ways and realize that they are able to accomplish difficult tasks. Practitioners who see it as their job to fix their clients are not working from an empowerment perspective because it is not possible to give someone a sense of power or empowerment. Practitioners who use an empowerment perspective relate to clients as partners and recognize that clients are the experts on their situation, their challenges, their strengths and capacities, their choice of what they will work on, their timing and pace, their goals, and their preferred way to work. In these client-practitioner partnerships, practitioners bring professional expertise and resources, and clients provide personal expertise and the energy for change. For example, practitioners can provide resources such as a space to meet, observations, information, and a supportive climate that can be useful as people begin the journey toward empowerment (Hardina, 2005; Simon, 1994). Practitioners may identify opportunities that can be empowering, such as teaching others or helping and supporting others. In AA groups, the role of sponsor is empowering to the sponsor.

Practitioners can also help people discover their strengths, identify their goals, and develop a plan to reach their goals. This type of collaborative work allows clients to accept responsibility for change and therefore experience a greater sense of empowerment. It can be particularly empowering for clients to work in a group because they will have the opportunity to help and support others, to take on tasks that might seem too challenging for any one person, to share experiences and competencies with others, to learn from others, to develop skills with others, and to get feedback from numerous people (Cheung et al., 2005; Dodd & Gutierrez, 1990; Home, 1999; Lee, 2001).

HOMEWORK EXERCISE 2.15 | CASE EXAMPLE

- What are your hunches about situations that Hector and Carol experienced as empowering?
- What ideas do you have about an experience that could be empowering to Julian?

- What kind of activity or challenge could the practitioner offer Hector that might be empowering?

THE DUAL PERSPECTIVE
Written by Carol Hostetter
Defining the Dual Perspective

Most of us who are involved in the helping professions benefit from one type of privilege or another in our lives, whether it is due to our race, gender, social class, sexual orientation, religion, or abilities. Being a member of the dominant group in at least one of these areas makes it challenging for us to empathize with members of a marginalized group and understand their perspectives on life. Experiencing even briefly what it means to be in a marginalized group can help you recognize unjust power structures and privileges. Below is an experiential exercise that can lead you to a place of reflection, self-awareness, and/or open-mindedness regarding what it is like to be on the receiving end of racism. It can help us feel, on a first-hand level, how our society may contribute to oppressing people. If you decide that you would like to try the guided imagery, ask a trusted friend or colleague to slowly read the following statement while you close your eyes and reflect. If you are an African-American student, you have lived the experience of being a minority and do not need to do this exercise. Consider sharing some of your own unique life experiences with other students.

> Imagine that you are exactly who you are, but the world around you has changed. As you look around your campus, you see that the vast majority of students are African-American. The majority of your professors are African-American. When you look at your state government, the governor and lieutenant governor are African-American. The majority of people in the statehouse are African-American. Looking beyond your state, to Washington, DC, you see that the vast majority of people in power are African-American. Of the nine Supreme Court justices, eight are African-American.
>
> Coming back to your community, you decide to apply for a job, and the business owners and the people taking applications are almost all African-American. You decide you need a loan, and the bank tellers and loan officers are African-American. You need to rent an apartment, and the landlords you meet with are African-American. You drive on the highway and realize you have started to speed—sirens flash, and the police officer who comes to your car is African-American. You decide to fight the ticket, so you go to court and the judge is African-American. You go grocery shopping, and the managers are African-American. If you are not African-American, you have a hard time finding hair products for yourself—you might find them within a small section marked "ethnic." And while you are looking for that section, you might feel that people are watching you closely in the store to see if you shoplift. Take a moment more and look around this world, and just notice what you feel and what you are aware of. Then return your attention to the present.

After doing the exercise, you may have many feelings depending on your background and life experiences. You may have an *aha* moment in which you suddenly empathize with African-Americans in our society or you may think that you could live comfortably in the world described by the guided imagery. Some people say, "I just couldn't get into it." Allowing yourself to participate fully in guided imagery, especially in a public setting, can feel like an emotional risk. Whatever your reaction to this exercise, it will be helpful to find a safe person with whom to share your thoughts and feelings.

After completing the exercise, imagine it again with a different twist. This time the dominant group in the world is women or people with a homosexual orientation. That world would look very different to most of us.

What is happening in this guided imagery? It is a concrete way to understand the concept of the dual perspective. Dr. Leon Chestang (1972) created this concept to explain the two worlds experienced by a person born outside of society's dominant group. The **dual perspective** views an individual as interacting and adapting to two surrounding systems or environments: the nurturing environment and the sustaining environment (Norton, 1978). The **nurturing environment** is composed of family, friends, and close associates at school or work. The **sustaining environment** consists of the people encountered in the wider community and broader society. Ideally individuals are accepted, respected, and supported within both environments. Although most Euro-Americans experience these two environments as fitting together, other ethnic and racial groups experience a poor fit between them.

Chestang (1972) described life for a typical African-American boy. His family is part of the nurturing world, the world where he is known as a unique individual and is loved for who he is. This world might contain not just his family, but also his neighborhood, including local stores, parks, and the church his family attends. Eventually, however, he must venture outside the nurturing world into the sustaining world—the world in which he will be educated, earn a living, and deal with the economic and political realities of life. In the sustaining world, he is more likely to be seen as an *African-American male,* not as a unique individual. Therefore, he must develop two views of reality—that is, a dual perspective. He must constantly evaluate disappointments in life, such as not being selected for a job, to determine whether they are based on his qualifications or on racism from the dominant culture. He must constantly shift between his *home culture* and the dominant culture to choose acceptable behavior in each situation.

A useful assignment is to apply the dual perspective concept to someone who is gay or lesbian. If the boy in our example is gay, chances are he is born into a world that does not understand and accept him. He must then create his own nurturing world as he grows up—not an easy feat in a heterosexist society. Similarly, you may apply this approach to a girl born into a family that is not female-affirming. In her family she might feel less valuable than her brothers. At school she might be encouraged to excel. Consider the perspective of a child who has a disability. The child might be loved and accepted at home and ridiculed in school.

Applying the Dual Perspective

Norton (1978) defined the dual perspective as "the conscious awareness on the cognitive and attitudinal levels of the similarities and differences in the two systems ..." (1978, p. 9). She points out that it is difficult to perceive the structural barriers that those in other groups experience. When we engage in practice with people who are "other" than ourselves, it is essential that we develop an awareness of their lived experience. As practitioners we need to examine our own attitudes related to the similarities and differences of our own nurturing and sustaining environments as well as those of our clients (McDonald & Coleman, 1999).

Our society discriminates widely on the basis of race, with different prejudices applied to people of different races. In addition to race, widespread discrimination exists on the basis of gender, abilities, sexual orientation, religion, age, appearance, and other factors. As you learn to partner with clients in the helping process, a "multiple model" of oppression that takes into account all types of oppression will help free you from society's prejudices (McDonald & Coleman, 1999, p. 32).

HOMEWORK EXERCISE 2.16 | CASE EXAMPLE

Consider Hector's background of having a mother who is Caucasian and a father who is Mexican-American.

- What comments might Hector have heard growing up?
- Where could Hector feel he was "at home" and nurtured?

- When Hector is at college, what "world" does he inhabit? How might that world change when he goes home on break?
- What are your hunches about the additional challenges Hector faces by having to live in "two" worlds?

TABLE 2.2 | THEORIES OF HUMAN BEHAVIOR

Theory/ Perspective	Practitioner Strategies	Concepts	Assumptions of Theory
Constructivism	Help clients identify existing constructs and develop new ones.	Practitioners need to be aware that the worldview of clients may be very different from their own.	Individuals describe experiences in terms of personal constructs—explanations of events that become the lens through which they see the world.
Ecological Perspective	Help clients recognize the barriers to achievement of goals. Help clients think about the advantages and disadvantages of various solutions in making decisions about how to achieve these goals.	Person-environment fit refers to the fit between individual needs, goals, and rights and the traits and functioning of the physical and social environment. Adaptation is the result of processes to sustain or raise the "fit" between people and their environment.	Humans are both influenced by and influence their environment, and human behavior must be viewed in terms of the interactions between people and their environment.
Family Systems	Focus on strengths, not deficits; on solutions rather than problems, and on the potential for individual and family growth and continued positive social change.	Systems are organized by the relationships among the system parts. All of the parts combined produce an entity that is greater than the sum of these parts.	The whole is greater than the sum of its parts. Changing one part of the system will result in changes to other system parts. Families change over time and individuals assume different roles in response to these changes. Individual dysfunction may be reflective of relationship problems.
Strengths	Start with past successes and look at the qualities and strengths through which the client was able to achieve these successes. Explore client competencies, capacities, abilities, and resources and focus on future possibilities.	Everyone has the capacity to develop new resources, to make positive changes, and to use their competencies to solve problems. Problems are described as challenges, since challenges can be seen as opportunities for growth. All environments, no matter how unfavorable, contain usable resources.	Every person has undiscovered or forgotten abilities.

Resilience	Resources in the individual, family, racial/cultural group, spiritual beliefs, and society enable one to adapt in times of stress.	Resilience qualities include a positive outlook on life. Seeing a mistake as feedback, not failure. Trust that others can be of help. Focus on the present rather than the past or future. The willingness to prevail even when it seems too difficult to go on.	Identify, access, and build upon resilience strengths of the individual or group. Teach and help develop qualities that increase resilience.
Empowerment	Empowerment results from using competencies in a setting where new abilities are learned through life experience, rather than from advice provided by "experts."	Empowerment has internal and external components. Internal components involve a sense of control over one's motivation, cognition, and personality, and a belief that one can make effective decisions, solve problems, achieve goals, and have an impact on one's environment. External components include knowledge, competencies, skills, information, opportunities, and resources that allow one to take action and actively advocate for change. Life stressors are the result of issues perceived as exceeding personal and environmental resources available to manage them. Behaviors are not seen as maladaptive, but as attempts to improve the person-environment fit.	Recognize that clients are the experts about their own particular situation, challenges, strengths, what they would like to change, the timing and pace, and their preferred way of working. Practitioners and clients are partners working together.
Dual perspective	When people are born outside the dominant societal group, they exist in two worlds of reality—the nurturing world of their own societal group and the sustaining group in which they must be educated, make a living, and deal with the economic and political realities of life.	Those who differ from the majority racially, in sexual orientation, disability, etc., will be viewed in terms of that difference rather than as individuals. To understand the client's worldview, practitioners must view interactions from the dual perspective.	Consider how the dominant society might influence clients' beliefs, sense of competence, and ability to make changes in their lives. In keeping with this idea of dealing with two views of reality, practitioners need to work to increase their awareness of the influences of racism, prejudice, and stereotypes.

It is important for practitioners to recognize that life is viewed differently by people in marginalized groups. When practitioners consider the dual perspective, they are able to better understand how our culture maintains the dominant group's power by objectifying the "other." When working with clients from a minority group, it is important for the practitioner to be aware of the day-to-day challenges these clients face and to keep in mind that their clients are living in two worlds, the nurturing world and the sustaining world. Minority clients must continually go back and forth between these worlds.

EXPECTED COMPETENCIES

In this chapter, you have learned about several perspectives that can help you better understand how you and your clients think, feel, and make choices.

You should be able to define the following terms: adaptations, compelling forces, constructivist perspective, dual perspective, ecological perspective, empowerment, force field, life stressors, nurturing environment, personality, person-environment fit, personal construct, protective factors, resilience, restraining force, risk factors, social constructivist, system, system theory, strengths perspective, sustaining environment.

You should now be able to:

- Give an example of how a personal construct might influence a decision.

- Describe how the ecological perspective would provide a broader view of a client.
- Compare and contrast a strengths perspective with a deficit-focused view.
- Give two examples of how the dual perspective provides a deeper understanding of a marginalized group of people.
- Explain several ways that a family functions as a system.
- Explain what is necessary for a person to gain a sense of empowerment.
- Explain the relationship between risk factors, protective factors, and resilience.

VALUES, ETHICS, AND LEGAL OBLIGATIONS

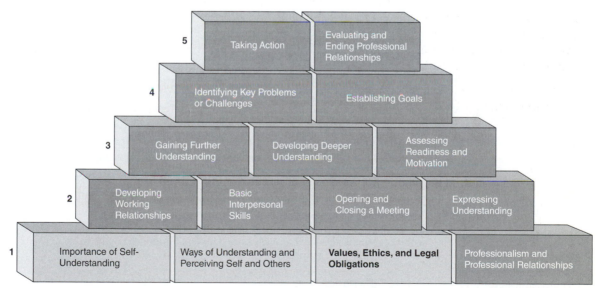

CHAPTER 3

© Cengage Learning 2013

Questions to consider as you read this chapter:

- What should I do when my personal values conflict with the values of my profession?
- What are my profession's ethical guidelines and practices?
- What are the most common ethical issues in the helping professions?
- What do I need to know about the legal obligations of practice?

This chapter covers practice behaviors related to ethical guidelines, practices, standards, and legal obligations. *You will learn the importance of:*

- Knowledge of ethical, legal, and professional standards and guidelines
- Application of ethical concepts and legal issues regarding professional activities with individuals and groups
- Ethical conduct demonstrated in behavior that reflects professional values, ethics, integrity, and responsibility
- Awareness and application of ethical decision making and ability to demonstrate the importance of an ethical decision model applied to practice

PERSONAL VALUES

In Chapter 1 you learned how your culture, race, ethnicity, gender, sexual orientation, family of origin, spirituality and religion, stage of life, socioeconomic status, disability and ability, and stresses and demands have influenced your development. All of these experiences influenced your personal values. **Values** are preferred conceptions of people, preferred outcomes for people, and also preferred ways of dealing with people (Levy, 1973). Personal values influence your view of the world, your personal and professional philosophies and choices, and your view of how people change. The decisions of practitioners are shaped in part by personal values. Personal values reside in a variety of domains, including religion, health, marriage and family, education, role of government, birth and death, and honesty. For example, you may have been raised in a family that believes that people should be self-sufficient and do whatever it takes to support themselves. Maybe you learned to obtain an education or believe that everyone has the capacity to "pull themselves up by their bootstraps."

HOMEWORK EXERCISE 3.1 | YOUR VALUES

As you complete the following sentences, think about what each sentence says about what you value.

The disability I most fear for myself is _____.

The circumstance under which I would wish for death is _____.

The "difference" in others I find most upsetting is _____.

The loneliest group of people is _____.

The "difference" within myself I am most proud of is _____.

The "difference" within myself I am most ashamed to admit to is _____.

One behavior I believe is a sin is when people _____.

One behavior I believe is evil is when people _____.

(Sommers-Flanagan & Sommers-Flanagan, 2007)

Your behavior is determined by your values and beliefs. Your decision to continue your education beyond high school and your choice of profession has been influenced by your personal values. Your beliefs affect what types of interventions you choose for your clients, the population you select to concentrate on, your interactions with clients and colleagues, and how you handle therapeutic power.

PROFESSIONAL VALUES

Each profession has a set of professional values that guide and direct the work of a professional and inform their professional code of practice. Professional values often include principles of respect, self-determination, social justice, and professional integrity (Powell, 2005). Social workers, counselors, psychologists, marriage and family therapists, psychiatrists, nurses, and other helping professionals have ethical codes of conduct. These codes generally include the general goals or objectives of the profession as well as enforceable ethical guidelines and reflect the values of the profession. It is essential that your professional ethics guide your behavior as a practitioner, even when your personal values clash with your professional values.

Areas where personal values may conflict with professional values include religion, health, marriage and family, education, role of government, birth and death, and honesty. For example, different religions have core values associated with beliefs about life and death, including how to live, eat, dress, and interact socially and sexually with others. Conflicts may occur when asked to pray with a client or when asked specifically about beliefs about heaven or hell, allowing death without extensive medical intervention or do not resuscitate orders, etc. Marriage and family values may also present a conflict in beliefs about who can marry, rights of parents, embryos, and biological and adopted children. Conflicts may also arise around values of honesty or deception. Is it okay to lie to save another person's self esteem or money? When interacting with clients as a professional, the values of your profession must be used, even when they are in conflict with your personal values. Most practitioners choose not to share their personal values with clients so that the practitioner's personal values will not influence client's decisions.

ETHICAL STANDARDS

An important part of your education is to become familiar with the code of ethics for your chosen profession. While codes of ethics vary among the different professions in clarity, purpose, and specificity, they serve several functions. The codes contain statements about the ideals of the profession at its finest. They also serve to define the profession and those it is designed to serve. **Ethical codes** provide an explanation of what can be expected in the interactions between both professionals and clients, and professionals and other professionals. Most importantly, they contain statements about what the professionals must and must not do. The website of each professional organization includes information about its code of ethics. Below are the web addresses of a number of organizations within the helping professions:

- American Association of Marriage and Family Therapy
  http://www.aamft.org/resources/LRMPlan/Ethics/ethicscode2001.asp

- American Counseling Association
  http://www.counseling.org/Resources/CodeOfEthics/TP/Home/CT2.aspx
- American Psychiatric Nurses Association
  http://www.apna.org/aboutapna/mission.html
- American Psychological Association
  http://www.apa.org/ethics/code2002.html
- Association of Addiction Professionals
  http://naadac.org/documents/index.php?CategoryID=23
- International Association of Marriage and Family Counselors
  http://www.iamfc.com/ethical_codes.html
- National Association of Social Workers
  http://www.socialworkers.org/pubs/code/code.asp
- National Organization for Human Services
  http://nationalhumanservices.org/ethics

As a practitioner you should study your profession's code of ethics and keep a copy of the code of ethics available to review. Each practitioner is responsible for following professional ethical guidelines in every situation. The agency where the practitioner is employed may have rules that differ from the stipulations of the practitioner's code of ethics. For example, the code of ethics of many disciplines do not allow practitioners to maintain relationships with clients after ending their professional relationship, but agencies that employ practitioners may or may not forbid such relationships. When there is a conflict or inconsistency between the agency rules and the professional ethical standards, practitioners are obligated to follow the ethical standards of their profession.

There are commonalities among all the ethical codes of each of the disciplines. These include professional competence and integrity, confidentiality, prohibition of boundary violations, assessment, and informed consent.

PROFESSIONAL COMPETENCY AND INTEGRITY

Professional competence includes practicing within the scope of competence based on education, training, professional credentials, and professional experience. Think about all the different reasons people seek help from your profession. How would you assess the type of competence you would need to help them with these various concerns? There are several factors to consider in assessing your competence. As you consider your competence to work with a client you need to ask yourself the following questions.

- Do I understand the current research literature related to this client?
- If you answered yes to the previous question: Am I able to appropriately understand and use the skills considered most effective for this client?
- If you answered yes to the previous question: Am I ready and able to do whatever is necessary to effectively work with this client?
- If you answered yes to the previous question: Am I physically and emotionally able to work well with this client? (Anderson & Handlesman, 2010; Welfel, 2006)

If you answered "no" to any of the above questions, you will need to consider appropriate action such as conferring with your supervisor or another professional or referring the client to another practitioner with the appropriate competence. You should be aware of your own personal issues and assess your feelings about your competency in working with certain clients. For example, if you or someone close to you recently suffered a miscarriage, working with a woman considering an abortion might not serve either of you well. However, some professionals believe that personal experience related to problems is helpful and others think it adds to the stress of being a practitioner. For example, if you or someone you know well has a serious problem with alcohol does that make you a more effective counselor to people with alcohol problems or does it mean that your personal issues could be mixed up with the client's situation? As a professional you are expected to continue increasing your competence throughout your career. Additional courses, workshops, degrees, certificates, practicum or internship experience, readings, and supervision are all good ways to enhance your competence and help you to decide when your personal experiences are limiting your ability to act in a competent manner.

One of the most important aspects of professional competence requiring professional self-awareness is cultural competence. **Cultural competence** in the helping professions is defined as the application of the cultural knowledge about individuals and groups of people to the standards, policies, practices, and attitudes in the helping process to result in better outcomes (Mizrahi et al., 2001). According to the U.S. Census Bureau (2009), by 2050 the Hispanic population will double, the Asian population will increase by 80%, while the Caucasian population is projected to decrease by about 6%. With this level of population diversity, plus the many cultural and ethnic groups in the United States, cultural competence is essential. A multicultural competent helping professional possesses the following: awareness of one's values, biases, pre-conceived notions, personal limitations, and assumptions about behavior. A culturally competent practitioner must be committed to ongoing education to better understand the worldview of all of his/her culturally diverse clients while withholding negative judgment, and to applying this knowledge in the use of appropriate interventions, strategies, and skills in working with such clients (Sue & Sue, 1990).

Just as your culture has influenced your values, the same is true for clients. Being culturally competent means being aware of how others interpret their environment, how they see the world, and how they function in it. Culture also influences client's perceptions about what works, what doesn't work, what is helpful and what is not, as well as what makes sense and what doesn't. All of these influence your work together. Since each person, family, neighborhood, and community is unique, it makes sense to ask clients to explain their own situation. For example, Asian Americans do not all think or behave in the same way, and not all Christians share identical beliefs. Diversity includes differences in race, socioeconomic status, ethnicity, age, physical capabilities, spirituality, acculturation, gender, and educational experiences. In Chapter 5 you will see a list of movies that you can use to increase your empathic understanding of different cultures and challenges.

Think about the ethnic group with which you most identify. What do you like about your ethnic identity? Which social or cultural factors in your background may contribute to barriers in relationships with clients from other groups? List some of the values of your ethnic group. Which of these values do you also hold? Which of these values do you no longer believe in?

CONFIDENTIALITY

Confidentiality may be the most vital of the professional obligations thought to be necessary to the process of mental health and counseling work (Sommers-Flanagan & Sommers-Flanagan, 2007). **Confidentiality** in the helping professions means information shared by the client with the therapist in the course of treatment is not shared with others. In addition to the legal aspects of confidentiality discussed later in this chapter, additional reasons for confidentiality include the potential for stigma, moral obligation for helping professionals, and modeling.

Stigma

Historical views of mental illness, psychology, and psychiatry led to in stigmatization of counseling, resulting in some clients' fearing they will be seen as "crazy" if they seek counseling (Farber, Berano, & Capobianco, 2004). Seeking professional mental health counseling also carries a stigma in some cultures as it is viewed as a failure of families or the church to take care of their own. It might cause the family to lose face or result in a sense of shame for the client's family or community (Cuellar & Paniagua, 2000).

Clients might also feel ashamed for seeking help from a counselor or therapist, as it makes them feel weak because of their inability to solve their own problems regardless of their family, religious, or cultural background (Frank & Frank, 1991). They may also worry about what others might assume about them or have concerns about how seeking help might affect their career or family life.

When stigma is a factor, clients need confidentiality not only to cover the content of the sessions, but also the professional relationship itself. Even if stigma is not a concern, some clients are very private and do not want others to know anything about their private lives.

Moral Obligation and Modeling

One aspect of behaving as a professional is to act with discretion and keep one's word. Failing to do so can harm clients and your profession. Gossiping or discussing clinical work to entertain others or to make you seem more important breaks with moral and ethical standards for a professional.

As a clinician, you are modeling some of the characteristics of other intimate relationships. The clinician is in a position of an authority so should behave in ways that are respectful, honest, and collaborative. This behavior provides an environment for healing and an example of what is ideal in future relationships (Benjamin, 2003).

Technology and Confidentiality

As new technology enhances and changes the way we communicate, confidentiality issues become more complex (Sommers-Flanagan & Sommers-Flanagan, 2007). Consider how cell phones, fax machines, answering machines, computers, and the internet impact our ability to maintain client confidentiality. The use of answering machines and fax machines requires you to send information over which you have no control once it is sent. Confidential information may be sent to agencies in the form of referrals and to insurance companies to access benefits. There have been reports of computers sold with accessible data despite the fact the hard drives had been wiped clean of data. Laptop computers are stolen. Email messages are sent to the wrong address and/or to more recipients than was intended.

It is important to use common sense as technology changes. Of course, just as you would never leave client files open on your desk, computers need to be set up with password protection and firewalls. Passwords should be changed often. Files should be backed up on a flash drive daily. Your computer should be protected with a high quality virus protection program that is updated often.

If you will be contacting clients by email, make sure they know this through the informed consent process. Consider carefully what you say in the messages and remember once a message is sent, it may be around forever as you have lost control over it. A clear explanation of ethics related to technology is provided in the ACA Code of Ethics, Section 12. As technology evolves, it will be important to continue to evaluate confidentiality issues as they are impacted by technology.

PROHIBITION OF BOUNDARY VIOLATIONS

Cautions about boundary violations in the helping professions are outlined in most codes of ethics. Practitioners are responsible for maintaining the boundaries of the relationship. **Boundaries** are defined as borders that separate some type of entity (for example, parents, children, systems, client, service providers, and health care workers). **Relationship boundaries** are the limits set in relationships. Think of the boundary that exists between parents and children. Parents have specific roles as the providers of support and nurturance for children. There are legal and moral standards related to these boundaries including those related to incest, abuse, and neglect. *Crossing a relationship boundary* involves doing something that is beyond the usual boundary of the relationship. If the boundary crossing is used to benefit the client, it may be acceptable (Lazarus, A., 2003; Pope & Keith-Siegel, 2008). For example, depending on the client, the use of touch—shaking hands, or reaching out to touch an arm or hand particularly to comfort a grieving client—may be appropriate (Barnett, 2007). On the DVD toward the end of the beginning meeting with an individual, the practitioner holds the client's hands. Do you think the practitioner is crossing a boundary? If so, does this boundary crossing benefit the client? Or maybe holding the client's hands is a *boundary violation*. A boundary violation occurs if the practitioner does something that exploits, harms, or violates the client in some way (Gutheil & Brodsky, 2008; Lazarus, 2003). In the case of touch, what may be appropriate and helpful for one client could be a boundary violation for a different client. For example, clients who have been physically abused might consider any kind of touch as a violation (Barnett, 2007). Although you intend to be supportive when you touch a client, you may not know how he/she interprets the touch.

Most of us see a difference between "good touch" (handshaking, patting the arm) and "bad touch" (sensual hugs or stroking). However, touch is not that easily dichotomized as good or bad depending on the circumstances and persons involved. Touch may be viewed as one method to communicate comfort, but it also may have erotic potential or be misinterpreted as an erotic or romantic invitation. There are cultural mores around touch, and touch can carry nonverbal signals of power and hierarchy (Sommers-Flanagan & Sommers-Flanagan, 2007). There are also gender differences in touch, with women tending to use touch to comfort and men using it to show power (Woods, 2004). Given this gender difference and cultural variance on who can touch whom safely, it is particularly important for men to evaluate all touching beyond a handshake with greater care than may be necessary for women.

In all helping relationships, maintaining appropriate boundaries is an essential part of developing a trusting relationship with a client (Gelso & Hayes, 1998; Rogers, 1958). In order to maintain boundaries, practitioners need to explain the rules of a professional relationship to their clients at the beginning of the relationship and also remind clients of these boundaries as needed throughout the relationship. Relationship rules involve protecting confidentiality, ensuring that the needs of the client take precedence over those of the practitioner, and clarifying assumptions that the client may have about any interactions outside of the professional one.

Violations to relationship boundaries often involve having more than one type of relationship with a person. For example, a parent's relationship with a child should meet the needs of the child. If the parent develops another type of relationship with a child, for example a sexual relationship, that second relationship violates appropriate boundaries. At one time, ethical codes defined dual relationships as occurring when an individual had two types of relationships with individuals. Currently ethical codes refer to such relationships as multiple relationships. **Multiple roles relationships** are relationships in which an individual has two or more types of relationships (either simultaneously or sequentially) with another person. When helping professionals were asked about the most challenging ethical concerns they faced, they often cited dual or multiple relationships (Pope & Vetter, 1992; Strom-Gottfried, 1999). Codes of ethics of most of the helping professions explicitly caution against multiple relationships.

Helping professionals need to consider potential harm and potential benefit when multiple relationships or crossing boundaries are possible. Younggren and Gottlieb (2004) suggest the following questions when considering multiple relationships:

- How *necessary* is this multiple relationship?
- What is the *potential harm* to the client from this dual relationship?
- If the harm seems unlikely or avoidable, what *benefits* would come from the additional relationship.

- What is the potential *risk* to the helping relationship from the dual relationship?
- Is it possible to evaluate it objectively? (pp. 256-57)

Here is another set of questions to use if you are faced with possible boundary problems. Ask yourself:

- Is there some other way to handle this situation without crossing a boundary? If there is another way to handle the situation, use it. If not, ask yourself
- Is crossing this boundary meeting my needs or those of the client? If it is meeting your needs rather than the client's needs, is there another way to get your needs met? If there is no other way to meet your needs, it is up to you to talk to your client and figure out the best way to manage the situation. Consider this possibility: your son wants to play on the only soccer team in town and the coach is your client. What would you say to your client?
- If the boundary crossing is meeting the client's needs, ask yourself if crossing this boundary could possibly cause pain or be exploitative to your client either now or in the future. If crossing this boundary could cause harm now or in the future, don't do it. If not, ask yourself if you would be comfortable telling your supervisor and colleagues that you crossed this boundary. If not, it is probably not a good idea. If you are still unsure, ask your supervisor for a recommendation.

HOMEWORK EXERCISE 3.3 | ANALYZING POTENTIAL MULTIPLE RELATIONSHIPS

Use any of the above questions to analyze the following case:

Alfonso has just been given information about a new client who is scheduled to see him later today. The client is a 17 year old boy whose parents have specifically requested that he be assigned to Alfonso. They said, "Alfonso is the only person we want to work with our son." Alfonso recognizes the client's name as a boy who is in his 15 year old son's scout troop. As the troop draws from the local high school population, Alfonso knows the family lives near him and the boy attends his son's school in addition to being in the same scout troop.

Personal Relationships that Predate the Professional Relationship

When your friends, family, partners, coworkers, and even casual acquaintances discover you are studying to be a helping professional, they may decide to talk to you about their concerns. While it is okay to share information about what you are learning and to use your improved listening skills to enhance your personal relationships, it is not ethical to enter into professional relationships with friends or family members. Your friendship would make being an unbiased practitioner impossible. Trying to work with friends or family members is a dual relationship and should be avoided. One option is to express your concern or understanding: "That sounds like a troubling problem. I can suggest someone who might be able to work with you on that problem." If you choose to work with your friend or coworker and he was disappointed with your work together, he has grounds for a malpractice case. Your decision to enter into a helping relationship with him is a violation of your profession's code of ethics.

HOMEWORK EXERCISE 3.4 | RESPONDING TO FRIENDS

If you are at a social gathering and a friend of yours says, "I really think you should talk to Joan. She is drinking a lot tonight and I have seen her driving after leaving another party when she was drunk." Write down two responses that let your friend know you heard her concern and care about her, but are at the party as a friend, not as a professional.

Multiple Relationships during the Professional Relationship

After beginning work with a client, it is not unusual to find that your lives intersect in unpredictable ways. Since the relationship with the practitioner is different from other types of relationships, anytime you enter into a second type of relationship with a client you are crossing the boundary of the professional relationship. You might attend a new Sunday school class and discover a client also attends the class. You might go on a Yoga retreat and find a client is also attending the retreat. While such overlapping relationships may seem more likely in rural settings or small towns, they also occur in urban areas. Each of these situations require that you reassure the client that confidentiality will be strictly maintained and explore their feelings about the multiple relationship. In addition to talking with the client, you should consult with colleagues or supervisors on how to minimize the potential problems of these multiple roles.

In rural areas it is often difficult to avoid multiple relationships. For example, if your child needs the services of an orthodontist, and the only orthodontist in town is a client of yours, what are you going to do? It can be quite difficult to be the practitioner in one situation and the consumer of a service in another situation. The practitioner is responsible for exploring the impact of these two very different relationships with the client; however, even with your best efforts problems may occur. What if you decide to take your child to the orthodontist who is your client and you aren't satisfied with his work? It is inappropriate for you to discuss your personal problems with your client, so how would you handle your concerns? Even though it would be less convenient, it might be better to go to an orthodontist in another town. If you decide to go to the orthodontist who is your client, you will be responsible for handling the complications that may be involved and for explaining why you made the decision to be in such a relationship.

Another challenge during the relationship with a client is self-disclosure, or how much information about yourself you should share. Self-disclosure is a natural part of the dominant culture in the United States. As a new helping professional, you may feel uncomfortable with the lack of reciprocity as a client discloses and you listen but do not self-disclose. It may be difficult not to respond to clients with statements about similar life experiences, reactions, or shared interests. In fact, sometimes clients will directly ask you about personal aspects of your life, such as "Do you believe in God?" or "Don't you think abortion is just wrong?"

From an ethical standpoint, self-disclosure should always be in the best interest of the client, not the practitioner. While you may choose to answer some personal questions, you should first obtain more information from the client as to what leads them to ask the question and then answer when appropriate. It may be helpful to ask them how they would feel if you answered in a particular way so that they can evaluate how it might affect your relationship. For some, it is an issue of wanting to feel closer to you, and for others whether they can feel safe if you are different in some way. Answering personal questions can begin the move into a personal relationship or create a distance because of your differences (Pipes, Holstein, & Aguiree, 2005). As with gift-giving, thoughtful and appropriate self-disclosure can be beneficial to the helping relationship (Zur, Bloomgarden, & Mennuti, 2009). Self-disclosure is viewed differently in other cultures (Kim et al., 2003; Simi & Mahalik, 1997). For example, in some Native American tribes, silence is seen as showing respect. Self-disclosure will be discussed further in Chapter 15.

Sexual Relationships

Despite the prohibition of sexual relationships between practitioners and clients by all of the helping profession codes of ethics, such relationships do occur. In fact, the most common ethical complaints filed are related to sexual relationships (Pope, Ketih-Spiegel, & Tabachnick, 2006). In two studies of practitioner-client sex conducted with a sample of psychologists, 7%–8% of the practitioners reported that they had engaged in sexual intimacy with their clients (Holroyd & Brodsky, 1977; Pope, Levenson, & Schover, 1979). Consequences from such a relationship to a client include cognitive dysfunction (attention, concentration, flashbacks, intrusive thoughts, and unbidden images), identity and boundary disturbance, sexual confusions, rage, and feelings of guilt, depression, and emptiness. Clients may also be at increased risk for suicide or self-destructive feelings (Pope, et al., 2006). Besides being unethical, there are also legal consequences for the practitioner that will be discussed later in this chapter. Thus it is vital for a practitioner to remember that the power differential is always a factor in practitioner-client relationships, making the practitioner solely responsible for keeping the sexual intimacy boundary intact. You might find it interesting to watch the film "Mr. Jones" in order to see some very blatant boundary violations by a practitioner with her client.

Multiple Relationships Following the End of Professional Relationships

There are several factors to consider in post-professional relationships although most codes of ethics do not directly prohibit relationships such as friendship, teaching, or business relationships. However, in order to avoid possible damage to the client, there are several factors to carefully consider before entering such a relationship:

- Even though the professional relationship has ended, the power differential remains. Most helping professionals believe that once a person is a client, they should always be considered a client (Lamb, Catanzaro, & Moorman, 2004).

- Some of the good work you accomplished during the professional relationship may be damaged when you are seen in a different light, as a person with shortcomings and vulnerabilities of your own.
- Some clients return for more professional help and prefer to see the same professional. If you now have another type of relationship, this would not be ethical.

Clients often hope to create a personal or friendly relationship with you when you have finished your work together. This is very understandable from the client's point of view. An example might be a young woman you are seeing. You have been compassionate, a good listener, helpful, and totally focused on her so she would like to have you as a friend. In addition to the fact that this type of friendship is not appropriate for your client, it is also not likely to be satisfying to you. Your client has a limited view of you as one who listens and focuses on her and her issues. It is desirable to have a more equal balance in personal relationships. In addition, your client also has a very limited view of what you are like outside of your role as practitioner.

HOMEWORK EXERCISE 3.5 | WHAT TO SAY TO A CLIENT WHO ASKS YOU TO GO TO LUNCH

Pretend you have seen a client for some time and are now ending your professional relationship with the client. The client thanks you for being so helpful and says, "I would really like to get to know you better. How about going to lunch with me sometime next week?" Write out two possible responses to your client.

Behaviors with Boundary Implications

Certain behaviors, such as accepting gifts, fall into a gray area concerning boundaries. Self-disclosure and touch, discussed previously in the chapter, are also gray areas. If your agency has a policy forbidding receiving even small gifts from clients and you believe that accepting small gifts is appropriate, you should consider challenging the agency rule. There are times when not accepting the gift might hurt the helping relationship. Cultural norms of some clients may dictate that they offer you a small gift when they come or food when you make a home visit. In Asian cultures, gifts are used to show respect and gratitude (Cuellar & Paniagua, 2000). For many Native Americans, gift-giving expresses honor for the recipient and the act of gift-giving is viewed as a sacred privilege (Herring, 1996). Families from many different cultures have traditions around gift-giving that may be rooted in past generations while the family has no idea why the tradition arose. Exploring the cultural meaning of gift-giving with clients may enhance your understanding of the client and aid in your work together.

Some practitioners believe that accepting small gifts can be a way of respecting cultural traditions or creating a relaxed atmosphere. When practitioners make home visits, accepting a cup of coffee or something to eat can be a way of showing respect. In group meetings, members may bring snacks for everyone. Having snacks is usually an accepted way of creating a comfortable environment. When clients cannot afford to pay for services, they may want to give practitioners small gifts as a way of expressing their gratitude. The problem with accepting gifts is that it can change the nature of the relationship. For example, as a young professional, one of the authors directed a camp for low income senior citizens. She faced the daily challenge of seniors who wanted to give her things or take care of her in some way. To them, she was about the same age as some of their grandchildren and she was very nice to them. What are some of the problems you think might have occurred if she had accepted gifts from one of her senior campers? How do you think that might have changed her relationship with that camper?

HOMEWORK EXERCISE 3.6 | GIFT-GIVING

Think about the role of gifts in your family and in your community. When do people give gifts? What is expressed through the giving of gifts? What happens if a gift is refused or seems to be unappreciated?

In summary, boundary issues range in severity from casual overlap in clubs and activities to sexual relationships between client and practitioner. Practitioners should always be aware of the potential harm to clients and their professional reputation from boundary violations and constantly evaluate such potential relationships from an ethical standpoint.

HOMEWORK EXERCISE 3.7 | BOUNDARY ISSUES DISCUSSED IN CODES OF ETHICS

Find the sections that discuss the various areas related to boundaries in your profession's code of ethics. You may have to search in several areas as they may be discussed in multiple parts. Make a list of the headings and specific language that guide a practitioner when considering boundary issues.

ASSESSMENT

Most of the helping professions include a section on assessment/evaluation/testing in their codes of ethics to help practitioners consider the ethical issues when assessing clients. These standards include the following:

- The assessment procedure or instrument should be within your scope of practice, education, and training.
- Throughout the assessment process, clients should be fully informed about the procedure and be included in the procedure in a collaborative way.
- Appropriate instruments or procedures should be selected based on the assessment question both the practitioner and client want to answer.
- Assessment instruments and procedures used should be standardized and include normative data appropriate for culturally diverse or disabled clients.
- When administrating, scoring, and interpreting instruments, appropriate procedures should be adhered to and any technology used for this should be within the competence of the practitioner.

- Clients should be given a clear and complete explanation of the assessment results.
- All test and interview data should be kept secure and released only to individuals who are competent in interpreting the data. (Adapted from Sommers-Flanagan & Sommers-Flanagan, 2007.)

INFORMED CONSENT

All of the codes of ethics of helping professions include a section on informed consent. **Informed consent** means full disclosure of the purposes, goals, techniques, and procedure rules for assessment and counseling approaches used, in language that is understandable to the client. An explanation about boundaries, informed consent, licensure, confidentiality, and record-keeping practices and policies needs to be provided at the first session with clients and updated as appropriate during the professional helping process.

HOMEWORK EXERCISE 3.8 | INFORMED CONSENT

How does the code of ethics for your profession address the issue of informed consent? List four standards that relate directly to this ethical principle.

LEGAL OBLIGATIONS
Written by Heather A. McCabe

In addition to the ethical obligations, helping professionals should know the legal obligations under which they must operate and the consequences of a legal breach. Legal violations are distinct from ethical violations, although a breach of professional ethics increases the likelihood of losing a malpractice challenge. Many helping professionals may feel that as long as they do good work and have good intentions they will be protected from challenges to their practice (Barker & Branson, 2000). In the recent past, at least for malpractice, this may have been true, but increasingly helping professionals have faced both ethical and legal challenges (Reamer, 1995). These challenges range from instances of inappropriate sexual relations with clients to inadequate documentation.

Ethical Violations and Licensing

Professionals must practice in accordance with the code of ethics for their specific profession. Codes of ethics are put into place in order to ensure protection for clients, but at the same time, following the code of ethics can provide some comfort to professionals hoping to avoid ethical challenges.

Ethical challenges are generally brought before a state licensing board, although they may also be brought to your professional organization. Licensing boards are housed in administrative agencies of state governments. In ethical challenges, the proceedings are between the licensing board and the professional. The person who alleges the violation may be called on to provide information, but they are not the party bringing a "suit" as in civil proceedings for malpractice. The licensing agency in each state is generally charged with defining the role of the professional licensing board, including the types of penalties incurred when an ethical violation is substantiated. In addition to the ethical rules, the licensing agency administrative rules provide specific guidance regarding how licensing may be obtained and maintained.

The licensing boards hold administrative investigations and hearings. The state agency has an attorney and the professional may also choose to be represented by an attorney. If the licensing board finds that an ethical violation has occurred, they will stipulate sanctions. The most common sanctions are reprimands and letters of admonishments, revocation of or refusing to renew license, probation and supervision of practice, surrendering of certificate or license, fines, CEU completion or documentation, suspension of license, and evaluations for substance dependence or mental health (Boland-Prom, 2009).

Although the licensing rules vary by state, documented information about ethics complaints from the licensing bodies of 27 states provided information about the most commonly alleged ethical violations to licensing boards throughout the county. The most serious offenses in each case of ethical violation were ranked by frequency. The top five in order are: dual relationship and boundary violations (sexual and nonsexual), license related problems (including CEU non-compliance), crimes, basic practice issues (e.g., confidentiality and documentation issues), and below standards of care (Boland-Prom, 2009).

Duties to Clients

When a practitioner-client relationship is established, the practitioner has obligations or duties to the client (Barker & Branson, 2000). Some of these duties are outlined below:

- *Duty to care:* Clients have the right to the provision of a reasonable standard of care. The practitioner is expected to carry out professional responsibilities in a competent manner. Professional competence includes availability to clients, ability to take action when there is danger to self or others, and appropriate record keeping.
- *Duty to respect privacy:* There are personal and symbolic areas that practitioners must not violate with clients. These include respecting the physical space that belongs to clients as well as not forcing them to reveal more information than they choose to disclose about themselves or their situation.
- *Duty to maintain confidentiality:* Sharing information about a client with a third party is a breach of confidentiality unless a waiver is signed by the client or other responsible party. Communication with a social worker may or may not be considered privileged by the court. A general privilege has not been extended to the social work profession; however, many states have created a statutory privilege (Dietz, Jacobs, Levin, Martin, Morris, & Zakolski, 2010). A social worker should research and know the law for the state in which he/she practices.

- *Duty to inform:* The practitioner is required to inform prospective clients about the nature and extent of the services being offered as well as the legal obligations of practitioners concerning the reporting of abuse or neglect of children, elders, and dependent adults. There is also an obligation to explain the qualifications of the practitioner and the possible risks as well as benefits of treatment.
- *Duty to report:* All states have laws concerning the reporting of child abuse, child neglect, molestation, and incest. Vulnerable populations covered by these laws include the elderly, children, and people who are physically or mentally disabled.
- *Duty to warn:* Most practitioners are legally obligated to reveal confidential information concerning a client's stated intent to harm another. The breadth and extent of how this law is to be carried out can vary by state or local jurisdiction (Anderson & Handelsman, 2010; Dolgoff, Lowenberg, & Harrington, 2005; Donovan & Regehr, 2010; Glosoff, Herlihy, & Spence, 2000; Knapp, Gottlieb, Berman, & Handelsman, 2007; Reamer, 2001; Strom-Gottfried, 2008).

A thorough discussion of legal obligations is beyond the goals of this book. The previous references are excellent sources for additional information.

Legal Limits of Confidentiality

Confidentiality is not absolute in the helping relationship due to legal concerns about certain kinds of information that is revealed in sessions. The now-famous Tarasoff court case from the 1970's has influenced changes to the reporting laws in several states. The case involved a young man who went to a counselor at his college and told the counselor that he intended to kill a young woman, Tatianna Tarasoff. The counselor reported the threat to the campus police, resulting in the young man being assessed at a mental facility. He was found to be rational and prior to discharge made a promise not to kill Tatianna. Sometime later he did carry out his threat to kill her and her parents sued the college. The case was dismissed in a lower court, but the California Supreme Court ruled that the counselor had a duty to go beyond contacting the proper authorities and also warn the intended victim. This decision is reflected in California state law, but in other states, Texas, for example, the state laws have not required nor found it appropriate for the counselor to warn the possible victim. The nature of what must be shared varies from state to state and has continued to change over time as a result of court rulings. Therefore, it is important to keep up to date on your own state laws concerning confidentiality requirements and exceptions.

Civil Legal Challenges

Unlike ethical violations, which are brought before an administrative licensing board, legal challenges are brought before a civil court. These civil challenges are often called malpractice claims. **Malpractice** is defined as negligence in which a professional fails to follow generally accepted standards of their profession resulting in injury to a client. When a case is brought before civil court, the person bringing the claim (the plaintiff) must prove four elements before they can recover damages:

1. That the professional owed the client a duty to conform to a particular standard of conduct;
2. That the professional had an obligation to follow defined standards of care;
3. That the professional breached that duty by some act of omission or commission in the professional practice;
4. That the client or others suffered measurable damage or injury and;
5. That the professional's conduct was the direct or proximate cause of the damage (Barker & Branson, 2000; Houston-Vega, 1996; Reamer, 1994).

Each of these elements must be proven by a preponderance of the evidence for the plaintiff to prevail. Following the state and federal guidelines suggested for civil claims should reduce the chance of criminal claims, although there may be occasions where a helping professional is brought before a criminal court.

While there is some variation in the laws by states, the top five reasons clients in the United States sue are: incorrect treatment, sexual impropriety, breach of confidence, failure to diagnose/incorrect diagnosis, and suicide of patient (Reamer, 1995). The first two claims categories encompass two-fifths of all claims. While incorrect treatment is the most frequent complaint, the most costly complaint is sexual impropriety.

There are several consequences of malpractice claims. If the practitioner loses in court, he/she may be fined for the actual damages the plaintiff incurred (for example, fee paid for follow up counseling to help the person recover) and/or punitive damages (money awarded above the actual damages as a means to punish the professional for their behavior). In addition, there may be loss of licensure, loss of reputation, and future difficulties in obtaining malpractice insurance. Malpractice claims can become public depending on the nature of the offense. Even when the plaintiff does not win in court, the process of a court case can be damaging financially, emotionally, and professionally (Barker & Branson, 2000). To alleviate these damages, some professionals choose to settle before a case goes to court regardless of whether or not the case may be won or lost. It is important to minimize the risk of a malpractice case when possible.

State and federal laws provide additional guidance for professionals. The Health Insurance Portability and Privacy Act (HIPPA) regarding privacy of patient information and child maltreatment laws regarding reporting requirements are just two such examples.

MINIMIZING RISK OF ETHICAL AND LEGAL CHALLENGES

There are steps that can be taken to minimize the risks of ethical and legal challenges and to protect yourself from liability (Barker & Branson, 2000; Bullis, 1990; Green & Cox, 1978; Reamer, 1995; Smith, 2003). Common elements include adherence to up to date practice methods, good documentation practices, and maintenance of appropriate boundaries with your clients (no dual relationships)

Upholding these three standards will go a long way toward ensuring appropriate practice. However, there are sometimes questions about what the most accepted practice for a specific issue is at the current time. Is there a point in time when an outside relationship with a former client is ever appropriate? Could your thorough documentation standards ever become a problem for your client in a legal proceeding records request?

HOMEWORK EXERCISE 3.9 | LEGAL CONFLICTS

Sometimes one set of legal duties of a practitioner conflicts with another. Think of situations in which the duty to warn might conflict with the duty to maintain confidentiality. In what situations do you think it is essential to break confidentiality with a client? What do you think would be the most difficult aspect of sharing information without the client's consent?

Helping professionals, like other professionals, are increasingly seeing ethical and legal challenges to their work. Understanding these challenges and possible risk management strategies can go far to reducing the chances of malpractice. Staying current in treatment methodologies, ethical and documentation standards, and maintaining boundaries in client-practitioner relationships will serve to minimize risks for practitioners.

ETHICAL DECISION MAKING

As you discovered in the discussion above, some actions are clearly unethical for practitioners, such as engaging in a sexual relationship with a client, practicing outside of your scope of competency, fraudulent billing, violation of reporting laws, and breach of confidentiality or refusal to provide records, while many other situations are not so clear cut. While knowledge of your profession's code of ethics is very important, it should be considered the foundation for ethical decision-making. You may encounter ethical dilemmas or a choice involving "two or more relevant but contradictory ethical directives: when every alternative results in an undesirable outcome for one or more persons" (Dolgoff, Loewenberg, & Harrington, 2005, p 258). Learning to appropriately handle ethical dilemmas is a career long task. In this section you will learn some principles used in ethical decision-making.

Reamer (1995) describes two principles that can guide practitioners in resolving ethical dilemmas. The first is **beneficence**, meaning that professionals should take actions that are intended to help or benefit others. The second principle, **non-maleficence**, means that professionals should act without malice in order to do no harm. You are probably familiar with these principles from the Hippocratic Oath, historically taken by doctors as an ethical statement to guide their medical practice. Practitioners more inclined towards beneficence are likely to be more proactive than those favoring non-maleficence. Using beneficence and non-maleficence, the practitioner considers whether the benefits of a certain intervention outweigh the risks.

HOMEWORK EXERCISE 3.10 | USING BENEFICENCE AND NON-MALEFICENCE

Think about a situation involving a neighbor in the area that your community center serves who reports that an elderly person is living alone and has medical problems. The neighbor is worried about the person's health. When you talk to the elderly person, you discover that the neighbor is correct, and it seems that the elderly person is not eating what you think is a good diet. When you tell the elderly person about an assisted living facility that he/she qualifies to live in, the person says he/she likes living alone and "No one is going to make me move to some miserable assisted living place." List the benefits and risks related to this ethical dilemma.

There are several ethical decision-making models available for use in ethical decision making, but practitioners often must make difficult decisions without a lot of time to consider complex models. We find the Congress (2000) particularly helpful in resolving ethical dilemmas. You will recognize elements from the principles discussed above in the model.

ETHIC Model of Decision Making

E   **Examine** all of the relevant client, personal, agency, professional, and societal values (including personal, societal and cultural, agency, client, and professional values)

T   **Think** about ethical standards of your professional code of ethics and relevant laws

H   **Hypothesize** about all the possible consequences of different decisions

I   **Identify** all who might benefit and all who might be harmed (it is often necessary to research potential consequences of possible decisions on all those involved)

C   **Consult** with supervisors and colleagues as you begin to formulate choices (when a supervisor, colleague, or consultant is involved, the final decision must take their thoughts into consideration) (Congress, 2000, p. 10)

When examining values, make sure professional values rather than personal values are used in the decision making. Sometimes personal values and professional values conflict. In this situation, the professional values should be used in decision-making. Client values are also important, especially with clients from other cultures. Sometimes values, ethics, and laws agree with each other and sometimes they conflict, such as the need to respect the confidentiality of the client and the laws that say you must report certain behaviors that clients share (child abuse). There may be a conflict between professional values and agency values (i.e., the professional value of client confidentiality and the use of computers to efficiently record client information without adequate safeguards to protect confidentiality). Congress added A: Advocate to the original model (2008). Identifying and advocating for adequate services, particularly for the most vulnerable populations, is an important aspect of the code of ethics in some helping professions.

In considering the ethical standards outlined in your profession's code of ethics, identify those sections that seem to be applicable to the current situation. If the dilemma is over what type of treatment might be appropriate for a client, sections about competence and responsibilities to clients might be helpful. Federal, state, and local laws may also impact the situation.

In considering all of the potential consequences of the various decisions, you would be using teleological reasoning. With a dilemma involving a dual relationship, listing the pros and cons for entering into the relationship versus not entering into it can be helpful.

In weighing benefits and harm to clients and others involved, it may become clear that the dilemma is difficult just because there is only a choice between two negatives or two possible positives. Consulting with a supervisor or colleague for all of the above steps may provide additional insight. Ethical dilemmas can be presented at a case conference or team meeting.

HOMEWORK EXERCISE 3.11 | ETHIC MODEL OF DECISION MAKING

Apply the Congress ETHIC model to the following case:

Jonna is a 16 year old high school student who has been working with a school counselor for the past six months. Over that period of time, Jonna has improved her grades, made new friends at school, and her father, a single parent, reports her behavior has also improved at home with fewer conflicts with her 13 year old brother and himself. During the last session, Jonna stated that she is going to start dancing at a strip club a few nights a week, using a fake ID that shows her to be 18 years old. What should the counselor do?

EXPECTED COMPETENCIES

In this chapter, you have learned about professional ethics, values, and legal obligations.

You should be able to define the following terms: (listed in the order that they were covered): values, ethical codes, cultural competence, confidentiality, boundaries, relationship boundaries, boundary violations, multiple role relationships, informed consent, malpractice, ethical dilemmas, beneficence, and non-maleficence.

You should now be able to:

- Explain the differences between professional and personal values.

- Describe the purpose of a code of ethics and why it is important to be knowledgeable about your profession's code.
- Explain what professional competence is and why it is an important part of ethical practice.
- List three reasons confidentiality is important to practitioners and their clients.
- Describe two boundary violations and why they are included in most of the codes of ethics for the helping professions.
- Give two reasons for being aware of the legal obligations as a practitioner.
- Explain the steps in resolving an ethical dilemma.

PROFESSIONALISM AND PROFESSIONAL RELATIONSHIPS

CHAPTER 4

Level 5:
- Taking Action
- Evaluating and Ending Professional Relationships

Level 4:
- Identifying Key Problems or Challenges
- Establishing Goals

Level 3:
- Gaining Further Understanding
- Developing Deeper Understanding
- Assessing Readiness and Motivation

Level 2:
- Developing Working Relationships
- Basic Interpersonal Skills
- Opening and Closing a Meeting
- Expressing Understanding

Level 1:
- Importance of Self-Understanding
- Ways of Understanding and Perceiving Self and Others
- Values, Ethics, and Legal Obligations
- **Professionalism and Professional Relationships**

© Cengage Learning 2013

Questions to consider as you read this chapter:

- How do I need to act in order to be the best professional I am capable of being?
- What is involved in developing a professional identity?
- How is professional supervision different from the way I was supervised by managers in the past?
- How are professional relationships different from other relationships?

This chapter covers practice behaviors related to professionalism and professional relationships. *You will learn the importance of:*

- Being professional
- Maintaining respectful, productive relationships with colleagues in your own and other disciplines
- Using supervision and consultation appropriately
- Engaging in career-long learning
- Advocating for change
- Understanding the nature of professional relationships

In the previous chapters you have learned about the importance of self-understanding, gained an awareness of some of the ways we perceive our world, and studied the values and ethics that guide professional conduct. In this chapter you will learn what it means to be a professional and about the unique nature of professional relationships. As a practitioner, an essential part of your education is to learn about and develop the ability to demonstrate professional behavior. Using these behaviors you can form and maintain appropriate professional relationships.

ACTING IN A PROFESSIONAL MANNER

One of the challenges for any new practitioner is learning what it means to be professional. As you have learned in the previous chapter, professional values and ethics should guide all professional behavior. While your values and ethics influence your professional responsibilities, some of these guidelines differ from your personal values and ethics. When in professional situations, you need to demonstrate behavior that follows the values and ethical guidelines of your profession.

A **professional** is a person who has specialized training for a particular career and who acts in conscientious, appropriate ways in the workplace. *Conducting yourself as a professional* can be a challenging process that involves many behaviors, including how you talk and how you present yourself. *Dressing appropriately* is one aspect of professionalism. The dress code for practitioners varies from site to site. In some situations you will be able to dress casually, such as when you are working with children in schools or recreation centers. Other locations require more business type of attire. In many locations you wear business clothes at meetings with outside professionals and wear more casual clothing at other times. A good rule is to notice what other professionals are wearing and dress in a similar manner. Of course, you can also ask about appropriate professional clothing.

It is important that your personal hygiene and clothing reflect positively on you as a professional. Men and women need to be sensitive to styles of dress that may be offensive. Tight slacks or shirts and implied or direct sexual dress, such as blouses that reveal too much cleavage or are transparent, are inappropriate in professional settings. Short skirts and shoes that are too casual or too dressy are generally seen as unprofessional.

Other aspects of professional behavior are being *organized and timely, and accurately recording meetings*. As a student you have probably already developed the ability to organize important documents or assignments so that you can easily find them when necessary. You have certainly learned the importance of completing assignments on time and you know how to take notes. As a professional your ability to organize important paperwork; to keep factual, easily understood notes and records about your work; to respond to clients as quickly as possible; and to meet deadlines will be part of your professional behavior. Other professionals and clients need to know they can count on you to follow through on tasks in a timely manner.

Being prepared for meetings is also an important aspect of professional behavior. In meetings you will be expected to be an active participant who shares ideas, thoughts, and opinions. Being a thoughtful participant in discussions is expected, and that includes listening attentively, raising questions, and critically considering issues being examined.

Being a professional is a challenging job. It requires awareness of yourself and your actions both when you are working with clients and when you are not (Cottone & Tarvydas, 2003; Elman, Illfelder-Kaye, & Robiner, 2005; Shepard & Morrow, 2003). Although technically what you do when you are not at work may be considered off the job, conducting yourself as a professional means that your *professional and personal life sometimes overlap*. In public places colleagues or clients who know you are a professional may observe you and expect appropriate behavior from you. No matter whether you are driving, at the movies, at the grocery store, or in other public places, you are still expected to act in a responsible manner. Becoming a professional means that people will observe and judge your actions, both on and off the job. Many practitioners are licensed by the state in which they reside and this licensure can be affected if you are charged with crimes such as domestic violence or drunk driving, even though these crimes are committed outside the times you are actually with clients (Bucky, Callan, & Stricker, 2005; Katsavdakis, Gabbard, & Athey, 2004; Remley & Herlihy, 2001; Sherman & Thelan, 1998).

People frequently ask, "What do you do?" and once you have told them your profession, you may be more critically judged on your interpersonal behavior. Sometimes after people know you are a professional practitioner, they think you are analyzing and judging them. If you hear them yell at their children, they may make some comment implying that they think you are judging them. Developing some comment to put your friends at ease is helpful. For example, "I am not trying to figure you out. I only do that when I am on the job."

Professional conduct includes not only following the rules of your workplace but also *behaving as a mature adult*. For example, openly expressing your anger in a loud or hostile way is not acceptable. Even if you feel like it, behaviors such as whining, blaming, criticizing, and pouting when things don't go your way are inappropriate.

As a professional, thinking about the impact of what you say is important. Besides using the skills that you will learn about later in this book, your language needs to be culturally appropriate, age appropriate, understandable by your client, and, of course, not offensive to your client. When talking to colleagues or your supervisor, you can be a bit more relaxed in your use of language; however, using professional language rather than slang will be a better reflection on you.

Honesty and integrity are important aspects of professional behavior. Integrity is expressed in what you do and honesty in what you say. Acting in a professional way, and following the ethics of your profession and the rules of your workplace, demonstrates integrity. Deciding how to express yourself with honesty and sensitivity can be challenging at times. For example, with a client who is often late to appointments, you could say, "I know that you have to travel by bus to come to our sessions and that the buses are not always reliable. I am disappointed when you are late because it limits the amount of time we have together and the amount of work we can accomplish. I hope that you will take an earlier bus in the future." An example with a supervisor might be, "My client often agrees to tasks to be worked on between meetings and then doesn't complete the tasks. I ask about the tasks and then don't say anything when she says she didn't do the task. I need help in knowing how to handle this and other similar situations. I think I should be more assertive." If you think that your supervisor is not providing the support you need, you could say, "I appreciate the new information that you shared with me, and it would also be helpful to know what I am doing well."

Being a professional means *knowing how to communicate information* to clients of all ages and backgrounds as well as to a fellow practitioner. For example, with a child who has attention difficulties, you might decide to talk to the child about the behaviors that are contributing to his/her difficulty in the classroom. You could say, "It seems like what is going on with your friends sometimes is more interesting than what the teacher is saying. I wonder if it might be helpful to sit in the front of the room so it would be easier to pay attention to the teacher." With a teacher or parent you may want to use more formal terminology. A teacher is more likely to respond to the following, "I think Herbert is easily distracted by the activity of others in the classroom. He seems to have some problems paying attention when he can see what his friends are doing. If you haven't tried it, you might find it helpful to have him sit in the front of the classroom." When dealing with the child's physician, you might use a different language yet: "Dr. Smith, as a result of a classroom assessment and discussions with Herbert's teacher and parents, I believe Herbert may have Attention Deficit Hyperactivity Disorder. Will you please evaluate him for a diagnosis and possible medication?" In each case you are being honest and choosing a language appropriate to each situation.

HOMEWORK EXERCISE 4.1 | COMMUNICATING WITH HONESTY AND SENSITIVITY

Imagine that you are angry with an older woman client who has been critical of you. How would you address this issue with honesty and sensitivity? Write down two possible ways of communicating to your client.

PROFESSIONAL ROLES

The *role of the helping professional* is not as clearly defined as the roles of other professionals because situations vary so much, training is not standardized among the various helping professions, and the clientele is so diverse. Unlike the medical profession, for example, the role of the practitioner is often situation dependent. A hospital-based social worker will have expectations and roles that are different from a school social worker. Medical personnel generally have the same expectations regardless of setting. Practitioners may be employed by a mental health agency, a family care agency, a social service agency, a school, or a health care facility. Each type of agency or setting has different expectations. Also, there is considerable diversity among clients with regard to factors such as age, gender, race, personal background, culture, socioeconomic status, sexual orientation, and level of ability or disability. Practitioners' roles vary with different clients. Additionally, practitioners will be working with individuals, groups, families, and organizations. Although basic professional behavior is the same and many of the same skills are used, the role of the professional will be different with an individual than with an organization.

Maintaining a professional role means different things with different clients. For example, you may play games with children or adolescents when working with them, but the purpose of the game is different than it would be if you were playing the same game with a friend. With your friend, your purpose might be to relax and have fun together. With a client you may have fun, but your purpose in playing the game might be to create a comfortable atmosphere that would allow your client to talk more freely. With a group of children, the purpose of the game might be to help the children learn to get along with other children. Playing the same game with an adult client would probably be inappropriate. It is up to you as the practitioner to keep the relationship focused and purposeful. To do this requires a clear understanding of your role in the relationship.

Professional roles are different based on level of training or education. Education for helping professionals includes associate, bachelor, masters, and doctoral level programs. Certification and licensure requirements are state, federal, and profession specific.

Practitioners with a graduate degree might have several different roles, including working independently in private practice, being a counselor or educator, being a supervisor, being a consultant, and/or being the director or administrator of a program or agency. Graduate degreed practitioners may also be in the role of mediator. A **mediator** provides an impartial forum for disputing parties (individuals, groups, communities, and organizations) to discuss areas of disagreement or misunderstanding and hopefully reach an acceptable resolution. Mediators use all the foundational skills you are learning and require additional training in skills that are particularly useful in opening and improving communication between parties in disputes.

Generalist workers have a broad range of roles that usually includes some supervision from a graduate degreed practitioner. Generalists have a number of roles. **Case management or coordination** involves providing interagency coordination and monitoring of services. The role of **broker** involves informing and linking clients with the services and resources needed. Depending on the needs of the client, in the broker role the practitioner may work with the client to help alleviate possible fears or lack of information about the services needed. The practitioner may make the initial appointment to the referral destinations. Professionals with an associate degree generally work with and may receive supervision and training from generalist or graduate degree practitioners. At any level, practitioners may be in the role of an **advocate** working to obtain services for clients or to improve political and/or social environmental conditions.

ADVOCATING FOR CHANGE

Being professional goes beyond what you do in your interactions with colleagues and clients. It also includes being aware of the social, political, economic, and cultural factors that impact individuals, families, groups, and institutions, and advocating for their betterment. As we discussed in Chapter 1, race, culture, physical disability, sexual orientation, and socio-economic class have broad impacts on individuals, families, and groups. Clients who aren't part of the dominant majority often have limited access to adequate schools, health care, jobs, and housing. People from different cultures may not speak English. Services for non-English speaking clients are often not available or very limited. People with physical or mental limitations sometimes do not get the level of skilled services they need. Socio-economic status can be a barrier to gaining services. In many areas, services for those who cannot afford to pay and/or do not have adequate insurance are very limited. The groups and individuals who have trouble accessing services are sometimes identified as *underserved*. These underserved people are usually in oppressed and vulnerable groups.

As a professional you need to advocate for adequate services for all (Congress, 2009). This means gaining knowledge about local, state, and national policies, particularly those that impact clients you serve. Depending on your professional discipline and area of practice, you will want to advocate for improvements in such areas as the health care system, the welfare system, public schools, etc. You also need to be involved with issues related to laws regulating insurance and managed care, as well as legislation related to such areas as licensure and practice concerns. Since each of the helping professions views the role of advocacy differently, you should review your code ethics to learn the specific requirements of your discipline, as well as the requirements at any site where you are employed.

Finding out who has influence to change the laws in your city, county, and state is essential. Contacting these legislatures about your concerns is part of professional behavior. In many cases you will need to work with a group of concerned professionals as you advocate for improved services and just laws. For example, if you live and/or work in an area where street violence is affecting a large number of people, you might choose to be involved in working to develop systems that protect people in these neighborhoods. If you live or work in an area where there is substantial air pollution due to industry or other problems, advocating for legislation to clean up the area is important. All threats in the environment are a consistent source of stress and need to be addressed.

As a student you can join your local, state, or national professional organization and become involved with promoting improved services and safe and healthy life conditions. Student membership in professional organizations is often inexpensive. With membership you receive newsletters informing the membership of important issues. Donations of time, skill, and/or money to professional organizations are part of being a responsible professional, as is being actively involved in promoting good services and social justice. Besides being actively involved in promoting changes that will enhance your clients' lives, you may be in a position to encourage your clients to become active advocates. Remember what you learned in Chapter 2 about strengths, resilience, and empowerment. Your clients can build on their strengths and become powerful change agents. Recall the material on empowerment. Taking on challenging projects can lead to an increased sense of personal competence and power.

Advocacy often involves working for *institutional change*. Fortunately, when working with institutions you will use the same skills you will be learning for working with individuals. In every situation, connecting with individuals is important as you work to create a cooperative atmosphere. If you are advocating for institutional change, you will work with a team of people. For example, as students you may think your school should make changes. As you have probably realized, getting an institution like a university to make changes requires a group of people working together. At one university, groups of faculty lobbied for a child care center on campus and eventually got a state of the art child care center. If you are working in a community that has no after-school programs for children, you may need to work with a group of people from the community to advocate for such a program. The after-school program may result in fewer gang problems and so benefit the entire community. You have probably read or heard about neighborhoods that cleaned off a trash-filled lot and developed a community garden or playground. As the neighbors saw their community improving, other improvements often followed. In attempting to change larger systems, you begin by getting to know the involved people and evaluating the challenges they are facing. Coming to agreement about goals, they will work together to achieve what may take considerable time. Once the goals have been established, you will help the individuals in the group agree on the steps to achieve the goals and support them as they take those steps.

HOMEWORK EXERCISE 4.2 | YOUR ROLE IN ADVOCACY

After reviewing your code of ethics, describe your professional expectations related to advocacy. Besides professional expectations, your personal values will influence what role you take as an advocate. Describe how you expect your personal values to influence the role you take as an advocate.

DEVELOPING A PROFESSIONAL IDENTITY

Developing a **professional identity** involves recognizing your identity as a professional and knowing what it means to be a practitioner of your particular discipline. Each discipline (social work, counseling, psychology, mental health counselor, etc.) has its own areas of expertise or scope of practice. **Scope of practice** involves knowing what activities, knowledge, and skills are identified by licensing boards and professional organizations as related to your discipline. You need to know and to abide by the guidelines set by your profession.

Although it is important that you identify the ethics, values, and skills special to your discipline, the general public does not understand differences between disciplines and often sees no difference between a social worker, psychologist, psychiatrist, and a counselor. Part of your responsibility as a professional is to define your area of competence for your clients. They may ask you to write a prescription without realizing that you are not a physician or nurse practitioner, and so are not allowed to write prescriptions. They may ask you to make a home visit when this is not either your area of training nor allowed by your place of employment. Knowing your professional identity and working as a team with other disciplines is part of professional behavior.

HOMEWORK EXERCISE 4.3 | EXPLAINING YOUR DISCIPLINE TO A CLIENT

What is unique or special about your discipline? Write a paragraph describing the focus of your discipline.

MAINTAINING RESPECTFUL, PRODUCTIVE RELATIONSHIPS WITH COLLEAGUES

Many settings employ professionals from different disciplines who *work together in teams*. Each team member brings his/her own professional, cultural, and individual way of assessing a situation. Each team member's perceptions should be considered and discussed in order to best serve clients. Working cooperatively and productively in interdisciplinary teams is an important aspect of being a professional. In many situations this means that you will need to learn the language of another profession. For example, if you are working with doctors, you will have to learn some medical terminology as well as at least basic information about pharmaceuticals. If your background is social work and you are working with psychologists, some knowledge about the meaning of psychological tests will be important.

Each profession has its own language and special training. Professional organizations and state licensure laws define the curriculum and requirements for each helping profession. Each profession's code of ethics discusses appropriate relationships and behavior among colleagues. It is up to you to know and follow your profession's standards.

To work most effectively together requires knowledge of and respect for the other professionals' expertise. For example, at a school the teacher may notice that the work of a child has deteriorated rapidly. Every school has different professionals available to work with the teachers. Some schools have school social workers and school counselors. Others have a counselors or social workers. With a child that needs extra help, the teacher might ask the school social worker or counselor to talk to the child. After talking to the child, he/she might visit the parents.

If needed, the practitioner would refer the parents to a community agency for services, to a mental health agency for counseling, and/or to a specialized agency for drug and alcohol treatment. Either the school counselor or social worker would coordinate all the referrals and services and might suggest that the school psychologist test the child for possible problems. After doing the testing, the school psychologist might refer the child to a child psychiatrist or to the child's pediatrician to evaluate whether medication is needed. The child might also be referred to a mental health counselor. All of these professionals would work together for the best interests of the child and family. Cooperation and close communication are essential between the various professionals serving this client.

Each profession assesses issues from a different perceptive and is trained in different methods or approaches of working with clients to achieve their goals. Just as there are a variety of effective ways to reach a career destination or a place, different professionals working toward the *same goal might use different methods*. Suppose you have a woman who is referred to you for a substance abuse problem. After working with the client to determine the goal, professionals with different training will very likely approach goal achievement in different ways. Even within the same profession, each person gains expertise in different theoretical approaches. One of your challenges as a beginner is to gain competency in a particular approach or approaches and respect for the many other effective approaches.

HOMEWORK EXERCISE 4.4 | DIFFERENT APPROACHES TO A CLIENT

Pretend that you are working in an agency and have just learned that your team is going to be working with a single, unemployed mother with two children under 5 years old.

- *As a social worker* your first thought may be to wonder whether this woman has adequate resources to provide for herself and her children. What else might you think about as you consider working with this woman?
- *As a psychologist* your first thought may be to have the client complete an assessment inventory to determine whether she is depressed. What else

might you think about as you consider working with this woman?
- *As a counselor* your first thought may be to find out what kind of support the women has. What else might you think about as you consider working with this woman?
- *As the team leader* your first thought might be about ways to encourage the team to work together effectively. What else might you consider when working with this team?

From your discipline's point of view, write down what you would think about before seeing this woman.

USING SUPERVISION AND CONSULTATION

Another important aspect of professional behavior is practicing within your *area of competence*. Earlier in this chapter we defined scope of practice as knowing what activities, knowledge, and skills are identified by licensing boards and professional organizations as related to your discipline. Your area of competence is within your scope of practice. In most states the professional organization and licensing board will identify the broad scope of possible practice for each profession. As a beginning practitioner, your area of competence, or area of practice in which you have the knowledge and skills to provide effective services, will be narrower. You may have taken a number of courses or workshops on working with individuals who have problems related to drugs and alcohol and have had experience working with clients who have these problems. You could consider working with this population as an area of competence.

The ability to reflect on what you are doing and evaluate your skills and competency is a necessary attribute of a professional. When you are practicing something new, you may over or underestimate your skills. Learning to accurately assess your expertise is part of professional behavior. Think about drawings you did as a child. Your parents may have put might put them up on the refrigerator. They might have been very good drawings for a 5 or 6 year old child. If you were to look at those drawings now you would see many problems with them. As you learn more, your expectations go up. As you practice the skills in this book, your expectations will increase and so will your ability to evaluate your use of these skills.

When beginning as a professional, your supervisor will help evaluate your level of competency by providing feedback about your use of skills. The use of supervision is critical in order to provide meaningful and helpful services to our clients. Hopefully your supervisor will listen to or watch examples of your work or observe you working with clients. Getting direct *supervision* of your work is an important way to improve your professional skills. Self-reports or transcripts of your work are also helpful, although it is easy to miss important areas.

Talking to your supervisor about what you are doing well and about your mistakes or challenges can be very beneficial. Your supervisor can help you figure out how to rectify the problem, learn from your mistakes, and improve your skills. You will get the most from supervision by engaging in non-judgmental self-reflection that leads to you sharing your successes and your missteps. Feelings of shame can inhibit your learning process. Remember that you are a beginner, and beginners make mistakes. The less critical and more curious you can be about your experiences, the more quickly you will be able to become the best practitioner you can be. Comments to yourself or others such as, "I wonder what I was thinking when I did not ask my client to talk about what led to their tears." are more productive than, "Maybe I am just not cut out for this kind of work. I totally blew it when I didn't follow through with my client." The second comment may accurately express your discouragement and/or self-critical attitude but doesn't show insight into your work with the client.

Consultation involves meeting with an expert who can help you solve a particular dilemma or problem. Consultants may be brought in to assist with many kinds of problems. They are often used in relation to difficult ethical dilemmas. As you know from the previous chapter, when facing an ethical dilemma, there are a series of steps to take to figure out the best resolution possible. If, after thoughtfully taking these steps, you, your supervisor, and your colleagues are still unsure about the best course of action, seeking assistance from an ethical consultant should be considered. As a person with advanced training in ethics and the law, an ethics consultant can provide additional information and points of view related to the dilemma. If two people have different ideas about how to resolve the dilemma, an ethics consultant can be a mediator. Ethical consultants also provide education and training regarding specific difficult ethical issues and/or the intersection of ethics and the laws of a particular area (Reamer, 2007).

ENGAGING IN CAREER-LONG LEARNING

Being a professional means being dedicated to on-going learning or professional development. In all professions there is an obligation to evaluate your practice and to continue to develop and enhance your skills (Ford, 2006; Orlinsky et al., 2005). Each profession sets ethical guidelines for remaining current with best practices, being involved in continuing education, and constructively evaluating your work. In most states there are licensing requirements for continuing education. As you learned in Chapter 3, on-going development of multicultural competence through increased self-awareness of one's own cultural values and biases, sensitivity to other cultural perspectives, and learning how to incorporate this knowledge in working with clients is important. Also, it is essential to continue learning appropriate ways to work with people with a wide range of diversities such as age, sexual orientation, gender, class, religion, and physical or mental ability. Maintaining your knowledge of ethical standards and laws that effect your practice is so important that many professions require at least some continuing education hours related to ethics every year.

UNIQUE NATURE OF PROFESSIONAL RELATIONSHIPS

The relationship between a practitioner and client is different from other types of relationships you have experienced. Each type of relationship (parent/child, husband/wife, friend/friend, and teacher/student) has its own qualities and either stated or unstated rules about how each person should behave. Some relationships involve people who are equals, such as a husband and wife, and others involve people who have different levels of responsibility and control, such as a parent and child. When people establish new relationships, there is a tendency to try to fit them into a pattern similar to an established relationship. Clients sometimes begin by treating the relationship with the practitioner as the same as a relationship with a friend or with an authority figure, such as a parent, doctor, teacher, or school principal. It is up to the practitioner to explain the unique nature of this particular professional relationship.

Although relationships may have some qualities in common, there are also distinct differences. Some of these differences involve who has the most power and/or responsibility for the relationship, whether it involves a payment for services, how often you meet and for how long, and whether there is mutual sharing of personal information. Some relationships have unique meeting locations. For example, teachers and students generally meet in classrooms whereas doctors and patients usually meet in offices, clinics, or hospitals. Practitioners often meet with clients in the practitioner's office; however, meetings sometimes occur in the client's home, at a community center, or in an agency conference room.

Relationships between practitioners and clients are unique in a number of ways. Although the practitioner is responsible for structuring the relationship and for making it work as effectively as possible, the relationship is also collaborative in many ways (Kottler, 2003; Krupnick et al., 2006). The client and the practitioner agree on times to meet and decide together on the focus of meetings. One of the key differences you may have noticed when you have worked with a professional (doctor, lawyer, counselor) is that the conversations are much more *goal-oriented* than they are in most personal relationships. One of the challenges of being a practitioner is keeping the interaction focused on finding solutions for the stated problems. It is all too easy to slip into a social conversation and accomplish very little. If the client wants to chat about local events, the practitioner might join the conversation very briefly before bringing the meeting back to the identified purposes. Remember that relationships between clients and practitioners should be *purposeful*.

Relationships between clients and practitioners are *time-limited*. Sometimes the practitioner and client agree in the beginning that they will work together for a certain period of time. Other times the relationship ends when the goals are achieved. The length of the relationship may be limited by financial considerations. For example, a neighborhood group may want a practitioner to help them create plans to improve their neighborhood, but they only have a limited amount of money to pay for services. Unless other arrangements are made, the relationship may have to be concluded when the financial resources are depleted. As in all professions, practitioners may do pro bono work, or professional work done without pay. Many practitioners also work for reduced fees when necessary or as a part of their contribution to the profession.

The relationship with a practitioner is a **fiduciary relationship,** meaning the client has confidence in the practitioner based on the particular expertise or superior knowledge and education of the practitioner. The client expects the practitioner to be competent and to put his/her interest first. The relationship is unequal with the practitioner having more power than the client. Practitioners' authority comes from their knowledge, position, and resources. This authority should not be used to dominate or control clients but to provide help to them. Since you have more power in the relationship than clients, you also have more responsibility. Clients see you as the expert, so what you say carries considerable weight and has more influence than what someone else might say.

Because this is an unequal relationship, the practitioner has certain obligations. The practitioner has a specific role in responding to the clients' needs. The practitioner will learn much more about the client than the client learns about the practitioner. It is not the client's role to take care of the practitioner or to listen to the practitioner's personal complaints, such as what a difficult day it has been, not getting a raise, or being in a minor accident. However, all of these are concerns that might be shared by the client. Clients come to the practitioner with problems to solve and, in order to get help, share information about the problems, expecting the practitioner to be helpful. This sharing puts the client in a vulnerable position. The practitioner's influence is increased by the client's vulnerability or needs. Think about a time when you were in trouble and told someone about your problems hoping that person would help you. You may have experienced a sense of vulnerability.

Another aspect of maintaining a professional relationship involves setting aside your personal opinions, judgments, and values and focusing on understanding a situation or problem from your client's point of view. If you are talking with a friend who is struggling with a difficult decision, you might say, "If I was in that situation, this is what I would do." As a friend, it is fine for you to share your ideas. When you are in a professional relationship talking with a client who is struggling with a difficult decision, you need to set aside what you would do in that situation and think about the situation from the client's point of view. What are the client's values, beliefs, and opinions related to this decision? Your role is to help your clients make the best decisions possible using their values and beliefs. As a professional you must recognize and acknowledge your personal values and not allow them to influence your professional behavior.

Practitioners also have responsibility for monitoring the emotional side of the relationship. If there is tension, anger, sexual attraction, hurt, or other feelings in the relationship between the practitioner and client, the practitioner needs to discuss these feelings with the client. For example, many practitioners choose to end meetings by asking clients how they are feeling about the relationship with the practitioner and their work together. If challenges are identified, these can be discussed. Table 4.1 provides a comparison of the characteristics of several types of relationships.

TABLE 4.1 | CHARACTERISTICS OF DIFFERENT TYPES OF RELATIONSHIPS

	Friendship	Parent/Child	Intimate Partner	Practitioner/Client
Information sharing	Both directions	Depends on the circumstance of the interaction.	Free flow in both directions is often expected.	Practitioner shares very little personal information and client shares a great deal.
Responsibilities	More or less equal	Parent has more than child: teaching, socializing, helping child solve problems, etc.	Varies by culture, but generally shared.	Practitioner has the responsibility to fulfill all agreements with client and to problem-solve with client.
Financial commitment	Little or none	High when child is still a dependent.	Depends on the culture, age, and accepted responsibilities for each role.	Practitioner is paid for time by client/insurer/government/agency, etc.
Length of relationship	Mutually determined	Usually only ended by death.	Depends on desire of each person.	Determined by the goals or agreements established by practitioner and client. When goals are accomplished, relationship ends.
Time spent together	Mutually determined	Considerable	Considerable	Practitioner determines with client.
Availability	Mutually determined	All the time	Much of the time	Scheduled between practitioner and client.

HOMEWORK EXERCISE 4.5 | UNDERSTANDING PRACTITIONER-CLIENT RELATIONSHIPS

Think about relationships you have had with professionals (doctors, lawyers, teachers, etc.). List words that describe the role of the professional and the role of the client or student. Underline those words that you believe fit with the practitioner-client relationship.

EXPECTED COMPETENCIES

In this chapter, you have learned about being a professional, using supervision and consultation, engaging in career-long learning, maintaining respectful relationships with colleagues, advocating for change, and maintaining professional relationships.

You should be able to define: advocate, broker, case management, consultation, fiduciary relationship, mediator, professional, professional identity, and scope of practice.

You should now be able to explain:

- At least three behaviors related to being professional.

- How using supervisors and consultants can be helpful.
- Why engaging in career long learning is important.
- The importance of maintaining good relationships with colleagues.
- The importance of advocating for change.
- The differences between professional and personal relationships.
- Four unique aspects of a client-practitioner relationship.
- What maintaining professional roles and boundaries involves.

BUILDING PROFESSIONAL RELATIONSHIPS

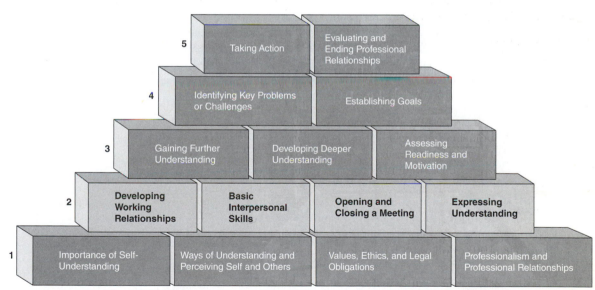

© Cengage Learning 2013

5 Taking Action | Evaluating and Ending Professional Relationships

4 Identifying Key Problems or Challenges | Establishing Goals

3 Gaining Further Understanding | Developing Deeper Understanding | Assessing Readiness and Motivation

2 Developing Working Relationships | Basic Interpersonal Skills | Opening and Closing a Meeting | Expressing Understanding

1 Importance of Self-Understanding | Ways of Understanding and Perceiving Self and Others | Values, Ethics, and Legal Obligations | Professionalism and Professional Relationships

Whether practitioners are working with a small system such as an individual or a family or a large system like an organization, they need to understand the change process. This process includes the following phases: (a) preparing to meet with the client; (b) beginning the first meeting; (c) building a collaborative relationship with the client; (d) exploring strengths, capacity, resources, stress and demands, support systems, and challenges of the client; (e) defining the focus of the work or identifying problems and goals; (f) planning for goal achievement and taking action to achieve goals; and (g) evaluating goal achievement, creating plans for maintaining progress, and ending the process. Chapters 5 through 15 focus on the knowledge and skills necessary to facilitate each step of the change process. Each chapter builds on the previous chapters and adds additional knowledge, practice skills, and practitioner qualities and identifies the strengths brought by the client.

The chapters in Section II focus on the interpersonal qualities and skills involved in building effective relationships with clients. Chapter 5, Developing Working Relationship, explains each of the core interpersonal qualities, warmth, empathy, respect, and genuineness, that are necessary for building a relationship with clients and identifies inappropriate behaviors. Chapter 6, Basic Interpersonal Skills, describes the basic skills of attending or fully focusing on clients, using good observational skills, listening attentively, and conveying warmth. Chapter 7, Opening and Closing a Meeting, introduces structuring skills including preparing to meet with clients, beginning a meeting, explaining important aspects of the helping process such as confidentiality and legal obligations, and closing a meeting. Chapter 8, Expressing Understanding, focuses on the crucial practice skills related to expressing empathy including reflecting feelings, reflecting content, reflecting content and feelings, reflecting meaning, and summarizing.

DEVELOPING WORKING RELATIONSHIPS

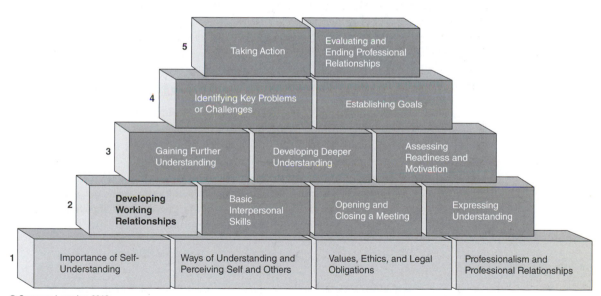

CHAPTER 5

© Cengage Learning 2013

5 | Taking Action | Evaluating and Ending Professional Relationships

4 | Identifying Key Problems or Challenges | Establishing Goals

3 | Gaining Further Understanding | Developing Deeper Understanding | Assessing Readiness and Motivation

2 | **Developing Working Relationships** | Basic Interpersonal Skills | Opening and Closing a Meeting | Expressing Understanding

1 | Importance of Self-Understanding | Ways of Understanding and Perceiving Self and Others | Values, Ethics, and Legal Obligations | Professionalism and Professional Relationships

Questions to consider as you read this chapter:

- How do I build a good relationship with my clients?
- What kinds of responses are inappropriate with clients?

In this chapter you will learn the importance of:

- Demonstrating warmth, empathy, respect, and genuineness as you build working relationships with clients
- The relationship between the practitioner and client in determining the outcome of the work
- Understanding the kinds of behaviors that are not appropriate in professional relationships

Client Attributes Necessary

- Willingness to join in a working relationship

To begin the process of working together, clients must be willing to talk about what motivated them to see the practitioner. Even clients who are court ordered to see a practitioner have a choice, although not a very good one. Clients may have to choose between following the court order to work with a practitioner or going to jail or losing custody of their children. In such cases, the client may be mainly interested in discussing his/her distress and anger about having to see a practitioner. The client demonstrated the ability to make a good decision by choosing to go to the practitioner over going to jail.

This chapter covers practice behaviors related to the core interpersonal qualities necessary to build helping relationships. In order to be helpful and effective, practitioners must be able to establish working relationships with clients. In this chapter we will focus on the core interpersonal qualities that are necessary for building rapport and creating a solid working relationship that supports change. Besides knowing what is appropriate in helping relationships, you will also learn what doesn't work and isn't appropriate in practitioner-client relationships. Just as with buildings, without a solid foundation, a relationship will not last or serve its purpose. No amount of knowledge and skill will make a difference if you are unable to establish effective relationships with your clients. In following chapters you will learn appropriate ways to express and demonstrate each quality.

USE OF SELF

One of the first things to consider regarding developing working relationships is *you*. How will you present yourself and behave in a professional working relationship? You need to develop the ability to appropriately use yourself in professional relationships. As you know from the previous chapters, the focus of working relationships is the client. You need to learn ways to set aside your own feelings and concerns in order to fully focus on the client. As you learned in Chapter 1, awareness of your beliefs, stereotypes, biases, prejudices, etc. is essential and necessary to keep these from influencing your relationships with clients (Hayes, Gelso, & Hummel, 2011). As a practitioner, your role is to be accepting and understanding of the client's beliefs, perceptions, stereotypes, biases, prejudices, life experiences, etc. If you are a person who sometimes speaks impulsively, you will need to learn to thoughtfully consider the impact of what you say to clients. Learning how to professionally use yourself in working relationships is essential (Bennett-Levy, 2006).

HOMEWORK EXERCISE 5.1 | PROFESSIONAL USE OF SELF

Think about a client whose beliefs are very different from your own. Maybe you think abortion is wrong and your client is considering getting an abortion. Maybe you think undocumented immigrants should be deported and your client is an undocumented immigrant. It may be that you think homosexuality is immoral and your client is homosexual. Maybe you believe all people should be accepted and your client is a member of a white supremacist organization. What are your ideas about what you will need to do to establish accepting, working relationships with your clients?

Who you are as a practitioner and the types of relationships you create with clients is as important as what you actually do and say during your time with clients. Since you will be using yourself in the process of working with others, it is important to consider aspects of your personality that help you become an effective practitioner. Personal qualities or traits useful to practitioners include being accepting, caring, concerned, conscientious, creative, dedicated, empathic, flexible, friendly, honest, intelligent, intuitive, kind, likable, open to new ideas, positive, respectful, sensitive, tolerant, and warm (Littauer, Sexton, & Wynn, 2005). These characteristics are listed alphabetically, not in order of importance. Each quality and trait is significant. Since you are interested in this field, you have probably already developed many of these qualities. Here are ways that some of these qualities may be demonstrated when working with clients:

Accepting: responding with a smile, nod, or encouraging word
Conscientious: being attentive to requests the client makes such as returning a phone call or accessing a needed resource
Creative: helping clients find multiple ways to achieve their goals
Flexible: understanding the life situations that may require a change in plans
Intuitive: thinking about what might be beyond the surface of what clients have said
Open to new ideas: working collaboratively with clients to include all possible ideas or approaches
Sensitive: being aware of and responding to the feelings of others

HOMEWORK EXERCISE 5.2 | CURRENT ASSETS AND ASSETS TO DEVELOP

Take a moment to think about which of the listed personal qualities and traits you already possess. Which would you like to develop? Create two columns labeled "Current Assets" and "Assets to Develop." In the Current Assets column, list your qualities and traits that will be useful in the role of practitioner. In creating the Current Assets column, it may be helpful to think of what others have found positive about you as well as aspects that you like about yourself. Include an example of how or when you experienced yourself exhibiting this asset. Under "Assets to Develop," list qualities and traits you need to develop to be an effective practitioner. You might want to include characteristics that previous teachers or supervisors have encouraged you to cultivate.

HELPING RELATIONSHIPS

When working with individuals, couples, families, groups, and communities to facilitate change, the quality of the relationship between the practitioner and the client is critically important. **Helping relationships** are relationships in which the attitudes, thoughts, and feelings expressed by the practitioner are intended to be helpful to the client (Brill & Levine, 2005; Gelso & Carter, 1994). Carl Rogers (1951) identified the importance of this relationship several decades ago. Since that time, many studies have shown that the outcome of counseling is largely determined by the quality of the relationship (Flaskas, 2004; Keijsers, Schaap, & Hoogduin, 2000; Lambert & Barley, 2002; Littauer et al., 2005). A positive working relationship is necessary in order to be effective (Bachelor & Horvath, 1999; Bennett-Levy, 2006).

Clients identify the relationship with their practitioner as the essential factor in their success (Hopps, Pinderhughes, & Shankar, 1995; Littauer et al., 2005; Smith, Thomas, & Jackson, 2004). For the practitioner, knowing how to connect with each client in a meaningful way is an essential condition for a successful outcome (Anderson, Ogles, Patterson, Lambert, & Vermeersch, 2009; Wiebe, 2002). This should come as no surprise. We all know from our own experience that it is easier to work with someone when you sense a positive connection with that person.

HOMEWORK EXERCISE 5.3 | QUALITIES IN HELPING RELATIONSHIPS

Think of recent times when you talked to a professional or someone in a position of authority. What qualities in the other person helped you to talk comfortably with that person? What qualities or behaviors in that person invited you to feel hurried, nervous, unimportant, or not heard?

Now think of a time when you were distressed and needed to talk with someone. Describe the relationship and the person with whom you would have felt comfortable expressing yourself. Think about the qualities in group relationships that invite you to feel open, comfortable, and/or safe. Make a list of at least five qualities that are important to you in group relationships.

As you know from your life experience, relationships develop in the interactions between two or more people. In successful relationships each person must be engaged and involved. Although we will focus on the practitioner's contribution to the relationship, the client's contribution is equally important. As clients begin to feel safe, accepted, not judged, and listened to and understood, they may decide to be involved and engaged in the relationship. With involvement will come a willingness to openly explore their problems and collaborate with the practitioner (Horvarth, Del Re, Fluckiger, & Symonds, 2011). Within the safety of this relationship, the practitioner and client will develop a partnership or alliance. A strong partnership involves the client feeling comfortable and safe with the practitioner, experiencing agreement on goals, and trusting the process (Baldwin, Wampold, & Imel, 2007). Such alliances have been shown to be crucial for effective work with clients (Bedi, 2006; Dore & Alexander, 1996;

Farber & Lane, 2002; Krupnick et al., 1996; Orlinsky, Grawe, & Parks, 1994; Shirk, Karver, & Brown, 2011; Thomas, Werner-Wilson, & Murphy, 2005).

A strong working relationship is important when working with larger systems (Friedlander, Escudero, Heatherington, & Diamond, 2011). When practitioners work with a group of people, they need to build empathic, respectful, genuine, collaborative relationships with each member of the group (Burlingame, McClendon, & Alonso, 2011). We know a highly successful practitioner who works exclusively with large corporations. His success stems in large part from his warmth, humanness, and genuine concern about the people with whom he works, together with his ability to communicate these factors to individuals in the group as he works with the larger system.

CORE INTERPERSONAL QUALITIES

Warmth, respect, empathy, and genuineness or congruence are the core interpersonal qualities or facilitative conditions essential for the development of good working relationships between clients and practitioners (Anderson et al., 2009; Rogers, 1957, 1961). These qualities are what the practitioner brings to the relationship. Although beginning practitioners often think that methods, approaches, or skills are the critical factors in achieving good client outcomes, clients surveyed in many research studies reported that the relationship qualities of warmth, respect, genuineness, empathy, and acceptance were most important (Beutler, Machado, & Allstetter-Neufelt, 1994; Flaskas, 2004; Krupnick et al., 1996; Littauer et al., 2005; Metcalf, Thomas, Duncan, Miller, & Hubble, 1996; Smith et al., 2004). Appropriately expressing these core qualities is necessary for developing trust and safety in relationships. Being understanding or empathic, listening attentively, and showing respect for the other person helps to create a climate of trust and safety that is necessary for the development of collaborative, working relationships (Farber & Doolin, 2011; Kolden, Klein, Wang, & Austin, 2011).

Warmth

Practitioners who are kind and accepting in a nonjudgmental way are perceived as warm. In contrast, people who appear detached, rejecting, and judgmental are experienced as cold. In accepting, warm relationships that are non-possessive, a climate of safety and trust develops that encourages clients to openly discuss, think about, and begin to explore their challenges and new ways of being and acting (Farber & Lane, 2002; Krupnick et al., 2006; Lambert & Bergin, 1994). Without this sense of acceptance, clients may not continue in the relationship.

It is important to realize that what is experienced as an expression of warmth in one culture may be perceived differently in another. Awareness of your own culture's ways of expressing warmth as well as that of your client's culture is very important. For example, in Ethiopia people greet each other by touching their cheeks together and kissing. Usually they do this on one cheek, the other cheek, and back to the first cheek. This expression of warmth is used the way some people in the United States use hugging. Recognizing how warmth was expressed in your family of origin influences how you perceive the need for warmth in relationships.

Appropriate expressions of warmth, caring, compassion, or concern in a professional relationship are similar in some ways to expressions of warmth in friendships. Practitioners express warmth verbally by showing interest, acceptance, and concern for their clients. Warmth may be expressed nonverbally by smiling or using whatever facial expression fits with what the client is expressing, by being interested, and by giving your full attention to the client. Warmth can also be expressed in your tone of voice. Even gestures can be perceived as open and inclusive or as closed and exclusive (Beresford, Croft, & Adshead, 2008). In the next chapter, you will practice attending behaviors that express warmth nonverbally.

HOMEWORK EXERCISE 5.4 | EXPRESSING WARMTH

In the next few days pay attention to people you think of as warm and people you perceive as cold or aloof. Make a list of actions that express warmth and another list for coldness. Now go back over your lists and circle the ways of expressing warmth that you believe would be appropriate in a professional relationship. For example, a person who runs up and hugs his/her friends would probably be considered warm, but that behavior would not be appropriate in a professional relationship. What about the person who calls others "honey" or "dear"? While you may consider that an expression of warmth, do you think that would be appropriate in a professional relationship?

Empathy

Empathy is the ability to understand another person's emotions, feelings, thoughts, and behavior from that person's viewpoint. Brain research has discovered that humans have the ability to create the internal states or emotions of another person and to assume "the perspective of the other person" (Siegel & Hartzell, 2003, p. 76). This capacity to understand and guess the intention of the other person has been essential to survival. Through the evolutionary process, we learned to survive by being able to "read minds" in social settings to determine if someone was a friend or foe (Iacoboni, 2009; Siegel & Hartzell, 2003).

As we attune to another person's internal state, a feeling of being connected develops. If parents and caretakers communicate with a child in a way that is attuned to the child's needs and indicates accurate understanding, the child will grow up wanting to and being able to connect with others (Decety & Lamm, 2006; Siegel & Hartzell, 2003). This desire for connectedness remains throughout life.

Neuroscience has shown that almost everyone has some capacity to understand and share the feelings of others (Elliott, Bohart, Watson, & Greenberg, 2011; Gibson, 2006). People interested in helping professions have generally developed more ability to be empathic than the general population; however, as a helping professional you will need to your enhance your ability to be empathic. Being empathic has been described as walking a mile in another person's shoes, but that is only part of empathy. True empathy is more like walking a mile in another person's shoes and experiencing the world as the other person would experience it. Being empathic involves having the willingness and flexibility to put yourself in the other person's reality (Gibson, 2006). Being empathic can be described as imagining yourself in the same situation as the other person, understanding that person's feelings, and seeing the situation from that person's point of view. Empathy involves understanding the other person's assumptions, beliefs, and/or worldview. Remember what you learned in Chapter 2 about the constructivist perspective. Each person's view of reality and truth is unique. Being empathic involves appreciating the way that others perceive or construct their world. Understanding the worldview, meanings, beliefs, or inner world of another person requires putting aside your ways of viewing life and truly tuning into the other person's reality.

One of the challenges of being empathic is that it requires understanding another person's subjective experience while maintaining the capacity to differentiate from that person. Taking on someone else's pain does not help the other person and is not empathy. If you as a practitioner did take on or experience your client's pain, the client would still be in pain, but you would be less effective, less objective, and less willing to fully connect because you would now need to attend to your own emotional distress. You can be empathic without taking on or experiencing another person's pain (Gerdes & Segal, 2009).

Empathy is not the same as pity or sympathy. Pity involves sorrow or grief aroused by someone else's suffering. Often it implies a one-up position. When you offer pity, you may be seeing the other person as weak, vulnerable, helpless, and/or incompetent. When you feel pity, you tend to think: "you poor thing." Sympathy involves feeling affected by whatever affected the other person. In personal relationships sympathy and even pity may be appropriate. Your feelings may be affected by a friend or family member who is having a painful experience.

In addition to being empathic by listening attentively to what your clients are telling you and, making every effort to comprehend what they are experiencing from their viewpoint, it is also important to express your understanding of your clients' experiences, including both painful and positive feelings. In Chapter 8 you will learn ways to express empathy and empathic understanding.

HOMEWORK EXERCISE 5.5 | EMPATHY

In the next few days look for ways people express empathy. If you do not find any expressions of empathy, what are your thoughts about why that might be true? After three conversations, think about how you expressed empathy or might have expressed empathy. Write down these expressions of empathy and talk with someone in your class about your experiences being empathic.

Developing Your Ability to Be Empathic

A challenge for practitioners is learning to be empathic with people whose backgrounds—including types of problems, age, experiences, race, or culture—are very different from their own. Developing the ability to be empathic is a lifetime task. Some good ways to develop understanding and empathy include the following:

- reading novels and professional literature about people from different backgrounds

- joining in activities, talking to, and getting to know others who have different experiences
- attending classes or workshops focused on specific groups of people
- traveling to different countries and spending time with local residents
- doing volunteer work in communities or neighborhoods very different from your own
- watching popular movies about people who are different from you

Anything that allows you to broaden or deepen your understanding of other people's experiences can enhance your ability to be empathic.

HOMEWORK EXERCISE 5.6 | DEVELOPING UNDERSTANDING AND EMPATHY

Select a movie about a situation (racial group, age group, sexual orientation) or life challenge with which you are unfamiliar (see Box 5.1 for a list of movies). As you watch the movie, focus on one character whose experiences, life situation, and background differ from your own. Your goal is to empathize with that character. Think about how that character is experiencing what is happening. What are your hunches about that character's thoughts? What are your guesses about how the character is feeling (e.g., angry, sad, scared, glad, troubled, frantic, anxious, etc.)? What might have led the person to experience those feelings? Make every effort to see the situation from the character's point of view rather than how you would perceive the same situation. Write a couple of paragraphs in the first person as the character in the movie. For example, instead of saying "I think the character felt sad," write as the character: "I feel angry when I think about my family putting me here" (*Girl, Interrupted*).

Write your thoughts about the aspects of the character that you would find difficult or easy to empathize with. Keep in mind that it is inappropriate to make generalizations about a group of people based on a character in one movie, but it is possible to get a sense of what it would be like to have experiences beyond your own.

| BOX 5.1 | MOVIES ABOUT DIVERSE GROUPS AND CHALLENGES |

• *Real Women Have Curves*	a second-generation Mexican-American girl
• *Hoop Dreams*	an inner-city poor African-American boy
• *Mystic River*	an inner-city white boy who is sexually abused
• *Girl, Interrupted*	a white teenage girl who is mentally ill
• *American History X*	a white boy in a neo-Nazi group
• *Bend It Like Beckham*	a second-generation Indian girl living in London
• *I Am Sam*	people with developmental disabilities
• *Radio*	
• *My Family*	a Mexican-American family living in L.A.
• *What's Eating Gilbert Grape*	a white, rural family dealing with issues related to poverty, autism, obesity, depression, and suicide
• *Soul Food*	an African-American family facing serious illness and death

BOX 5.1 | **MOVIES ABOUT DIVERSE GROUPS AND CHALLENGES** (*continued*)

• *Sleeping with the Enemy* • *What's Love Got to Do with It*	women struggling with partners who are physically abusive
• *The Notebook* • *On Golden Pond* • *Driving Miss Daisy* • *Iris*	people facing challenges related to aging
• *28 Days* • *Losing Isaiah* • *When a Man Loves a Woman* • *Gracie's Choice*	women with drug and alcohol problems
• *Boys Don't Cry* • *Boys on the Side* • *Philadelphia* • *Brokeback Mountain* • *The Crying Game* • *Desert Hearts* • *Longtime Companion* • *Milk*	people dealing with issues related to discrimination and sexual orientation
• *As Good as It Gets*	a white man who is dealing with obsessive-compulsive disorder
• *A Beautiful Mind*	a white man who has schizophrenia
• *Children of a Lesser God*	a white woman who is deaf
• *My Left Foot*	a person with cerebral palsy
• *The Green Mile* • *Dead Man Walking* • *The Shawshank Redemption*	men in prison
• *The Saint of Fort Washington*	people who are homeless
• *Monster's Ball*	the struggles of a single African-American mother
• *The Soloist*	African-American man who is homeless, has schizophrenia, and is a talented musician
• *Joy Luck Club*	a second-generation Asian-American woman
• *Eat, Drink, Men, Women*	challenges in a Taiwanese family
• *Amreeka*	divorced Palestinian woman and her son
• *Rhapsody in August*	Japanese children visit grandmother who lived through bombing of Nagasaki

(*continued*)

BOX 5.1   MOVIES ABOUT DIVERSE GROUPS AND CHALLENGES (*continued*)

• *Stand and Deliver*	teacher in a low income Hispanic neighborhood
• *Four Little Girls*	challenges African-Americans have faced
• *Do the Right Thing*	
• *Ghost of Mississippi*	
• *The Long Walk Home*	
• *The Celebration*	upper middle class, Danish, multi-generational family dealing with incest and violence (subtitles)
• *Yesterday*	rural African family, both parents HIV positive (subtitles)
• *Tuesdays with Morrie*	a white man diagnosed with Lou Gehrig's Disease
• *Rain Man*	a white man diagnosed as an autistic savant
• *Lars and the Real Girl*	a white man dealing with a mental illness
• *Cyrus*	a white single mother who has devoted her life to her 21 year old son
• *The Diving Bell and the Butterfly*	A white man adapting to being mute and paralyzed
• *Pieces of April*	white middle class family, oldest daughter estranged from family, mother ill and dying, aging grandparent
• *Precious*	African-American teenager living on welfare, pregnant as a result of incest
• *The Namesake*	first generation Indian man
• *City Island*	a white blue collar family dealing with a grown son recently released from prison
• *As It Is in Heaven*	a white Swedish community with issues related to impact of bullying on a child and domestic violence (sub-titles)
• *Winter's Bone*	a poor white Appalachian family, father missing and mother mentally ill
• *Goodnight, Mister Tom*	a white, British family, single, mentally ill mother, neglect and abuse of children
• *Children of Heaven*	a poor Iranian family struggling to manage
• *Lost in Translation*	challenges faced by white adults
• *Up in the Air*	
• *Life as a House*	
• *Million Dollar Baby*	
• *Edward Scissorhands*	
• *Eternal Sunshine of the Spotless Mind*	
• *American Beauty*	a family facing challenges

Respect

Respect involves acceptance, or as Rogers (1958) said, "unconditional positive regard." Unconditional positive regard is expressed by affirming and appreciating clients without condoning their harmful behaviors. It means looking for the good in others and seeing their strengths. Respectful practitioners communicate their regard for clients' thoughts, feelings, and abilities. They notice, acknowledge, and highlight their clients' strengths, capabilities, resilience, coping ability, potential, and resources.

Practitioners who always need to be the expert may not be experienced as respectful. It is better to realize and share with clients that they are the experts on their lives. Instead of telling a client, "Your family isn't good at problem solving" (as if you were the expert on his/her family), practitioners should be tentative in expressing their thoughts about the client. For example, a practitioner might suggest, "I wonder if your family hasn't learned to solve problems together." If the client finds this suggestion incorrect, respectful practitioners openly admit their mistake.

Being respectful involves being polite and following appropriate cultural norms. Practitioners must be able to work respectfully with clients from many diverse backgrounds. This involves learning about a client's background and knowing how people from that culture treat each other when showing respect (Witty, 2007). Ways to demonstrate and express respect will be covered in Chapter 9.

HOMEWORK EXERCISE 5.7 | RESPECT

Write a paragraph describing ways you demonstrate respect for yourself and other people. Now notice how others express respect. Also notice if certain groups of people receive more respect than other groups of people. In groups, notice whether certain types of people (men or women, older or younger, people of different races) seem to receive more respect.

Genuineness

Genuine behavior is behavior that is sincere and authentic. Being genuine in a professional relationship involves being real and allowing your humanness and uniqueness to be seen by clients (Kolden, Klein, Wang, & Austin, 2011; Thwaites & Bennett-Levy, 2007). Being natural, honest, and forthright is experienced as genuine. Practitioners who seem stiff, formal, unapproachable, distant, or phony are experienced by clients as inauthentic. When the practitioner always has to be right and is unwilling to admit making mistakes, this can also be experienced by the client as an inability to be authentic. In response, clients are likely to be reluctant to acknowledge their own errors. Ways to demonstrate and express genuineness will be covered in Chapter 10.

HOMEWORK EXERCISE 5.8 | GENUINENESS

You probably know some people whom you consider "fake." What do those people do and say that makes you see them as fake? You also probably know some people whom you consider honest, forthright, open, or genuine. What do those people do and say? You can ask other people what they notice that leads them to think someone is fake or genuine. Now make a list of the qualities and behaviors that relate to being fake and those that relate to being genuine.

COMMON MISTAKES

In addition to understanding the core interpersonal qualities for developing good working relationships, it is important to learn about common mistakes that can disrupt working relationships (Patterson, Williams, Edwards, Chamow, & Graur-Grounds, 2009). Blaming, arguing, reacting defensively, and attempting to pressure clients indicate a lack of respect. Deciding what changes clients need to make or what their goals should be rather than working with them collaboratively is disrespectful and ineffective. Consider how hard you would work to reach a goal someone else set for you. Maybe there was a time when someone told you that you had to get an A in a class and you didn't want to work hard enough to get an A.

Working harder than the client to solve the client's problems indicates a lack of respect for the client's skills or a lack of understanding of the circumstances that may be hindering the client's ability to make changes. Doing the thinking for clients may indicate that the practitioner doubts the client's abilities to think and solve problems. When practitioners find themselves offering one suggestion after another despite the client's lack of receptivity, they are working too hard. Although you may do some of these things in your relationships with friends and family, it is important that you find ways to avoid this kind of behavior with clients.

As you practice and develop the skills needed to be an effective practitioner, it is important that you become aware of responses that are commonly used in conversations but are not appropriate for practitioners to use. Many of these responses may appear to be helpful and are often used when someone is trying to solve a problem for another person. As a practitioner, your role is to work collaboratively with clients to help them define their problems and goals and to help them find ways to solve problems and achieve goals. Rather than taking over, parenting, preaching, or judging clients, your goal should be to demonstrate your respect for your client's strengths, capacity, and resources as you help them find their own unique ways of responding to their challenges. The following are mistakes that are commonly made by beginning practitioners.

Offering Advice

It is common in everyday conversations to offer advice whether it is asked for or not. Beginning practitioners often think they should be able to provide immediate help, so they offer suggestions on how to solve the presenting problems. It is inappropriate for you as a practitioner to offer advice until you have fully understood the people involved, their challenges and situation, and collaborated with the clients on setting goals. Offering advice before you know what the clients have already tried can be experienced as not respecting their strengths and capacities. Also, providing recommendations before you and the client have identified goals is not helpful. For example, even if you think your client is lonely and should meet new people, suggesting that your client join a group in order to meet people would not be appropriate unless you and your client agreed on a goal of meeting people, you had asked about ways your client had tried to meet people, and you had asked if your client wanted a suggestion. Offering advice reinforces the practitioner as the authority and expert instead of demonstrating the belief that the client is able to solve problems and is the expert on his/her situation.

Reassuring

Reassuring is another response that is generally inappropriate even though it seems supportive. Reassurance is generally not based in reality. Saying "it will be okay" sounds nice but is inappropriate unless the practitioner knows for sure that it will be okay.

The purpose of offering reassurance to people is often to reduce their pain. As a practitioner you need to remember that the pain clients feel about their problem can motivate them to solve the problem. If the pain is about a loss, it is a natural response that will decrease with time. Negating the importance of the clients' pain can lead them to feel that they are not fully understood or respected. Telling someone "it will all work out in the end" sounds positive but may communicate that you don't understand how troubled they are right now. This kind of reassurance is not based in reality. You do not know what is going to happen in the future.

It is common for people to say things like "Don't worry about it." This statement indicates that people have or should have the capacity to stop worrying on command and/or that their worries are not significant. Think about a time when you were really worried and someone told you not to worry about it. Did that comment make you feel listened to? Did the comment reduce your concerns in any way? In your experience, has telling others not to worry helped them to quit worrying? Generally, this type of comment has the effect of minimizing the importance of their concerns. Although it is intended to be reassuring, telling someone who is worried not to worry sounds like telling him/her not to feel what he/she is feeling.

Offering Excuses

Offering excuses for the client's situation may appear to demonstrate understanding but can discourage the client from considering ways to improve or change the situation. For example, a practitioner might tell a client, "You have a learning disability that keeps you from being successful in school." The label of learning disability may be accurate, but it would be better to say, "I understand that you have a learning disability and want to find new methods of learning that will work for you." The statement, "How could you be a good parent with a poor example set by your own parents?" is making an excuse for the client's lack of parenting skills. Instead, the practitioner could say, "I understand that you do not want to parent your children the way your parents parented you. It sounds like one of your goals is to learn better ways to parent." Rather than making excuses, practitioners need to help clients set goals and find ways to achieve those goals.

Asking Leading Questions

Leading questions are questions that give advice. This type of question has the same effect as giving advice and should not be used, at least until the practitioner and client have established clear goals (Baxter, Boon, & Marley, 2006; Collins, 1990). An example of a leading question is, "Have you considered talking in a calm voice to your partner?" Imbedded in the question is advice. If clients want advice or suggestions, they will ask. Practitioners should help clients figure out ways to achieve their goals and create opportunities for them to try new capacities or new ways of thinking and feeling. An overarching goal is often for clients to gain a sense of empowerment so they can act in new and more effective ways. When practitioners give advice or try to quickly fix the problem, they may believe they are being helpful, but giving advice will not lead to a greater sense of control, capacity, or empowerment for clients.

Dominating through Teaching

In Chapter 14 we will discuss examples of appropriate times for practitioners to teach or provide information to clients. Teaching in a way that is dominating or pushy is inappropriate. It can suggest that there is only one right way to do something. Think about how you would feel if you had not asked for a suggestion about how to study better and someone told you, "When you study, you must underline the key sentence in each paragraph and develop a written outline of everything you read." Communicating in a dominating way tends to invite people to feel shamed or rebellious and to withdraw or become defensive and argue. Implying there is only one way to resolve an issue can lead to clients shutting down their own thinking and not searching for their own answers.

Labeling

Labeling is a sophisticated way to judge, criticize, or blame another person and is not helpful. Identifying a person as passive-aggressive, developmentally delayed, at risk, or resistant tends to limit the practitioner's view of the client's ability to change. While many practitioners consider labeling clients to be inappropriate at any time, others believe that labels can be useful. However, they insist on using person-first language—meaning you first speak about the person. For example, "He is a person who has acted in passive-aggressive ways" rather than "Working with that passive-aggressive person is difficult." You could say, "I have found working with Tom, who has been labeled passive-aggressive, to be difficult." Even though a label may accurately describe some aspect of a person, it doesn't portray the whole person.

Interrogating

Asking clients one question after another makes them feel as though they are being interrogated. Remember that your task as a practitioner is to understand and work with your clients. Instead of listening to the client and expressing empathy concerning their situation, beginning practitioners often ask too many questions. "Why" questions are particularly problematic because they sometimes imply judgment and also invite defensiveness. Think about how you feel when someone asks you, "Why haven't you completed that task?"

HOMEWORK EXERCISE 5.9 | UNHELPFUL RESPONSES YOU MAY HAVE EXPERIENCED

Think about a time when something was bothering you and you went to a friend to talk about it. Describe your reaction to the following hypothetical responses and label the mistake that each response demonstrates.

- "Let me tell you how to fix your problem."
- "Something just like that happened to me and ———— is what I did to solve the problem."
- "Everything will be fine after a few days."
- "Everything happens for a reason."
- "You are never given more than you can handle."

- "Think of it as a growth opportunity."
- "There must be an important lesson in this for you."
- "I am sure it will all work out in time."
- "Have you considered doing ....?"
- "I just read an article about that kind of a problem so I know that you should do ...."

Do these responses invite you to continue talking to the person, or do they make you want to end the conversation? What if the friend had simply listened to you or expressed understanding? Do you think you would have continued to share with that friend?

EXPECTED COMPETENCIES

In this chapter, you have learned about the essential interpersonal qualities needed for developing effective relationships with clients.

You should be able to define the following terms: empathy, genuine behavior, helping relationships, and respect.

You should now be able to:

- Name and describe the four core interpersonal qualities identified as essential to the development of a working relationship with a client.
- Name, describe, and give an example of each of the seven common practitioner mistakes.

BASIC INTERPERSONAL SKILLS

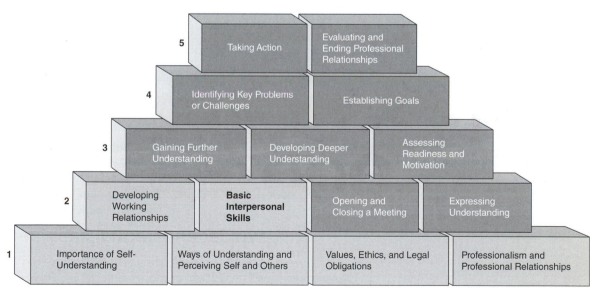

CHAPTER 6

© Cengage Learning 2013

The pyramid diagram contains the following blocks:

5 Taking Action | Evaluating and Ending Professional Relationships

4 Identifying Key Problems or Challenges | Establishing Goals

3 Gaining Further Understanding | Developing Deeper Understanding | Assessing Readiness and Motivation

2 Developing Working Relationships | **Basic Interpersonal Skills** | Opening and Closing a Meeting | Expressing Understanding

1 Importance of Self-Understanding | Ways of Understanding and Perceiving Self and Others | Values, Ethics, and Legal Obligations | Professionalism and Professional Relationships

Questions to consider as you read this chapter:

- What does it mean to truly listen?
- How would you rate your ability to be observant? Why is that important in helping relationships?
- How do you show that you are fully present and attentive in a relationship?

This chapter covers practice behaviors that are necessary skills in forming a relationship with individuals, families, groups, and organizations. *You will learn the importance of:*

- Accurately observing
- Effectively attending
- Actively listening
- Conveying warmth

Client Attributes
- Willingness to communicate as openly as possible

CORE INTERPERSONAL SKILLS FOR HELPING

As you learned in the previous chapter, warmth, empathy, respect, and genuineness are core qualities that form the foundation for effective professional relationships. While these qualities are vital, practitioners must also master a number of interpersonal skills that invite clients to feel more comfortable communicating openly. Good professional relationships rest on accurately observing, effectively attending, and actively listening (Ackerman & Hilsenroth, 2001).

BEING A GOOD OBSERVER

Observing means noticing all the behaviors that accompany communication. Some people are naturally excellent observers, while others tend to focus on the content of what is being said and pay less attention to other modes of communication. These other forms of communication are called non-verbal communication. **Non-verbal communication** includes such things as facial expressions, breathing patterns like sighing, gestures, movement, and posture. Research has shown that much of the meaning in any communication is expressed nonverbally (Contarello, 2003; Gordon, Druckman, Rozelle, & Baxter, 2006; Van Buren, 2002).

Being a good observer increases understanding of what clients are communicating. Careful observations supplement what the client tells you verbally; sometimes intensifying what is being said and sometimes contradicting it (Westra, 1996). If the client expresses one message nonverbally and a different message verbally, the inconsistencies should be noted because what is communicated nonverbally is closer to the actual meaning. For example, if a client clenches his fist and hits the table while saying he is not angry, the discrepancy between what he is doing and what he is saying needs to be noticed. Practitioners often comment on contradictions. For example, the practitioner might say, "I heard you say you aren't angry and noticed that you clenched your fists and hit the table." If practitioner pauses after that comment, the client may choose to explain his/her behavior.

Good observers pay attention to many aspects of behavior. Facial expressions can express any emotion or show no expression. No expression or facial movement is called flat effect, and may indicate depression. Other expressions of depression are little body movement and/or slumped posture. Sadness may be expressed by crying, by sighing, by looking down, or by a slight change in the amount of moisture in the person's eyes. Stress may be expressed with muscle tension, by movement, and sometimes by shallow breathing. Looking away may indicate that the person is thinking or remembering or may be hesitant about relating. Some gestures like clenched fists may indicate stress, frustration, anger, or anxiety. Since nonverbal communication is unique to each culture and even to each individual, careful observation only gives clues about possible feelings. When people are experiencing strong feelings, their skin tone may change color, darkening or looking rosier than usual. This skin color change usually starts at the chest and moves up to the face. Sometimes only the neck darkens or a spot appears on each cheek. These observations will provide information about emotions the client may be experiencing and the intensity of these feelings.

HOMEWORK EXERCISE 6.1 | BEING A GOOD OBSERVER

Sit in a public place for five minutes and watch two people who are sitting and talking to each other. Write down what you notice about facial expressions, eye movement and eye contact, body position and movement, breathing pattern, muscle tone, gestures, and skin tone changes. Use descriptive words rather than evaluative words. For example, you might say that his mouth was turned down; he mostly looked at the floor; sat slumped in his chair, leaning way back, rarely shifting position; sighed a few times; and seldom moved his hands. There were no indications of tension and no skin tone changes. You might guess that he is depressed (an evaluation); however, he might be troubled, tired, or have a headache (evaluations). Just describe what you see, no evaluations. Also note your reactions as you are observing. Were there ways that you distracted yourself from paying attention and noticing behaviors? Here are some questions to stimulate your thinking about what you observed.

1. *Facial expression:* What did you see on the person's face? Did she have tears in her eyes? Was her mouth turned down? Was her brow wrinkled? Did she have circles under her eyes? Did she smile a lot?

2. *Eye movement and eye contact:* Did she look mostly at the floor, up at the ceiling, all around the room, or directly at the other person? Did she stare?

3. *Body position and movement:* How was she sitting? Was she leaning back against her chair, slumped over, slouched, upright and stiff, legs crossed, feet flat on the floor, legs curled under her, legs uncrossed, or ankles crossed? What about movement? Did she hardly move at all, move only slightly, or move around most of the time? Did she nod her head or swing her legs? Did her movement change, maybe sitting up straight and stiff in the beginning and later leaning back?

4. *Breathing pattern:* Did her breathing seem normal or did she often sigh, take deep breaths, or breathe in a shallow way?

5. *Muscle tone:* What did you notice about muscle tone? Perhaps her fists were clenched or her jaw seemed tightly closed. Maybe she was slumped or her face looked slack. Did her muscle tone change? If so, in what ways?

6. *Gestures:* What was she doing with her hands? Did her hands stay in her lap folded together? Were her hands moving around most of the time? Were her hands held together in tight fists? Did she make circles with her hands as she talked or rotate her arms so her palms faced up?

7. *Skin tone changes:* Did you notice any change in skin tone? If there was a skin tone change, describe it.

Observing in Groups

When working with groups of people, practitioners need to observe each member of the group. In a group or family meeting, observing everyone is challenging. Observing provides the practitioner with additional valuable information that helps to understand and decide how to respond to clients. In groups, the practitioner should not only look at the person speaking but also scan the other group members (Jacobs, Masson, & Harvill, 1998; Rutan & Stone, 2001; Saiger, Rubenfeld, & Dluhy, 2008). Scanning encourages clients to speak to one another rather than to the practitioner exclusively. If a client is speaking to the practitioner and the practitioner begins to glance at others in the group, the client will generally follow the practitioner's example and look at group members. If there are two group leaders, one leader can scan the group while the other leader is talking. Thoughtful observation is important to all types of groups (task groups, agency teams, or leadership teams). By observing group members' behaviors, the practitioner may notice such things as one member looking at the ceiling, another member whose eyes are closed, someone whose fists are clenched, and so on. If you notice someone who is leaning forward, sighing, and has a wrinkled brow, you might wonder whether something being discussed might be troubling. Of course, it could also be that the person has a headache, is worried about money, had a fight with his/her spouse, or is thinking about something unrelated to the group. Practitioners can guess about the meaning of non-verbal behaviors and may choose to ask if their hunches are accurate. For example, the practitioner might say, "I noticed that several folks in the group have their eyes closed. I wonder if you are getting tired of discussing this topic."

Observing in Community Groups and Organizations

Being a good observer in larger groups requires considerable practice. There may be several levels of interaction in larger groups (Northhouse, 2010). This could include smaller groups within the larger group. These small groups may be reacting with different thoughts or feelings than the larger group. If it is a group of families, individuals within families may be observed to have different expressions or actions. If you are consulting with an organization, there may be a hierarchy of people who have their own agendas exhibited in differing behaviors. It will be important to take note of as many behaviors as you can in order to figure out such things as who is the informal leader, who silently challenges the authorities; who seems to have power; and who feels slighted. There may be in-groups and out-groups who participate in different ways. Pay particular attention to behaviors and expressions that seem different such as someone who is fidgeting a lot, facial expressions incongruent with others in the group, shoulders hunched, mouth pinched, eyes closed, looking around at others, and so on. Depending on the agenda for the meeting, you may or may not decide to respond to these different behaviors. Observations can help you determine whether to change the topic, whose questions need answering, or what to change to make the meeting more effective.

ATTENDING TO CLIENTS

Attending involves being completely focused on the client. The process of attending is not a new experience. Think of a time when you were watching an exciting movie and were so focused on the movie that you forgot about everything else (your headache, the time, what you had to do later). Often we believe we are paying full attention to other people, but actually are only partially attending. We may hear what the other person is saying while doing something else such as glancing at the TV or a magazine. You miss part of what is being communicated if you aren't looking at the person and focusing on him/her. The use of attending is the foundation of any positive relationship (Anderson, Ogles, & Weiss, 1999; Cooper, 2007).

Attending is communicated in many ways. Although different cultures communicate involvement in different ways, there are some basic behaviors that generally convey that you are attending (Norcross, 2010). Readiness to be involved and to be fully present can be communicated in several ways. Leaning very slightly forward with a comfortable, relaxed position indicates attention and concern to most people. You can be relaxed and comfortable without leaning way back as if you are resting rather than being attentive. Sitting in an open and accessible way tends to express acceptance. Practitioners who fold their arms tightly across their chest may be experienced as being closed off or distant.

Facial expressions are particularly important ways to communicate attending. The practitioner's facial expression should be congruent with whatever is being discussed. If the client is talking about something sad or serious, the practitioner's face should express concern or somberness. For most people this comes naturally, but some people smile or even laugh when serious topics are being discussed. If smiling in sad situations is something you know that you do, think about what your smile may be communicating to your client.

Maintaining regular eye contact is another way of showing that you are paying attention. However, those from Asian and Northern European countries prefer a non-gaze or peripheral gaze (Wang De-Hua, 2007). Gender issues influence the meanings of different types of eye contact. The length of time a man looks "into" a woman's eyes or how a woman lowers her eyelashes can be interpreted as having sexual connotations.

Any type of distracting behavior draws attention to itself and away from the process. Nervous behaviors such as playing with a pencil, pen, or rubber band; rocking or turning in a chair; drinking from or fiddling with a water bottle; and moving about a lot may distract clients and invite them to think you are nervous, troubled, or not paying attention. These behaviors may be interpreted by clients as impatience or boredom, leading the client to cut short what he/she wanted to communicate. Think of a time when you had several things you wanted to discuss with a teacher and the teacher was tapping a pencil or pen on his/her desk. What effect did that have on you? Did you forget some of the things you planned to say? Did you feel hurried to finish and leave?

Another way to communicate involvement or interest is minimal encouragement. **Minimal encouragement** involves repeating one or more words a person says, nodding, or saying something like "Uh-huh." Minimal encouragement tells the other person you are paying attention to them. Repeating one or more of the last words in the client's sentence can be an effective method of offering minimal encouragement. For example, if the client said, "I am worried about what my manager will say," the practitioner might say, "Your manager?" thus letting the client know he was heard and inviting him to continue (Duggan, 2006).

Practitioners use the same behaviors to communicate attending with groups and organizations. With a large group or an audience, making eye contact with individuals and scanning the group demonstrates attending. Think about how you feel when your teacher looks at you. If your attention had been drifting, that look from the teacher might invite you to once again think of yourself as an important member of the class. When leaders or teachers look directly at individuals, it tends to increase interest and participation (Clark, 2003; Northhouse, 2010).

HOMEWORK EXERCISE 6.2 | ATTENDING

Pick a time when you are talking to someone and practice using as many attending behaviors as you can.

- sit leaning forward in an open, relaxed way
- maintain appropriate eye contact
- have a congruent facial expression
- minimize distracting behaviors
- offer minimal encouragement

After the conversation write down how you felt and what you were thinking. Which behaviors came naturally? Which behaviors were harder to do? Which behaviors did you forget to use? How did attending feel to you? What are your hunches about how the other person felt in response?

LISTENING

Listening involves fully focusing on what the other person is attempting to communicate. Listening is a step beyond attending and is one of the most important things practitioners do. In our busy society, we often do not listen to one another. Listening involves not only hearing the words but also making every effort to understand the meaning the other person is trying to convey and to understand the implications of what the other person is saying (Baum & Gray, 1992; Cooper, 2007; Friedman, 2005). Feeling genuinely listened to helps the client develop a sense of trust, be more inclined toward self-reflection, and experience respect and caring from the practitioner.

Listening as a practitioner is different from listening in conversations in social or work situations. To facilitate listening, practitioners must refrain from typical conversational behaviors such as talking about oneself, changing the subject, asking a lot of questions, and avoiding silence. Although listening may seem simple, it can be difficult because it requires that the practitioner pay complete attention to what the client is saying and doing, rather than to what the practitioner is thinking. When practitioners are focusing on listening to their clients, they limit their responses to minimal encouragement such as "uh-huh" or "mm" or one or two words of acknowledgment while listening. Other valuable ways to demonstrate listening will be addressed in Chapter 8.

Listening involves noticing the client's communication style, including tone, volume, and speed of delivery. Listening to the way a client communicates includes noticing pauses, silence, and changes in his/her usual patterns of speech. As you listen, you will notice the client's style of speaking. Some clients are clear, direct, and easy to understand. Others ramble and are hard to follow. Some use jargon or colloquialisms that you may not understand. Some have trouble expressing themselves in the practitioner's language. Others use a narrative style, communicating in a story form. Some speak in a confused or circular manner, jump from one topic to another, and/or do not complete their explanations. Whatever way the client talks, it is up to you as the practitioner to listen carefully in order to understand the meaning of what the client is communicating.

Whatever communication style clients use, it is important to give clients plenty of time to express their thoughts and feelings. Thus, part of listening is to slow the pace to allow some silence and resist the temptation to talk in order to keep the conversation moving. If the client is speaking very quickly, it may be useful to ask them to slow down a bit so both of you can think more about what is being said.

Even when practitioners are fully focused on listening, they may not understand the client because they misinterpret the client's words, lack knowledge about the client's culture, or are influenced by personal biases and prejudices (Norcross, 2010). A client may say, "I was so angry." Your natural interpretation is to think what "so angry" means to you, but you don't know what "so angry" might mean to your client. In Chapter 10 you will learn ways to gain further understanding of clients' possible meanings. A wife may say to her husband that she is "upset" and neither he nor you may know exactly what "upset" means to her. She could be hurt, angry, sad, or some other feeling. Different cultures and even different families express feelings differently. For example, if a child says, "I don't want to," it can be heard as rebellion or disrespect or just a statement concerning the child's wishes. It all depends on your ideas about a child's appropriate behavior.

Physical challenges also affect listening. If you or your clients have physical limitations, this may change communication patterns (Duggan, 2006). You may need to rearrange the room so you are facing someone who has limited vision. If the client is hearing impaired and cannot read lips, sign language or an interpreter is needed. It may be useful to more regularly ask someone with limited hearing what he/she has heard you say. Being open and direct in addressing these differences is often the best way of responding to the unique needs of people who are deaf, visually impaired, or have other physical challenges.

Listening in groups, including families, small groups, community groups, and organizations, is critical to understanding the dynamics in the group (Jacobs, Masson, & Harvill, 2009a). Good group leaders know that listening is essential to understanding the agenda of the group. As the leader models listening, other members of the group may follow the leader's example. As group members begin to listen respectfully to each other, trust and understanding develop (Northhouse, 2010).

HOMEWORK EXERCISE 6.3 | LISTENING

In a conversation with someone, listen carefully to what the person says. Focus on listening more than talking. After the conversation, write down a summary of what the person said. Describe the person's:

- tone or volume (for example, the person spoke very softly),
- speed of delivery (most of the time the person talked quickly, and then when talking about his problems in class talked much slower), and
- style of speaking (such as "he tended to ramble, but I was able to understand him," or "he talked in a direct, logical manner," or "he jumped from one topic to the next," etc).

Now do this again with another person. In what ways were these conversations different from your usual conversations?

Think of a time that you felt someone was really listening to you. What was the experience of being listened to like for you? List three reasons that you sometimes don't listen to people?

EXPRESSING WARMTH

In Chapter 5 you learned about the importance of expressing the core interpersonal qualities. **Warmth** is expressed by conveying caring and interest to clients through your demeanor. Warmth is shown in the way the practitioner looks at the client, pays attention to the client, and/or has a facial expression of concern or acceptance. The practitioner's tone of voice and way of sitting can express warmth and caring. With a visually impaired person, it is particularly important to express warmth in your tone of voice.

In general observing, attending and listening to a client are aspects of conveying warmth (Norcross, 2010). However, observing, attending, and listening can be done mechanically and accompanied by a facial expression of detachment. Think about a time when you met with a professional person, a doctor, teacher, or lawyer who seemed to be observant, attentive, and listening but seemed cold or uncaring in his/her approach to you. How did you feel then with that person? How comfortable were you in openly talking with that professional?

Warmth may be expressed by a handshake at the beginning or end of a meeting. However, any type of touch, even a handshake, may be prohibited between men and women of certain faiths. The more orthodox the faith, the more he/she may abide by stricter rules about contact. This is true of some Muslims, some Jews, and some Christians. Physical contact is seen as an intimate exchange and not an acceptable way of expressing professional caring (Wang De-hua, 2007). Racial and ethnic differences and age influence how physical contact is understood. It may be okay to put your arm around a young child, but in many cultures it is inappropriate to use physical contact with others.

In the exercise at the end of this chapter, you will evaluate your ability to appropriately express warmth. For each quality, an evaluation scale is included to help you specifically identify how well you demonstrate each quality. When doing the practice exercises, you may find that you are so focused on using skills correctly that you do not express as much warmth as you would naturally express. As using professional skills becomes more natural for you, expressing warmth will become easier and begin to feel more authentic.

The following scale is used to evaluate expressions of warmth.

Warmth Evaluation Scale

Level 1: The practitioner communicated *little or no concern* for the client and appeared cold, detached, stiff, and/or mechanical.

Level 3: *At least half the time,* the practitioner verbally and nonverbally communicated concern and caring appropriate to the unique needs of the client.

Level 5: The practitioner's facial expression and posture *consistently* communicated concern and caring appropriate to the unique needs of the client.

HOMEWORK EXERCISE 6.4 | Expressing Warmth

For the next few days, pay attention to ways that you and other people express warmth. List four specific ways that people express warmth that you think would be appropriate in a professional relationship. What about other people's behavior communicates that they are cold, detached, or lack warmth? Also notice situations where the expression of warmth might be inappropriate, such as hugs that are too close, looking at another too long so as to suggest flirtation, or patting on the head or back.

DVD Example: Warmth

Watch the beginning meeting with the individual.

- Identify expressions of warmth between the practitioner and the client.
- What did you like about how the practitioner expressed warmth to her client?
- Identify any expressions of warmth that you thought were inappropriate.

USING INTERPERSONAL QUALITIES AND SKILLS IN PRACTICE INTERVIEWS

Remember what you read in the Introduction to this book about teaching-learning methods used in this book. You are now ready to begin doing the Practice Exercises. Starting with this chapter, practice exercises will be included to provide you with opportunities to use the skills that make up professional practice. Beginning practitioners need to practice using professional skills and expressions of core interpersonal qualities until they can use the skills and core qualities comfortably (Bennett-Levy, 2006; Weick, 1993). As you gain mastery of these skills, you will be able to use them easily and increase your ability to focus on understanding your client's reality challenges (Harvey, 2007; Mahoney, 1986; Vodde & Gallant, 1995).

By completing the practice exercises, you will move from "knowing about" skills to "knowing how" to appropriately use the skills. Using skills in simulated situations has been shown to be the best way to develop expertise (Bennett-Levy, 2006; Stone & Vance, 1976; Vinton & Harrington, 1994; Vodde & Gallant, 1995). As with learning any new behavior or skill, you may feel awkward, be afraid of making mistakes, or be hesitant about trying new behaviors. Initial feelings of awkwardness, discomfort, or tension as you use new skills are common with any learning process. Think about a group of skills that you learned some time ago, such as learning to drive. Take a minute to think about what it was like when you first drove a car, maybe with an instructor or parent. Now think about the time when you first drove alone. You may remember feeling tense and nervous and thinking that driving was a lot of work. It certainly didn't feel natural and comfortable. If you had to drive on a highway, you might have made mistakes and probably would have felt scared. Think about what driving is like for you now. For most of us, the skills of driving are so automatic that we don't think about what we have to do. As with driving, repeated practice develops your confidence and sense of competence until these skills seem natural.

In addition to practicing skills, these exercises teach you to do self-assessment and self-evaluation. Self-evaluation is a very important aspect of a professional career. Experienced and competent practitioners engage in a process of constant self-assessment and self-evaluation. They regularly define goals related to professional development and identify both their strengths and areas for growth related to skill development and knowledge acquisition (Bernotavicz, 1994; Orlinsky et al., 2005).

The practice exercises in this book provide opportunities to apply the skills you are learning and to get immediate feedback. In these exercises you will be working with a single client. Although these same skills are used with families and groups, it is easier to start by practice with a single client.

In the practice exercises, you will form a group with two of your classmates. The three of you will take turns playing the roles of client, practitioner, and peer supervisor. In other words, each person will have an opportunity to experience being a client, a practitioner, and a peer supervisor.

Client role: In the role of client, you will discuss a problem in your life. Keep in mind that these will be short meetings. There will not be enough time to fully explain your situation. The goal is to allow the practitioner to practice using skills. Resolving your challenges is not the goal. You can discuss a challenge that occurred in the past, but in your role as client act as if the challenge is current. You should have a confidentiality contract with your classmates. Anything discussed in these practice sessions is confidential just like anything discussed with clients is confidential. If you have never been a client, being in this role will help you understand something about the vulnerabilities of being a client. After each practice meeting, the person in the role of the client will give feedback to the practitioner, focusing on whether he/she felt understood by the practitioner. It is helpful if the client describes the specific behaviors that contributed to the experience of feeling understood.

Practitioner role: The practitioner will practice demonstrating the skills for the particular exercise. After each practice meeting, the practitioner will identify what he/she perceives as his/her strengths and weaknesses.

Peer supervisor role: During the meeting, the peer supervisor will observe the client, listen to the client, and keep track of time. After the practice meeting, the peer supervisor will give the practitioner feedback on his/her use of skills related to the practice meeting. In the role of peer supervisor, you will learn to evaluate the appropriate use of skills and interpersonal qualities. Although the many tasks of the peer supervisor are challenging, you will benefit from closely observing fellow students and giving constructive feedback. As the peer supervisor, you will be the mirror reflecting back to the practitioner his/her strengths and areas for growth. The goal of the peer supervisor is to help the practitioner improve by identifying what the practitioner is doing well along with areas to be improved.

As a peer supervisor it is important to give specific, clear, direct, and accurate feedback (Campbell, 2006; Rosenbaum & Ronen, 1998; Wilkerson, 2006). It is not helpful to say, "You did a fine job." Instead, the peer supervisor should tell the practitioner specifically what he/she did that was positive or negative, and when possible, tell the practitioner what impact he/she seemed to have on the client. For example, "You leaned toward your client and looked directly at her. After you did that for a while I noticed your client seemed to relax." Or, "You frequently fidgeted with your pencil. I noticed your client looking at the pencil. I think your behavior might have been distracting to your client."

When talking to the practitioner, focus on the behavior, not on the person. Do not make guesses, judgments, or interpretations about his/her actions. For example, you might say, "You leaned back in your chair and looked at the ceiling" rather than "You didn't pay attention to your client."

The final task of the peer supervisor is to complete the evaluation form related to the practice exercise. This evaluation system has been used successfully by both undergraduate and graduate students (Baez, 2003; Chang & Scott, 1999; Menen, 2004; Pike, Bennett, & Chang, 2004; Wilkerson, 2006).

Remember that mastering new behaviors requires practice. Some skills may seem easier to master and others more difficult. With some exercises, you may need to repeat practice exercises several times to adequately master the behaviors and skills. Since each practice exercise adds new behaviors and skills, it is important to become comfortable with one group of skills before moving on to the next practice exercise.

PRACTICE EXERCISE 1 | ATTENDING, OBSERVING, LISTENING, AND EXPRESSING WARMTH

Exercise Objectives
- To practice communicating to a client your readiness to listen, willingness to focus on work with the client, warmth, and overall involvement with the process. These behaviors say to the client: "I am fully present and ready to be with you."
- To heighten your awareness of the nonverbal ways clients communicate.
- To practice listening to what the client is trying to communicate.

Step 1: Preparation
Form groups of three people. Each person will have the opportunity to play the roles of client, practitioner, and peer supervisor. Each meeting will last about five minutes.

Client Role
- Think about a problem that involves some reasonably strong feelings that you feel comfortable talking about for a few minutes. These exercises

will be more authentic if you talk from your own experience.

Practitioner Role
- Think about important things to observe in the client and to do in the interview.
- Review the behaviors involved in attending and important things to observe in the client. (See evaluation form.)

Peer Supervisor Role
- Review the behaviors involved in attending in order to evaluate the practitioner's use of these behaviors during the interview (See evaluation form).
- Prepare to observe and listen to the client and to keep track of time.

Step 2: The Client Meeting

Client Role
- Tell your story for five minutes.

(continued)

PRACTICE EXERCISE 1 | Attending, Observing, Listening, and Expressing Warmth (*continued*)

Practitioner Role
- Use the attending behaviors to communicate involvement.
- Observe all aspects of the client's communication.
- Listen, remaining silent except to express minimal encouragement. Rather than thinking about what to say to client, the practitioner should focus on attending, observing, and listening.

Peer Supervisor Role
- Watch the practitioner's behavior and check each attending behavior consistently used by the practitioner.
- Check off the items for each type of attending behavior used by the practitioner. *Each check mark is worth one point.*
- Observe the client's behavior.
- Keep track of the time and alert the practitioner and client at the end of five minutes.

Step 3: Feedback
Purpose: Receiving immediate constructive feedback helps students enhance their practice skills. Using this evaluation system, the peer supervisor monitors the skills used by the social worker. The client, social worker, and peer supervisor identify strengths and areas for growth in the social worker.

Client Role
- Share experience of the practitioner.
  - In what ways did you think the practitioner was attentive?
  - Did you think the practitioner was listening to you?

Practitioner Role
- Evaluate yourself related to attending, observing and listening.

Peer Supervisor Role
- Give the practitioner one point for each attending behavior consistently used. Record the feedback in the practitioner's textbook for future reference.
- Ask the practitioner about observations of the client related to each of the following: facial expression, eye movement and eye contact, body posture and movement, breathing patterns,

muscle tone, gestures, and skin tone changes. Ask for descriptions rather than evaluation.
- Give the practitioner a check mark for each area that he/she was able to describe adequately.
- Ask the practitioner to summarize what he/she heard the client say. Ask the practitioner any of the following questions:
  - Did you notice any shifts in the conversation?
  - Did you hear any changes in the volume and speed of the client's speech?
  - How would you describe the client's speaking style? For example, the practitioner might say, "The client had a clear, direct, logical way of speaking. His volume was rather quiet, but he tended to talk louder when discussing his son. He spoke slowly and deliberately."
  - Did you forget to listen at any time? If so, when? Any ideas about why you stopped listening?
  - Did anything happen that made it hard for you to listen?
  - Discuss the listening scale with the practitioner and decide on an appropriate score.

Listening: Content and Process Evaluation Scale
Level 1: The practitioner did not summarize any of the major elements of content or describe anything about the client's way of speaking.

Level 3: The practitioner summarized *four elements* of content but did not describe anything about the client's way of speaking.

Level 5: The practitioner summarized all the major elements of content and accurately and fully described the client's way of speaking, including communication style, volume, and speed of delivery.

- Ask the practitioner to discuss ways he/she demonstrated warmth.

Discuss the warmth scale with the practitioner and decide on an appropriate score.

Warmth Evaluation Scale
Level 1: The practitioner's facial expressions and posture communicated *little or no concern* for

PRACTICE EXERCISE 1 | ATTENDING, OBSERVING, LISTENING, AND EXPRESSING WARMTH (*continued*)

the client and appeared cold, detached, stiff, and/or mechanical.

Level 3: At least half the time, the practitioner's facial expression and posture communicated concern and caring and appeared relaxed and appropriate to the unique needs of the client.

Level 5: The practitioner's facial expression and posture *consistently* communicated concern and

caring and appeared relaxed and appropriate to the unique needs of the client.

- Add all the individual points and the points on the scales to get the total score.
- Record the feedback in the practitioner's textbook for future reference.

EVALUATION FORM

Name of Practitioner_____

Name of Peer Supervisor_____

Directions: Under each category (in italics) is a list of behaviors or skills. Give one check mark, worth one point, for each skill used by the practitioner.

Building Relationships

Attending

Give one point for each behavior used by the practitioner.

1. Open and accessible body posture   _____
2. Congruent facial expression   _____
3. Slightly inclined toward the client   _____
4. Regular eye contact unless inappropriate   _____
5. No distracting behavior   _____
6. Minimal encouragement

Observing

Give one point for each item accurately described by the practitioner.

1. Facial expression   _____
2. Eye movement and eye contact   _____
3. Body position and movement   _____
4. Breathing patterns   _____
5. Muscle tone   _____
6. Gestures   _____
7. Skin tone changes   _____

Active Listening Skills Content and Process

Using the following listening scale, evaluate the accuracy and completeness   _____
of the practitioner's ability to summarize what the client said and to describe
the client's way of speaking, including such things as speaking style, vocal tone
and volume, and speed of delivery.

(*continued*)

PRACTICE EXERCISE 1 | ATTENDING, OBSERVING, LISTENING, AND EXPRESSING WARMTH (*continued*)

Listening Evaluation Scale

> Level 1: The practitioner did not summarize any of the major elements of content or describe anything about the client's way of speaking.

> Level 3: The practitioner summarized four elements of content but did not describe anything about the client's way of speaking.

> Level 5: The practitioner summarized all the major elements of content and accurately and fully described the client's way of speaking, including communication style, volume, and speed of delivery.

On the following line write the score, from 1 to 5, for listening.   _____

Core Interpersonal Qualities

Using the scales in Appendix A, evaluate the appropriateness and effectiveness of the practitioner's expression of warmth. Write the score from 1 to 5 for warmth.

Warmth Evaluation Scale

> *Level 1:* The practitioner communicated *little or no concern* for the client and appeared cold, detached, stiff, and/or mechanical.

> *Level 3: At least half the time,* the practitioner verbally and nonverbally communicated concern and caring appropriate to the unique needs of the client.

> *Level 5:* The practitioner's facial expression and posture *consistently* communicated concern and caring appropriate to the unique needs of the client.

Score for warmth   _____

Total score   _____

EXPECTED COMPETENCIES

In this chapter, you have learned skills for attending, observing, and listening, all of which invite clients to be actively involved in the process. You have also learned the importance of warmth in relationships with clients. These are the beginning skills you need to be competent in forming relationships with clients.

You should be able to define the following words: observing, non-verbal communication, attending, listening, and warmth.

You should now be able to:

- Describe three things to observe as you listen to clients.
- List three ways to attend or communicate involvement to clients.
- Compare typical conversational behavior with listening in the practice setting.
- Demonstrate attending, observing, listening, and warmth.

OPENING AND CLOSING A MEETING

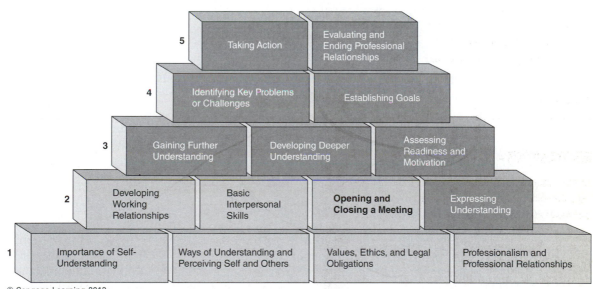

CHAPTER **7**

5	Taking Action	Evaluating and Ending Professional Relationships	
4	Identifying Key Problems or Challenges	Establishing Goals	
3	Gaining Further Understanding	Developing Deeper Understanding	Assessing Readiness and Motivation
2	Developing Working Relationships	Basic Interpersonal Skills	**Opening and Closing a Meeting**	Expressing Understanding
1	Importance of Self-Understanding	Ways of Understanding and Perceiving Self and Others	Values, Ethics, and Legal Obligations	Professionalism and Professional Relationships

© Cengage Learning 2013

Questions to consider as you read this chapter:

- What should you do to prepare for the first meeting with a client and subsequent meetings?
- What should be discussed in the first 10 minutes of an initial meeting?
- How do you describe confidentiality to your clients?
- How might summarizing a meeting help in closing it?

This chapter covers practice behaviors related to preparing for, beginning, and ending meetings. *You will learn the importance of:*

- Preparing for meetings with individuals, families, groups, and organizations
- Effectively communicating information about the process of working together, including: confidentiality, the practitioner's role, details about the meeting
- Effectively and appropriately summarizing and ending meetings with individuals, families, groups, and organization

Client Attributes

- Willingness to attend scheduled meetings and the courage to begin the process of discussing challenges with a practitioner

Practitioners are responsible for preparing for and structuring meetings with clients. In this chapter we will cover skills and techniques needed for beginning the first meeting and subsequent meetings and ending a client session. Developing effective skills in these areas is essential to the success of the entire process. For some clients, the first meeting with a practitioner is frightening. It takes considerable courage to schedule a meeting with a practitioner and then to follow through by coming to the meeting. Feelings of fear and uncertainty are also true for families beginning to work with a practitioner. This is a completely new experience for children and many adults. Individuals joining a group or attending a community or organization meeting for the first time are also often quite hesitant. Although it may not feel strange and foreign to you as a practitioner, consider how the client may feel as he/she begins this process of working with a practitioner.

PREPARING FOR WORK

It is important to prepare before each client meeting. *Preparing* involves getting ready to meet with the client by doing such things as obtaining available client information; collecting supplies, forms, or possible referral information; and possibly talking to a supervisor or co-worker about the client. When preparing for a meeting, it is particularly important to think about the possible purposes of the meeting and what might be accomplished in the meeting. When preparing for a meeting with a task, community, or psycho-educational group, practitioners should plan the agenda, decide what topics will be covered, think about how to help people get acquainted, and begin to think about possible plans for future meetings.

Preparation involves considering the physical arrangements of the building, the waiting room, and the room where you will be meeting. What physical barriers or impediments might individuals face? Is there a waiting area? If so, how comfortable is the waiting area in terms of chairs and/or bathroom facilities? Are there adequate accommodations for those with physical limitations, such as those using wheelchairs or those needing particular chairs because of back problems? Do you have appropriate accommodations for those who are blind or hearing impaired? Are there enough chairs for a family or group to be seated? Are there toys or various types of literature available that are appropriate to the individuals or group you are going to be seeing? Beyond the waiting area, the same questions needed to be answered about the area where you will be meeting with clients. If these issues are not addressed, they can affect communication in multiple ways. Clients may think you are not sensitive to the needs of others or a competent planner. If this is a counseling meeting, is the space private? What is the lighting like? Can participants see each other easily? It is difficult to work with a family if the room does not have appropriate chairs and toys if needed. If you are working with a group, what configuration of chairs will facilitate your goals? For example, in a psycho-educational group, the chairs could be in rows if you plan to lecture. If you want to facilitate discussion, putting the chairs in a circle might be better. When working with an individual, most practitioners think it is more conducive to open discussion to sit across from a client rather than behind a desk. Are there tissues conveniently placed and a clock that both you and the client can see? These are all important issues to consider before you start working with any clients.

Depending on the information about the client that is available before you meet, you may need to learn more about client issues, such as schizophrenia, homelessness, chronic illnesses, and so on. If the client belongs to a cultural group you are not already familiar with, gaining at least an initial understanding of that cultural group is essential. As you learned in Chapter 1, culture influences language, behaviors, rules, and ways of understanding others. In the constructivist section of Chapter 2, you learned that culture provides a framework of assumptions for understanding and giving meaning to events, and communicating that understanding to others. Gaining basic knowledge of each client's culture is vital to developing an effective relationship. Information about other cultures can be gained by reading literature written by authors from other cultures, learning about the relationship of your own culture to other cultures, talking to key resource people from other cultures, and using other resources to get more information if needed. For example, books about diversity are listed on the websites of the American Psychological Association (http://www.apa.org), the National Association of Social Workers (http://www.socialworkers.org), and the American Counseling Association (http://www.counseling.org). Additional information can be found by searching the web for information on a specific culture. Of course, general information about a cultural group will not apply to all individuals, but it will give the practitioner a starting point for understanding the client's worldview.

HOMEWORK EXERCISE 7.1 | PREPARING TO MEET WITH A NEW CLIENT

Assume that you are a practitioner at a junior high school. One of the teachers has referred Paco, a 14-year-old Native American boy, to you. Although Paco is a good student, he has been quiet and withdrawn recently. His teacher thinks something might be bothering him. Write down your ideas about what Paco's first thoughts may be when he sees you. How do you think Paco might be feeling about meeting with you? What concerns do you have about meeting with Paco?

After gathering as much information as possible, the practitioner should consider how the client might be feeling about the meeting. Clients are often anxious and uncomfortable about the first meeting. They may feel embarrassed about asking for help. Practitioners should take some time for preparatory empathy, or thinking about feelings and concerns the client may be experiencing (Gerdes & Segal, 2009; Shulman, 1992). Even in task group or organizational meetings, participants may be hesitant or uncomfortable about the first meeting.

Preparing mentally involves doing whatever is necessary to set aside possible distracting thoughts and getting ready to fully focus on the client (Littauer, Sexton, & Wynn, 2005; Viederman, 1999; Williams et al., 2003). Each person has a different way of letting go of personal concerns so these concerns don't interfere with focusing on the client. Some practitioners find that making "to do" lists of personal tasks helps them clear their minds. For some, walking around or eating helps them to be more alert. Taking a minute to meditate or take a few deep breaths is helpful to others. At times, practitioners need to take a moment to reflect on how their meeting with the previous client went, reassure themselves that they did the best they could, and move on to being fully engaged with the next client.

HOMEWORK EXERCISE 7.2 | PREPARING TO BE FULLY PRESENT

Think about what you have done in the past to let go of thoughts about yourself in order to focus on someone else. Imagine that you received a troubling phone call just before a meeting with a client or that your previous session left you feeling unsettled. What might you do to calm your mind about your own problems and concentrate on your client?

BEGINNING A FIRST MEETING

Setting the Tone

Beginning meetings appropriately is essential, since first impressions are established quickly and often have lasting effects on relationships (Jacobs, Masson, & Harvill, 2009c). Whether you are leading a group for the first time, meeting with colleagues to discuss a problem at your agency, meeting with a community leader, or meeting with a new or returning client, the first few minutes are vital in creating an atmosphere conducive to productive work together (Jacobs, Masson, & Harvill, 2009c). Remember that how you greet your clients when you first come into contact with them is an important aspect of connecting with them. If you must identify your client from a group of people in the waiting room, be aware of issues of confidentiality. If clients check in with a receptionist, that person can point out your clients so that you can introduce yourself without using their name. You might say something like, "I am Jesse Melendez and I think you are here to meet with me today." If it is not possible to previously identify your clients, then be aware of the loudness of your voice, your eye contact, and how you address them. In this case you might say, "I am Jesse Melendez. Are you Ms. Chen?"

The practitioner is responsible for beginning the meeting. The beginning of a first meeting can be awkward, especially with a group or family. In the first meeting, people may feel uncomfortable and wonder what other group members and the practitioner are thinking about them. Often in first meetings, people are judging others and feeling judged. Clients may initially feel confused and uneasy, as well as hopeful about the possibility of getting help to resolve their challenges (Hanna, 2002; Jacobs, Masson, & Harvill, 2009c). Structuring and organizing the initial meeting promotes trust and creates an atmosphere of safety.

In these critical first few minutes, the practitioner should invite the client to introduce him or herself and state how he/she wants to be addressed. It is inappropriate to assume that clients are comfortable having the practitioner use their first name. In cross-racial relationships it is particularly important for the practitioner to begin with last names and only use first names if the client requests the use of first names (Proctor & Davis, 1994). It is appropriate for the practitioner to follow the lead of the client. If the client prefers first names, you can invite him/her to use your first name. With families it is important to determine how the parents want other adults addressed. Some want their first names used but want their children to address you by your last name. Inquiring about their preferences shows respect (Jacobs, Masson, & Harvill, 2009c).

Explaining the Process

People tend to feel more comfortable with professionals who fully *explain the process*, including what they are going to do and what will be expected of each person participating in the meeting. In first meetings it is important to explain the purpose of the meeting, describe what will happen during the meeting, discuss limits of confidentiality, cover any ground rules for the meeting, and ask clients if they have any questions. Here are some examples of explaining the purpose of the meeting.

- *To a psycho-educational parenting group:* "The purpose of our meeting today is to discuss various ways to parent your children."
- *To an individual client:* "In this first meeting I hope to understand some of the challenges that you are facing."
- *To a family:* "In this meeting I want to get acquainted with each of you and learn something about the challenges your family is facing."

Practitioners should provide basic information about the meetings, such as where they will take place and how long the meeting will last. For example, you might say,

- *To an adult client:* "We will be meeting in my office."
- *To parents during a home visit:* "Let's talk together in your kitchen."
- *To a task group:* "I have reserved the conference room for our meeting."
- *To an adult client in the first meeting:* "Since this is our first meeting, it will be 90 minutes. Subsequent meetings will be about 50 minutes."
- *To a counseling group:* "As I told you when we discussed this group, our group meeting will last 90 minutes."
- *To a community task group:* "We agreed to meet for 2 hours."

Since many clients have not met with a practitioner before and do not know what to expect, it is helpful to explain something about what typically happens in a first meeting. When meeting with an individual, the practitioner might explain that he/she will be mostly listening but also asking some questions to better understand the client. For example, you might say:

> "I want you to know a little about how our sessions will be set up. We will usually meet for fifty minutes. During this first meeting I will be mostly listening in order to understand what brought you to our clinic. I will ask questions when I am unclear about what you have said and I hope you will do the same with me. In each session we will work together to find new ways to deal with the problems you have presented. I hope that you will begin thinking about each of our meetings before you come. Coming to a session knowing what you want to talk about or how you want to use the time will help us use our time together wisely. Do you have any questions?"

In beginning an initial meeting with a child or adolescent, it is important to cover the essential material in a way that the child or adolescent can clearly understand. Children and adolescents may not have been told why they are meeting with the practitioner. As with all clients, you need to cover basic education about the practitioner and client roles. They certainly need to be told how long the meeting will last. For example, with a 9-year-old child you might say:

> "I am glad you are here today. We are going to be talking about the problems you have had at school with sitting in your chair when your teacher is talking. Sometimes we will talk and sometimes we might play a game. I may also ask you questions about what you think and feel about your teacher and your problems in class. We will usually meet for about a half an hour. After that time I will ask your mother to come in and we will talk with her as well. How does that sound to you? (Pause) Do you have any questions?"

Beginning meetings with families and groups is similar in many ways to beginning with individuals. When working with families, it is important to provide the basic information using words that the children will understand. After going over the initial information, each person is often asked what he/she expects or hopes to change or accomplish. In initial family meetings it is particularly important to ask about expectations. You might want to say, "How would you like your family to be different?" or "What is hard for you in your family?" The practitioner might say to a family, "I hope each of you will share your thoughts and feelings about what is happening in your family." Sometimes children have not been told the truth about the meeting. They may have been told that they were going to see a doctor and think they are going to be examined, or they may have been told they were going out for a treat like ice cream. Parents may have unrealistic expectations, such as that the practitioner's role is to "make my child behave." After hearing these expectations, the practitioner can discuss realistic expectations with the family. For example, you might say:

> "I know that you would like to have a happy family. Sometimes people think that coming here to talk about family problems with me will fix things. Families make changes when all of the family members work together to do things a bit differently. Each of you is important in making your family feel better. I know sometimes it seems

like when you come for help that the practitioner will make things better but here we will work as a team to accomplish your goals. Do you have any questions?"

Or you might want to say:

"I know that you have been trying your best to work out the problems. It is important to know that all of us have to work together to change things in your family. I am here to help guide and sometimes suggest other ways of doing things. We will all work together to create the kind of family you want. Do you have questions?"

Starting with a task group, the practitioner might say, "In this first meeting, I see my role as helping everyone get acquainted, leading the discussion about the purpose of the meeting, and inviting everyone to discuss possible ground rules for our work together." Practitioners often include some discussion about the client's role in the work. Some group practitioners open meetings with exercises that invite members to get acquainted or check in with the group. These exercises help group members feel more comfortable sharing their thoughts, feelings, and experiences with each other. An example of a beginning group exercise is to invite members to form pairs to discuss topics such as likes and dislikes related to music, movies, food, etc.; something unique about themselves; one fear about being in this group; one thing they hope to achieve by being in this group; and/or one thing they hope that the group will accomplish. When the pairs rejoin the group, each person introduces his/her partner and tells the group something about their conversation.

HOMEWORK EXERCISE 7.3 | BEGINNING A FIRST GROUP MEETING

Think about groups in which you have participated. Write down one way a group leader began his/her group meetings. Discuss whether you think his/her way of beginning effectively set a comfortable tone for the group meeting. If you believe the group was started in a way that was not effective, discuss what you remember about what made it seem ineffective.

Now that you have read about opening a meeting, seeing how different practitioners open a first meeting will give you chance to evaluate several styles of opening. As discussed in the Introduction, watching and evaluating different practitioners gives you a better understanding of how to use practice skills.

BEGINNING SUBSEQUENT MEETINGS

After the first meeting, there are many ways a practitioner may start a meeting. Some practitioners choose to begin meetings by waiting for the client to initiate the conversation, thereby giving the client the responsibility for setting the direction of the meeting.

A common beginning phrase is "Where would you like to start?" Another way to begin a meeting is by saying, "Let's begin by discussing the progress you have noticed since our last meeting" (DeJong & Berg, 1998; Knight, 2006). This beginning sets a positive tone and establishes expectations to look for improvements, to continue the work between meetings, and to believe in the possibility of ongoing positive change. Practitioners can take the opposite approach and ask clients about difficulties they experienced between meetings. However, this approach invites clients to look for problems and to believe that the practitioner expects them to have encountered problems since the last meeting. The practitioner may identify the topic of the meeting: "In our last task group meeting, we decided to begin this meeting by discussing how the new agency policies might affect low-income clients."

Beginning with a summary of the previous meeting is also effective. For example, when working with a task group, the practitioner might begin by saying, "In our last meeting, we decided to move ahead with planning for the neighbor-hood park. Let's start by discussing ideas you have had since our last meeting about how to proceed with that project." The practitioner may choose to begin with an observation or reflection about the previous meeting. For example, a group leader might say, "As I was thinking about our last meeting, I became aware that a few individuals didn't say much, and I'd like to begin by offering those people an opportunity to share their thoughts with us."

EXPLAINING CONFIDENTIALITY

One of the most important elements to address at the beginning of the first meeting with individuals, families, or groups is confidentiality of their sessions with you (Beahrs & Gutheil, 2001; Neitzke, 2007). You need to assure clients that information shared with you will be keep confidential, secure, and not shared with others unless they sign a consent form. As you learned in Chapter 3, there are limits to confidentiality and practitioners need to be sure that clients clearly understand these limits. Perhaps the most difficult area for clients to understand is the mandated reporting of possible harm to self or others, suspected child abuse (sexual or physical) and neglect, and elder abuse. The practitioner's responsibility to report these concerns to the proper authorities may cause clients to think that they cannot trust the practitioner. In response to such a report, the client may end the relationship. Clients may believe that the practitioner does not understand the reasons for their actions and statements and feel betrayed by the practitioner. Clients do not think of the many forms of abuse when practitioners state that they must report if clients are a threat to themselves or others. Parents who neglect their children may not be aware of societies' standards related to child care. For example, parents of chronically ill children may not realize that not following medical directions or regimens is consider child neglect. Most parents do not see themselves as abusers but as disciplinarians. The same may be true of people who neglect or abuse elders or dependent adults.

It is helpful to begin your discussion of confidentiality by covering the legal limits of your state, including the name of the state in your explanation. For example, you might say, "By California law I am required to provide you with information concerning the limits of confidentiality" (Neitzke, 2007; Pope & Vasquez, 1998). Sharing this information helps to put the boundaries of confidentiality in a context that clients can more easily understand. When explaining confidentiality it is important to tell clients that if you see indications of abuse or neglect, you are required to refer the client to the appropriate agency for additional services.

Most agencies will have a statement of confidentiality and informed consent that clients must sign before or during the first appointment. If the client is able to read and understand this material, it can reduce the amount of time spent explaining these issues. However, it is still the responsibility of the practitioner to be sure that their client understands written or spoken communication on this subject. Underage clients and clients with limited cognitive ability may need extra help in understanding the concept of confidentiality. Clients whose first language is not English may also have trouble fully understanding material written in English.

Another important piece of information to communicate involves who the actual client is and how records are kept (Fisher, 2003; Hedges, 2000; Neitzke, 2007). For example, if a client is mandated by the court to see a practitioner, it is important that the client knows from the beginning to whom the practitioner must report. All of this information must be communicated at the first meeting. Box 7.1 provides an example of opening remarks that a practitioner might offer at the beginning of a meeting.

Minors and Confidentiality

When the person coming to the practitioner is considered a minor (the definition of a minor varies from state to state), the parents or guardians usually have the legal right to know what happens during meetings (Fisher, 2003; Haslam & Harris, 2004; Neitzke, 2007). Practitioners must learn their state's laws regarding sharing information with parents. The extent of the information revealed depends upon the laws, the agency rules, the practitioner, and the situation. Many practitioners tell parents or guardians that they will only reveal information if the child's behavior is a threat to self or others, such as being sexually promiscuous, using drugs excessively, threatening to run away, having been abused or neglected, or feeling suicidal or homicidal. For example, the practitioner might say, "I prefer to work in the following way with adolescents. I will not tell you about the other details of our sessions so that (name of child) can be frank with me about his/her feelings. If I think he/she is a danger to himself/herself or others, I will share that information that with you. If you (the parent) tell me about something he/she did, I will tell him/her that I have talked to you. Is this acceptable to you? (Pause) What concerns do you have about not knowing everything (name) has shared with me?" Turning to the adolescent in the room you might say, "How does this plan sound to you?" (Pause) "If there is something I think your parents need to know, I will tell you what I am going to tell them or include them in our session so you can tell them." It is particularly important for adolescents to understand the types of information that will be shared with their parents or guardians. Some practitioners routinely include parents at the end of sessions with children and/or meet with parents regularly to share what they are working on with the child. Of course, this plan must also be shared with the child.

| BOX 7.1 | **EXAMPLE OF WHAT A PRACTITIONER MIGHT SAY AT THE BEGINNING OF A MEETING** |

Hello, my name is Juanita Brown. I am a counselor here at the ABC agency. I understand your name is Mrs. Otsuka. Did I pronounce your name correctly? Would you prefer using first or last names? Since you prefer first names, please call me Juanita.

Today, we will be meeting here in my office for 50 minutes to discuss the challenges you are facing. I will be listening to you and asking you some questions in order to get to know you and understand your situation. Sometimes I will summarize what I am hearing to be sure that I have understood you accurately.

Even though we have just met, I hope that you will decide to be open and honest as you tell me about the challenges you are facing. How does that sound to you? (Pause) If you have any questions either now or at any time, I hope you will bring them up.

I want you to know that everything you say to me will remain confidential within the agency unless you give me written permission to share information with someone else. There are only a few exceptions to that rule regarding confidentiality. First, I am a mandated reporter, which means that if there is or has been any suspicion of physical, emotional, or sexual abuse of a child, elderly person, or incapacitated adult, I am required by law to report that information to the proper authorities. Also, if you tell me something that indicates that you are a danger to yourself or someone else, I am required to take appropriate steps to ensure the safety of those involved. Would you like to talk more about the issue of confidentiality?

Confidentiality in Groups

Working with clients in groups raises additional issues of confidentiality. While practitioners understand confidentiality, clients may not. Nor do clients have professional ethical standards to uphold. Just as with individual clients, it is best to discuss the limits of confidentiality at the first meeting. The purpose of the group and the setting in which it meets can make a difference. In a counseling or support group, there are several questions to discuss. If a client in a group reveals personal information to the group, are other group members free to share it with their family members or friends after the meeting has ended? Are group members free to discuss information from the group meeting in smaller groups if they meet for coffee after the group meeting has ended? Most practitioners recommend that the group members agree to not discuss information covered in meetings with anyone outside the group or with each other after the meeting has ended. One way to state this is, "I want you to know that I as your leader cannot share what you have said outside of this group and I will not discuss anything said here with any member should we meet for an individual meeting. If you talk about the group, I recommend that you only talk about yourself and never refer to others in the group. How does that seem to you? (Pause) Okay, let's talk about what you might say if someone asks you what happens in group?" Even with such agreements, you need to tell group members that you cannot guarantee that group members will honor these agreements. Clients must be warned that information revealed in the group might not be kept confidential.

In task groups, community groups, and organizational groups, the rules about confidentiality are different. In some situations, group members may need to get feedback from others between one meeting and the next. In these situations, group members may prefer to have a confidentiality agreement or agree that certain topics will be confidential.

ADMINISTRATIVE CONTRACTS

In addition to providing verbal explanations to clients, many counseling organizations require that formal written *administrative contracts* be given to clients during the first meeting. Practitioners should go over the administrative contract with clients and ask clients if they have questions about any of the information in the administrative contract.

Administrative contracts may include any or all of the following information:

- Detailed descriptions of the nature and the limits of confidentiality
- Explanation of when disclosure is required by law
- What to do in case of emergencies
- Payment terms
- Confidentiality of records and e-mail communications
- Rights of the client to review records
- Telephone and emergency procedures
- Cancellation policies
- Information about the practitioner's qualifications, training/education, and licensure should be given to the client.

An example of an administrative contract is presented in Box 7.2

BOX 7.2 | **INFORMED CONSENT**

Confidentiality

Everything you share with your counselor is confidential, except information pertaining to child abuse, dependent adult abuse, or intent to do harm to yourself or another. In these cases the law mandates counselors to report to appropriate agencies. All records related to clients will be kept secure and confidential. You have the right to review your record. If you want information shared with others, you will be asked to sign informed consent for release of information.

Treatment of a minor requires parental or guardian consent. Parental input and conjoint sessions will be sought as they serve the interests of the minor client. Progress on agreed-upon goals may be discussed. No specific information will be shared without the consent of the minor client unless it relates to harm to the client or others. By signing below, you give consent for treatment of the minor client.

_____   _____

Name of Minor   Name of Parent or Guardian

                                                         _____   _____

                                                         Parent or Guardian's Signature   Date

Policies and Procedures

- *There will be no sexual or non-therapeutic business contact of any kind between counselor and client.*
- Sessions are generally 45–50 minutes long and are scheduled weekly.
- Fees are due at the beginning of each session unless otherwise agreed.
- There will be a $30 charge for returned checks to cover bank costs.
- There will be fees for letters, forms, or phone calls beyond 5 minutes. These fees will be discussed and agreed upon before the charges are made.

(*continued*)

| BOX 7.2 | **INFORMED CONSENT** (*continued*) |

- Emails that take more than 5 minutes to read and respond to will be charged at a rate of $1.00 per minute.
- You must cancel 24 hours in advance, or a partial fee will be charged:
  - If you neglect to cancel, you will be charged half of your usual fee. Insurance will not cover any of this charge.
- At the conclusion of counseling, the client and practitioner will evaluate their work together.
- Our Center does not provide emergency services after office hours or on weekends. Should an emergency arise, please call 911, your healthcare provider, or go to a hospital such as Lakeside Hospital (800-xxx-xxxx) or St. Mary's Hospital (800-xxx-xxxx)

<u>Client Agreement</u>

I have read, understand, and agree with the above statements.

I agree to a fee of _____ per session.

I have been given the opportunity to clarify any questions and have received a copy of this disclosure agreement.

_____   _____ _____

Name of Minor   Name of Counselor   Date

_____ _____

Client/Parent or Guardian's Signature   Date

Any administrative contracts that you use with clients will be part of the case record. The case record includes other forms the client has completed and ongoing records documenting the practitioner's work with the client. Each discipline has different requirements related to documentation and record keeping, and each agency has policies and guidelines related to documentation and record keeping. Practitioners must learn and follow the documentation guidelines set by their agency.

CLOSING A MEETING

The last few minutes of any meeting are almost as important as the first few minutes. Practitioners may choose to discuss several topics near the end of a meeting. As you near the end of a session, you will want to discuss the possibility of future meetings, to review what was covered in the meeting and any tasks that were agreed upon, and to request feedback. An example might be, "It is time for us to end this meeting. Today we discussed your need to seek a job as soon as possible and what previous difficulties you have experienced in job hunting. How was this discussion helpful to you? You decided to contact your local vocational rehab agency and to apply to one temp agency." It is up to the practitioner to assure that the meeting ends on time.

Because the decision to ask for help may be contrary to some client's personal or cultural beliefs, at the end of the first meeting the practitioner might discuss the client's feelings about seeking help. Some clients may view seeking help as a sign of weakness or failure. Others might be apprehensive about what their friends or family members will think if they learn about the client attending counseling sessions. Supporting clients' courage in seeking help can give them more permission and determination to continue in the process with you. You might say, "You have shown a lot of strength in identifying the problems that you are struggling with, deciding to get help, and having the courage to follow through with your appointment. How are you feeling about being here today? (Pause)" Closing meetings on a positive note might include supporting the client's decision to seek help at this time; providing support and praise for the client's accomplishments; and/or expressing realistic hope about possibilities for the future. Here is one way to say this, "I am impressed with the courage and determination you showed in coming to talk with me. I believe you have been open in your discussion of the challenges you are facing. I am looking forward to continuing our work together." When these elements are included in closing a meeting, clients are more likely to return for the next meeting (Jacobs, Masson, & Harvill, 2009b; Safran, Heimberg, & Juster, 1997).

Since people seeking help often feel self-critical and insecure, closing the session with a focus on client strengths can help enhance a sense of hope. The power of hope is an essential aspect of the work (Hillbrand & Young, 2008; Meyer et al., 2002). Most adults seeking the input of a practitioner have lost hope and need to be supported in finding and seeing change possibilities (Hillbrand & Young). As part of closing the first meeting, the practitioner might say "You have shared a lot about the challenges you are facing and some of the discouragement you have felt. I believe that coming here is a positive step in working towards resolve these challenges."

After the first meeting, the responsibility for ending a meeting may be given in part to the client. If this is the practitioner's preference, it is important to have a clock the client can see and to explain that it is up to them to decide what is most important to cover during the meeting. The client can then decide how to work within the time constraints. However, if the client loses track of time, you will be responsible for ending the meeting. Observing how a client responds to the time limits will tell you about him/her. Some will be anxious not to overstep the allotted time and others will push against the time limit. If a client has great difficulty honoring the time period, it is wise to take this up as an item of discussion at the beginning of the following meeting. The practitioner might say, "I know that it is sometimes hard to stop a meeting when we are still discussing important things. However, we will end at 7:30. I will stop our discussion at 7:15 allowing time to review what we have talked about in this session and plan our next session."

When the meeting ends, practitioners may ask for client reflections. Asking clients to reflect on their experience is also good as a part of closure (Strachan, 2007; Yalom, 1995). For example, "We discussed appropriate ways to express anger today. What are your thoughts and feelings about this discussion? (Pause)" Another topic for reflection is possible unresolved issues. It is helpful to identify unfinished business and to note that it can be addressed in the future. For example, the practitioner might say, "At the end of today's meeting you mentioned problems with your mother. We can talk about those problems next week if you'd like."

To allow ample time to close the meeting, the practitioner may interrupt the flow of the meeting to begin the closing process and complete the meeting on schedule. If, for some reason, you are going to have to change the meeting length, this should be addressed as soon as possible. If you don't know until the day of the meeting, then let the clients know at the beginning of the session. The more you can prepare clients for what will be happening, the more comfortable they will feel. For example, you might say to a group, "I have an emergency with a client whom I need to meet with later. Unfortunately I will have to end our meeting a half an hour early. Ten minutes before the end of the meeting we will summarize what we have accomplished and plan for our next meeting."

Examples of Closing Statements

- "How would you like to end today?"
- "We have 10 minutes left today."
- "This seems like a good place to stop for today."
- "We've talked about some important things today. Although we need to end for now, it seems like it might be helpful to continue our discussion next time."
- "We have 15 minutes left. Do you have any closing thoughts about our meeting today?"
- "Let's talk about what we have accomplished today."
- "What did you find most helpful in our work today?"
- "I would recommend that we meet weekly for the next four weeks and then evaluate our progress. Does that plan sound okay to you?"
- "We are about out of time and have covered most of the points on our agenda. I think this is a good point to end."
- "Shall we meet again next week at the same time?"

Another issue in closing meetings is being sure you are aware of cultural differences in how clients interpret the ending of meetings. Some cultural groups are not used to defined time limits (Ponterotto, Casas, Suzuki, & Alexander, 2010). Some people with Native-American, African-American, and Hispanic cultural backgrounds may be used to continuing to work until everyone is comfortable or think the issues have been resolved. They may experience more defined time limits as rude, rejecting, or insensitive. Practitioners should discuss time limits as often as seems necessary. You might say, "I know we haven't resolved the problem we have been discussing and it is hard to stop this session before making a final decision. As I shared with you at our first meeting, we will conclude our meetings after two hours. Please remember any further questions you have so we can discuss them at our next meeting."

HOMEWORK EXERCISE 7.4 | CLOSING

Just as there are differences between beginning everyday conversations and beginning professional meetings, there are differences in the way they end. Even in everyday conversations, there is some closure. Notice how you end three different conversations. Write down what you said to close each of the conversations. Now write what you remember about the way a meeting with a professional ended. You can use the ending of a meeting with a teacher.

DVD Example: Opening and Closing a Meeting

Watch the beginning meeting of the family and group.

- What did you like about the way the practitioners opened the meeting?
- What aspects of confidentiality were discussed by the practitioners?
- Identify specific ways the practitioners could have improved the opening of the meeting.
- What did you like about the way the practitioners closed the meeting?
- Identify specific ways the practitioners could have improved the closing of the meeting.

WORKING WITH CASES

Remember what you learned in the Introduction about the teaching-learning methods used in this book. Starting with this chapter, you will have another opportunity to further integrate what you are learning and to begin using your knowledge in relation to an actual client situation. As you remember from the Introduction, modified problem-based learning involves working on a section of a case at a time. As you work with the case, you will identify relevant issues related to the case, identify additional information needed to work effectively with the client in the case, and apply the concepts you are learning. Just as in the real world, there are often no right answers to the problems and challenges in the case. Two individuals or groups working on the same case might generate different answers to the questions that follow each section of the case.

CASE | ## CASE, PART 1: HIDEKO ASKS FOR HELP

In this first section of the case you will be using what you have learned about preparing to meet with a new client and what you have learned about opening a meeting. New sections of the case will be introduced in Chapters 10, 11, 13, 14, and 15.

Susan is the office manager for a community mental health center. She pre-screens all new clients. She receives a call from Hideko who is requesting assistance with her "personal problems." Hideko said that she has felt "run down" recently. Hideko said that the hospital social worker who saw her mother during her mother's recent hospitalization suggested that she seek counseling. Hideko lives at home and is in the second year of a medical genetics PhD program. Susan passes the information to Viviana, who is scheduled to meet with Hideko the next week. Viviana, a licensed clinical practitioner, is a slight, 40-year-old Mexican-American woman who is 5 feet tall and has short, dark hair.

Some of the information completed by the client before the first appointment:

Occupation: <u>Unemployed full-time graduate student</u>

Last year of school completed: <u>First year of PhD program in medical genetics</u>

Marital status: <u>single</u>

List anyone else living in household: <u>father and mother</u>

Father's name: <u>Katashi</u>   age: <u>62</u>

Mother's name: <u>Nobuko</u>   age: <u>57</u>

Siblings' names: <u>brother, Akikiko</u>   age: <u>32</u>

Have you ever been in counseling before? Yes____ No __x__

List all medications and supplements you are taking: <u>Multi-vitamin pill</u>

(continued)

CASE | CASE, PART 1: HIDEKO ASKS FOR HELP *(continued)*

In the past month, have you ever thought you ought to cut down on drinking or drug use?

Yes __No_x__

In the past month, has anyone else suggested that you should cut down on your drinking or drug use?

Yes___No_x__

In your own words, what has been troubling you? I am run-down and have little energy. It seems like I am working all the time. Besides graduate school, I help with caring for my mother and do a lot of the house work and cooking.

Questions: Put yourself in the role of practitioner and answer the following questions.

1. What is the role of the practitioner in this type of agency or setting? (Consider visiting a similar agency and talking to a practitioner. You might also want to read the job description of practitioners in this type of agency.)
2. What will you need to do prepare to meet with this client? Include any additional information you will need to better understand the client.
3. What are your preliminary impressions related to the case?

4. What are the key facts in the case?
5. What do you plan to say in the first few minutes?
6. What are your thoughts about the purpose of this first meeting?
7. How will you describe the purpose of this meeting to the client?
8. Write out your opening statement to this client.
9. What issues of confidentiality might occur with this client situation?
10. What initial reactions might this client have when meeting with you for the first time?
11. How will you build a relationship with this client?
12. How might your own spiritual, gender, or culture influence interactions with this client?
13. What concerns do you have about working with this client? Think about any possible prejudices or stereotypes related to this client.

Now that you have thought about opening a meeting with Hideko, you are ready to practice opening a meeting in a role play with fellow students. Although these new skills may seem challenging at first, your preparation with the case example will help you to attend, observe, listen, open, and close the role play meeting.

PRACTICE EXERCISE 2 | OPENING, LISTENING, AND CLOSING

Because these skills require considerable practice to master, you will be using and evaluating the use of attending, observing, and active listening as well as the skills introduced in this chapter. In the practice exercises, each set of skills will be included at least twice.

Exercise Objectives
- To practice opening and closing meetings.

Step 1: Preparation
Form groups of three people. Each person will have the opportunity to play the roles of client,

practitioner, and peer supervisor. Each meeting will last about 10 minutes.

Client Role
- Think about a problem that you encountered in the past. These exercises will be much more authentic if you talk from your own experience.

Practitioner Role
- Think about important things to observe in the client and to do in the interview.
- Review the behaviors introduced in this chapter and the previous chapter (see evaluation form).

PRACTICE EXERCISE 2 | Opening, Listening, and Closing (*continued*)

Peer Supervisor Role
- Review the behaviors introduced in this chapter (see evaluation form).
- Prepare to observe and listen to the client and to keep track of the time.

Step 2: The Client Meeting

Client Role
- If the experience you plan to discuss happened more than a year ago, give the practitioner the necessary basic information, e.g., "This happened when I was a junior in high school."
- Except for the beginning and closing, you will be doing most of the talking. The only verbal skill the practitioner will use during the meeting is minimal encouragement.

Practitioner Role
- Use the opening and closing skills.
- Attend to the client, observe the client, and listen to the client.

Peer Supervisor Role
- Watch the practitioner's behavior, check each attending behavior consistently used by the practitioner, and notice the client's behavior.
- Keep track of the time and alert the practitioner and client when 9 minutes have passed so the practitioner has time to close the meeting.
- Check the attending behaviors used by the practitioner.
- Check the opening and closing skills used by the practitioner.

Step 3: Feedback

Purpose: Receiving immediate constructive feedback helps students enhance their practice skills. Using this evaluation system, the peer supervisor monitors the skills used by the social worker. The client, social worker, and peer supervisor identify strengths and areas for growth.

Client Role
- Share how you experienced the practitioner.
  - Did you feel understood?
  - Was the practitioner warm?
  - What did the practitioner do particularly well?
  - In what ways could the practitioner improve?

Practitioner Role
- Evaluate your use of skills related to opening and closing meetings.

Peer Supervisor Role
- Give the practitioner one point for each attending behavior used consistently.
- Ask the practitioner to describe each item under observation. Give the practitioner one point for each area that he/she was able to describe adequately.
- Ask the practitioner to summarize what he/she heard the client say. Using the listening scale in Appendix A, evaluate the accuracy of the practitioner's summary of what the client said and description of the client's speaking style, volume of speaking, and speed of delivery. Discuss with the practitioner the appropriate score for listening. Discuss with the practitioner the appropriate score for warmth (see scale in Appendix A).
- Add all the individual points and the points on the scales to get the total score.
- Record the feedback in the practitioner's textbook for future reference.

Evaluation Form

Name of Practitioner_____

Name of Peer Supervisor_____

Directions: Under each category (in italics) is a list of behaviors or skills. Give one point for each skill used by the practitioner.

(*continued*)

PRACTICE EXERCISE 2 | OPENING, LISTENING, AND CLOSING *(continued)*

Building Relationships

Attending

Give one point for each behavior used by the practitioner.

1. Open and accessible body posture _____
2. Congruent facial expression _____
3. Slightly inclined toward the client _____
4. Regular eye contact unless inappropriate _____
5. No distracting behavior _____
6. Minimal encouragement _____

Observing

Give one point for each item accurately described by the practitioner.

1. Facial expression _____
2. Eye movement and eye contact _____
3. Body position and movement _____
4. Breathing patterns _____
5. Muscle tone _____
6. Gestures _____
7. Skin tone changes _____

Active Listening Skills Content and Process

Using the listening scale in Appendix A, evaluate the accuracy and completeness of the practitioner's ability to summarize what the client said, and describe the client's way of speaking, including such things as speaking style, vocal tone and volume, and speed of delivery. On the following line write the score, from 1 to 5, for listening. _____

Opening and Closing

Beginning Skills (for a meeting)

Give one point for each topic covered by the practitioner.

1. Introduced yourself and your role. _____
2. Sought introductions. _____
3. Identified where the meeting will be held. _____
4. Identified how long the meeting will last. _____
5. Described the initial purpose of the meeting. _____
6. Explained some of the things you will do. _____
7. Outlined the client's role. _____
8. Discussed ethical and agency policies. _____
9. Sought feedback from the client. _____

Closing Skills (for a meeting)

Give one point for each topic covered by the practitioner.

1. Identified that the meeting was about to end. _____
2. Provided a summary of the meeting. _____

PRACTICE EXERCISE 2 | Opening, Listening, and Closing (*continued*)

3. Reviewed any tasks that the client agreed to complete. _____
4. Discussed plans for future meetings. _____
5. Invited client feedback about the work. _____
6. Asked client about any final questions. _____

Core Interpersonal Qualities

Using the scales in Appendix A, evaluate the appropriateness and effectiveness of the practitioner's expression of warmth. On the following lines write the scores, from 1 to 5, for warmth, empathy, respect, and genuineness.

Score for warmth _____
Total score _____

EXPECTED COMPETENCIES

In this chapter you have learned about preparing, opening, and closing a meeting with individual clients, groups, and families.

You should now be able to:

- Summarize the important elements of confidentiality in working with clients.
- Summarize key activities you need to do to prepare for a meeting.
- Give an example of how you might open an initial meeting with an individual and with a group.
- List the important elements to include when you open a meeting with a new group or client.
- Give an example of how you might open a second meeting with a family.
- Give two examples of how you might close a meeting.
- Demonstrate opening and closing a meeting.

EXPRESSING UNDERSTANDING

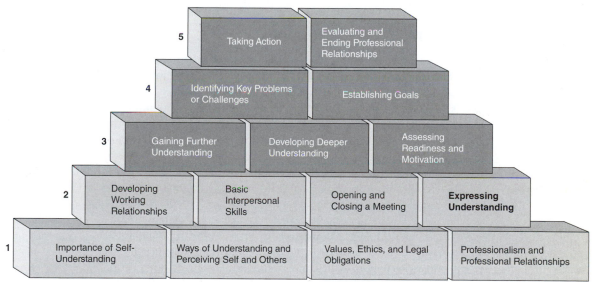

CHAPTER 8

© Cengage Learning 2013

5 Taking Action | Evaluating and Ending Professional Relationships

4 Identifying Key Problems or Challenges | Establishing Goals

3 Gaining Further Understanding | Developing Deeper Understanding | Assessing Readiness and Motivation

2 Developing Working Relationships | Basic Interpersonal Skills | Opening and Closing a Meeting | **Expressing Understanding**

1 Importance of Self-Understanding | Ways of Understanding and Perceiving Self and Others | Values, Ethics, and Legal Obligations | Professionalism and Professional Relationships

Questions to consider as you read this chapter:

- What are effective ways to demonstrate that you understand what your clients are saying to you?
- Why is it important to express your empathic understanding?
- What is the value of summarizing what a client has told you?

This chapter covers practice behaviors related to expressing understanding and empathy. *You will learn the importance of:*

- Using interpersonal skills that express understanding and empathy in order to relate effectively and meaningfully with individuals, groups, and/or communities
- Being aware of your feelings and using affective skills to respond to your clients' feelings
- Using expressive skills to show understanding

Client Attributes
- Willingness to discuss thoughts and feelings about challenges

In order for this process of building a relationship to continue, clients must be willing to discuss their thoughts and feelings about their challenges and concerns. It is important to remember that openly discussing concerns with a stranger requires considerable strength on the part of the client.

THE IMPORTANCE OF BEING EMPATHIC

Being empathic involves connecting with clients by attuning to their thoughts and feelings. It requires considering the content and feelings of what is shared and possible meaning for clients (Siegel, 2010). Empathic practitioners "attend to what is not said and is at the periphery of awareness as well as what is said and is the focal awareness" (Norcross, 2010, p. 119). As discussed in Chapter 5, empathy involves making every effort to understand others from their point of view. Remember what you learned about constructivism in Chapter 2. Each person's view of their experiences and their world is unique. Being empathic involves learning enough about another person or family to understand their views and the meaning they give to events in their life.

Empathy is *seeing* the world as that person sees it, not as you would see it if you were in his or her place; *feeling* the way that person feels about a situation, not as you would feel if you were in that situation; *understanding* the meaning that person is giving to events, and grasping the *assumptions* that influence his or her particular worldview. By being empathic you can learn to connect with people from different backgrounds and experiences. Whether clients have a background, experiences, and problems similar to yours or not, developing understanding and empathy requires very thoughtful, carefully listening.

The sense of being understood is essential to establishing relationships with clients (Gibson, 2006). In order to share personal thoughts and feelings, clients need to feel understood. Empathic understanding is the foundation for the practitioner-client relationship, whether this relationship is with an individual, a family, a group, or a community organization. Practitioners who are perceived as empathic and who collaborate with clients are the most effective (Horvath & Bedi, 2002; Meier, Barrowclough, & Donmall, 2005).

EXPRESSING EMPATHIC UNDERSTANDING

In this chapter you will learn ways to express your empathic understanding. Extensive research supports the importance of expressing empathic understanding to clients (Decety & Moriguchi 2007; Pfeifer et al., 2008). The basis for empathic communication is the ability to join with or connect with another person (Decety & Lamm, 2006; Seigel & Hartzell, 2003). Expressing empathy means communicating an understanding of another person's experience, behavior, viewpoint, meanings, and/or feelings. Empathy is not expressed by saying, "If I were you," or "I know just how you feel;" rather it involves restating in your own words your understanding of what your client is expressing. As your client experiences feeling understood, he/she will be more likely to be open and trusting. Expressing empathic understanding invites clients to share more of their thoughts and feelings. This process of restating what you understand also helps clients who are having trouble expressing themselves.

As you express your empathic understanding, you will be validating the client's experience. Empathic practitioners accept the validity of their clients' point of view and understand their experiences and concerns (Gerdes & Segal, 2009). Often clients have been told that their view or understanding of a situation is wrong, stupid, silly, and/or ridiculous. This is particularly true when the client has been in an abusive relationship (Chang, 1996; Meier et al., 2005), or if the client is in a less powerful position such as a child, an elderly person, or a member of an oppressed group (Fivush, 2004; Harvey, 2007). Being validated is very helpful to clients.

Students often say they feel awkward or uncomfortable expressing empathic understanding. This discomfort is reasonable considering our societal norms about interpersonal communication. Generally, it is considered more acceptable to simply nod or say something like "mm-hmm" when listening to someone instead of sharing what you heard. As a practitioner, you may assume that your clients feel understood, but the best way to ensure that your clients know you understand is to share what you have heard, beyond saying, "I understand." When practitioners summarize a client's story, they create an opportunity for the client to correct any misunderstandings and to elaborate or explain further. To invite active participation in meetings with any type of group, practitioners need to respond with some indication of hearing and understanding each person who speaks. It is useful to have other group members also express empathic understanding, showing that they have grasped the meaning of what other people are saying.

HOMEWORK EXERCISE 8.1 | LISTENING FOR EMPATHIC RESPONSES

During a conversation with at least two other people, pay attention to the process of the conversation. Does one person let the other person know that he/she was heard? Is there any expression of understanding? Do you have a sense that they are truly listening to each other or even paying attention to each other? How can you tell whether each of them is listening or not? Are they in a serial conversation in which one person talks and then the next person starts talking without really connecting to what the first person said?

Skills to express empathic understanding include reflecting content, reflecting feelings, reflecting feelings and content, summarizing, and exploring meanings. Using these skills allows the practitioner to express understanding of the client's feelings, thoughts, opinions, points of view, values and expectations, worldview, situation, and challenges.

REFLECTING CONTENT

When **reflecting content**, practitioners restate their understanding of what the client has said. As practitioners reflect back their perception of the clients' reality, clients realize that the practitioner is trying to understand. If the practitioner's understanding is not correct, the client can correct any misunderstandings. In these exchanges between practitioners and clients, practitioners gain a deeper understanding of their clients. Clients experience being listened to, and may clarify their thinking as they explain their situation to their practitioners. Reflecting what clients have said helps them know that you are trying to understand them. Practitioners sometimes begin reflecting comments with "Are you saying …," "What I hear you saying is …," "As I understand it …," or "It sounds like …." Just repeating what clients have said can seem like parroting and may be offensive.

Examples of Reflecting Content
- *Client in a group*: "I am just not sure if we are ready to make this decision."
  Practitioner: "It sounds like you think we should do more exploration before committing to this course of action."
- *Family member*: "I just don't know what to do any more. It seems like we have been hit with one thing and then another."
  Practitioner: "It sounds like your family has experienced lots of challenges recently."
- *Adult client*: "I have really tried to make this marriage work, but I don't love him anymore and just don't want to be with him."
  Practitioner: "As I understand it, you are considering ending this relationship."
- *Child:* "Mom is sick a lot and then she is gone at the hospital. It is awful at my house."
  Practitioner: "When your mom is sick, I bet you are not sure what is going to happen."
- *Adult client*: "I used to love all the traveling I did for work but it is different now."
  Practitioner: "It sounds like the traveling that your job requires has been very difficult for you since your baby was born."

HOMEWORK EXERCISE 8.2 | REFLECTING CONTENT

In the next few days, listen for comments that reflect content. Since this skill is rarely used in regular conversation, you may not find any examples. Write down five reflecting content comments that you could use to let someone know that you understand what he/she is saying.

REFLECTING FEELINGS

As a practitioner, it is important to be attuned to the emotional experience of clients (Eagle, Migone, & Gallese, 2007; Siegel & Hartzell, 2003). **Reflecting feelings** requires that the practitioner use empathy to join with, attune, and understand the client's feelings, and to communicate this understanding (Fosha, Siegel, & Soloman, 2009). You can know how another person is feeling by how your body and/or your mind responds. It can be confusing to separate what you are feeling *about* what your client is saying from what you believe your client is feeling. For example, you might be feeling sad listening to a client express his frustration and anger about his child's behavior. Your feeling may be due to a past experience you have had or to your concern about the child. As a practitioner you need to develop an acute awareness of your feelings and your client's feelings in order to accurately reflect the feelings of your clients.

The skill of reflecting feelings may take you time to develop but is important to understand. Many clients do not state their feelings in words such as, "I feel angry." Practitioners need to be aware of body language, tone of voice, and/or facial expressions that indicate what clients are feeling. It is not enough to think about how the client may be feeling. Practitioners should express their hunches about how clients may be feeling. For example, "I noticed you clenching your jaw and looking troubled. I wonder if you are feeling angry."

Reflecting feelings allows the client to experience being understood at a core level (Bennett-Levy, 2006; Egan, 2002). Reflecting feelings is a very different experience from the way a friend might respond. A friend might say, "I know exactly how you feel," whereas a practitioner responds, "You seem to be feeling sad" or "I wonder if you're sad about that."

Reflecting feelings requires that the practitioner understand the client's feelings even though the practitioner may not have had the same feelings or similar experiences. After reflecting feelings or content, the practitioner can ask, "Am I understanding you correctly?" or "Did I get that right?" These questions invite the client to correct any possible misunderstandings.

Reflecting feelings may be accompanied by (a) a softer voice or leaning forward to imply deeper connection if the client is expressing fear, shame, or sadness, or (b) more firmness if the client is expressing anger, disgust, or dismay. Expressing understanding or acceptance of a client's feelings should be accompanied by congruent facial expressions. How would you feel if a friend smiled and seemed happy when you were telling him/her about a sad situation? It is also important to reflect the intensity of what the client is feeling by changing your voice tone or using words that emphasize the strength of the feelings. An example is, "I hear you are *really, really* angry about that." You may also use a scale such as, "On a scale of 1 to 10 it sounds like your level of anger is a 9. Is that right?"

Many people do not readily express feelings or even know the names for what they are experiencing. If parents do not express feelings, their children may not be able to label feelings they are experiencing. You may need to suggest names for feelings. As long as you share your hunches in a tentative voice, clients will probably be comfortable correcting you. You may need to reassure clients that you appreciate their willingness to correct any misunderstandings. Some feelings are not as acceptable in some cultures or families, so that clients may be hesitant to express these unacceptable feelings. The longer you work with particular clients, the more you will be able to correctly guess what their feelings might be.

Examples of Reflecting Feelings

- *Client*: "You know, I haven't heard from any of them. If they are busy, they could at least email me."
  Practitioner: "It sounds like you feel sad about that."
- *Client* (sounding angry and speaking with a tight jaw): "I feel like we just aren't getting anywhere."
  Practitioner: "You seem to be feeling impatient with me and our progress."
- *Client on a team:* "Some of the people on this team just aren't carrying their weight."
  Practitioner: "I'm guessing that you are feeling kind of frustrated."
- *Child family member (looking scared):* "When they start fighting and yelling, I just run up to my room."
  Practitioner: "I wonder if you feel kind of scared."
- *Client*: "Yesterday, out of the blue, I was one of the people they laid off. I am not sure what I am going to do."
  Practitioner: "Wow, what shocking news. You look like you are feeling quite worried and upset."

In common conversation, people often believe they are reflecting feelings when they are expressing thoughts, opinions, or judgments. This kind of sharing generally starts with "I feel that …" rather than "I feel (followed by an expression of feelings)." For example, the following are not ways to express feelings:

- "I feel that you aren't paying attention to me." (thought, judgment)
- "I feel that this assignment is too hard." (thought, judgment)
- "I feel that you children should clean up your room." (directive)
- "I feel that you always misunderstand me." (thought, judgment)
- "I feel that this group is terrific." (thought, judgment)
- "I feel that you have lots of strengths." (thought, judgment)

Reflecting Feelings in Families and Groups

In groups, practitioners may encourage members of the group to reflect feelings (Northouse, 2010). This is also a good approach when working with families. In either case, the practitioner can prompt people by asking, "How do you think (name of the person) might be feeling?" It is helpful for group members or family members to be encouraged to reflect feelings. This helps the individual who is talking realize that he/she is understood. Reflecting feelings is a valuable skill for them to learn. It is important for the practitioner to model expressing empathy by reflecting feelings. Creating an atmosphere in which people are comfortable and value being corrected is helpful. The practitioner can accomplish this by demonstrating a willingness to share hunches and expressing appreciation for being corrected without being embarrassed. Some people would rather be silent than risk making a mistake, so the practitioner's role modeling this is important. Encouraging those in groups to share hunches increases their comfort and willingness to do this in other situations.

Examples of Reflecting Feelings in Families and Groups

- "The group seems hesitant to talk about the fact that we didn't get the grant we applied for. I wonder if folks are feeling discouraged."
- "I sense low energy in the room, almost sadness. Is anyone else experiencing this feeling?"
- "Several members of the family seem angry with each other. Is that true?"
- "You folks look a bit tired tonight, or are you having some other feelings?"

HOMEWORK EXERCISE 8.3 | REFLECTING FEELINGS

Reflecting feelings may seem awkward because it is something people in our society rarely do. Remember that any new behavior feels uncomfortable at first. Reflecting feelings requires that you have a good vocabulary of "feeling words." Make a list of six words that are additional ways to express each of the following feelings: sad, mad, scared, glad. Put each list in order from the most intense expression of the feeling to the least intense expression of the feeling.

In three different conversations, think about what you might say to reflect feelings. Write down your ideas about what you could say. At least once in a conversation express your understanding by reflecting what you believe the person is feeling. Notice how the person responds.

REFLECTING FEELINGS AND CONTENT

Frequently practitioners reflect both feelings and content in the same sentence. **Reflecting feelings and content** is a skill involving attuning to the client to understand both what they are saying and how they are feeling, and then communicating that understanding. Using this skill allows the practitioner to include more information in the reflective comment. Reflecting content or reflecting feelings in the beginning of a relationship with a client is especially helpful as the practitioner is learning about the client's situation. As the practitioner has more understanding of the client, he/she may use the technique of reflecting feelings and content. For example, with a client who looks like she is about to cry, and who has expressed considerable distress about her sister's angry behavior toward her, the practitioner could say, "You seem quite sad as you talk about what is going on between you and your sister." Reflecting both feeling and content demonstrates deeper understanding of the client's situation.

Examples of Reflecting Feelings and Content

- *Adult client*: "Can you believe it? She just left me a note telling me to leave. She hadn't said anything about me leaving."

    Practitioner: "It sounds like you were shocked when your wife told you that she wanted you to leave."

- *Adult client*: "Ever since I was laid off, I just mope around. I am just at a loss."
  Practitioner: "So in a way you are grieving about losing your job."
- *Group at a picnic*—one person didn't show up and didn't let them know
  Practitioner: "It seems like most of you are feeling hurt and a little angry that Mary Ann didn't show up for the picnic."
- *Child*: "It is no fun to watch football games since Dad left."
  Practitioner: "So before your dad left, the two of you used to watch football games together and now you feel sad and really miss him whenever the football games are on."

HOMEWORK EXERCISE 8.4 | REFLECTING FEELINGS AND CONTENT

Think back to the movie you watched for Homework Exercise 5.6, Developing Understanding and Empathy, in Chapter 5. Write down five comments reflecting feelings and content that you could make to the movie character you focused on.

Each practitioner develops a different style related to using reflecting skills. Some practitioners use mostly reflecting feelings and content and others tend to use reflecting feelings or content. Many practitioners attempt to express what is not being explicitly discussed by the client. If the client is talking about the facts related to a situation, the practitioner may make a reflecting comment that involves a hunch about the client's feelings. For example, if the client is unemotionally talking about a terrible fight with her husband and the practitioner notices that her eyes are tearing up, he/she might say "It seems like you are feeling quite sad." If the client seems focused on his/her feelings, the practitioner may make a comment about possible facts in the situation. For example, with a client who is focusing on her anxiety and distress related to her job, after reflecting feelings, the practitioner might say "I know from what you've told me that you are ambivalent about this job. Although it is stressful, you believe it is important." Moving beyond what the client has stated often helps the client gain new understanding or insight.

All types of reflective comments are essential. Reflecting comments help clients understand the connection between their thoughts and their feelings. The most important reason for offering a reflecting comment is to let the client know that he/she is understood.

SUMMARIZING

Summarizing is another way to express empathic understanding. Summarizing is the same as reflecting but generally covers more information. The skill of **summarizing** involves listening to considerable information provided by the client and communicating understanding of that information. Sometimes clients have so much information to share that practitioners listen for some time before making a reflecting comment. When the practitioner does make a statement, it might be a summary of the many things the client has been talking about.

In the dominant culture in the United States, it is considered rude to interrupt. However, at times practitioners may interrupt a client after hearing quite a bit of information. This helps assure that the practitioner understands correctly and hasn't missed important points. It is okay to say, "Just a minute, I want to see if I understand what you are telling me." You can then summarize what you have heard. If you aren't sure you understood correctly, you might stop the client and summarize your understanding, followed by "Do I have that right?"

As you learned in Chapter 7, summarizing is often a good way to indicate your empathic understanding when you close a meeting. Since there are often many points of view in a group or family, reflecting and summarizing comments are particularly important when meetings include more than one client (Jacobs, Masson, & Harvill, 1998; Littauer, Sexton, & Wynn, 2005; Seligman, 2004). To assure that all members have a complete understanding of key points, a summary at the end of the meeting is essential. Using a closing summary, the practitioner will outline the key points of a whole meeting. With a family or group practitioners may choose to identify particular points or to note what key members have said. They may also ask questions after a summary such as, "Did I miss anything important?" or "Does anyone want to add anything?" These questions let people know the practitioner is willing to be corrected.

Examples of Reflecting Comments and Summarizing

- *Client:* "I am really trying hard in school, but I just can't seem to get the grades I want."

  Practitioner: "You sound discouraged because even though you are working hard, you are disappointed with your grades." (reflecting feelings and content)
- *Client:* "When I'm angry with my friend, I tell her how I feel and then she does the same thing again."

  Practitioner: "It sounds like you are unhappy because your friend has ignored what you told her about how you feel." (reflecting feelings and content)
- *Practitioner*: "As I remember our last meeting, we focused on how distressed you felt about your wife's roller coaster behavior toward you. When she is being friendly, you feel good and get more work done, and when she is distant, you worry and have trouble sleeping and focusing at work. Is that how you remember it?" (summarizing to an individual)
- *Practitioner*: "We have discussed both sides of the issue and noted the pros and cons of each direction we could go. I appreciate how difficult this discussion has been for some of you. It appears that some members of the group seem to be troubled when people disagree with each other." (summarizing to a group)
- *Practitioner*: "Everyone in the group seems relieved that we have agreed to keep all the information confidential." (reflecting feelings and content to a group)
- *Practitioner*: "Jaime and Mary, you seem to be ready to take charge of some of the family problems. It has been hard to disagree with your children on what should happen next. I can imagine that you children are upset because you think that your opinions don't count." (summarizing to a family)

Using your movie character from Homework Exercise 5.6, Developing Understanding and Empathy, in Chapter 5, write down three summarizing comments that you could make. Make a summarizing comment about what happened in the first part of the movie, near the middle of the movie, and at the end of the movie.

REFLECTING MEANING

Reflecting meaning is a skill in which the practitioner expresses his/her understanding of the underlying meaning of what the client is discussing. Reflecting the meaning of an event is not as straightforward as understanding its content or the feelings related to it. To understand meanings, practitioners need to not only be good observers of the behavior and tone that accompanies the content, but also must listen for the possible meaning a client is giving to a situation, action, thought, or feeling. For example, earlier in this chapter we mentioned a client who was upset that her sister was angry with her. The practitioner continued to listen in order to understand the meaning the client was giving to this event. As the practitioner listened, it became clear that although the client had not been close to her sister since the death of their mother, she longed for a better relationship with her sister. In an attempt to express the meaning of this situation to the client, the practitioner said, "It sounds like when your sister acts in uncaring ways, you feel particularly sad because now she is your only close living relative. Is that right?"

When working with clients who come from a different background than your own, it is particularly important to express your tentative understanding of their meaning. This gives clients a chance to further explain (Siegel, 2010). For example, if a college student from the dominant U.S. culture doesn't work up to his potential in college, it may be interpreted as a lack of maturity or not working hard enough. However, if a college student from a Chinese-American background doesn't get excellent grades in college, his performance may mean that he is a disgrace to his family.

Think back to what you learned in Chapter 2 about the constructivist perspective. We are constantly involved in constructing or giving meaning to our reality. The meaning we attach to an event will depend on many factors, including our cultural background, education, mental stability, family, age, and experience (Badenoch, 2008). It is up to the practitioner to understand what meaning or meanings clients are giving to situations. For example, a well-educated white male client felt he was a failure because his boss seemed unfriendly toward him and only focused on the areas in which he needed to improve. There were many other possible interpretations of his boss's behavior, but this was the meaning that made sense to this client. An African-American male client with almost straight A's in a graduate program focused on the fact that another student was getting higher grades than he was. He interpreted this to mean that he wasn't working hard enough.

Examples of Reflecting Meaning
- *Client*: "I thought we had a good marriage until my husband told me that he lost his job and had spent our family money on seeing call girls. We are very

religious and want to put this marriage back together." (while ringing her hands and looking worried)

> *Practitioner*: "I hear you value your marriage and at the same time are shocked and worried about your husband's behavior. Is that right?"

- *Counseling group member*: "I really enjoy spending time with the man I am dating, but my job is so demanding these days that I am feeling stressed and worried about getting everything done."

  > *Practitioner*: "It sounds like you really value time with George and also want to do a good job at work."

- *Family member*: "Since Bob (the father) lost his job, it seems like we go from one stress to the next all the time. It is like everyone is worried most of the time, not at all like it used to be."

  > *Practitioner*: "So the stress related to Bob being unemployed is affecting everyone. Sounds like you are longing for the fun times you used to have in your family."

- *Task group member*: "Finishing this project is taking forever! I am sick of having to do so much extra work. I wonder if it is worth it."

  > *Practitioner*: "You sound frustrated and kind of discouraged, too. It sounds like you wonder if the project is as important as you once thought. Is that right? (pause for response) How are the rest of you feeling?"

HOMEWORK EXERCISE 8.6 | REFLECTING MEANINGS

When talking to someone who is different from you in cultural background, age, gender, and/or experience, write down what you could say to express your understanding of what you think the person means or intends to communicate. For example, you might say, "It seems like you are doing a lot of thinking about whether to continue in your current job. Is that right?" In another situation you might express, "I understand that it is really a challenge to juggle all the things you are doing."

REFLECTING UNDERSTANDING OF DIVERSITY ISSUES

Sensitivity to diversity issues and the meaning that the client gives to situations provides a framework for a positive working relationship. When developing relationships, it is important to deal directly with diversity variables. For many clients, having a worldview similar to that of the practitioner is more important than differences such as age, ethnicity, race, gender, sexual orientation, education, and physical differences. However, for some clients, obvious differences between the practitioner and client may be a barrier to developing an empathic relationship (Tronick, 2009). Language differences present significant challenges even if the client speaks the same language as the practitioner. In the United States, slang words and phrases can vary from one region to another as well as from one generation to another. "Gay," "bitch," or "suck" can be used in multiple ways acceptable to some and not to others depending on the meaning given. If the client is using a second language rather than his/her native language, she may not be fluent enough to express how she feels. This is further compounded when English is the second language for the practitioner as well. Language differences will obviously influence the nature of communication and perhaps the ability to understand each other either. When language differences exist, it is particularly important to frequently reflect or summarize. After hearing the summary, the client can be encouraged to correct any misunderstandings. This process may need to go both ways, so that the practitioner also asks the client if he/she has understood what the practitioner said.

When your clients are from a different ethnic group, age, gender, religion, or physical ability, it is important to express empathy (Siegel, 2010). Even when we share common feelings and thoughts, the meaning of experiences may be different for clients. For example, conveying that you understand the challenges of someone who has a physical limitation that you yourself have not experienced can be challenging. The client may think "How can you possibly understand when you have never faced this difficulty?" When clients are obviously from a different race or socioeconomic background, they may wonder if the practitioner is able to understand them. It is helpful to ask clients to give examples of what they have experienced. You might say:

- "I hear that you feel angry about the struggles you have faced. I'd like to hear more about those struggles."
- "You seem sad about how you were treated. I'd like to hear more about what happened."
- "I can see how troubled and very sad you feel about your child's illness. I'd like to hear more about what this experience has been like for you."

Your goal is to understand how your clients feel, what they experienced, and what meaning that experience had for them. For example, if you have a situation in which your client looks concerned and is wringing her hands, and she says, "I've never talked this much with a white woman, but I guess it will be okay." Your observations might lead you to say, "I can understand that it might be hard to talk with someone like me. Let's begin by talking about what it is like for you to be talking to me." Verbally reflecting feelings, content, and/or meaning helps clients know that you do "get" who they are and what they have experienced and that it's safe to talk about what they have experienced.

As you have learned in this chapter, when clients feel understood, they are likely to continue talking about their situation and further explore their challenges. The next practice exercise focuses on expressing understanding by reflecting feelings, reflecting content, reflecting feelings and content, summarizing, and exploring meanings. Using these skills will encourage your clients to explore their situation more fully. You will also evaluate your ability to appropriately express warmth and empathy. An evaluation scale is included to help you specifically identify how well you demonstrated each quality. When doing the practice exercises, you may find that you are so focused on using new skills correctly that you do not express as much warmth as you would naturally express. As using professional skills becomes more natural for you, expressing warmth will become easier and begin to feel more authentic.

EVALUATING EXPRESSIONS OF EMPATHY

At this point you can see how each group of skills, or building block, rests on the previous building blocks. As you learned in Chapter 6, careful observation, listening, and attending are important ways to demonstrate that you are focused on your client. Appropriate demonstrations of warmth invite clients to feel comfortable. You learned in Chapter 7 that opening a meeting sets the tone for the meeting and that summarizing at closing reflects understanding of main points. In the next practice exercise you will demonstrate your ability to use all of these skills and to express empathy. Adding empathic understanding increases the client's sense of connection to the practitioner (Badenoch, 2008). It is important to remember that openly discussing concerns with a stranger requires considerable strength on the part of the client. When reflecting skills are used, clients feel safer sharing their thoughts and feelings. When you express warmth along with reflecting empathic understanding, the communication is more impactful.

HOMEWORK EXERCISE 8.7 | EXPRESSING EMPATHY

Think of a time when you felt that another person really understood you.

- How did he/she convey this to you?
- In what ways did he/she let you know that they grasped where you were coming from?

- Challenge yourself to think of how you would be empathic to someone who has very different values and beliefs from yours.
- Write a sentence that conveys understanding another person's position even though you don't agree with that person's position.

As you will see on the following scale, the more often you communicate understanding of the client's experience and feelings, the more your client will experience you as empathic.

Empathy Evaluation Scale

Level 1: *Once during the meeting* the practitioner communicated an understanding of the client's experience and feelings with enough clarity that the client indicated agreement.

Level 3: *Three times during the meeting* the practitioner communicated an understanding of the client's experience with enough clarity that the client indicated agreement.

Level 5: *Five times during the meeting* the practitioner communicated an understanding of the client's experience with enough clarity that the client indicated agreement.

 DVD Example: Expressing Empathic Understanding
Watch the exploring sections of the family and group meetings.

- Identify examples of expressing understanding by reflecting feelings, reflecting content, reflecting feelings and content, reflecting meaning, and summarizing in both meetings
- What did you like about the way the practitioners used the expressing understanding skills?
- Identify any specific ways the practitioners could have improved their use of expressing understanding
- What score would you give each practitioner related to expressing empathy?

PRACTICE EXERCISE 3 | EXPRESSING EMPATHIC UNDERSTANDING

Because these skills require considerable practice to master, you will be using and evaluating the use of skills involved in observing, listening, attending, beginning, and ending meetings as well as the skills introduced in this chapter. You will also evaluate your demonstration of warmth and level of your demonstration of empathy.

Exercise Objectives
- To practice reflecting content, feelings, feelings and content, meanings, and summarizing.
- To practice expressing warmth and empathy in appropriate and effective ways.

Step 1: Preparation
Form groups of three people. Each person will have the opportunity to play the roles of client, practitioner, and peer supervisor. Each meeting will last about 10 minutes.

Client Role
- Think about a problem that you encountered in the past. These exercises will be much more authentic if you talk from your own experience.

Practitioner Role
- Think about important things to observe in the client and to do in the interview.
- Review the behaviors introduced in this chapter and the previous chapters (see evaluation form).

Peer Supervisor Role
- Review the behaviors introduced in this chapter (see evaluation form).
- Prepare to observe and listen to the client and to keep track of the time.

Step 2: The Client Meeting
Client Role
- If the experience you plan to discuss happened more than a year ago, give the practitioner the necessary basic information, for example, "This happened when I was a junior in high school."
- Talk for a brief period, pausing to give the practitioner a chance to respond during the

telling of your story. Remember that your role is to give the practitioner an opportunity to practice these skills. Working on whatever problem you discuss is not the goal.

Practitioner Role
- Use the skills of reflecting content, reflecting feelings, reflecting feelings and content, reflecting meanings, and summarizing.
- Listen to the client and observe the client's nonverbal communication.
- Open and close the meeting.
- Remember that your goal is to practice the skills. Even if this was a real interaction with a client, it would be inappropriate to begin working on problem solving until you thoroughly understood the situation and had set goals with the client.

Peer Supervisor Role
- Watch the practitioner's behavior and check each attending behavior consistently used by the practitioner.
- Observe the client's behavior.
- Keep track of the time and alert the practitioner and client when 9 minutes have passed so the practitioner has time to close the meeting.
- Check off the skills used by the practitioner in opening and closing the meeting.
- *Write down each of the practitioner's statements.* Writing out each practitioner statement is difficult but critical in order to accurately identify statements, to give solid feedback, and to effectively evaluate the practitioner's work. You may abbreviate, use a form of shorthand, or just write the first group of words in the statement, or you can tape record the interview and transcribe or listen to the tape.

Step 3: Feedback
Purpose: Receiving immediate constructive feedback helps students enhance their practice skills. Using this evaluation system, the peer supervisor monitors the skills used by the social worker. The client, social worker, and peer supervisor identify strengths and areas for growth.

(continued)

PRACTICE EXERCISE 3 | EXPRESSING EMPATHIC UNDERSTANDING *(continued)*

Client Role
- Share how you experienced the practitioner.
  - ○ Did you feel understood?
  - ○ Was the practitioner warm and empathic?
  - ○ What did the practitioner do particularly well?
  - ○ In what ways could the practitioner improve?

Practitioner Role
- Evaluate your use of skills related to reflecting content, reflecting feelings, reflecting feelings and content, reflecting meanings, and summarizing.

Peer Supervisor Role
- Give the practitioner one point for each attending behavior consistently used.
- Give the practitioner a check mark for each area he/she was able to describe adequately.
- Ask the practitioner to summarize what he/she heard the client say and to describe the client's way of speaking.
- Go over the listening scale and decide on the appropriate numerical score.
- Give the practitioner one point for each beginning item covered and each closing item covered. It is not likely that the practitioner would use all of the closing skills.
- Based on your notes, give the practitioner feedback on the use of reflecting the client's feelings,

content, feelings and content, and meanings, and summarizing. Give the practitioner a point for each reflecting comment. For example, if the practitioner reflected feelings three times, he/she would get three points after reflecting feelings.
- Discuss with the practitioner the appropriate score for warmth and empathy.

Empathy Evaluation Scale

Level 1: Once during the meeting the practitioner communicated an understanding of the client's experience and feelings with enough clarity that the client indicated agreement.

Level 3: Three times during the meeting the practitioner communicated an understanding of the client's experience with enough clarity that the client indicated agreement.

Level 5: Five times during the meeting the practitioner communicated an understanding of the client's experience with enough clarity that the client indicated agreement.

- Add all the individual points and the points on the scales to get the total score.
- Record the feedback in the practitioner's textbook for future reference.

EVALUATION FORM

Name of Practitioner_____

Name of Peer Supervisor_____

Directions: Under each category (in italics) is a list of behaviors or skills. Give one point for each skill used by the practitioner.

Building Relationships

Attending

Give one point for each behavior used by the practitioner.

1. Open and accessible body posture   _____
2. Congruent facial expression   _____
3. Slightly inclined toward the client   _____

PRACTICE EXERCISE 3 | EXPRESSING EMPATHIC UNDERSTANDING (*continued*)

4. Regular eye contact unless inappropriate
5. No distracting behavior   _____
6. Minimal encouragement   _____
                                                               _____

Observing

Give one point for each item accurately described by the practitioner.

1. Facial expression   _____
2. Eye movement and eye contact   _____
3. Body position and movement   _____
4. Breathing patterns   _____
5. Muscle tone   _____
6. Gestures   _____
7. Skin tone changes   _____

Active Listening Skills Content and Process

Using the listening scale in Appendix A, evaluate the accuracy and completeness
of the practitioner's ability to summarize what the client said and describe the
client's way of speaking, including such things as speaking style, vocal tone and
volume, and speed of delivery. On the following line write the score, from 1 to 5,
for listening.   _____

Opening and Closing

Beginning Skills (for a meeting)

Give one point for each topic covered by the practitioner.

1. Introduced yourself and your role.   _____
2. Sought introductions.   _____
3. Identified where meeting will be held.   _____
4. Identified how long meeting will last.   _____
5. Described the initial purpose of the meeting.   _____
6. Explained some of the things you will do.   _____
7. Outlined the client's role.   _____
8. Discussed ethical and agency policies.   _____
9. Sought feedback from the client.   _____

Closing Skills (for a meeting)

Give one point for each topic covered by the practitioner.

1. Identified that the meeting was about to end.   _____
2. Provided a summary of the meeting.   _____
3. Reviewed any tasks that the client agreed to complete.   _____
4. Discussed plans for future meetings.   _____
5. Invited client feedback about the work.   _____
6. Asked client about any final questions.   _____

(*continued*)

| PRACTICE EXERCISE 3 | EXPRESSING EMPATHIC UNDERSTANDING *(continued)* |

Expressing Understanding
Expressing understanding is so important that for this group of skills one point
should be given for each time the practitioner used one of the skills.

1. Reflected feelings
2. Reflected content
3. Reflected feelings and content
4. Summarized
5. Reflected meanings

Core Interpersonal Qualities

   Using the scales in Appendix A, evaluate the appropriateness and
   effectiveness of the practitioner's expression of warmth and empathy.
   On the following lines write the scores, from 1 to 5, for warmth
   and empathy.

   Score for warmth
   Score for empathy
Total score

EXPECTED COMPETENCIES

In this chapter you have learned about expressing
empathy using skills such as reflecting client feelings, reflecting content, reflecting feelings and
content, summarizing, and reflecting meaning.

   *You should be able to define the following
   words and phrases:* reflecting content, reflecting
   feelings, reflecting feelings and content, summarizing, and reflecting meaning.

You should be able to:

*   Demonstrate expressing empathy by
    o   reflecting feelings
    o   reflecting content
    o   reflecting feelings and content
    o   summarizing
    o   reflecting meanings

EXPLORING AND ASSESSING WITH CLIENTS

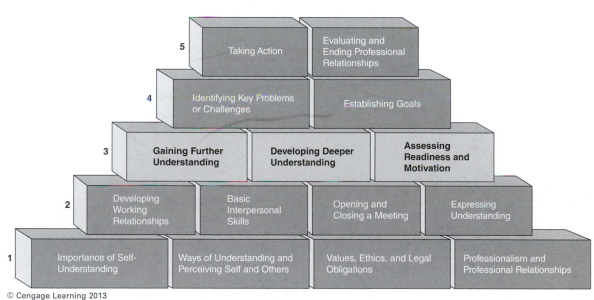

5	Taking Action	Evaluating and Ending Professional Relationships		
4	Identifying Key Problems or Challenges	Establishing Goals		
3	Gaining Further Understanding	Developing Deeper Understanding	Assessing Readiness and Motivation	
2	Developing Working Relationships	Basic Interpersonal Skills	Opening and Closing a Meeting	Expressing Understanding
1	Importance of Self-Understanding	Ways of Understanding and Perceiving Self and Others	Values, Ethics, and Legal Obligations	Professionalism and Professional Relationships

© Cengage Learning 2013

Building on the relationship skills covered in Section II, you will learn practice skills in Section III related to exploring, assessing, elaborating, and gaining a deeper understanding of clients. Chapter 9, Gaining Further Understanding, presents information about using questions to learn more about the challenges and situation of clients and about ways to demonstrate genuineness. Chapter 10, Developing Deeper Understanding, introduces ways of seeking more in-depth information, focusing on strengths and positive factors, and demonstrating respect. The focus of Chapter 11, Assessing Readiness and Motivation, is learning how to identify clients' readiness to change and level of motivation for change as well as factors that may make change more difficult. This process of exploration is collaborative. Clients need to be willing to think about and discuss their thoughts, feelings, resources, strengths, and situations related to their challenges.

Gaining Further Understanding

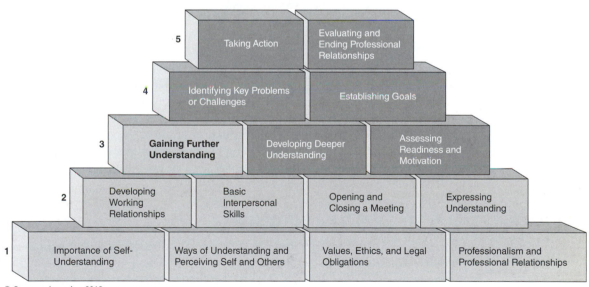

5	Taking Action	Evaluating and Ending Professional Relationships		
4	Identifying Key Problems or Challenges	Establishing Goals		
3	**Gaining Further Understanding**	Developing Deeper Understanding	Assessing Readiness and Motivation	
2	Developing Working Relationships	Basic Interpersonal Skills	Opening and Closing a Meeting	Expressing Understanding
1	Importance of Self-Understanding	Ways of Understanding and Perceiving Self and Others	Values, Ethics, and Legal Obligations	Professionalism and Professional Relationships

© Cengage Learning 2013

Questions to consider as you read this chapter:

- How do practitioners know when to use different types of questions?
- What types of questions should you use to gain more information about clients?
- What are appropriate ways to demonstrate genuineness to clients?
- How does expressing understanding fit with using questions?
- What are the key topics that practitioners need to understand?
- How can you avoid the common mistakes related to using questions?

This chapter covers the differences between open-ended and closed-ended questions and how to further your understanding of clients. You will also learn ways to demonstrate genuineness to clients. *In this chapter you will learn the importance of:*

- Inviting your clients to collaborate with you in the exploration of their problems and challenges
- Using open-ended questions to further understand your clients
- Gaining a thorough understanding of the problems and challenges your clients face
- Gaining a thorough understanding of the broader situation or environment of your clients
- Demonstrating genuineness to your clients

Client Attributes
- Willingness to explore further

Reflecting and summarizing are excellent ways to let clients know that they have been heard and understood (Bennett-Levy, 2006). After expressing your empathic understanding of your client, you may decide to ask a question to direct the client to focus on a particular area or to invite the client to say more about some topic. As a practitioner, you need to fully understand your client's concerns. If you have effectively built a beginning relationship by expressing understanding, your client may be ready to share more information. Of course, exploring will be successful only if the client is willing to share further information.

USING QUESTIONS TO EXPLORE FURTHER

Asking questions to get information is a skill that most people use, so it comes naturally when you are in the role of practitioner. Before asking questions it is important to express understanding by reflecting feelings, reflecting content, reflecting content and feelings, reflecting meanings, and/or summarizing. Asking questions without expressing understanding first may be experienced as "grilling" or interrogating. Although you may be more comfortable asking questions than expressing empathic understanding, it is important to express empathy first and to avoid asking many questions. Reflecting shows that you are interested in more than "just facts." If you pause after your empathic comment, the client will often continue discussing what is important to him/her without the need for a question from you. Questions asked without a thorough understanding of what the client has just said can also be confusing to the client or change the direction of the conversation inappropriately.

Open-Ended Questions

Open-ended questions are defined as questions that are broad and require more than one or two word answers. They invite clients to think and reflect and to express their opinions and feelings. Open-ended questions are broad enough so that clients can decide how to reply (Boardman, Catley, Grobe, Little, & Ahluwalia, 2006). Open-ended questions generally begin with *who, what, when,* or *how*. When these words are used, the questions are usually open-ended. An example of an open-ended question is "How do you feel about that?" Sometimes request statements have the same kind of messages as open-ended questions. For example, statements that begin with "Tell me about."

Examples of Phrases That Begin Open-Ended Questions:
- Will you tell me more about ...?
- Will you tell me more about how you feel when ...?
- Who could help with ...?
- What seems to help when...?
- How important is ...?
- Will you explain more about ...?
- Tell me more about what happened when...

Examples of Open-Ended Questions:
- Tell me about who has helped you with this problem
- How have other people helped you with this problem?
- What led you to seek help at this time?
- Tell me about improvements you have noticed since our last appointment.
- What would your life be like if this problem wasn't going on?
- How have others you know solved this type of problem?
- Who have you talked to about this problem?
- How did it help to talk to others about the problem?
- Tell me about what it feels like to have this problem.
- How have you solved other problems in your life?
- What do you understand about the kind of help I might offer you?
- Tell me about what you have done to work on this problem.

Some questions are open-ended and go beyond what the client has expressed. If practitioners ask questions using language that the client has not used, this may limit rather than expand the area of exploration. For example, if the client has not mentioned anger and the practitioner asks, "What is it about the situation that makes you angry?" the practitioner has assumed that the client is feeling anger related to something in the situation. It would be more appropriate to ask something like, "When you think others are not taking you seriously, how do you feel?"

HOMEWORK EXERCISE 9.1 | OPEN-ENDED QUESTIONS

Write down five open-ended questions that you might use if your client is:

- An adult
- A 10-year-old child
- A frail older person living in a nursing home

- A family
- A psycho-educational group
- A larger system such as a community group, an agency, or a neighborhood.

Closed-Ended Questions

Closed-ended questions are questions that can be answered with one word such as yes or no. Using closed-ended questions is appropriate when the practitioner needs to obtain specific information (Gorske & Smith 2009). Examples of such questions are "How old are you?", "What is your address?", and "How many other people live in your house?" When practitioners need to obtain specific information related to eligibility requirements, discharge needs, and immediate needs, the use of closed-ended questions is appropriate. Closed-ended questions give you facts, are easy to answer, and keep control of the conversation with the practitioner. If you want to invite the client to explore a topic more fully and be more engaged, an open-ended question is more effective.

Skilled practitioners choose the type of question to ask based on their goals. Beginning practitioners often overuse closed-ended questions. Since closed-ended questions ask for limited and very specific information, they do not invite clients to fully explore a topic and may indicate that the practitioner is not interested in obtaining more information. Using closed-ended questions may imply a practitioner's need to be in control rather than to work collaboratively with the client.

If clients treat open-ended questions as closed-ended questions by giving one-word responses, you need to encourage them by saying, "Tell me more about...." Adolescents are often masters at giving one-word answers to open-ended questions. For example, if you say, "Tell me more about the problems you are having at school," they just shrug their shoulders. In Chapter 12 you will learn more about working with clients who may not want to talk with you.

Examples of Closed-Ended Questions:

1. When did this problem start? (could answer with a date)
   Changed to open-ended question: Tell me about how this problem developed.
2. What do you like about school? (could be answered with one or two words, for example "recess")
   Changed to open-ended question: Tell me about some of the things you liked at school today.
3. What do you do when your husband comes home drunk? (could be answered with "scream at him")
   Changed to a more open-ended question: Will you tell me about what happens when your husband comes home drunk?

4. Do you check-in with each other at the beginning of your meetings? (could answer with yes or no)
   Changed to an open-ended question: Tell me about some of the ways that you begin your meetings.

5. Do you eat dinner together? (could answer with yes or no)
   Changed to an open-ended question: Tell me about what it is like in your family when you eat dinner together.

HOMEWORK EXERCISE 9.2 | CLOSED-ENDED QUESTIONS

In the next week pay attention to the kinds of questions people use. Write down ten questions that you hear in everyday conversations. Identify each question as closed-ended or open-ended.

COMMON MISTAKES WHEN USING QUESTIONS

Some ways of using questions are less effective than others. For example, you should not ask more than one question at a time. Asking several questions at once is confusing. Generally clients will just reply to one of the questions. Thus, the practitioner will not obtain potentially important information. For example, a practitioner might ask the client: "Is it hard for you to both work and study? How does your family feel about this?" Sometimes the second question is similar to the first question, but in this example there are two different questions. The first question focuses on the client's thoughts and the second question on his/her family's feelings. It would be better if the practitioner decided which question to ask first and just asked that question. The other question could be asked another time.

Multiple choice questions, which are usually closed-ended, can also inhibit the client's exploration. For example, "How do you feel about that – sad, confused, angry?" The client may respond with a one-word answer – sad. However, when clients are not used to expressing their feelings or reporting on them, asking a multiple-choice question initially may give them a larger vocabulary for describing what they are experiencing.

Although a rapid-fire questioning style is common in some cultures, this style fits with interrogation, not with creating cooperative, working relationships. Avoid asking one question after another, and remember to express understanding before asking questions.

Sometimes questions are used to inform or persuade clients about your point of view. For example, "Don't you think it is important for you to go back to school and complete your GED?" or "What do you think about trying to exercise more to decrease your depressed mood?" These types of questions should not be used until you are clear about the client's goals. Even then veiling your point of view in a question is not a good approach. Consider saying instead:

• "Since your goal is to get a job that pays an adequate salary, I'd suggest that you explore getting your GED. What are your thoughts about that?"

• "I know you want to learn ways to reduce your depression. I have read that exercising is often helpful when you are depressed. Is that something you might consider?"

Questions that begin with "why" often invite people to feel defensive. Some of you may remember questions such as "Why did you get in so late last night?" or "Why is your grade in Algebra so low?" This kind of question doesn't invite open discussion and is often experienced as attacking. People often don't understand why they behave as they do. Clients may hope that the process of counseling will help them understand the reasons for their behavior. This lack of understanding is particularly true for children (Ellis, 2006). Sometimes it is also more important to find ways to change an undesirable behavior than to understand why it is done.

HOMEWORK EXERCISE 9.3 | MULTIPLE QUESTIONS

In the next few days pay attention to the types of questions people ask you and the questions you ask others. You will probably hear some open-ended questions, some closed-ended questions, and some multiple questions. Identify which type of questions you use most frequently. Notice how people respond to multiple questions.

IMPORTANT AREAS TO LEARN ABOUT

Two broad areas that are generally important to learn more about in counseling situations are *problems or challenges* and *situation or environment*. When telling their story, clients usually discuss these broad topics but may not fully cover each area. It is up to the practitioner to notice what is not being discussed and to explore those areas.

Learning about the Problems or Challenges

To better understand the client's challenges, one important area to explore is the history of the problem. The practitioner might say, "I understand you haven't had this problem for very long. (Pause) When did this problem begin?" In some cases understanding why the client decided to see a practitioner at this time is important. Often there is some precipitating event that leads to the person making an appointment. The practitioner might say, "I wonder what happened that led to you deciding to seek help now." Another critical area to explore is the client's previous attempts to solve the problem. Exploring this area gives clients an opportunity to talk about what they have tried. A practitioner might say, "I know you are working on this problem by coming to talk to me. (Pause) What other things have you done to try to resolve this problem?"

In many cases, the practitioner may not fully understand the severity and frequency of the problem. The practitioner might say, "It sounds like this challenge has been very troubling to you. (Pause) How often does this problem occur?" Another way to ask about the seriousness of the problem is to use a scaling question that invites the client to rate the severity of the problem on a 1 to 10 scale. The practitioner could say, "This situation sounds very difficult. On a scale of 1 to 10, with 1 being one of the worst problems you have ever faced and 10 being almost no problem, what number would you give this problem?" Another example of gaining more information about the severity of the problem is to say, "I understand you are very troubled. On a scale of 1 to 10, with 1 being very troubled and 10 being not troubled at all, how problematic is this challenge for you?"

Learning about how the problem affects the client is also essential. Usually clients talk about how they feel about having a problem. If not, the practitioner might say, "I understand that this problem is happening more and more frequently. (Pause) How are you feeling about having this problem?" The practitioner also needs to learn about how the problem is affecting the person's functioning. The practitioner might say, "I hear that you are very worried about your son. I wonder if your concern is affecting other areas of your life, like your ability to sleep." The pain of many problems can cause appetite loss, insomnia, inability to concentrate at school or at work, irritability, withdrawal, crying easily, etc. As a practitioner it is important for you to understand how having this problem is affecting other aspects of the client's life.

HOMEWORK EXERCISE 9.4 | LEARNING ABOUT PROBLEMS OR CHALLENGES

Think about a problem in your life, either current or in the past. If a practitioner were working with you on this problem, what five open-ended questions would help the practitioner gain an understanding of your problem? List the questions followed by an explanation of why you selected each question.

Learning about the Situation or Environment

As you remember from the discussion of the ecological perspective in Chapter 2, people and their environment are continuously interacting, adapting, and evolving. Some people interact well and feel comfortable in their environment. For others the fit with their environment is negative and impacts their ability to meet their needs and achieve their goals. Since clients' overall life situation or environment affects their ability to work on problems, practitioners need to understand their clients' life situation and environment. Practitioners need to understand how well clients are adapting and fitting into their environment. To gain this understanding, practitioners may ask about available social support (neighbors, friends, church, etc). Practitioners should learn about what the client likes (or dislikes) about his/her neighborhood, church, work group, etc. For example, a client who recently moved to a new area and has few friendships is in a different situation from a client who lives near friends and/or family. The practitioner could say, "So you just moved here a couple of months ago. I wonder if you have had time to meet people who might be helpful as you work on this problem."

Since problems usually also affect people other than the client, part of learning more about the situation involves asking about others who may be affected by the problem. Asking about the effect of the problem on others helps the practitioner gain a better understanding of the client's situation. For example, the practitioner might say, "I understand that you are very troubled by the problems on your job.

I am guessing that your challenges at work are affecting other people in your life. Will you tell me about others who may be affected?"

As each of you know from your experience, the people in your family usually have the most impact on you. As you remember from the discussion of family systems in Chapter 2, practitioners need to learn about how members of a family are affecting each other. For example, a practitioner might say to client who is away from home at college. "I understand you are the first person in your family to go to college. I wonder if your mom and dad understand the challenges of being a full-time college student and also working part time."

The ecological perspective also reminds the practitioner of the importance of learning about life stressors (traumatic events, illnesses and deaths, and major changes and transitions). In Chapter 1 you learned that anything that upsets your normal routine is stressful. Stress becomes a problem when a person experiences more stressful events than he/she can cope with adequately. At that point the person becomes more vulnerable to accidents, illness, and inappropriate behavior. We all have demands in our lives, but we only experience these demands as problems when the level of demands is higher than we can comfortably handle. Individuals, families, and groups with sufficient resources are able to handle the disruption of high levels of stress better. However, even with sufficient resources, high levels of stress over long periods of time can cause emotional and physical disturbances. Clients who are living in poverty are under constant stress that affects all parts of their lives and often affects their view of themselves. To a family living in poverty, the practitioner might say, "I know that you are working two jobs and still having trouble paying your bills. I imagine that is an everyday worry for you. (Pause) Tell me more about the challenges you are facing." In order to better understand the demands and stresses in the client's life, there are several areas to consider:

- Number of children and other people in the household
- Job demands
- Care-taking responsibilities for family members
- Deaths, illnesses, and major health challenges
- Current or past traumatic events in their family or community
- Changes such as moving, job changes, marriage or divorce, new relationships, and relationship break-ups
- Demands related to attending school, church involvement, and volunteer activities

---

HOMEWORK EXERCISE 9.5 | PERSONS AND THEIR ENVIRONMENT

- Think of someone you know who has been a caretaker for a seriously ill close relative for a long period of time or someone who has been dealing with another type of long-term stress. List what you have noticed as indications that

the person is having trouble coping. Write a reflecting comment and five open-ended questions a practitioner could use to gain further information about this client.

Understanding the many environments that clients may be living in is important. Remember what you learned in Chapter 2 about the dual perspective. If you are working with clients who live in both a nurturing environment and a sustaining environment, they have to be more cautious and are more stressed than those clients who are part of the dominant majority. Think of an immigrant who is of the Muslim faith. That person may feel safe at home and at risk whenever he/she leaves home. As the practitioner you might say, "I know there have been attacks against Muslims in this town. I imagine that has felt very scary for you. (Pause) Will you tell me what it has been like for you since the attacks?" Or to a Mexican-American client living in an area with considerable discussion about sending illegal immigrants back to their own country, the practitioner might say, "It seems like Mexican-Americans are being targeted around here. (Pause) Tell me what that has been like for you."

GENUINENESS

Clients are more likely to feel comfortable exploring further with a practitioner they trust and believe is genuine. As discussed in Chapter 5, being genuine involves being natural and sincere rather than stiff, and being fully present rather than thinking about something else, such as what to say next. People are experienced as genuine who seem authentic, candid, forthright, and honest.

HOMEWORK EXERCISE 9.6 | Characteristics and Behaviors Associated with Genuineness

Think of someone you experience as genuine. Write a description of what that person does that makes you think he/she is genuine. Now think of someone you experience as insincere or not genuine. Write a description of what that person does that make you think he/she is not genuine.

Genuineness Evaluation Scale

Level 1: The practitioner appeared stiff, tense, distracted, and/or detached from the process most of the time, and responses were obviously not connected to the client's feelings; flat affect.

Level 3: The practitioner appeared sincere and relaxed, but not clearly connected to or focused on the process.

Level 5: The practitioner appeared sincere, relaxed, focused on the client, and selectively shared personal reactions to the client's feelings, comments, and behavior.

DVD Example: Open and Closed Questions and Learning about Problems and Situation

Watch the exploring sections of the individual, family, and/or group meetings.
- Identify examples of
  - expressing understanding
  - using open and closed questions

- ○ learning about problems
- ○ learning about situations
- • What did you like about the way the practitioners used questions?
- • Identify any specific ways the practitioners could have improved their use of questions.
- • Rate each practitioner's expression of genuineness?

PRACTICE EXERCISE 4 | GAINING FURTHER UNDERSTANDING AND EXPRESSING GENUINENESS

Because these skills require considerable practice to master, you will be practicing using and evaluating skills you have learned related to opening and closing a meeting, reflecting feelings, reflecting content, reflecting feelings and content, reflecting meanings, summarizing, and expressing warmth and empathy, as well as the skills introduced in this chapter. In the practice exercises each set of skills will be included at least twice.

Exercise Objectives

- • To practice expressing understanding before using questions, to use open-ended and closed-ended questions appropriately, and to ask one question at a time.
- • To practice gaining further information about problems and challenges and the situation and environment.
- • To practice expressing genuineness in appropriate and effective ways.

Step 1: Preparation

Form groups of three people. Each person will have the opportunity to play the roles of client, practitioner, and peer supervisor. Each meeting will last about 10 minutes.

Client Role
- • Think about a problem that you encountered in the past. These exercises will be much more authentic if you talk from your own experience.

Practitioner Role
- • Think about important things to observe in the client and to do in the interview.
- • Review the skills introduced in this chapter and the previous chapter (see evaluation form).

Peer Supervisor Role
- • Review the skills introduced in this chapter (see evaluation form).
- • Prepare to observe and listen to the client and to keep track of the time.

Step 2: The Client Meeting

Client Role
- • If the experience you plan to discuss happened more than a year ago, give the practitioner the necessary basic information, e.g., "This happened when I was a junior in high school."
- • Talk for a brief period, pausing to give the practitioner a chance to respond during the telling of your story. Remember that your role is to give the practitioner a client to practice with. Working on whatever problem you may be facing is not the goal.

Practitioner Role
- • Listen to the client and observe the client's nonverbal communication.
- • Use the skills of expressing understanding before using questions, using open-ended and closed-ended questions appropriately, and asking one question at a time.
- • Listen for gaps in information related to problems and the environment and ask questions to gain further information.
- • You can stop the meeting at any time to get suggestions from the persons in the role of client or peer supervisor.
- • Remember that your goal is to practice the skills. Even if this was a real interaction with a client, it would be inappropriate to begin working on problem solving until you thoroughly understood the situation and had set goals with the client.

(continued)

PRACTICE EXERCISE 4 | GAINING FURTHER UNDERSTANDING AND EXPRESSING GENUINENESS (continued)

Peer Supervisor Role
- Keep track of the time and alert the practitioner and client when 9 minutes have passed so the practitioner has time to close the meeting.
- Check off the items for opening and closing the meeting.
- **Write down each of the practitioner's statements.** Writing out each practitioner statement is very difficult but critical in order to accurately identify statements, to give solid feedback, and to effectively evaluate the practitioner's work. You may abbreviate, use a form of shorthand, or just write the first group of words in the statement, or you can tape record the interview and transcribe or listen to the tape.

Step 3: Feedback

Purpose: Receiving immediate constructive feedback helps students enhance their practice skills. Using this evaluation system, the peer supervisor monitors the skills used by the social worker. The client, social worker, and peer supervisor identify strengths and areas for growth.

Client Role
- Share how you experienced the practitioner.
- Did you feel understood?
- Was the practitioner warm, empathic, and genuine?
- What did the practitioner do particularly well?
- In what ways could the practitioner improve?

Practitioner Role
- Evaluate your use of skills related to expressing understanding before using questions, using open-ended and closed-ended questions appropriately, asking one question at a time, and gaining further information about problems and the situation.

Peer Supervisor Role
- Check off the items for opening and closing the meeting.
- Based on your notes, give feedback to the practitioner on the use of reflecting the client's feelings, content, feelings and content, and meanings, and summarizing. Give the practitioner a point for each reflecting comment. For example, if the practitioner reflected feeling three times, he/she would get three points after reflecting feelings.
- Discuss with the practitioner the appropriate score for demonstrating the skills for expressing understanding before using questions, using open-ended and closed-ended questions appropriately, and asking one question at a time.
- Give the practitioner one point for expressing understanding before using questions, using open-ended and closed-ended questions appropriately, and asking one question at a time.
- Give the practitioner one point for each topic related to problems or challenges that was adequately discussed whether the practitioner asked about the topic or not. The practitioner doesn't need to ask about areas discussed by the client, just those topics the client does not discuss. Remember that these are only 10 minute interviews, so the practitioner will not have the time to fully cover each area.
- Give the practitioner one point for each topic related to situation or environment that was adequately discussed whether the practitioner asked about the topic or not. The practitioner doesn't need to ask about areas discussed by the client, just those topics the client does not discuss. Remember that these are only 10 minute interviews, so the practitioner will not have the time to fully cover each area.
- Discuss with the practitioner the appropriate scores for warmth, empathy, and genuineness.

Genuineness Evaluation Scale

Level 1: The practitioner appeared stiff, tense, distracted, and/or detached from the process most of the time, and responses were obviously not connected to the client's feelings; flat affect.

Level 3: The practitioner appeared sincere and relaxed, but not clearly connected to or focused on the process.

Level 5: The practitioner appeared sincere, relaxed, focused on the client, and selectively shared personal reactions to the client's feelings, comments, and behavior.

(continued)

PRACTICE EXERCISE 4 | GAINING FURTHER UNDERSTANDING AND EXPRESSING GENUINENESS (*continued*)

- Identify any inappropriate response made by the practitioner (see evaluation form). One minus point for every inappropriate response.
- Add all the individual points and the points on the scales to get the total score.
- Record the feedback in the practitioner's text-book for future reference.

EVALUATION FORM

Name of Practitioner_____

Name of Peer Supervisor_____

Directions: Under each category (in italics) is a list of behaviors or skills. Give one point for each skill used by the practitioner.

Opening and Closing

Beginning Skills (for a meeting)

Give one point for each topic covered by the practitioner.

1. Introduced yourself and your role. _____
2. Sought introductions. _____
3. Identified where meeting will be held. _____
4. Identified how long meeting will last. _____
5. Described the initial purpose of the meeting. _____
6. Explain some of the things you will do. _____
7. Outlined the client's role. _____
8. Discussed ethical and agency policies. _____
9. Sought feedback from the client. _____

Closing Skills (for a meeting)

Give one point for each topic covered by the practitioner.

1. Identified that the meeting was about to end. _____
2. Provided a summary of the meeting. _____
3. Reviewed any tasks that the client agreed to complete. _____
4. Discussed plans for future meetings. _____
5. Invited client feedback about the work. _____
6. Asked client about any final questions. _____

Express Understanding

Expressing understanding is so important that for this group of skills one point should be given for each time the practitioner used one of the skills.

1. Reflected feelings _____
2. Reflected content _____
3. Reflected feelings and content _____
4. Summarized _____
5. Reflected meanings _____

(*continued*)

PRACTICE EXERCISE 4 | Gaining Further Understanding and Expressing Genuineness *(continued)*

Gaining Further Understanding

Questioning Skills

Give one point for each skill used by the practitioner.

1. Expressed understanding before asking questions.
2. Asked open-ended questions when appropriate.   _____
3. Asked one question at a time.   _____
4. Asked closed-ended questions when appropriate.   _____
    _____

Learning about Problem/Challenge and Situation

Give one point for each topic adequately discussed.

Problems or Challenges

Previous attempts to solve problem
History of the problem(s)   _____
Severity or intensity of the problem(s)   _____
Feelings about having the problem(s)   _____
Effects of the problem(s) on other areas   _____
    _____

(such as health, sleeping, and ability to function at school or work)

Situation

Effect of the problem on other people
Available social support and strengths in the environment   _____
Interactions with family   _____
Other demands and stresses in the situation/environment   _____
    _____

Common Mistakes or Inappropriate Responses (subtract 1 point for each)

(offering advice, reassuring, offering excuses, asking leading questions, dominating
through teaching, labeling, and interrogating)   _____

Core Interpersonal Qualities

Using the scales in Appendix A, evaluate the appropriateness and effectiveness
of the practitioner's expression of warmth, empathy, respect, and genuineness.
On the following lines write the scores, from 1 to 5, for warmth, empathy, respect,
and genuineness.

Score for warmth
Score for empathy   _____
Score for genuineness   _____
Total score   _____
    _____

EXPECTED COMPETENCIES

In this chapter, you learned to use questions to gain further understanding of the client and learn about challenges, problems, situations and environments.

You should be able to define the following words: open-ended questions and closed-ended questions.

You should now be able to:

- Explain the difference between closed-ended and open-ended questions and give examples of each.

- Give examples of questions that explore:
  - previous attempts to solve the problem
  - the history of the problem
  - severity or intensity of the problem
  - feelings about the problem
  - effects of the problem on functioning
  - the situation and environment of the client
- Demonstrate gaining further understanding related to problems and situations.
- Demonstrate expressing genuineness.

DEVELOPING DEEPER UNDERSTANDING

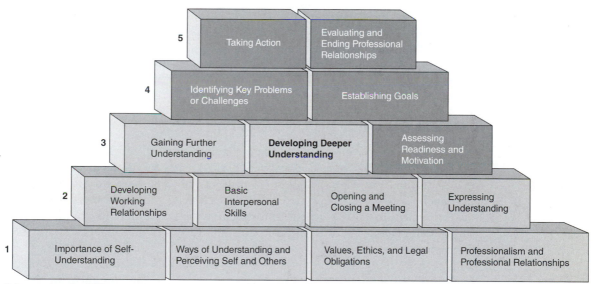

© Cengage Learning 2013

Questions to consider as you read this chapter:

- What can you do to move from surface to deeper understanding?
- What are appropriate ways to demonstrate respect to clients?
- How can you learn more about client's strengths?

This chapter covers practice behaviors related to developing further and deeper understanding of your clients. *You will learn the importance of:*

- Understanding the basis of the conclusions your clients' have made
- Seeking clarification to understanding clients better
- Clarifying the meanings of such things as the words clients use and the situations they describe
- Exploring and identifying possible patterns of behavior
- Allowing silence
- Acknowledging and learning more about your clients' strengths

Client Attributes
- Willingness to explore thoughts, feelings, conclusions, and strengths

In this chapter, you will continue to develop your ability to use your professional skills in order to more fully understand clients. Clients need to be willing to look more deeply and share more fully. This level of exploration is only possible if the client experiences their relationship with practitioners as safe and trusting. In this chapter you will learn the skills related to seeking clarification and gaining deeper understanding. You will also learn about the importance of allowing silence so clients can reflect on the process before moving further and about the need to acknowledge and focus on clients' strengths.

THE NEED TO DEVELOP DEEPER UNDERSTANDING

In ordinary conversation, people often communicate in verbal shorthand, only discussing topics in a superficial way. We rarely ask for more information. We tend to assume that other people use words in the same way we do, that others can somehow fill in the information that is left out, and that others understand how our conclusions are reached. Unfortunately these assumptions are often incorrect. Communicating in this surface way often leads to misunderstanding. As a practitioner, it is important to listen for gaps in information, notice points and words that are not clear, and ask about how conclusions are reached. Since practitioners need to fully understand their clients, it is important for them to gain as complete an understanding of their clients as possible. This complete understanding includes learning about strengths and resources as well as about problems and challenges.

Seeking Clarification

Seeking clarification is a skill that involves using questions to invite clients to thoroughly explain their thoughts and feelings with more specific details. When clients thoroughly explain their behaviors, feelings, and experiences, the nature of the problem, challenge, or situation will be clearer to the practitioner and to the client. Often when practitioners are unclear about what clients are saying or meaning, the clients are also confused. For example, if a client says, "I'm depressed," the client may be repeating what someone else has said or may be using the word "depressed" to mean something very different from what the practitioner means. The practitioner should not assume that depression means the same thing to the client as it does to the practitioner. Of course, as you learned in the previous two chapters, it is important to express your understanding of what the client is saying first. Often the practitioner will express understanding using one of the reflecting skills and pause to give the client time to explain further. If the client doesn't continue, the practitioner may ask a question to gain further understanding. The practitioner might ask for more information by saying, "I understand that you are feeling depressed. (pause) What is depression like for you?" In a group meeting, several people may agree that the clients of the agency are not treated with respect. It is up to the practitioner to explore further by making a remark such as, "I hear that you are concerned about how your clients are being treated. (pause) Will you give me examples of ways that clients are not treated with respect?"

When seeking clarification, practitioners can explore the meaning of words and body language. For example, the practitioner might say, "I noticed that several people in the group began looking at the floor when we started discussing who was willing to go and talk to the mayor. (pause) Will one of you tell me more about what you are expressing by looking at the floor?" (exploring meaning of body language). The practitioner might explore the meaning of a word and say, "You mentioned that people in this family are often angry at each other. (pause) Will you give me an example of what happens when people are angry in your family?" (exploring the behaviors related to anger).

Exploring the basis of conclusions drawn by the clients is another area that often needs further exploration by the practitioner. For example, if a member of a task group says, "Okay, I guess that I will have to do all the work of putting together the PowerPoint presentation," the task group leader might say, "It sounds like you think you will have to prepare the presentation by yourself. Will you tell us what happened to make you decide that you would have to do all the work of putting the PowerPoint presentation together?" A family member might say, "Our family is just hopeless." The practitioner could respond "I hear that you are feeling very discouraged. Will you tell me what has been happening recently that led you to feel hopeless?"

Examples of Questions to Seek Clarification

Client: "He is always getting mad at me over nothing."

    Practitioner: "I am guessing you are feeling mistreated by him." (pause) Followed by possible questions:

- "Tell me about what he did the last time he got mad at you." (asking for further information)
- "How often was he mad at you yesterday?" (asking for further information)
- "Would you give me an example of a time when he got mad at you over nothing?" (asking for further information)
- "What does he do when he is mad at you?" (exploring behaviors described as "mad")

Client: "I just know she doesn't love me anymore."
    Practitioner: "You sound sad." (pause)
    Followed by possible questions:

- "Would you tell me how you know she doesn't love you anymore?" (asking for basis of conclusion)
- "What has she done or said that makes you believe that she doesn't love you anymore?" (asking for basis of conclusion)
- "If she did love you, what would she do?" (exploring meaning of "love" to the client)

Client in a task group: "I think the other people in this group just don't care about whether this project gets completed on time or not."
    Practitioner: "You sound kind of frustrated and maybe discouraged." (pause)
    Followed by possible questions:

- "Will you tell me what you have noticed that makes you think others don't care about whether this project gets completed on time or not?" (asking for basis of conclusion)
- "Will the rest of you tell us your thoughts about people's commitment to completing this project on time?" (asking for further information)
- "What are some things you think the people in this group could do to show that they were invested in completing the project on time?" (asking for further information)

Child in a family meeting: "I just know that mom doesn't like me."
    Practitioner: "I wonder if maybe you are feeling kind of sad or maybe mad." (pause)
    Followed by possible questions:

- "Will you tell me what makes you think that your mom doesn't like you?" (asking about basis of conclusion)
- "Mom, I doubt if you agree with your daughter. What ideas do you have about what might have led her to that conclusion?" (asking about basis of conclusion)
- To the child, "What is happening when you think mom doesn't like you?" (asking for further information)

Using questioning to expand and clarify is particularly important with families and groups because it encourages interaction among members as they expand on their thoughts and feelings. Using clarifying questions can lead to everyone having a clearer picture of what is being communicated. Clarification can also increase awareness of similarities and differences among members.

Examples of Clarifying Questions in Groups
- "Several people mentioned thinking this neighborhood is going to the dogs. Will you give me some examples of what you mean?" (basis of conclusion)
- "I understand that you would like the agency to be more efficient. Will you tell me what you believe will be different when it is more efficient?" (meaning of efficient)

- "I heard several folks say that you thought that doing group assignments would not work. What do you think doesn't work about group assignments?" (basis of conclusion)
- "It sounds like you believe that people in this family don't feel close to each other. Will you tell me what happens when people don't feel close to each other in this family?" (meaning of close in this family)

HOMEWORK EXERCISE 10.1 | SEEKING CLARIFICATION

Read each of the following sentences and write a reflecting statement followed by two questions you might ask to get more information.

1. No one in this neighborhood cares about the drug problems.
2. I just know that my teacher doesn't like me and is going to give me a low grade.
3. I know the other kids in this group will be mean to me.
4. The people in this agency don't really care about the clients.
5. My mother had a nervous breakdown, so she can't help how she acts.
6. My parents just don't understand kids. They won't let me do anything.
7. In this family we just don't communicate very well.
8. I think the problem is that she just won't honor my boundaries.

The next time you are in a conversation with several other people, pay attention to whether people take time to ask about what the other person means or whether they just wait until one person has stopped talking so they can start talking.

Client's Role in Clarification

The practitioner may be highly skilled at noticing missing information and asking clarifying questions, but to go further with exploration, the client must also be willing to explore more deeply. This willingness to explore more deeply is generally based on feeling comfortable or safe with the practitioner. As you know from your life experiences, some people develop a sense of trust very quickly while others are more hesitant. Experiences of abuse, oppression, and mistreatment often lead people to be cautious about trusting. If clients are not willing to explore more deeply, practitioners should not push them but rather accept what they are ready to do. Asking clients to talk about their hesitancy to share information may be helpful. The practitioner should also consider his/her possible role in the client's caution. When clients resist exploring further, it may be an indication that the practitioner is trying to move too quickly or is asking too many questions. Asking one question after another feels like being interrogated, and no one likes being interrogated. Perhaps the practitioner has tried to gain further information before adequately establishing a trusting relationship with the client. Some people have not had the opportunity to explore their thoughts and feelings or be introspective. It may take them some time to develop this ability. If the client seems uncomfortable exploring further, the practitioner should go back to expressing understanding in order to build a trusting relationship.

Allowing Silence

Sometimes allowing silence is the best way to invite clients to elaborate further. It is important to allow clients time to think and process what has been said. The practitioner may have said something or asked something that the client needs time to consider. Although allowing silence may seem awkward to beginning practitioners, it is an appropriate and respectful response, particularly at times when the client is expressing strong feelings and needs time to reflect.

Silence allows time for emotions to be experienced and/or thoughts to become clarified. Allowing silence is a nonverbal response that has been described as one of the most useful interventions available to practitioners (Belkin, 1984; Beutow, 2009; Moursund, 1993). When it appears that clients need time to deal with what has been said, practitioners should allow some silence. It is important to remember that some topics, particularly those that involve intense or strong feelings, require more time to process. Sometime in the course of talking to a practitioner, clients will say something that involves new insight or understanding for them. When this happens, it is helpful to allow for them to think about what they just said. In addition, although you may process information quickly and be ready to respond almost immediately, this is not true of all people. Some people need quiet in order to think about what they are feeling and decide what to say. Practitioners need to be sensitive and allow clients the time they need to think.

As with other responses, silence should be used purposefully. Some clients consider silence an indication of lack of interest or even rejection. Practitioners should observe nonverbal clues that could indicate that the client is uncomfortable with the silence. Clients who are mandated to be in the session may not want to talk. Some practitioners choose to remain silent because they believe that the client will decide to talk when he/she is ready. Each situation and each client needs to be thoughtfully considered.

Sometimes it is important to ask about the silence. For example, the practitioner might say, "What were you thinking about during the silence?" During a silent period, the practitioner may look at the client or decide not to keep eye contact as a way to give the client more space.

Examples of Allowing Silence

1. *Individual client:* "I don't know why I get sick so often … maybe it is the stress in my life, the fast pace …"
   Practitioner: (silence, giving the client time to think about her comment)
2. *Group member:* "I'm not sure where we should go from here, but it seems like we need to make a decision."
   Practitioner: (silence, giving group members time to reply)
3. *Family member:* "I really wish that we could do something together without fighting."
   Practitioner: (silence, giving other family members time to respond on their own)

HOMEWORK EXERCISE 10.2 | ALLOWING SILENCE

Think about your own experience with silence when you are with other people. Are you comfortable with silence, or do you feel anxious or uncomfortable if a conversation stops? In one conversation in the next few days, try allowing 10 seconds of silence rather than immediately starting to talk if there is a pause in the conversation. How did you feel during the silence? If silence is uncomfortable for you, you might try counting slowly to ten and encouraging yourself to be quiet for the whole 10 seconds.

FOCUSING ON STRENGTHS AND POSITIVE FACTORS

To develop a deeper understanding of clients you need to focus on their strengths, resources, and positive factors as well as their challenges. You learned about the strengths perspective and the importance of learning about, acknowledging, and focusing on clients' strengths in Chapter 2. Also in Chapter 2, you learned about the resilience perspective and how important positive factors are in coping with difficult challenges. Although clients generally want practitioners to fully explore and understand their challenges before moving on to exploring positive factors and strengths, listening for, highlighting, and asking about strengths is important. Whether the client is an individual, a family, a group, or neighborhood, looking for positive factors and strengths is essential. Often it will be the clients' strengths and positive factors that will help them resolve their problems.

By turning the focus to strengths and positive factors in their life, practitioners help clients begin to feel hopeful, positive, and/or more able to cope. There are many ways to invite clients to turn their focus from problems to strengths and positive factors. For example, the practitioner might say, "It sounds like you are feeling quite anxious and having trouble sleeping since these problems with the man you are dating began. (pause) I'd like to change the direction for a few minutes and learn more about what is going well in your life."

Identifying Strengths and Positive Factors

As you are listening to clients, begin to identify their abilities and resources, their capacity to cope in difficult situations, what they have achieved, their willingness to keep trying, and the positive factors in their life. Commenting on strengths and positive factors invites clients to change their perspective from what is wrong in their life to what is positive in their life. This shift in focus often invites clients to feel hopeful. Highlighting what clients have already achieved shows that the practitioner understands and supports the efforts they have made (Anderson, Ogles, Patterson, Lambert, & Vermeesch, 2009; Saleebey, 2002c).

Below are some areas to consider when thinking about a client's strengths, positive factors, capacities, and resources:

- Past ability to solve or manage problems
- Level of resilience (this includes such things as positive outlook, trust in others, confidence in ability to cope, positive self-esteem, and strong cultural identity)

- Common sense or ability to use past experience and knowledge to figure out what to do
- Support from friends, neighbors, church, family, community
- Financial support
- Eligibility for social service support
- Adequate housing
- Safe area to live
- Adequate schooling
- Ability to obtain or maintain employment

Examples of Comments that Focus on Strengths and Positive Factors

- *To a group:* "It seems like each of you contributed a great deal of time to make this project such a success."
- *To children in a family:* "As I listen to you talking about how you have managed during the time your mom has been sick, I am aware of how capable you are. You have pitched in to help with the laundry, house cleaning, and cooking."
- *To an individual:* "I know that standing up for yourself is new for you. However, it sounds like you were clear and assertive with your boss."
- *To a couple:* "I think that figuring out that you need help and getting it shows you each have a lot of commitment to your relationship."
- *To a family:* "I am sure that coping with George's illness has been painful and maybe exhausting. Having friends bring dinner and help with the children must have been very helpful."
- *To a couple:* "What a shock it has been to lose everything in a flood! I know you have really appreciated the help of the Red Cross, the loan from your parents, the money from your insurance, and the willingness of your friends to let you live with them until you find a place."

HOMEWORK EXERCISE 10.3 | IDENTIFYING STRENGTHS

Think of someone in your life who saw and identified one of your strengths. What was that experience like for you? Now think about a time when something you didn't do well was noticed and highlighted, while something you did well seemed to be ignored. An example might be when you were a child and got nine out of ten spelling words right on a test. Were you told, "Good job! You got nine right." Or instead, were you asked, "Why did you miss one?" As a practitioner, do you want to be the person who focuses on the one word that was missed or on the nine words that were correct?

Now think about three friends or family members. Identify one or more of their strengths.

Review the list of positive factors in Chapter 2. List 3 positive factors in your life related to each of the following areas: individual, family, community, and socio-cultural.

Questions to Learn about Strengths and Positive Factors

Besides acknowledging strengths and positive factors they hear from clients, practitioners should go further and ask about additional strengths and positive factors. Here are a few examples of possible questions and statements that can be used to invite clients to identify strengths and positive factors.

Examples of Questions to Explore Strengths and Positive Factors

- What do you do well?
- What are you good at?
- What do you like about yourself?
- What do other people say they like about you?
- How have you made it through the challenges you faced in the past?
- What are some things that you did as a child that you were proud of?
- When you were a teenager, what did you do that you felt good about?
- What does your family do that is fun?
- What does your family do that you all have to help with?
- Tell me about the people in your life who have helped you out.
- Tell me about the relatives that you like.
- Who has your family turned to for help in the past?
- Tell me about friends who have helped you in the past.
- Tell me about (neighbors, people at work, people in your church, etc.) that you count on.
- What are some good things that this (organization or neighborhood) has been able to do?
- Tell me about a time that you helped someone else.
- What are some of the ways that people in your family help each other?
- If someone else had a problem similar to yours, what would you suggest that person do?
- Think of someone that you know who has solved a problem similar to yours. What did that person do that might work for you?

HOMEWORK EXERCISE 10.4 | ASKING QUESTIONS ABOUT POSITIVE FACTORS AND STRENGTHS

Write down five additional questions you might use to find out about strengths or positive factors. (*Hint:* You can ask about strengths and achievements in the past, including qualities needed to accomplish certain tasks or goals. For example, "Tell me about the strengths and skills that you used when you learned to drive.")

Connecting Strengths and Empowerment

Ultimately, practitioners often hope their clients will become empowered. As you remember from Chapter 2, individuals and groups that have achieved a sense of empowerment know they have knowledge, skills, competencies, and resources to make decisions, solve problems, and achieve goals. As people use their strengths and resources to face and deal with problems and challenges, they gain confidence in their ability to continue to actively manage challenges. Practitioners who partner with clients to understand challenges and to identify strengths, resources, and positive factors create opportunities for clients to enhance their sense of empowerment. After making a reflecting statement, practitioners may ask questions that invite clients to identify ways in which they have actively participated in solving problems and in so doing enhanced their confidence or sense of empowerment.

Examples of Questions that Focus on Empowering Experiences
- Tell me about something you completed that seemed difficult.
- Of the things you have already done to resolve this problem, tell me about what has worked well, even for a brief period of time.
- What are some of the things you learned from dealing with past challenges?
- What skills helped you solve previous challenges?
- How have you resolved previous challenges?

HOMEWORK EXERCISE 10.5 | LEARNING ABOUT EMPOWERING EXPERIENCES

In homework exercise 2.14 you identified an experience that was empowering to you. Using that experience or another empowering experience, identify three reflecting comments a practitioner could make to you that would demonstrate that the practitioner understood how important that experience was for you or how much you learned from dealing with that experience.

DEMONSTRATING RESPECT

Focusing on strengths is a way of demonstrating respect. In Chapter 5 we discussed the importance of showing respect in relationships with clients. Respect can be expressed through expressing understanding and validating the client's story; by showing interest in the client's thoughts, feelings, wants, needs, and goals; by creating and maintaining a collaborative environment; by asking about strengths, resources, potential, and capacities; and by identifying strengths. Using language that expresses a belief that clients can change and are able to solve their problems also shows respect (Corey, 2009).

Examples of Statements that Demonstrate Respect
- With all the trained professionals in this group, I am confident we can find a way to resolve this. (respecting strengths)
- "You've tried to solve this problem. Will you tell me about other things you have considered, but haven't used yet?" (showing interest in the client's thoughts and asking about strengths and potential)
- "You seem quite angry about how your boss has been behaving. It must be a tough place to work. How do you think I might help you?" (validating the client's story and showing interest in his/her wants and needs)

- "When you resolve this problem, what are some things that will be different in your family?" (expressing belief in the client's ability to change)
- "You have told me about the many ways you have worked on this challenge. Who else in the agency might be willing to work with us to resolve this problem?" (validating efforts and asking about resources)
- "As I understand it, you have done a lot of thinking about the problems this organization is facing. You have talked to a number of people about their understanding of the problem and have decided to commit time and energy to resolving this problem. You have taken some important steps in problem solving." (summarizing and identifying strengths)

Respect Evaluation Scale

Level 1:   The practitioner did not invite discussion of and/or recognize the client's strengths, resources, and/or capacities, and/or showed a lack of respect for the client's abilities such as helping or providing answers that the client did not ask for.

Level 3:   *Once during the meeting*, the practitioner invited discussion of and/or recognized the client's strengths, resources, and/or capacities, and the practitioner did nothing that showed a lack of respect for the client's abilities such as helping or providing answers that the client did not ask for.

Level 5:   *Three times during the meeting*, the practitioner invited discussion of and/or recognized the client's strengths, resources, and/or capacities, showed positive regard for the client, and did nothing that showed a lack of respect for the client's abilities such as helping or providing answers that the client did not ask for.

HOMEWORK EXERCISE 10.6 | DEMONSTRATING RESPECT

Over the next few days, notice what people do or say that you believe demonstrates respect. Also notice what people do or say that you believe demonstrates a lack of respect. Write a list of five things that you noticed that demonstrate respect.

DVD Example: Developing Deeper Understanding

Watch the exploring and goal setting section of the individual meeting.
- List examples of seeking clarification.
- List examples of identifying strengths and/or positive factors.
- Identify examples of asking questions to learn about strengths and/or positive factors.
- What did you like about the way the practitioner used skills related to developing deeper understanding?
- Give specific examples of points where the practitioner could have made a statement or asked a question to develop deeper understanding.

- Identify any specific points where the practitioner could have identified a strength or positive factor.
- What score would you give the practitioner related to expressing respect?

CASE   CASE, PART 2: FIRST MEETING WITH HIDEKO

Using your skills related to expressing understanding, gaining further information, and developing deeper understanding, you are ready to do more work with Hideko.

Hideko enters the office and sits tentatively on the couch. Viviana notes that she is dressed casually and has medium-length hair. She is pale and doesn't appear to be wearing any makeup. She crosses her legs and tucks her hands under them. After covering the beginning information, including confidentiality issues (mandated reporting, etc.) and informed consent, Viviana asks Hideko to sign a release of information to the hospital social worker. Viviana thought it might help her to provide more effective treatment if she understood more of the stressors that Hideko was experiencing with her mother.

HIDEKO: "I'd be glad to sign the release of information form, but the hospital social worker doesn't know me very well. She sees me when my mother is in the hospital, and I sometimes talk to her about home health care for my mother. She suggested that I come see you after noticing that I looked more tired than usual. She said I sighed several times. When my mother was out of the room, she asked me if I was okay and I told her things weren't going very well. So she suggested that talking to someone might help."

VIVIANA: "I understand you are a graduate student, and it sounds like your mother has some health problems and you help with that. *(pause)* Will you tell me about what things aren't going well for you?"

HIDEKO: "Well … *(pause)* I've never been in counseling before so I don't really know what to say. Generally I can just step back and figure out what needs to be done and just do it, but this is different. Anyway, after what the hospital social worker said I thought it over and felt like talking to someone might possibly help."

VIVIANA: "So this is a very new experience for you. You're used to figuring out your challenges, but this is different. You mentioned that you've been having some "trouble." Would you tell me more about that?"

HIDEKO: "Well, I'm not sleeping very well, and it's just hard for me to keep up with everything. Last week I found myself staring into space during class. That is just not like me, and I can't allow myself to be so distracted and not succeed. I have always gotten top grades in the past."

VIVIANA: "You sound troubled… how long has this been going on?"

HIDEKO: "Hmm… I guess a couple of months now. It's frustrating. I'm sick of feeling like this. And I don't know what to do about it. I've never had this happen before …"

VIVIANA: "It sounds like you have been quite distressed. Tell me what was happening in your life a couple of months ago."

HIDEKO: "Well, my boyfriend and I broke up. He said I just never had enough time to be with him and he didn't see it getting any better." *(short pause— Viviana notices that Hideko looks very sad and is wringing her hands)*

VIVIANA: "It is painful for a relationship to end, particularly when it sounds like it wasn't what you wanted. Tell me more about what he meant about it not getting any better."

Hideko tells Viviana that she and her boyfriend dated for two years. She met him during undergraduate school. After graduation he took a job in sales. He understood that her classes were demanding, but had trouble with the fact that her family didn't accept him because he wasn't Japanese. She thought the biggest problem was that on top of everything else she had to spend a lot of time helping her mother, and didn't have much time to be with him. Hideko explained that her mother had been in a very serious automobile accident four years ago. Her mother had a "traumatic spinal cord injury and incomplete paraplegia. She also has lost bowel and bladder control." When the accident happened Hideko was in college. As the only daughter she felt it was her duty to care for her mother, so she told her mother she would drop out of school to take care of her. Her mother wanted her to continue going to school. In order to manage school and caring for her mother, Hideko transferred to a school near home and moved home to live. Although Hideko had planned to go on to graduate school, she decided to give that up because of the demands of helping her mother; however, both parents insisted that she continue her studies.

Her mother has not been getting better and has been in and out of the hospital. She is also often in pain caused by damage to nerve fibers. Hideko feels like she has to do well in graduate school and must help her mother. Nearly the only time she used to take off was the little time she had with her boyfriend. "He is right. I don't think it will get any better. It may never get any better." Hideko's eyes tear up as she says this.

VIVIANA: "You seem sad right now." *(pause … Viviana allows silence … Hideko begins to cry)*

HIDEKO: "I know I should be able to do all of this, but sometimes I just feel overwhelmed."

Later in the meeting, Viviana learned that both of Hideko's parents were born in Japan. The family has many relatives in Japan, and they visit Japan when possible. Hideko's parents speak in Japanese at home, so Hideko is fluent in Japanese. Hideko's parents are Buddhist. Hideko said that she isn't an active Buddhist but accepts much of what she has learned about Buddhism.

Questions
1. How has your initial perception of the client changed?
2. What new facts have you learned?
3. What are your current impressions or hunches about the case?

Expressing Understanding
4. Identify the statements the practitioner made that express understanding.

5. Write three additional things that the practitioner might have said to express understanding.
6. What happened in the interview that makes you think the client felt understood?
7. Write a summarizing statement that the practitioner might use with Hideko.

Gaining Further Understanding
8. List what you know about the following topics: history of the problem, previous attempts to solve the problem, severity and frequency of the problem, client's feelings about the problem, how the problem is affecting other people, how the problem is affecting the client's functioning, available social support, how the problem is affecting other people, how the problem is affecting people in the family, and stress and demands in the client's life.
9. For every area that you don't know about write an expressing understanding statement followed by an open-ended question to gain further information.

Developing Deeper Understanding
10. List the words and topics that need further clarification. Write what you would say to express understanding related to each item in your list. Write a question that could follow each of your previous statements.
11. What are your thoughts about whether the practitioner used allowing silence appropriately?
12. What do you already know about the client's strengths and resources (including cultural and spiritual resources)? Write two statements the practitioner could have made to identify strengths and/or positive factors.
13. What are three questions the practitioner could have used to identify further strengths and/or positive factors?

PRACTICE EXERCISE 5 | Developing Deeper Understanding and Expressing Respect

Because these skills require considerable practice to master, you will be using and evaluating the use of expressing understanding and using questions to explore as well as the skills of seeking further understanding. In the practice exercises, each set of skills will be included at least twice.

Exercise Objectives
- To practice developing deeper understanding.
- To identify and ask questions about strengths.
- To practice expressing warmth, empathy, respect, and genuineness in appropriate and effective ways.

Step 1: Preparation
Form groups of three people. Each person will have the opportunity to play the roles of client, practitioner, and peer supervisor. Each meeting will last about 10 minutes.

Client Role
- Think about a problem that you encountered in the past. These exercises will be much more authentic if you talk from your own experience.

Practitioner Role
- Think about important things to observe in the client and to do in the interview.
- Review the behaviors introduced in this chapter and the previous chapters (see evaluation form).

Peer Supervisor Role
- Review the behaviors introduced in this chapter (see evaluation form).
- Prepare to observe and listen to the client and to keep track of the time.

Step 2: The Client Meeting
Client Role
- If the experience you plan to discuss happened more than a year ago, give the practitioner the necessary basic information, for example, "This happened when I was a junior in high school."

- Talk for a brief period, pausing to give the practitioner a chance to respond during the telling of your story. Remember that your role is to give the practitioner a chance to practice these skills. Working on whatever problem you may be facing is not the goal.

Practitioner Role
- Use the skills related to expressing understanding and gaining further information.
- Also use the skills related to developing deeper understanding including: exploring the meaning of words and body language, exploring the basis of conclusions, allowing silence, identifying strengths, and asking questions about strengths.
- You can stop the meeting at any time to get suggestions from the persons in the roles of client and/or peer supervisor.
- Remember that your goal is to practice the skills. Even if this was a real interaction with a client, it would be inappropriate to begin working on problem solving until you thoroughly understood the situation and had set goals with the client.

Peer Supervisor Role
- Keep track of the time and alert the practitioner and client when 9 minutes have passed so the practitioner has time to end the meeting.
- *Write down each of the practitioner's statements.* Writing out each practitioner statement is very difficult but critical in order to accurately identify statements, to give solid feedback, and to effectively evaluate the practitioner's work. You may abbreviate, use a form of shorthand, or just write the first group of words in the statement, or you can tape record the interview and transcribe or listen to the tape.

Step 3: Feedback
Purpose: Receiving immediate constructive feedback helps students enhance their practice skills. Using this evaluation system, the peer supervisor monitors the skills used by the social worker. The client, social worker, and peer supervisor identify strengths and areas for growth.

PRACTICE EXERCISE 5 | DEVELOPING DEEPER UNDERSTANDING AND EXPRESSING RESPECT (*continued*)

Client Role
- Share how you experienced the practitioner.
- Did you feel understood?
- In what ways was the practitioner warm, empathic, respectful, and genuine?
- What did the practitioner do particularly well?
- In what ways could the practitioner improve?

Practitioner Role
- Evaluate your use of skills related to developing deeper understanding.

Peer Supervisor Role
- Based on your notes, give feedback to the practitioner on the use of reflecting the client's feelings, content, feelings and content, and meanings, and summarizing. Give the practitioner a point for each reflecting comment.
- Give the practitioner one point for each time he/she expressed understanding before using questions, used open-ended and closed-ended questions appropriately, and asked one question at a time.
- Give the practitioner one point for each topic related to problems or challenges and situation and environment that was adequately discussed whether the practitioner asked about the topic or not. The practitioner doesn't need to ask about areas discussed by the client, just those topics the client does not discuss. Remember that these are only 10 minute interviews, so the practitioner will not have the time to fully cover each area.
- Discuss with the practitioner his/her use of each of the skills related to gaining enhanced understanding.
- Give the practitioner one point for each skill used related to enhancing understanding.
- Discuss the practitioner's ability to demonstrate respect.

Respect Evaluation Scale

Level 1:   The practitioner did not invite discussion of and/or recognize the client's strengths, resources, and/or capacities, and/or showed a lack of respect for the client's abilities such as helping or providing answers that the client did not ask for.

Level 3:   *Once during the meeting,* the practitioner invited discussion of and/or recognized the client's strengths, resources, and/or capacities, and the practitioner did nothing that showed a lack of respect for the client's abilities such as helping or providing answers that the client did not ask for.

Level 5:   *Three times during the meeting,* the practitioner invited discussion of and/or recognized the client's strengths, resources, and/or capacities, showed positive regard for the client, and did nothing that showed a lack of respect for the client's abilities such as helping or providing answers that the client did not ask for.

- Discuss with the practitioner the appropriate scores for warmth, empathy, genuineness, and respect.
- Identify any inappropriate response made by the practitioner (see evaluation form). One minus point for every inappropriate response.
- Add all the individual points and the points on the scales to get the total score.
- Record the feedback in the practitioner's textbook for future reference.

(continued)

PRACTICE EXERCISE 5 | Developing Deeper Understanding and Expressing Respect (*continued*)

Evaluation Form

Name of Practitioner_____

Name of Peer Supervisor_____

Directions: Under each category (in italics) is a list of behaviors or skills.
Give one point for each skill used by the practitioner.

Expressing Understanding
Expressing understanding is so important that for this group of skills one point
should be given for each time the practitioner used one of the skills.

1. Reflected feelings   _____
2. Reflected content   _____
3. Reflected feelings and content   _____
4. Summarized   _____
5. Reflected meanings   _____

Gaining Further Understanding

Questioning Skills

Give one point for each skill used by the practitioner.

1. Expressed understanding before asking questions.   _____
2. Asked open-ended questions when appropriate.   _____
3. Asked one question at a time.   _____
4. Asked closed-ended questions when appropriate.   _____

Learning about Problem/Challenge and Situation
Give one point for each topic discussed.

Problems or Challenges

Previous attempts to solve problem   _____
History of the problem(s)   _____
Severity or intensity of the problem(s)   _____
Feelings about having the problem(s)   _____
Effects of the problem(s) on other areas (such as health, sleeping, and ability   _____
to function at school or work)

Situation

Effect of the problem on other people   _____
Available social support and strengths in the environment   _____
Interactions with family   _____
Other demands and stresses in the situation/environment   _____

Developing Deeper Understanding

Skills to Enhance Understanding
   Give one point for each skill used by the practitioner.

1. Explored the meanings of words and body language   _____
2. Explored the basis of conclusions drawn by the client   _____

PRACTICE EXERCISE 5 | DEVELOPING DEEPER UNDERSTANDING AND EXPRESSING RESPECT (*continued*)

3. Allowed silence
4. Identified strengths   _____
5. Asked questions about strengths   _____
                                                              _____

Common Mistakes or Inappropriate Responses (*subtract one point for each*)   _____

(offering advice, reassuring, offering excuses, asking leading questions, dominating through teaching, labeling, and interrogating)

Core Interpersonal Qualities
Using the scales in Appendix A, evaluate the appropriateness and effectiveness of the practitioner's expression of warmth, empathy, respect, and genuineness. On the following lines write the scores, from 1 to 5, for warmth, empathy, respect, and genuineness.

Score for warmth
Score for empathy   _____
Score for respect   _____
Score for genuineness   _____
Total score   _____
                                                              _____

EXPECTED COMPETENCIES

In this chapter, you learned to seek further and deeper understanding and clarify what clients are expressing.

You should be able to define the following word: seeking clarification.

You should now be able to:

• Give examples of questions that seek clarification and invite deeper understanding.
• Identify when allowing silence is useful.
• Give examples of identifying and exploring a pattern.

• Give examples of acknowledging strengths and positive factors.
• Give examples of questions to learn about strengths and positive factors.
• Demonstrate appropriately seeking clarification, identifying and exploring patterns, acknowledging strengths, and asking about strengths.
• Demonstrate expressing respect.

Assessing Readiness and Motivation

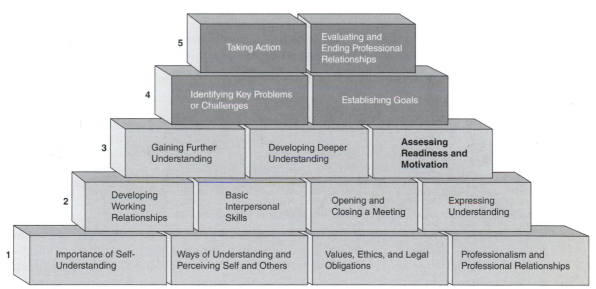

© Cengage Learning 2013

Questions to consider as you read this chapter:

- How do practitioners determine whether a client is ready to work on making changes, thinking about possibly making a change in the future, or following the suggestion of another person?
- What factors lead to strong motivation to change?
- What factors reduce motivation to change?
- What ways of thinking limit someone's ability to work on making changes?

This chapter covers practice behaviors related to assessment. *You will learn the importance of:*

- Applying two theories for assessing readiness to change
- Understanding and assessing motivation to change

Client Attributes
- Willingness to discuss readiness to do the work

After gaining deeper understanding of the client's situations, challenges, and strengths, the practitioner assesses clients' readiness to make changes and their motivation to change. As you gain further understanding of your clients, you will find that some clients agree to attending sessions with a practitioner but have no interest in making changes, some are just beginning to think about making changes, and others are ready to focus on changes. Still others have begun to solve problems and need help in taking the necessary steps to achieve their goals. Skillful practitioners explore clients' levels of readiness and motivation before deciding how to proceed in working with clients (Longshore & Teruya, 2006).

STAGES OF READINESS TO CHANGE

Based on research that studied how people modified their health habits, such as smoking cessation, weight reduction, and sobriety, Prochaska (1999) identified five stages of readiness to change. The stages-of-change theory has now been applied to many other problem areas (Alexander & Morris, 2008; Dowden & Andrews, 2000; Fishman, Taplin, Meyer, & Barlow, 2000; Kelch, 2010; Tambling & Johnson, 2008; Trevos, Quick, & Yanduli, 2000). To establish effective working relationships with clients, practitioners need to understand the readiness of the client to change and be prepared to work with the client at his/her stage of readiness. Although these stages are presented in a linear fashion, the process of change is more circular than sequential. People may move to the next stage for a while and then move back to a previous stage, possibly because of fear of making lasting changes or maybe because other demands are taking precedence. This theory of change focuses on the individual and does not take into account the environmental and situational forces that may either inhibit change or facilitate change (Hayes, Laurenceau, Feldman, Straus, & Cardaciotto, 2007).

Pre-contemplation

Pre-contemplation is the first stage of change. At this stage the person denies the problem and/or lacks understanding that the behavior is problematic. Since persons in this stage do not accept that they have a problem, naturally they do not see the need for change in their actions or feelings. They often do not see their behavior or situation as a problem that should be addressed, may not connect their problems with anything that can be changed, or may blame their problems on others. Clients in this stage sometimes see practitioners because someone else encouraged or required them to do so (Balmford, Borland, & Burney, 2008).

Examples of People in the Pre-contemplation Stage

- A person who abuses substances but, despite many arrests for driving under the influence, does not consider him/herself to have a problem that needs to be addressed.
- A gang that lives in a community with high levels of violence who believe they can continue perpetrating violence and not be personally affected.
- A husband who comes along to counseling because his wife thinks they have problems but who doesn't see any problems himself.
- A wife who wants to end the marriage and comes to counseling to ease her guilt. (Maybe she is going to counseling in order to tell herself, "I did everything I could to save the marriage, I even went to counseling.")
- A person who has had a serious health crisis and has been told to change his/her eating habits but states, "I have always eaten this way, and I am not going to change now."

Practitioners working with clients in the pre-contemplation stage should focus on raising their clients' awareness of the urgency of the issues and the pain or fear that these issues might cause. For example, the practitioner might say, "If you continue drinking, what do you think your life will be like in 5 years?" Practitioners may also attempt to engender hope that things can be different. For example, "I have worked with people who changed their eating patterns and become healthier." A person in this stage is not interested in setting goals because he/she has not accepted that he/she has problems that require making changes. While working with clients in this stage, practitioners invite clients to think about whether a change could improve their lives. Specific ways of working with people in each stage of change will be discussed in Chapter 12.

Contemplation

The second stage of readiness for change is **contemplation**. Contemplation is the stage that involves ambivalence or conflict between the pros and cons related to making a change. At this stage the individual or group is aware that there is a problem, but they are not quite ready to move ahead with making a change. In this stage people are thinking about the possible challenges and benefits of changing. It is helpful for the practitioner to discuss the client's perception advantages and disadvantages of changing. For example say, "As you think about giving up smoking mariju would be possible advantages and possible disadvanta change as a future possibility but not something to con state that "sometime" in the next six months or a year h making some changes (Principe, Marci, Glick, & Ablon, 2

Examples of Statements Made by Clients in the Contemplation Stage

- "I am just not ready to make any changes right now."
- "I have wondered if some of the problems on this team are because I am kind of dominating, but on the other hand, I think we get more accomplished because I am pushy."
- "My boss thinks I should get over my fear of making speeches, but I am just not sure if that is something I can do."
- "I keep getting sent to the principal's office for fighting, and then I can't play in the next football game. I don't like getting in trouble, but I have to stand up for myself."
- "We have talked about forming a committee to address some of the problems in this organization, but I wonder if we would really accomplish anything."

In working with clients who are at this stage, practitioners can help clients identify barriers or challenges to making changes and also strengths that will be helpful if they decide to make changes. Sometimes practitioners ask clients if there are small steps that they might consider that may lead to a greater willingness to change in the near future. In the case of a married couple who do not spend enough time together to develop a healthy relationship, the practitioner may choose to focus on the pleasure derived from the few times they are together or the joy they experienced in their relationship before they were married. Exploring these feelings may encourage the partners to think about changes they could make in order to spend more time together.

Preparation

The third stage of readiness for change is **preparation**. During this stage of change, clients are preparing to change by getting information about making changes, by taking small steps related to change, and by thinking about possible goals. Usually at this stage clients have thought about the steps necessary to achieve their goals. Often they have already made some progress and are planning to make more progress. Goals can now be set. Generally people need to be at this stage before a major change will be possible (Vito, 2010).

Examples of People in the Preparation Stage

- A person who has been told to prepare to move into a supervisory role and seeks counseling with the goal of gaining confidence in his/her ability to supervise other people.
- A task group that has decided to work on a particular problem and asks a practitioner to help them set realistic goals and develop an action plan.
- A couple who are committed to working out their problems and ask for help in learning to solve particular issues.

Working with people's readiness to change can be very challenging in the case of families and community groups since group and family members may be at different stages of change. Sometimes a loud naysayer will stop or slow down the whole process. It is then necessary to explore that person's hesitation or ambivalence about making a change. He/she is likely in either the pre-contemplation or contemplation stage. Sometimes people who are not ready to make a change will be willing to give up their resistance and allow the other group members to carry the project forward. In other situations, a person who isn't necessarily opposed to a goal but isn't willing to work to achieve the goal will choose to work on another committee or on a part of the project he/she can support.

Action

The fourth stage is the **action** stage. In the action stage, clients are ready to take specific steps and may even take steps with little or no support from the practitioner. Many people who are ready to make changes do so without seeking help. Those in the action stage may only need the practitioner's reinforcement, some new information, or help with developing plans. Clients in this stage are very rewarding to work with because they are ready to quickly set goals and take action (Katzman, 2010).

Examples of People in the Action Stage
- An obese client, when faced with life-threatening health issues, joins Weight Watchers, learns to follow the program, and loses a significant amount of weight.
- A parent, whose children have been removed from the home because the parent used harsh, abusive means of discipline, says that he/she will learn other ways to discipline, willingly goes to a parenting class, and talks with the practitioner about ways to use what he/she is learning.
- A child realizes that he/she will not be able to play on a team without earning passing grades and starts attending an after-school tutoring class in order to bring up his/her grades.
- A task group establishes a clear goal, identifies steps to achieve their goal, and talks with a practitioner about ways to work together most effectively.

If the practitioner assumes that clients are ready for action before they are really ready, the practitioner may become frustrated when there is no movement on proposed goals or when goals are hard to clarify. Clients may feel they should please the practitioner by taking steps they aren't ready to take. Because many clients are not ready to take action when they first seek the help of practitioners, it is important for practitioners to carefully assess each client's level of readiness rather than to assume that every client who comes for help is at the preparation or action stage and to proceed based on this assumption.

Maintenance

One of the most challenging stages is **maintenance**. This stage requires as much careful planning as the previous stages. The old problematic behavior was maintained because it was rewarding or comfortable. The pull to go back to the old ways is often quite strong. In order to maintain the new behaviors, clients need to develop ways to cope with temptations and to reward day-to-day successes. Sometimes clients celebrate achieving their goals without figuring out how to maintain these goals. Practitioners need to help clients explore how past successes have been maintained and develop ways to hold onto their current successes (Hanner, 2010).

Examples of Clients in the Maintenance Stage

- An organization develops more effective ways of problem-solving and plans regular meetings so potential problems can be addressed before they become bigger issues.
- An individual learns to stop procrastinating on projects and makes plans to check in with someone who will provide honest feedback about whether the problem seems to be reappearing.
- A person who has had serious problems with alcohol abuse continues to be involved with AA.
- A person has lost weight with the help of Weight Watchers and continues to attend meetings at least once a month.

Relapse/Termination

Relapse is not uncommon with any major change. In fact, relapse is so common that is sometimes identified as a stage of change that involves going back to the problematic behavior, not maintaining the goals. Clients need to be made aware of the possibility of relapse and helped to view relapse not as a failure but as a learning experience. Relapses can provide clients with the opportunity to learn ways to be increasingly successful in achieving their goals. When clients relapse they may go back to any one of the previous stages. Practitioners will have to assess which stage the clients are in as a result of their relapse and plan interventions accordingly (Cheney, McMenamin, & Shorter, 2010; Stoltz & Kern, 2007).

In Prochaska's (1999) Transtheoretical Model, *termination* is not the end of the process but rather the point in time when there is no temptation to return to the problematic behavior (Roe, Dekel, Harel, Fennig, & Fennig, 2006). As you know from your own experience, it may take a very long time before you have complete confidence that you will never go back to the problematic behavior. For many people it will always be important to stay focused on maintaining the change. For example, an ex-smoker may report occasionally wanting a cigarette years after quitting.

The stages of readiness for change are summarized in Table 11.1.

HOMEWORK EXERCISE 11.1 | STAGES OF CHANGE

Think about a situation in which you have a toothache. Identify the stage of change revealed in each of the following situations:

- After having the toothache for some time, you think, "Maybe I should do something about it, but going to the dentist is painful and expensive, so maybe I can wait."
- You actually go in for the dental appointment.
- You decide to follow the dentist's recommendations and get regular check-ups in the future.

- You think, "It's probably nothing serious and will go away on its own."
- You decide, "I am definitely going to call the dentist and make an appointment."

Now think about a change that you have made and identify each of the stages that you went through. Next, think about a current problem or issue. What stage of change are you in now for this problem or issue? What support would you need in order to move on to the next stage?

TABLE 11.1 | STAGES OF CHANGE

Stage of Change	Brief Description
Pre-contemplation	Does not consider the issue to be a problem.
Contemplation	Is thinking about the problem but ambivalent about whether to address it or not. No intention to change within the next 6 months.
Preparation	Intends to take action within the next 30 days and has taken some behavioral steps in that direction.
Action	Is ready to take action or has changed overt behavior for less than 6 months.
Maintenance	Has changed overt behavior for more than 6 months.
Termination	No temptation or desire to engage in unhealthy behavior in any situation, and 100% self-efficacy or confidence that he/she can engage in healthy behavior in all situations. Even under stress, when depressed, bored, lonely, or angry, still doesn't return to the previous habit.

ASSESSING STAGE OF CHANGE

The following questions help determine a client's stage of readiness for change (Medvene, Base, Patrick, & Wescott, 2007; Norcross et al., 1989).

- "Do you currently have a problem with ___?"
  - If the answer is "yes," the client is in the contemplation, preparation, or action stage of change.
  - If the answer is "no," the client is in the pre-contemplation or maintenance stage of change.
- If the answer to the previous question is "yes," then ask, "When do you intend to deal with the problem?"
  - If the answer is someday, the client is in the contemplation stage of change.
  - If the answer is in the next few weeks or some specific date in the near future, the client is in the preparation stage.
  - If the answer is "right now" or the client has already begun to deal with the problem, the client is in the action stage.
- If the answer to the first question is no, then ask, "What leads you to say that?"
  - If the client responds, "Because it is not a problem," the client is in the pre-contemplation stage of change.
  - If the client responds, "Because I have already dealt with that problem," the client is in the maintenance stage of change (Hanner, 2010; Prochaska, Norcross, & DiClemente, 1994).

After client statement of the problem, identify the stage of change that the client is describing to the practitioner.

- "I can't decide whether to continue in school or drop out."
- "I think the task group has reached our initial goals. What are we going to do to keep on track?"

- "Our family has done a lot of talking about all this fighting that has been happening recently. I'm tired of all the talking. Let's decide what to do to stop it."
- "My wife thinks I have a drinking problem, but I don't drink any more than many of my friends."
- "I think we have decided to work together to develop better services for our Mexican-American clients."

SOCIAL COGNITIVE THEORY

Another theory that can be used to assess readiness or ability to make changes is social cognitive theory. Social cognitive theory was developed by Bandura (1977) and originally called Social Learning Theory. This theory considers the impact of environmental, personal, and behavioral factors on readiness to change. Personal factors include everything from physical make-up and brain structure to cognitive capacity, beliefs, self-concept, goals, and emotions. Obviously, what you think and feel affects your behavior. For example, if you believe people are basically trust-worthy, you are more likely to act in a friendly manner toward them. How you act impacts personal factors. For example, if you focus on your studies and get good grades, your self-concept will be enhanced. We now know that behavior even affects brain structures (**Mathiak & Weber, 2006**). For example, studies of the brain have shown that behaviors such as being a cab driver or being the conductor of an orchestra lead to different brain structures. Of course, behavior also affects physical make-up. Think of the football player whose behavior leads to repeated knee injury.

Think about what you learned in Chapter 2 about empowerment. As people actively participate in projects that they haven't done before (behavior), their self-concept is enhanced and beliefs about their own abilities are increased (personal). Environment, as you know, includes such things as culture, family, social status, socioeconomic status, and social influences. Remember what you read in Chapter 1 about the impact of socioeconomic status on health and self-concept (personal). Personal and behavior factors impact the environment. Think about a fellow student who comes to class late, often whines and complains about the workload, and/or tries to dominate other students. That student's behavior affects the classroom environment. Consider groups of people whose goal is to improve their neighborhood (personal), who form a group to discuss ways to work together (behavior), and over time, change the neighborhood (environment). Most of us know a teenager whose rebellious behavior affected his/her family (environment). Personal, behavioral, and environmental factors interact and influence each other (Bandura, 1989; Tuvblad, Grann, & Lichtenstein, 2006).

HOMEWORK EXERCISE 11.3 | REFLECTING ON SOCIAL COGNITIVE THEORY

Identify at least one way in which the following factors interact in your life:

- personal and environmental
- environmental and behavioral
- behavioral and personal

When assessing a person's readiness or ability to make changes from the point of view of social cognitive theory, several dimensions are considered. First, does the environment support or encourage changed behavior? This may be difficult to determine. For example, one of the authors worked with a boy who was seriously disturbed. His parents were working with another practitioner. The parents said they wanted the child to get better, but every step the child took toward healthy behavior was undercut by his father.

Second, does the person believe he/she has the capacity to make the change? This belief, called **self-efficacy**, involves a person's belief in his/her ability to successfully handle a situation. Sometime clients come to practitioners wanting to make changes, but they don't believe they are capable of making the changes. Using a strengths perspective, the practitioner may choose to help clients recognize their strengths and resources. Practitioners may also work with clients to identify and take small manageable steps. As the client succeeds with taking small steps (behavior), their level of self-efficacy (personal) increases.

Third, along with believing in their capacity to make changes, clients must decide that there is more to be gained from making the change than from maintaining the current behavior. The practitioner may need to help the client evaluate the pros and cons related to changing behavior. This often involves identifying both immediate and long-term positive outcomes.

HOMEWORK EXERCISE 11.4 | ASSESSING SELF-EFFICACY

If you put self-efficacy on a scale from 1 (low) to 10 (high), what self-efficacy score would you give yourself related to getting an A in this course? A score of 10 means you have no doubts about your ability to get an A in this course. What is your self-efficacy score related to a college level calculus course? Your belief about your capacity to handle different challenges affects you in many ways. List five ways in which your belief in your capacity affects your behavior.

ASSESSING MOTIVATION TO CHANGE

In addition to assessing the client's level of readiness to change, practitioners must consider the client's level of motivation to change. The level of motivation is determined by taking into account all the factors that influence person, family, group, or organization to feel compelled to resolve an issue or problem, and those factors that influence them to maintain the status quo. Besides the personal factors discussed related to social cognitive theory, the amount of discomfort created by the problem or challenge also impacts motivation. As you know from your own experience, you only make an effort to address and resolve problems that are creating considerable discomfort. For example, remember the earlier homework exercise on a toothache. Most people would not take action for a minor ache that didn't last long. However, they would take action if the pain continued.

Environmental factors also influence motivation. Common environmental pressures include such things as peer group pressure, family encouragement or discouragement, court orders (such as steps required to regain custody of children), and societal pressure such as smoke-free workplaces.

HOMEWORK EXERCISE 11.5 | MOTIVATION FOR CHANGE

Think of a time when you thought you ought to make a change in one of your habits. What factors motivated you to make the change? What factors reduced your energy, enthusiasm, or motivation to make the change?

The type of relationship that the client has with the practitioner affects motivation. If clients experience practitioners as being genuine, providing regular feedback, having positive regard, and being focused on their issues, motivation tends to increase. If practitioners are aware that there is tension or a breakdown in their collaboration with clients, then addressing this problem non-defensively and making the necessary adjustments in their behavior enhances the motivation for change. In order to maintain motivation, it is important to not only notice possible problems in the relationship between the client and practitioner, but also to regularly ask for feedback from clients. Here are a few questions that practitioners can use (Norcross, 2007):

• "Would you tell me your thoughts about the progress you are making?"
• "Are you satisfied with the progress you are making?"
• "Are you satisfied with the way we are working together?"
• "How are you experiencing your relationship with me?"

Of course, if the client is dissatisfied in some way, it is important to explore the problem and work with the client to resolve it.

Discounting

An important step in determining a client's motivation to change is to assess whether the client is discounting the problem. **Discounting** is a cognitive distortion that allows individuals to avoid dealing with a problem by denying its existence or minimizing its significance (Forbes, Schmader, & Allen 2007; Melor & Sigmund, 1975). Motivation can be seriously limited by discounting. Individuals, couples, families, groups, and organizations all use discounting.

There are four levels of discounting. The most destructive type of discounting is thinking that there is no problem or denying that a problem exists. Examples of this type of discounting include an individual who thinks being 50 pounds overweight is not a problem, a family that believes disciplining children by hitting them with a belt isn't a problem, a task group that thinks the fact that they haven't started working on an assignment that is due in a few days is not a problem, and a business that thinks the fact that their product isn't completely safe is not a problem.

The next level of discounting involves thinking the problem is not significant but at least realizing it exists. This level is less serious but still prevents action toward solving the problem. Using the same examples, the overweight person could accept being 50 pounds overweight as a problem but not a serious one. The family might say that some people see hitting children with a belt as a problem, but it is not something for them to be concerned about because it doesn't happen very often, and besides their family has always disciplined in this way. The task group could say that getting started late is a problem but not a serious one because students work on things at the last minute all the time and they still get them done. The business could say that their product isn't completely safe but most people are not negatively affected so it's not important to change it.

There is no motivation to change a situation unless it is seen as a problem causing painful consequences and there is a belief that something can be changed to alleviate these consequences. Discounting the solvability of a problem, the next level of discounting, is not as serious as discounting the existence or the seriousness of the problem, but it still blocks motivation to make changes. At this level of discounting, the individual might say being 50 pounds overweight is a serious problem, but everyone in the family is overweight and there is nothing that can be done about it. The family recognizes that disciplining the children by hitting them with a belt is considered a serious problem by many people in their community, but they also believe that it is the only effective way to make their children behave. The task group could say, "We wanted to get a good grade on this project and knew that starting on it so late may mean that won't be possible, but everyone was too busy. We just couldn't do it any other way." The business could say that selling a product that is unsafe is taking a risk, but it is a profitable product and they don't know any way to improve its safety.

At the next level of discounting, the individual or group realizes that others have changed this behavior or situation, but they do not think they can change. The individual might state, "I am concerned about being overweight and I know that my friend lost weight recently, but losing weight isn't something I can do." The family could say, "We haven't been able to discipline our children except by hitting them, but our neighbors took a parenting course and learned several new ways to discipline their children." The task group might state, "For this assignment we weren't able to start working until right before the project was due, but some of the other groups in class somehow found enough time to work together before the project was due and they got a better grade than we did." The business might say, "We haven't found any way to be profitable except by continuing to sell an unsafe product, but there are other similar companies who have found alternative safe and profitable products." In each case, change is only seen as possible for others.

Clients who are discounting their ability to solve the problem may be at the contemplation level of readiness to change. They are beginning to think that the problem is solvable and may be wondering if they could solve the problem.

Think about what would happen if you just received a low grade on a paper. You might handle this painful situation by denying the problem: "It's nothing. Grades don't matter." Or you might minimize the significance: "One low grade isn't important." You could decide that nothing could be done about the problem: "That instructor is just a tough grader." Or maybe the problem could be solved, but not by you: "I know some people have gotten better grades after talking to the instructor about his/her expectations, but I can't go and talk to him/her. I am just too scared."

If a practitioner determines that clients are discounting at any level, the first step is to help them get to the point of accepting that the problem exists, is serious, and is solvable by the client. This process of working through the levels of discounting might take considerable time. Since most of us are uncomfortable with change, discounting to avoid facing problems is quite common. Sometimes clients avoid the pain of one set of problems with addictions or other avoidance patterns. For example, a soldier who was in violent situations during combat and now has regular nightmares and flashbacks may become addicted to alcohol or drugs to avoid the pain related to his/her memories. Discounting can be subtle. If practitioners are not careful, they can find themselves convinced that clients are correct in their perceptions. This is especially true if the practitioner has discounted a similar problem in his/her own life.

Some areas to consider when assessing discounting include the following:

- Does the client acknowledge that a problem exists?
- Does the client identify the problem as important or significant?
- Does the client believe that this type of problem can be solved?
- Does the client believe that he/she could possibly solve this problem?

HOMEWORK EXERCISE 11.6 | DISCOUNTING

Think of a problem in your life that you or someone close to you have been discounting. Discuss this situation with a partner. Talk about ways you or someone else have avoided dealing with the problem. Note how the significance of the problem may have been minimized, how you or the other person underestimated your personal ability to solve the problem, or denied that the problem could be solved. Was there a time when you denied the existence of the problem and found ways to avoid feeling the pain that problem was causing you?

OTHER FACTORS THAT INFLUENCE MOTIVATION TO CHANGE
Strengths, Capacity, and Resources

In addition to recognizing a problem and believing that change is possible, the client's capacity, resources, and strengths also have significant effects on the level of motivation to change. In Chapter 10 you learned to focus on positive factors and strengths in the client and the client's environment. Clients who have many personal strengths, good social support, and adequate resources tend to be more motivated than those with more limited strengths, social support, and resources.

Remember what you learned about resilience in Chapter 2. Resilience is an important strength. Clients who are more resilient are likely to be more motivated because they know from previous experience that they are able to cope with challenges. For example, think about the possible differences in motivation in the following two female clients. Both clients came to the agency with concerns about their adolescent sons who had begun to perform poorly in school. Both clients have full-time jobs. Client A is married, is active in her church, lives near her family, and earns an adequate income. She has a positive outlook on life and believes that other people are helpful. As a teenager she was in a serious automobile accident and was hospitalized for 2 weeks with multiple broken bones. As she worked through that trauma, she realized how resilient she could be. Remember back to what you read in Chapter 2 about empowerment related to dealing with challenges. By facing the challenges related to the accident, she also developed considerable personal strength. Client B is a single mother who recently moved to town and has a poverty-level income. Because of the many challenges she is facing, she is discouraged about her life and does not have much confidence in the goodwill of other people. It is fairly easy to guess that client A, with good support, resources, and resilience, may have more energy or motivation available to focus on how to best help her son than does client B.

HOMEWORK EXERCISE 11.7 | RELATIONSHIP OF STRENGTHS, CAPACITY, AND RESOURCES TO MOTIVATION

Talk to someone in your class about a time when your strengths, resources, and capacities enhanced your motivation to solve a problem. For example, think of a simple problem like an oil leak in your car. You will probably be more motivated to solve the problem if you have such resources as: a trusted mechanic, money to pay for the repair, and time to take the car in. Write a brief description of a problem you have had and a list of at least ten positive factors, strengths, resources, and capacities that enhanced your motivation to solve the problem. Also add a sentence about how solving the problem enhanced your sense of empowerment (hint: using the previous example, if this is the first car the person has maintained on his/her own, finding out that they could take care of repairs will enhance his/her capacity to manage independently).

Level of Stress and Demands

As you learned in Chapter 1, high levels of stress and demands affect all areas of your life. In Chapter 9 you learned about the importance of assessing levels of stress and demands. The level of stress and demands in a person's life also affects motivation. For example, if a student faces numerous assignments that are due at the same time that she is taking final exams, she might experience the demands as too high. If that student learned about a problem in her life, such as her mother being diagnosed with cancer, she might feel overwhelmed and unable to deal with all the demands. After getting past exam week and turning in her papers, the student would feel much less stress and would now be more motivated and able to deal with her feelings about her mother's illness. Clients who have faced extensive stress in the last year and have high demands in their current lives often have more trouble staying motivated to work on problems that go beyond dealing with the stress and demands they face on a daily basis.

Let's go back to Clients A and B who were discussed previously. We know that Client B recently moved to this area and that moving is very stressful. What if we found out that she had gotten divorced in the last year and, because of the divorce, her financial situation changed and now she has to work full-time for the first time in many years? Client A has not experienced significant stress in the last year. Empathizing with Client B, you might guess that the additional problem of her son not doing well in school could make her feel overwhelmed and unable to cope. She might need to focus on her feelings about the changes in her life before she would have adequate energy and motivation to work with her son.

HOMEWORK EXERCISE 11.8 | IMPACT OF STRESS AND DEMANDS ON MOTIVATION

Think of a time in your life when you faced high levels of stress and multiple demands. What if another problem was added, such as finding out that your partner was having an affair. At that point, the stress and demands might seem beyond your coping skills. What would you do? Would your motivation to get high grades decrease? Would you act in ways that are atypical for you, such as withdrawing, losing your temper over small things, or being irritable with your friends?

Hope

While high levels of stress and limited resources may weaken motivation, hope can serve to increase motivation and is critical to all practitioner-client relationships. After acknowledging clients' pain, practitioners help clients feel hopeful that change is possible.

Hope is created by many experiences. Think back to what you learned about worldview constructs in the constructivist section of Chapter 2. People who believe that they have the power and capacity to change, that other people will help them, and/or that they can succeed in the world are likely to be hopeful. As you remember, a sense of self-efficacy includes a belief in one's ability to make a change or a sense of capability to bring about a desired effect. Self-efficacy is an important element of hope (Bandura, 1989; Bodenheimer, Lorig, Holman, & Grumbach, 2002; Valle, Huebner, & Suldo, 2006). Another element of hope is having an **internal locus of control**. A person with an internal locus of control believes that his/her behavior will produce desired changes. An example of internal locus of control would be a student who says, "I am determined to get a good grade in this class. If I don't understand the professor's explanation, I am going to work with a group of other students in the class to understand the concepts and do well in the course." In contrast, a person with an **external locus of control** believes that there is no connection between his/her behavior and the desired outcome (Beyeback, Morejon, Palenzuela, & Rodriguez-Arias, 1996; Ng, Sorensen, & Eby, 2006). An example of external locus of control would be a student who says, "The professor never explains things clearly so there's no way I can do well in this class."

Various life experiences influence an individual's sense of hope. Martin Luther King, Jr., in his well-known speech "I Have a Dream," engendered hope in a community of people who had lost hope as a result of oppression. Others may have lost hope due to illness, poverty, discrimination, or continued experiences of rejection or failure. Considerable support from others may be needed to renew hope. Many clients come to practitioners because they cannot see any way to solve their problems. They feel hopeless and stuck. When hope is renewed, it provides energy to help them make changes.

Practitioners can help clients feel more hopeful. Practitioners bring their previous experience, education, and beliefs about change to any meeting with clients. When change is not as quick or easy as clients want, practitioners provide support and encouragement that change is possible. Mahoney (2003) calls those working in the helping professions "socially sanctioned protectors of hope" (p. 196). Without hope, practitioners may become discouraged and cynical as a result of continued work with difficult and painful situations. However, developing a positive future vision does not mean that practitioners gloss over pain or offer false reassurance of quick and easy solutions to problems (Murphy & Dillon, 2003). After practitioners have listened to and understood the client's pain and situation and have a relationship based on empathic understanding, the practitioner can focus on the potential within the person or the situation to help the client feel hopeful. Maintaining hope in the face of difficult problems is an important aspect of being an effective practitioner (Beresford, Croft, & Adshead, 2008; Hanna, 2002).

Another element of hope is the **placebo effect**. The placebo effect is the positive effect which occurs because of a person's belief in the intervention. Research on counseling and medicine consistently shows that when people believe that something will help them, it often is helpful. In medical research, a high percent of improvement has been shown to be due to the placebo effect (Cho, 2005; Kraemer, 2006; Wylie, 1996). In counseling situations, studies have demonstrated that clients who expect therapy to be successful experience more gains (Frank & Frank, 1991; Hill, 2006; Kim, Ng, & Ahn, 2005). Practitioners' belief in the efficacy of their methods has a powerful effect on clients' beliefs in these methods (Anderson et al., 2009; Wampold, 2001).

In situations when the client does not have positive expectations and is feeling discouraged about the possibilities for change, the practitioner can enhance hope by focusing on each small improvement made by the client. Another way to enhance hope is by focusing on what the future will be like after the problems have been solved. "The simple act of imagining a different future can free clients from a hopeless perspective" (Butler & Powers, 1996, p. 231). In studies of what clients identify as helpful, 58% reported that *acquiring hope* was important (Beresford, Croft, & Adshead, 2008; Murphy, Cramer, & Lillie, 1984; Steinglass, Bennet, & Wolin, 1987).

Let's go back to Clients A and B and add hope into the equation. We know that Client B has limited social support and resources and a heavy burden of stress and demands in her life. What if she is also feeling hopeless and says, "You know, my son has always had trouble in school. I never believed he'd be able to go all the way through high school." This low level of hope will further decrease her motivation. If the same client said, "My son is very intelligent. He has always been a good student. These problems started after we moved and he enrolled in this new school. I think there have just been too many changes in the last year for all of us." What level of hope does that statement indicate?

Below are some areas to consider when assessing levels of hope:

- The client's belief that he/she may be able to make needed changes
- Successes the client has had in resolving past challenges
- The client's belief in the practitioner's ability to help
- The client's belief in his or her ability to be effective, to reach goals, and/or to take action

---

HOMEWORK EXERCISE 11.9 | UNDERSTANDING THE EFFECT OF HOPE

Think of a time when you had a problem and felt confident and hopeful that you could resolve it. What was that experience like for you? What role do you believe that your hope for success played in your ability to solve the problem?

Now think of a time when you had a problem and felt hopeless about getting it solved. What was

that experience like for you? What role do you believe that your sense of hopelessness played in your ability to solve or not solve the problem? What if you had talked to someone who told you they had helped someone with a similar problem before and felt confident that they could help you? How would that have affected your level of hope?

CASE | ## CASE, PART 3: SECOND MEETING WITH HIDEKO

You are now ready to move ahead with assessing the stage of change and motivation in relation to Hideko.

VIVIANA: "We covered quite a bit of information in our first meeting. As you have thought about what we discussed, what are your thoughts about that meeting?"

HIDEKO: "Well, it was kind of a relief to tell someone about what is happening. I don't say much about all of this to many people. I don't want to complain about my mother. I know she is often in pain and feels very discouraged and depressed about this whole situation."

VIVIANA: "After all that your mother has been through, I can imagine she feels quite discouraged. Tell me more about the ways that you help your mother."

HIDEKO: "Well, I live at home so I can be around to help her. Sometimes we have nurses and aides to help, but that is expensive and my father hates to spend the money. Mother doesn't like having strangers in the house. I attend to her bowel and bladder care twice

a day. Dad helps sometimes, but he gets impatient and is often hurried. He is gone sometimes, too. He has to travel some for work. Mother doesn't like my brother to help with that kind of thing so it's my job most of the time. Because I am the daughter, my father and my brother expect me to take care of her. I am the one who usually takes her to the doctor or ER. Sometimes I am needed to translate for her as English is her second language. Of course, she often gets very painful bladder infections. You know how it is—my brother is the favored child so it is assumed that I will handle things."

VIVIANA: "So even though you are living at home and doing a lot to help, your brother is the favored child. That sounds difficult to me."

HIDEKO: "Oh, you get used to it. It has always been that way. I do something like getting very good grades and they hardly notice, and he does something and it is a big deal. I help every day and it is expected. He gets the groceries and they think it is wonderful. I mean I am glad that he helps. He has even taken her to the doctor a few times, but the burden is on me.

| CASE | **CASE, PART 3: SECOND MEETING WITH HIDEKO** (*continued*) |

My dad is busy supporting the family. As he says, he has to pay for everything, and it is his insurance that covers most of her medical bills."

VIVIANA: "Besides having so much to do, it sounds like you are burdened by feeling like your parents don't appreciate what you are doing. Is that right?"

HIDEKO: "Well, I feel that way sometimes, but then I feel guilty. They raised me and put me through college. I should be willing to help them. I am willing to help. Sometimes my mother is difficult. She can be pretty demanding and I hate it when she gets so depressed that she starts to cry, but I love her, too. Sometimes we still have fun. I can take her out in the wheelchair to go shopping or just for a ride to get her outside a bit. And she is a great cook. We have made some adaptations to the kitchen, so sometimes she is able to help with some of the cooking. My brother lives nearby and he often comes over for dinner."

VIVIANA: "So you are kind of torn between feeling it is your duty to help and also feeling unappreciated and like it is just too much to handle, right?"

HIDEKO: "Yes, I guess that is about right. It was easier when I had some time with my boyfriend. That was my escape. Maybe we could have stayed together, but my parents didn't approve of him. Besides not being Japanese, he doesn't have a graduate degree. I sometimes wonder if they will ever think anyone is good enough for me. Maybe they just want me to stay home and take care of them."

VIVIANA: "Having some breaks to be with your boyfriend must have been very helpful."

HIDEKO: "Yes, I just haven't been able to get back on track since he isn't in my life anymore."

VIVIANA: "It sounds like you are really sad and discouraged."

HIDEKO: "I just wish I could stop thinking about him so much. It makes me sad and then I get discouraged and don't feel like doing anything. I know lots of people break-up. It shouldn't be such a big deal. I just want to get back to being sure I do well in graduate school."

VIVIANA: "I am glad you decided to come in. We can work together to find ways for you to figure out how to deal with these challenges. We are about out of time for today. In our next meeting, let's spend some time talking about the goals you want to achieve. Does that sound okay to you?"

HIDEKO: "Yes, I will be thinking about my goals."

Questions

1. What new facts have you learned?
2. What are your current impressions or hunches about the case?
3. What additional information do you need prior to your next meeting with this client?
4. What did the practitioner do well in this session?
5. What, if any, mistakes did the practitioner make?
6. Identify the ways that the practitioner used skills to enhance understanding. What are additional ways that the practitioner could have enhanced understanding? Give specific examples of what the practitioner could have said.

Role play—The person in the role of Hideko will use the information you have to play the role. The practitioner should use expressing understanding, gaining further information, and developing deeper understanding skills. The practitioner should also assess Hideko's stage of change and level of motivation.

7. What two problems do you think Hideko is most concerned about?
8. Review what you learned in this chapter about assessing the client's stage of change. What is this client's stage of change? What information do you have to support your evaluation regarding the stage of change? What further exploration do you need to confirm that the client is in this stage of change?
9. Using the social cognitive theory, discuss the interaction between personal factors, environmental factors, and behavioral factors related to this client. How do you think these factors impact her readiness to change?
10. Discuss the client's level of motivation. What else would you want to explore to further determine level of motivation?
11. What are your hunches about possible discounting that the client may be doing? Define the level of discounting.
12. What strengths and resources did the practitioner in the role play identify in the client? What might the practitioner have said to further

(continued)

CASE | **CASE, PART 3: SECOND MEETING WITH HIDEKO** (*continued*)

highlight the client's strengths? What questions should the practitioner in the role play ask to further explore strengths?

13. What else have you learned about level of stress and demands that might be impacting level of motivation?

14. What do you believe is the client's level of hope? What information do you have to support that belief?

15. What did the practitioner in the role play say that might help Hideko believe that she could help her?

EXPECTED COMPETENCIES

In this chapter you have learned about assessing readiness to work on problems, and factors than influence motivation to change.

You should be able to define the following: the transtheoretical stages (pre-contemplation, contemplation, preparation, action, maintenance, and relapse/termination), social cognitive theory, self-efficacy, discounting, internal locus of control, external locus of control, and the placebo effect.

You should now be able to:

• Give an example of each of the stages of readiness for change identified by Prochaska.
• Explain the social cognitive theory way of assessing capacity to change.
• Give an example of a statement related to each of the four levels of discounting.
• Identify factors that influence motivation.
• Name two ways in which practitioners can invite hope in clients.

DEFINING THE FOCUS

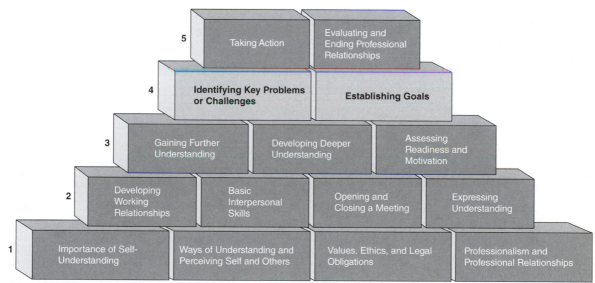

5 Taking Action	Evaluating and Ending Professional Relationships	
4 Identifying Key Problems or Challenges	Establishing Goals	
3 Gaining Further Understanding	Developing Deeper Understanding	Assessing Readiness and Motivation
2 Developing Working Relationships	Basic Interpersonal Skills	Opening and Closing a Meeting / Expressing Understanding
1 Importance of Self-Understanding	Ways of Understanding and Perceiving Self and Others	Values, Ethics, and Legal Obligations / Professionalism and Professional Relationships

© Cengage Learning 2013

In this section we address ways to clarify client issues. This is one of the most challenging stages for most new practitioners. Without an agreed upon understanding of problems and goals, clients are not likely to make changes. In Chapter 12, Identifying Key Problems or Challenges, you will learn skills to help clients identify the problems they are ready and motivated to work on. In Chapter 13, Establishing Goals, we discuss practitioner tasks that encourage clients to create general goals as well as goals that are *M*easurable, *A*ttainable, *P*ositive, and *S*pecific (MAPS). With goals that meet the MAPS criteria, clients and practitioners can easily evaluate ongoing progress.

IDENTIFYING KEY PROBLEMS OR CHALLENGES

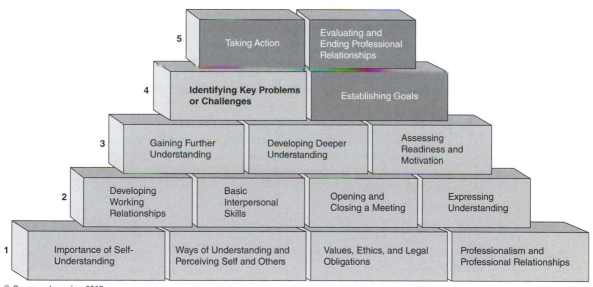

5 — Taking Action | Evaluating and Ending Professional Relationships

4 — **Identifying Key Problems or Challenges** | Establishing Goals

3 — Gaining Further Understanding | Developing Deeper Understanding | Assessing Readiness and Motivation

2 — Developing Working Relationships | Basic Interpersonal Skills | Opening and Closing a Meeting | Expressing Understanding

1 — Importance of Self-Understanding | Ways of Understanding and Perceiving Self and Others | Values, Ethics, and Legal Obligations | Professionalism and Professional Relationships

© Cengage Learning 2013

Questions to consider as you read this chapter:

- How can practitioners decide which interventions to use based on the clients' stage of change?
- What can practitioners do when clients are in a crisis situation?
- What can practitioners do when clients seem resistant to change?

This chapter covers practice behaviors related to identifying key problems or challenges. *You will learn the importance of:*

- Working collaboratively with clients to define the challenges or problems to be worked on
- Selecting and using interventions that are appropriate to the clients' stage of change

Client Attributes

- Willingness to move beyond blaming and to identify specific challenges to work on

After assessing the client's level of readiness and motivation, practitioners help clients identify their primary challenges or the challenges they want to focus on at this time. The process of helping a client move from statements such as "My life is just falling apart" or "This team will never be able to accomplish anything" to statements that are specific and clear can be difficult. Problem identification requires all the skills you have learned so far plus additional skills introduced in this chapter. For clients, the process of identifying the problems they are ready to work on may take courage. As we all know from our experience, looking honestly at our role in problems takes considerable strength.

UNDERSTANDING THE CLIENT'S PROBLEMS

Some clients come to a practitioner with a clear idea of the problem(s) they are ready to focus on. For example, the client may be an individual or a family working with a hospital social worker to find appropriate placement for an elderly parent who needs ongoing medical care. A child may request to work with a school counselor due to his frustration with getting several low grades in math. An agency team may be required to work together to figure out how to cut $10,000 from the budget. A neighborhood that is becoming so rundown that property values are falling may decide they must do something to turn the trend around. Even in situations where the problem seems obvious and clear, a skilled practitioner will fully explore the issues, knowing that there may be many other problems that also need attention in order to solve the problem identified by the client. To follow up on the example of the child who got low grades in math, exploration might reveal that his dad, who always encouraged him in math and is very good at math, separated from the family and moved out of town. Now the child rarely sees his father. If the practitioner accepted the low grades in arithmetic as the only problem to address, he/she might refer the child to a female math tutor. This intervention might not be helpful because the child's problem of missing the support and encouragement of his father would not be addressed.

Learning to help clients identify problems or challenges to be worked on can be a complicated process. To make it easier to conceptualize how to move from hearing clients discuss their problems to clearly identifying the problems and goals, it might be helpful for you to think through a process that may be more familiar, such as dealing with a leaky roof.

Imagine you are working for a home repair company. A couple comes to you complaining that their roof is leaking and asks you to fix the problem. There are a number of steps to take to determine exactly what you can and will do to help the couple with their problem. As you are exploring the problem, you should also be developing a relationship with the couple. Without some sense of trust and connection, the potential customers might go to another repair company. The problem exploration will probably include determining the answers to the following questions:

- What is the extent of the problem?
- How is the problem affecting the structure of the house and those who live in it?
- How long has the problem been in existence?
- How frequently does the roof leak, and how much water comes in?
- What has caused the problem?
  - Is it due to neighbors throwing rocks and breaking the roofing material so that even if it is fixed the neighbors may destroy the repairs?
  - Is it due to a lack of maintenance or the number of years since the roof was last repaired?
  - Is it a superficial problem or one that indicates that the entire roof needs to be replaced?
- How urgent is it that the problem be solved?
- Could the leak be an indication that the foundation is unsound and the entire house is sinking and shifting so that even if the roof is repaired, it will likely leak again?

As an experienced home repair consultant or roofer, you must also consider such things as the homeowners' financial and time constraints. You should consider the homeowners' ability to deal with the disruption of repairs as well as costs. Some homeowners do not have the money to do any repairs and must learn to live with the leak. It may be that no amount of money will fix the roof for long, and the homeowners will have to decide how they want to respond to this news. It may be that the homeowners have the money to do the repairs but not the desire to do a thorough repair job, or they may not be ready to do the whole repair at this time. Rather than moving forward, the people with the leak may decide to do nothing or may just postpone any changes due to a lack of motivation to fix the problem now since the rainy season is almost over. As discussed in the last chapter, the practitioner, like the roofer, needs to fully explore the clients' readiness to make changes and work with what the client is ready to do. If the people with the leaky roof told you that all they were ready to do was put a piece of plastic over the hole in the roof, you might say that in your professional opinion that would only be a temporary fix; however, you could not make the homeowners replace the roof.

To continue this leaky roof scenario, you would also need to think about possible goals and/or other solutions to the problem. You might think that the most appropriate goal would be to rework the foundation of the house so that it provides more support for the walls and subsequently, the roof. You might recommend a new roof if the foundation is strong. You would know that, if necessary, the homeowners could do as little as putting a piece of plastic over the hole in the roof. You could talk with the homeowners about the possible goals, but it is up to the people with the leaky roof to decide which goal is appropriate for them. The practitioner, like the roofer, must fully explore the problem and the clients' readiness to make changes before talking with the clients about possible goals. Once the decision has been made about which goal is appropriate at this time, the roofer or practitioner will discuss the process the homeowners or clients will use to achieve the goal and complete the work. An agreement is reached and a contract is signed.

The process of coming to an agreement about problems and goals involves doing a thoughtful and complete assessment. When clients do not take steps to solve the problem and reach their goals, it may be that the practitioner is focusing on a problem that is not important to the client or one the client is not yet ready to solve. Think back to what you learned in Chapter 11 about readiness to solve problems and levels of motivation. Using our roofing example, the homeowners may be in the contemplation stage and thinking about the pros and cons of solving the problem, but not yet in the action phase and ready to solve the roof problem. The first problem the homeowners might need to address is the fact that they spend more money than they make and therefore have no extra money to deal with emergencies like the roof leaking. The problem could be that the homeowners are stuck in low-paying jobs and just cannot get ahead financially until they work on the problem of having low-paying jobs. Many clients (or people who need roof repairs) do not seek professional help until the problems in their life have persisted for some time and seem overwhelming to them. Practitioners need to carefully explore all aspects of the problems that are troubling their clients.

DEALING WITH CRISIS

In most client situations, there is plenty of time to fully understand the problems and situation. However, in a crisis situation, the practitioner may have to take action quickly without fully exploring the problems. A crisis situation exists anytime the immediate problems are so serious that the individuals involved are in shock and/or are unable to cope with the situation. Crisis situations include such things as interpersonal violence (murder, rape, or bombings), major natural disasters (floods, tornados, fires, or hurricanes) or some forms of personal loss (unexpected death of a family member, or sudden abandonment by a significant other). At a time of crisis, practitioners need to focus on dealing with the immediate needs of those involved. After assessing the level of the crisis, the practitioner needs to determine the most effective immediate response. When clients are in shock or are unable to cope, the practitioner may need to be much more directive than usual. If the practitioner has no training in dealing with crisis or the client needs the services of another professional such as a police officer, physician, or a clergy person, the practitioner needs to refer the client to the appropriate professional. When the crisis situation is defused, clients will then be able to cope with the remaining challenges. In the future, you will want to learn more about crisis intervention and the numerous ways crises can be handled. For now, here are a few guidelines:

- Stay calm. Your ability to acknowledge the crisis and offer hope and help are essential. Slow breathing will help you stay calm. You should also remind yourself that you can seek the help of your supervisor or other professionals.
- The safety of everyone involved is your first priority. Creating that safety is your first task. You may need to seek the help of others such as your supervisor, other practitioners, or other professionals.
- At times of crisis it is particularly important to use all the skills you have learned so far: listen carefully, ask questions for clarification, and be empathetic and warm.

HOMEWORK EXERCISE 12.1 | DEALING WITH CRISIS SITUATIONS

Describe a time when you or someone you know experienced a crisis. What helped most in resolving the situation? How did others help? What happened once the crisis was over? Sometimes unresolved feelings from our own personal crises can hinder our ability to handle the crises faced by our clients. What unresolved crises from your life might hinder your ability to effectively help a client facing a similar crisis?

In every situation except a crisis, practitioners and clients need to fully explore person, problem, and situation and assess stage of change and motivation before defining the focus of their work together. Several new skills will be useful in this phase of work with clients. We will introduce these new skills by looking at the stages of change in which these skills are most helpful; however, you will find many other times when these skills are useful.

WORKING WITH CLIENTS IN THE PRE-CONTEMPLATION STAGE

Clients in the pre-contemplation stage do not see any need to make a change. They do not perceive their behaviors or feelings as problems. Practitioners working with clients in the pre-contemplation stage should focus on raising their awareness of the issues and the pain and fear that these issues might be causing. Practitioners may also attempt to engender the hope that things can be different. For clients in the pre-contemplation stage, practitioners work to help clients move toward contemplating that a change would improve their lives.

Blaming Others for the Problem

Sometimes people in the pre-contemplation stage begin the process of working with a practitioner by seeing the problems as belonging to or caused by someone else. When clients blame others for their problems, it is difficult to identify problems that they want to address. They stay focused on wishing they could change the behavior of others. When clients believe their problems are the fault of others, they may not believe that there are changes that they can make.

If they are blaming others, clients may identify problems by making statements like these:

"My boss doesn't support me."

"My husband doesn't communicate with me, and he drinks too much."

"The Child Protective Service worker is unfair to me."

"The judge threw the book at me."

If the client is a family, they may identify the problem as difficult in-laws, the high crime rate in the neighborhood, or prejudiced teachers at their children's school. If the client is a group of teenage boys referred to counseling by the probation department, they might identify the problem as laws that are too harsh, a "mean" probation officer, or someone "out to get them." If the client is a neighborhood group, they might see the problem as the city failing to spend any money on their neighborhood, limited jobs because of businesses moving out, or neighbors leaving junk in their yards.

The challenge for the practitioner is to listen empathically to the clients' narrative, explore and express understanding of the client's challenges, and encourage clients to realize that they only have control over themselves. Moving the focus from something clients cannot change to something the client can change gives clients the opportunity to effectively make changes. As we all have experienced, complaining about someone else's behavior can continue indefinitely without resulting in any changes in the other person's behavior. When practitioners focus on what their clients can do, they are not denying the existence of problems beyond their clients' control. The practitioner should express empathetic understanding of how difficult the situation is for the client. Hopefully clients will eventually be willing to work on the aspects of the problems that are within their control to change. Clients can learn to communicate effectively and assertively and invite others to make changes, but their work needs to focus on what they want to change about themselves.

Examples of Blaming Others for Problems and Ways to Respond

- If the client states that her boss is unfair to her, the practitioner might help the client see her part of the problem as her inability to figure out what she can do to be treated more fairly.
- If clients state that the problem is the city's failure to adequately maintain their neighborhood, the practitioner might help the clients to see their part of the problem as their lack of information about how to effectively lobby for services.

In both of the above examples, the practitioner is not denying that there is an external problem (the boss is unfair or the city is neglectful), rather, he/she is inviting the client to think about an aspect of the problem that the client has control over and can do something constructive to solve.

- If a mother is upset because her son is doing poorly in school and wants to make him bring up his grades, the practitioner will accept this as a valid concern and work with the mother to figure out what she wants to change about herself. The mother may be focusing too much on what the child is not doing or may not have encouraged him. She may not have discussed the problem with his teachers. The practitioner might want to work with the mother and son together or even with the whole family.

- If the client is a young single mother of three children who states that she doesn't have enough money for food and housing even though she works full time, the practitioner can work with her on her desire for more income so that she can better provide for her family and can tell her about whatever additional resources might be available to help her provide for her family. Many of us might say that part of the problem is the unavailability of adequate low-cost housing and the fact that the minimum wage is too low to support a family. However, in working with this particular client, our focus would be on the problem of helping her secure adequate housing and food for her family.

HOMEWORK EXERCISE 12.2 | BLAMING OTHERS FOR PROBLEMS

Seeing problems that others have is much easier than identifying and working on our own part of the problem. Think of some problem that you have (or have had) that involves at least one other person. If you are like most of us, you might have blamed the other person for the problem. Striving to be as honest as possible, identify your part of the problem or the aspect of the problem that you are willing to consider addressing. What might you change to contribute to the solution to the problem?

One method that can help clients to accomplish the various tasks required to move from one stage of readiness to the next stage is **motivational interviewing** (Miller & Moyers, 2006; Miller & Rollnick, 2002). Motivational interviewing is client-centered counseling that helps clients increase motivation by assisting them in exploring and resolving ambivalence about making changes. This type of interviewing is particularly useful in the early stages of change. Motivational interviewing involves four skills: rolling with resistance, identifying discrepancies, expressing empathy, and supporting self-efficacy. Rolling with resistance and identifying discrepancies are often helpful when working with clients in the pre-contemplation stage of client change.

Rolling with Resistance

Clients in the pre-contemplation stage have often been considered resistant because they are not ready to deal with problems identified by others as important. Pushing these clients to accept another person's view of the problem often strengthens their perspective rather than changing it. **Rolling with resistance** is a motivational interviewing strategy based on the assumption that clients have valid insights and ideas about their situation. With this technique, arguments for change are avoided. Instead, the practitioner expresses understanding of the client's viewpoint and asks the client what changes, if any, he/she wants to make.

Rather than opposing resistance, practitioners focus on accepting and understanding the client's point of view and indicate their willingness to work on the problem identified by the client. For clients in the pre-contemplation stage, the task may be helping the client decide whether a particular situation is a problem or not. When working with a teen who has been sent to the practitioner by his parents because he is not spending enough time studying, the practitioner might say, "I can see that you are having trouble deciding between hanging out with your friends and spending time studying. Sometimes it's hard to see the value of doing something that you don't particularly want to do. Is there any part of your parent's position about studying that makes sense to you?" A woman with two DUIs may say "My husband thinks I have a problem with drinking because I've gotten two DUIs, but since I only drink too much occasionally, I know I can control it, so it's not an issue." The practitioner might say, "I understand you don't think your drinking is a problem you need to work on. I am guessing that having two DUIs is troubling to you. What do you think would happen if you got a third DUI?" When working with a family who has been told they must make their 14 year old child go to school every day, the practitioner might say, "It sounds like you are really struggling with making enough money to pay your bills. I can see how also trying to figure out a way to be at home in the morning when your daughter should be leaving for school seems like too much to do. Is there some aspect of the problem with your daughter that you are particularly concerned about?" In the previous examples, the practitioner is looking for what part of the situation the client may be willing to work on.

HOMEWORK EXERCISE 12.3 | ROLLING WITH RESISTANCE

Think of a time in your life when you tried to convince someone to make a change he/she was resistant to make. For example, if a friend or partner said, "I don't care how much money I owe. I am going to get this great new car." You might have responded by saying, "Maybe you should wait until you have gotten yourself out of debt before getting a new car." What are your guesses about what the other person might say? Often when you push against resistance, the other person pushes back by making his/her position even stronger. In the above example, if you had said, "It sounds like you really want the new car but are also a bit concerned about how much money you owe," how do you think the other person would have responded to that statement?

Resistance often occurs when clients are required to see a practitioner and are resentful about having to see someone when they don't think they have a problem. Rolling with resistance with involuntary clients involves exploring their willingness to consider other problems. These clients are in the pre-contemplation stage for the problem requiring the referral, but they may be ready to work on another problem they themselves define. For example, if Child Protective Services requires that a mother see a practitioner to learn new systems of parenting, she might be angry at the system that is forcing her to see a practitioner. This anger might be expressed as resistance. When asked if there are any problems she would like to work on, she might say, "Get Child Protective Services out of my life." The practitioner could express understanding of the client's viewpoint by saying, "So you have been unable to figure out a way to get Child Protective Services out of your life, and you want to figure out how to do that. Do I have that right?" Now instead of the client and practitioner pushing against each other, they can work together. The client will probably realize that she will need to learn some new parenting methods in order to achieve her goal of getting Child Protective Services out of her life.

Here is another example of exploring other problems with clients. An adolescent boy was referred to group counseling because his probation officer wanted him to stop shoplifting and cutting school. When the practitioner talked to the boy about the problems in his life, he said he was upset that a girl in his math class didn't want to go out with him. The practitioner agreed that not being able to get a date with a girl he liked was a problem. She suggested that they could focus on that problem. As the work proceeded, the boy realized that truancy and shoplifting were not effective ways to interest this girl. As he worked on achieving his goal, he also changed the behaviors that led to the referral.

Identifying Discrepancies

Identifying discrepancies is another motivational interviewing strategy that can be used with all stages of change, but it is particularly helpful when working with clients in the pre-contemplation and contemplation stages of readiness. **Identifying discrepancies** involves pointing out an incongruity between the client's present behavior and something he/she values or wants. Often practitioners ask questions to invite the client to see the discrepancy. For example, an adolescent girl complained about being required to be in counseling after fighting a number of times in school. The practitioner invited the client to see the discrepancy by saying, "I know you've said that you hate coming here and think it is a waste of time. I understand that you think the principal has no right to make you see me just because you have been fighting in the halls. It sounds like you'd really like to stop coming to see me. If you really don't want to have to come here, what do you think has to change to make that happen?" The practitioner is accepting and acknowledging the client's frustration and inviting the client to see that she has the power to change the situation. Seeing the discrepancy between present behavior and what the client values may increase the client's motivation to consider making changes. Identifying discrepancies is a skill that can also be used with a family, group, or organization. With a family, the practitioner might say, "I know you think the agency had no right to put your child in foster care. What do you think will have to change for you to get your child back home?" With an organization, "I know that you have been complaining about having to attend these training meetings. What do you think would have to change to get your supervisor to decide that you have had enough training?"

HOMEWORK EXERCISE 12.4 | IDENTIFYING DISCREPANCIES

Think of three examples from your own life or from someone else's life when there has been a discrepancy between a stated value, wish, or hope and behaviors.

For example, maybe a friend has stated that she is going to lose 10 pounds, but when you are out to eat together she orders and eats a hot fudge sundae.

WORKING WITH CLIENTS IN THE CONTEMPLATION STAGE

Clients in the contemplation stage of readiness believe there is a problem. They recognize the advantages of changing but are also aware of the costs involved with these changes. With these clients, it is important for the practitioner to state or restate the problems or challenges to be sure there is a clear understanding. The practitioner may need to discuss the client's perception of both the advantages and disadvantages of making a change. The client may see making a change as a future possibility but not something to commit to right now. In working with clients at this stage, practitioners need to support the client's feelings of ambivalence about making a change, help clients gain a clearer understanding of what they want, and help them become aware of patterns and themes related to their problem.

Expressing Empathy

Expressing empathy is important with clients at all stages of change. The expression of empathy provides acceptance that facilitates change and is described as an essential skill in motivational interviewing. As you learned in Chapter 5, being empathetic is essential in building a relationship with clients. In Chapter 8 you learned skills for expressing empathetic understanding. For the client in the contemplation stage, accepting ambivalence as a normal part of change is particular important. A statement like the following indicates empathy for the client: "I understand that you think it would improve your health if you gave up smoking but that giving up smoking feels almost impossible." The practitioner does not have to agree with the client or have the same values in order to demonstrate empathy.

HOMEWORK EXERCISE 12.5 | EXPRESSING EMPATHIC UNDERSTANDING OF AMBIVALENCE

Read each of the following statements and write a possible response that would express empathic understanding of ambivalence.

- "I know I should start saving money, but there are just so many things I want to buy for the kids."
- "I really want to do well in school, but when I take time to finish all my assignments in the evening, I don't have any time left for my husband and children."

- "I know I sometimes drink a bit too much, but I work hard and deserve some time to just relax with my friends."
- "The doctor has said that my weight is in the obese range and making my joint problems worse. I would love to be the right weight, but I've tried so many diets and the diets just don't work."

There are two other skills that practitioners use with clients in the contemplation stage as well as in the preparation and action stages: advanced reflecting and noticing patterns and themes. With these skills the practitioner goes beyond what the client says to point out new possibilities or insights. It is important to have a good working relationship with the client and a solid understanding of his/her perspective before using advanced reflecting and noticing patterns and themes.

Advanced Reflecting

Advanced reflecting is another way of expressing empathic understanding by identifying the values, meanings, feelings, and expectations beneath or behind the expressed message. It is similar to what many call advanced empathy, additive empathy, or going beyond (Ivey & Ivey, 2003; Kuntze, van der Molen, & Born, 2009; Murphy & Dillon, 2003). When using advanced reflecting, the practitioner identifies values, meanings, feelings, and expectations related to the problem. In advanced reflecting, the practitioner considers what he/she knows about the client as well as the practitioner's experience, knowledge, observations, and feelings. Since practitioners might share what they *sense* is going on with the client rather than what they *know,* they often begin with "it seems like" to express the tentative nature of the comment.

Often practitioners will comment on feelings, meanings, and values that have only been implied in the clients' previous comments. These may be feelings that have been hinted at but not spoken, such as hurt, sadness, or fear that is felt along with the anger that was expressed. Think of a time in your life when what you expressed was anger, and what you felt was disappointment and anger. Sometimes advanced reflecting is used to give voice to something that is implied (Egan, 2007). For example, your client is talking about leaving his present job because his wife thinks he could make more money in another position. As the practitioner, you hear little enthusiasm or motivation to leave his present job. You might say, "I wonder if getting another job is something your wife wants you to do, but you are unsure about." Advanced reflecting can be used to help clients recognize what they really value, want, or need in a situation. For example, "It sounds like you value living within your means and feel troubled about the amount of credit card debt you and your wife have accumulated."

One of the purposes of advanced reflecting is to invite the client to have insight, self-awareness, and/or deeper understanding of his/her situation. This understanding is helpful as the client thinks about his/her part in the problem. Sharing intuitive hunches with clients can help clients gain a different perspective or a new understanding of their problems. Advanced reflecting skills also help clients move from focusing on the problems and challenges they blame on others to focusing on the meaning of the challenges in their lives. With more understanding, clients may be able to move from the contemplation stage to the preparation stage.

Examples of Advanced Reflecting
- "It seems like you feel angry because you value communication and he doesn't" (moving from focusing on the client's husband to identifying what the client values)
- "It sounds like you feel angry because you expect clear directions from your boss. Without clear directions you feel afraid of making mistakes." (moving from focusing on the boss to focusing on the client's need for clear directions)
- "It seems like you value open communication and haven't found a way to invite other members of this group to share openly." (moving from focusing on what the client thinks is wrong with the other group members to focusing on what the client values)

- "I hear that you are frustrated and think this group isn't accomplishing enough. It seems like you really want this task group to do well." (moving from focusing on what the client is frustrated about to what the client wants)
- "It seems like several folks in this agency are feeling impatient because the needs of the growing Hispanic population are not being adequately addressed by the agency. It sounds like addressing the needs of the Hispanic population is something many of you value and think is important." (moving from focusing on what is wrong with services at the agency to what the people in the agency value)
- "I'm wondering if you feel like you aren't getting much recognition at work. Being valued for your contribution seems to be important to your job satisfaction." (moving from what the people at work aren't giving the client to what the client wants)
- "I have a sense that the group really wants to deal with this issue, but you are afraid of hurting one another's feelings." (moving from what the group members are afraid of to what they want)
- "It seems like you folks in the neighborhood really want to get this problem solved but are feeling pretty discouraged right now because the process seems difficult." (moving from how hard the process is to what the people want)

As you read the above examples, you might think what the client wants, values, or expects should be obvious. Actually clients often begin the helping process by focusing on or blaming others and have not thought about what they want, value, or expect. Once they move to thinking about their own needs, they are in a much better position to figure out which problem to address.

HOMEWORK EXERCISE 12.6 | ADVANCED REFLECTING

Using the following list, indicate which statement is an advanced-reflecting statement and which statement shows reflecting feeling and content.

1a. Your family has been troubled and hasn't done fun things together ever since your dad moved out.

1b. You value the fun times you have had with your family and wish you did more fun things together now.

2a. In this group you seem frustrated because I haven't told you how I think this problem should be solved.

2b. My sense is that you were hoping that someone would give you the solution.

3a. I believe that you folks really wish this problem were solved.

3b. It seems like folks in the group are feeling a bit scared or hesitant to take the next steps in solving this problem.

4a. You expect your girlfriend to call you and are disappointed and worried when she doesn't call.

4b. When your girlfriend doesn't call you, you feel worried.

5a. As I understand it, your partner has gotten mad at you because you aren't spending as much time with him as you used to.

5b. You are feeling a lot of conflict because you value spending time with your partner and also think it is important to spend time on your studies so you will do well in school.

6a. I hear that the folks at this neighborhood meeting are feeling quite worried about the recent arrest of someone selling drugs in the neighborhood.

6b. You folks value living in a drug-free neighborhood and hope it will be possible to find a way to curb the sale of drugs around here.

Identifying Patterns and Themes

Practitioners listen for themes and patterns related to interacting, behaving, thinking, and/or feelings. Part of the practitioner role is to help clients see patterns or themes related to their problems so that they can move one step closer to the preparation stage.

Although themes and patterns are similar concepts, there are differences between them. A *theme* refers to an idea or point of view shared by several people. Noticing themes is particularly important when working with families and groups of all sizes and types. Practitioners working with families are more objective than the family members, and this allows them to see themes that the family might have missed. For example, when working with a family the practitioner might say, "As I see it, getting high grades is important to almost everyone in this family." With a group, the practitioner might say, "As I understand it, all of you want to get this project completed (shared thought), but some folks are able to work more hours than other folks are willing to work. It seems like this is leading to conflicts in the group. Is that right?" In a neighborhood group, the practitioner might say, "It sounds like most of you are quite concerned about your children's safety in the playground (shared feeling and thought). Maybe that is something you are ready to work on."

A *pattern* refers to a consistent way of thinking, feeling, or behaving. When pointing out patterns, the practitioner might comment on similarities between the client's words and nonverbal communication. For example, "When you were talking about your best friend moving away, I noticed your eyes tearing up. Maybe dealing with your feelings about your friend is something you might want to work on." The practitioner might identify a possible pattern and then invite the client to say more about the possible pattern, "I hear that you believe that people don't take you seriously (pattern). Tell me more about the kinds of situations in which people don't take you seriously." With a family the practitioner might say, "I understand you are very frustrated when your daughter becomes so angry that she screams at you and won't do what you ask her to do (pattern). I wonder if you have noticed particular situations that seem to set off these incidents with your daughter."

The practitioner might identify a possible pattern of behavior related to such things as a client who tries to escape, run away, or use some self-defeating behavior whenever he/she gets into difficult situations. In suggesting a pattern, the practitioner might say, "It seems like before meetings with your boss you become frightened when you think about things your boss might be critical about (self-defeating pattern). Then when you meet with your boss, you are hesitant and don't explain things clearly because you are scared. Does that sound right?" In another situation, the practitioner might say, "You like watching football games with your friends, but when you hang out with these friends it seems like it usually leads to drinking too much and you feel guilty later (self-defeating pattern). Is that how you see it?" Since the client might not be ready to hear or accept the pattern as valid, the practitioner should be tentative in the tone of voice he/she uses and ask a question to explore whether the client agrees that the identified pattern exists.

The practitioner might ask about possible connections between problems and thoughts, feelings, ways of coping, and other situations. For example, the practitioner might say, "I understand that you that you are concerned about how much money you spend and your high credit card debt (problem). What do you notice about how you are feeling when you spend more money than you think you should?" (connection between problem behavior and feelings) In another situation the practitioner might say, "I hear that you try to get your son to follow the rules by talking to him, but sometimes you lose your patience and spank him (problem behavior). Think back to the last time you lost your patience with him. What had been going on in your life that day?" (connection between problem behavior and other situations) By using these kinds of questions, the practitioner is trying to understand more about the client. Sometimes thinking about the answers to these questions helps clients gain better understanding of their challenges.

Examples of Identifying Patterns and Themes
- *Client:* "This paper has a life of its own. I've created a monster with it. I want it to be perfect, but I can't seem to get it right."
  - *Practitioner:* "In previous meetings you have mentioned having high expectations of yourself and then feeling afraid that you can't meet your expectations." (noticing a pattern)
  - *Client:* "Yeah … This seems to be a major part of my life! It's really troubling. I haven't been able to get past it."
- *Client:* "I feel so frustrated every time I talk with my mother. She always criticizes me."
  - *Practitioner:* "I have heard you mention getting very upset when you feel unappreciated by your mother, and you have also mentioned feeling unappreciated at work. Does this happen in other areas of your life?" (noticing a possible pattern)
  - *Client:* "I guess sometimes at home when my husband doesn't notice something I have done, particularly something out of the ordinary, like when I made drapes for the living room windows, I feel unappreciated and sometimes over-react."
- *Client:* "I know I can never do well on these exams. They just aren't my thing."
  - *Practitioner:* "Do you think there is a connection between your belief that you won't do well and the fact that you freeze up when taking exams?" (noticing a possible pattern)
  - *Client:* "I'm not sure whether I freeze up and fail or fail because I freeze up. I will have to think about that."
- *Group member:* "I just don't think it is safe to walk around here at night. It is too dark."
  - *Practitioner:* "Tonight I have heard several people talking about the need to have more streetlights in this neighborhood so it will be safer." (noticing a theme)
  - *Another group member:* "I agree we don't have enough streetlights around here."
- *Group member:* "I'm pretty scared about what is happening with my mother. I feel so alone." (silence in response from group)
  - *Practitioner:* "When Chanté brought up her fears about her mother's health, I noticed that everyone got quiet. I wonder if this is an area that is

a problem for several people in the group and might be hard to talk about." (noticing a possible theme).

- ○ *Another group member:* "I don't even like to think about my mother being ill, but I guess it might be good to talk more about it."
- *Agency professional:* "I think we need better phone service for emergencies."
  - ○ *A second agency professional:* "Well, I would like better coverage on the front desk."
  - ○ *A third agency professional:* "I want to be able to respond better to those who do not have adequate funds."
  - ○ *Practitioner:* "As I listen to you discuss the problems in the agency, it sounds like you want to improve services and have several ideas about what is most important. I wonder if this is something you are ready to work on." (noticing a theme)
  - ○ *Agency professional:* "Yes, I think we need to decide on which areas need attention first and begin on that."

HOMEWORK EXERCISE 12.7 | IDENTIFYING PATTERNS AND THEMES

Think about one self-defeating behavior that you recognize in yourself. Write down what you know about the pattern. For example, maybe you are trying to lose weight but when you go to the store you frequently buy cookies or other baked goods while telling yourself you are getting them for someone else and then end up eating too much of them yourself. Now think about any group that you are involved with and identify a theme in the group.

It is particularly powerful to relate the themes or patterns that clients experience in their day-to-day lives to what is happening between the practitioner and the client during their meetings. The practitioner might say, "It seems like your high expectations of yourself (pattern) have led you to believe that you need to have all the answers when you come into a meeting with me," or "You have said that when you are afraid you have difficulty talking (pattern). It seems like that might have happened here when I asked you to describe your past substance abuse." Noticing themes or patterns as they occur in the relationship between the practitioner and client can have a great deal of impact on helping clients move toward change.

WORKING WITH CLIENTS IN THE PREPARATION STAGE

Clients in the preparation stage are preparing to set goals and thinking about the steps necessary to achieve their goals. They may have already made some progress and have plans to make more. Goals can now be delineated more clearly, and the timing of beginning steps can be proposed. Generally people need to be at this stage before a major change is possible. Practitioners help clients at this stage by breaking the problem into smaller, more manageable parts and enhancing the clients' sense of self-efficacy by supporting their belief that they are capable of success in making the necessary changes.

Partializing

Clients in the preparation stage are ready to identify their role in problems and to begin setting goals. With these clients, it is important for the practitioner to state or restate the problems or challenges to be sure there is a clear understanding between the practitioner and the client. Often this communication will involve **partializing**, or breaking a complex problem into manageable parts. Because some problems can seem overwhelming, dividing a problem into smaller parts can make the problem seem more manageable. For example, if the client's problem is that she doesn't have enough money to pay the bills and feels scared, the practitioner might help the client see that the problem has several parts: the client has a minimum-wage job or is unemployed, the client's housing costs are too high, and/or the client is spending too much money on non-essential things. After dividing the problem into manageable parts, the practitioner may choose to work with the client to identify which difficulty should be addressed first. Sometimes it will be the problem that can be changed most easily. Sometimes the client may choose the problem that is causing the most pain. At other times it is the issue that will help solve other aspects of the problem. It is important to remember that the client's perception of what is manageable may be smaller than or different from what the practitioner might see as possible.

HOMEWORK EXERCISE 12.8 | PARTIALIZING

Think about a problem that you have faced or a problem that someone you know has faced or is facing. Write out ways to break the problem into several smaller, more manageable parts. You may want to challenge yourself to think of as many small parts as possible. It is important to generate these smaller parts of the problem since what seems like a manageable part to you may not seem so to others.

Supporting Self-Efficacy

Another motivational interviewing skill that is particularly useful in the preparation phase is supporting self-efficacy. In Chapter 11, you learned about the concept of self-efficacy, or the belief in one's capacity to influence events that affect his/her life (Bandura, 1994; Souvignier & Mokhlesgerami, 2006). When supporting self-efficacy, practitioners encourage clients to acknowledge and believe in their ability to carry out and succeed with specific tasks. The general goal is to enhance clients' confidence and capability to cope with obstacles and to succeed in making changes. A statement that recognizes what the clients have already accomplished and identifies their strengths can support their belief in themselves. The skill of supporting self-efficacy is the same as the skill of identifying strengths that you learned in Chapter 10.

HOMEWORK EXERCISE 12.9 | SUPPORTING SELF-EFFICACY

Think of someone who believed in your ability to overcome your problems or who recognized your strengths and capacities. How did that person communicate this to you? What influence did that person have on your life? If you can't think of an example in your life, think of an example from a family member or friend's life or even the life of someone you have read or heard about.

Problem Identification

All of the previous skills are necessary as practitioners move toward helping clients identify problems. If the client is an entire family, the practitioner might ask each person in the family what he/she wants changed in the family (problems). The same type of question could be asked about a larger system such as an agency or a neighborhood. For example, when working with a neighborhood, asking what they would like changed about the neighborhood (problems).

Even though as a practitioner you may think there is a clear understanding of the problem, you need to state your understanding to ensure that you and the client are in agreement. Since stating problems is not something that is generally done in ordinary conversations, many beginning practitioners feel awkward when stating the problem. As you experienced with previous skills, this awkwardness goes away with practice. When the client is ready to identify the problem and to work toward solving it, the practitioner states the problem in terms of something the client has so far been unable to achieve.

Examples of Practitioner Statements that Move from Reflecting Feeling and Content to Identifying the Problem   (Of course, after each statement, the practitioner would pause to give the client(s) an opportunity to respond.)

- "The way you see your boss managing the business is frustrating to you, and you wish he'd get organized." (reflecting feeling and content)

    "You wish that you could talk directly to your boss." (advanced reflecting)

    "Your inability to make recommendations to your boss is frustrating to you." (identifying the problem)
- "You sound disappointed in your friend because she frequently asks you for money." (reflecting feeling and content)

    "You have noticed that you sometimes say 'yes' and later regret it." (identifying a pattern)

    "When being asked for money by your friend, you are not happy with your inability to say 'no.'" (identifying the problem)
- "You feel unhappy because it seems like the people in your family don't listen to you." (reflecting feeling and content)

    "Having your family listen to you is very important to you." (advanced reflecting)

    "It seems like you haven't found a way to tell the folks in your family how important it is to you that they listen to you." (identifying the problem)
- "It sounds like some folks are disturbed because there hasn't been much openness in our group." (reflecting feelings and content)

    "I have heard several people say they wished for more openness in the group." (identifying a theme)

    "In this group it seems like folks have felt unable to be fully open with each other." (identifying the problem)
- "It seems like you are unhappy because the people in your family rarely spend time together." (reflecting feelings and content)

    "You really value spending time with your family." (advanced reflecting)

"It seems like your family hasn't been able to figure out a way to spend more time together." (identifying the problem)

- "I understand that all of the people at this neighborhood meeting are feeling very disappointed that you didn't get any of the city's redevelopment money for your neighborhood." (reflecting feelings and content)

"It sounds like most of you are interested in figuring out how to get a redevelopment grant." (identifying a theme)

"It seems like you haven't been able to figure out how to successfully apply for the redevelopment money that is available." (identifying the problem)

Examples of Possible Problem Statements Related to Individuals, Families, Groups, and Neighborhoods   Clients often think about problems in terms of what they want to stop doing. So the practitioners or clients identify what the client wants to give up such as "I need to stop drinking." In other cases clients think of problems as something they want to start doing. So the practitioner or client state the problem as a behavior they have not been able to accomplish such as "I need to complete my assignments on time." Stating a problem in positive terms is helpful because it is closer to a goal that needs to be stated as a behavior or feeling they would like to have. You will learn about effective goal setting in Chapter 13. In the following list of problems, some are stated as what the clients want to stop doing and some are stated as what the clients want to start doing.

You have not been able to:

- Assert yourself when your rights are being violated.
- Listen to others without interrupting. *Or* Keep silent when others are speaking.
- Find a job with a salary above minimum wage.
- Express your anger and/or frustration without being abusive. *Or* Express your anger and/or frustration in an appropriate way.
- Find time to spend with your children.
- Discipline your children without hitting them. *Or* Discipline your children verbally not physically.
- Find a way to work, do well in school, and spend time with your family.
- Stop giving in to your child. *Or* Set limits on how much you give to your child.
- Stop yourself from excessive drinking, eating, smoking, or spending money. Stop yourself from being overly critical and/or attacking others. *Or* Find ways to express your negative feelings to others in a different way.
- Stop yelling and verbally attacking people when you are angry. *Or* Express your anger in a way that communicates better with others.
- Trust men/women/people.
- Stop criticizing yourself. *Or* Find ways to praise yourself.

In your family you have not been able to:

- Communicate without yelling. *Or* Keep your voice at a normal level when sharing.
- Solve problems together.
- Agree on appropriate rules.

- Understand each other.
- Find an adequate place to live.
- Work together to reach goals.
- Deal with the grief you feel.

In this group we have not been able to:

- Trust each other with our feelings.
- Treat each other respectfully.
- Be honest about our thoughts about each other.
- Support each other.
- Clearly identify our goals.
- Agree on a leadership plan.

In this neighborhood we have not been able to:

- Reduce the crime rate. *Or* Find ways to make it safe.
- Find a way to clean up the parks or get more playgrounds.
- Work together to set goals.
- Find a way to get the city to fill the potholes in the streets.
- Figure out ways to accept the changes in the neighborhood from a racially homogenous neighborhood to a racially mixed neighborhood.
- Find ways to effectively work with the school administration and teachers to improve the local schools.

HOMEWORK EXERCISE 12.10 | IDENTIFICATION OF PROBLEMS

Write at least four examples of other possible problems individuals, families, groups, or community associations might have to deal with.

ETHICAL CONSIDERATIONS IN PROBLEM IDENTIFICATION

The stages-of-change model and motivational interviewing both support essential ethical principles related to autonomy and self-determination (Britton, Williams, & Conner, 2008; Ford, 2006). As a practitioner, it is important that you respect the rights of clients to make their own decisions about how they live their lives. Practitioners who believe clients have valid insights and ideas about their situation should demonstrate this belief by respecting the client's right to self-determination. Client decisions are influenced by culture, gender, age, and other factors that the practitioner may not fully understand. This right of autonomous self-determination should not be denied or interfered with by well-intentioned practitioners either through coercion or through undue influence. A practitioner's role is to support clients in the choices they make, even when the practitioner feels the client should make other choices. Ethically, practitioners should affirm the rights of clients to decide how to act as long as their behavior does not infringe upon the legal rights of others or actively endanger others (suicide, homicide, child abuse).

HOMEWORK EXERCISE 12.11 | PROBLEM IDENTIFICATION, AUTONOMY, AND SELF-DETERMINATION

Think of at least three times when you or someone you know was troubled about something and talked to another person about that concern. What if the other person said, "It seems to me your problem is ..." The other person then follows up with, "What you really should do about that is ..." The other person was probably trying to be helpful and was not in the role of practitioner.

Reflect on times when you have experienced this type of situation. How did you feel? What are your guesses about how a client might feel and what the client might think if that kind of discussion happened between a practitioner and client? Do you think the client would feel respected? Consider autonomy and self-determination. Would the client have thought the practitioner was respecting the client's autonomy and need for self-determination? If you had been the client, would you have continued working with the practitioner?

DVD Example: Identifying Problems

Watch the exploring and goal setting section of the family meeting.

- List specific examples of rolling with resistance, identifying discrepancies, advanced reflection, identifying a theme, partializing, supporting self-efficacy, and/or identifying problems.
- What did you like about the way the practitioner used skills related to developing deeper understanding?
- Give specific examples of points where the practitioner could have made a statement or asked a question to further or more specifically identify key problems.

PRACTICE EXERCISE 6 | IDENTIFYING PROBLEMS AND CHALLENGES

Exercise Objectives

- To practice using skills that reach for agreement about problems or challenges.

Step 1: Preparation

Form groups of three people. Each person will have the opportunity to play the roles of client, practitioner, and peer supervisor. Each meeting will last about 10 minutes.

Client Role
- Think about a problem you can discuss with the practitioner.

Practitioner Role
- Although practitioners sometimes move to identifying problems in the first meeting, this task is often accomplished in subsequent meetings. Begin this and subsequent meetings as you would

meetings after the first meeting. Review procedures for beginning a subsequent meeting in Chapter 6.
- Review the use of skills for identifying the problem: rolling with resistance, identifying discrepancies, advanced reflecting, identifying patterns and themes, partializing the problem, supporting self-efficacy, and stating the agreed upon problem.

Peer Supervisor Role
- Review the use of skills for identifying the problem (see evaluation form).
- Prepare to write down verbal responses of the practitioner and to keep track of the time.

Step 2: The Client Meeting

Client Role
- Tell your story, but stop talking after every few sentences to give the practitioner a chance to practice using his or her skills. At this point it is

PRACTICE EXERCISE 6 │ IDENTIFYING PROBLEMS AND CHALLENGES (*continued*)

helpful to be working with the same client, practitioner, and peer supervisor teams so the meeting can begin where the last meeting ended.

Practitioner Role
- Use all of the skills you have learned so far.
- Use any of the following skills as appropriate: partializing, advanced reflecting, identifying patterns and themes, identifying discrepancies, rolling with resistance, supporting self-efficacy, and stating agreement on problems.
- You can stop the meeting at any time to get suggestions from the persons in the role of client or peer supervisor.
- Remember that your goal is to practice the skills. Even if this was a real interaction with a client, it would be inappropriate to begin working on problem solving until you thoroughly understood the situation and had set goals with the client.

Peer Supervisor Role
- Keep track of the time and tell the practitioner and client when 9 minutes are completed so the practitioner has time to close the meeting.
- Check off the beginning subsequent meeting skills used by the practitioner.
- Write down each practitioner statement and question. You may abbreviate, use a form of shorthand, or just write the first group of words in the statement, or you can tape record the interview and transcribe or listen to the tape.

Step 3: Feedback
Purpose: Receiving immediate constructive feedback helps students enhance their practice skills. Using this evaluation system, the peer supervisor monitors the skills used by the social worker. The client, social worker, and peer supervisor identify strengths and areas for growth.

Client Role
- Share how you experienced the practitioner.
  - Did you feel understood?
  - Was the practitioner warm, empathic, genuine, and respectful?
  - What did the practitioner do particularly well?
  - In what ways could the practitioner improve?

Practitioner Role
- Evaluate your use of skills defining the focus of the work.
- Identify any inappropriate responses.

Peer Supervisor Role
- Give the practitioner feedback on his/her skills related to beginning subsequent meetings.
- Based on your notes, give feedback to the practitioner on his/her use of skills related to expressing understanding, gaining further information, and developing deeper understanding.
- Discuss with the practitioner his/her use of the skills of rolling with resistance, identifying discrepancies, advanced reflecting, identifying patterns and themes, partializing, supporting self-efficacy, and stating agreement on problems. Talk with the practitioner and client about additional ways the practitioner might have used these skills.
- Discuss with the practitioner any inappropriate responses made by the practitioner. One minus point for every inappropriate response.
- Discuss with the practitioner the appropriate scores for warmth, empathy, respect, and genuineness (all of the scales are in Appendix A).
- Add all the individual points and the points on the scales to get the total score.
- Record the feedback in the practitioner's book for future reference.

(*continued*)

PRACTICE EXERCISE 6 | IDENTIFYING PROBLEMS AND CHALLENGES (*continued*)

EVALUATION FORM

Name of Practitioner_____

Name of Peer Supervisor_____

Directions: Under each category (in italics) is a list of behaviors or skills.
Give one check mark, worth one point, for each skill used by the practitioner.

Opening and Closing

Beginning Subsequent Meetings

  Give one point for each topic covered by the practitioner.

  1. Asked client where he/she would like to begin.   _____
  2. Summarized previous meeting.   _____
  3. Identified tasks for this meeting.   _____
  4. Asked client about progress.   _____
  5. Asked client about homework.   _____
  6. Asked client about problems.   _____
  7. Made an observation about the previous meeting.   _____
  8. Did a check-in.   _____

Expressing Understanding

  Expressing understanding is so important that for this group of skills one
  point should be given for each time the practitioner used one of the skills.

  1. Reflected feelings   _____
  2. Reflected content   _____
  3. Reflected feelings and content   _____
  4. Summarized   _____
  5. Reflected meanings   _____

Gaining Further Understanding

Questioning Skills

  Give one point for each skill used by the practitioner.

  1. Expressed understanding before asking questions.   _____
  2. Asked open-ended questions when appropriate.   _____
  3. Asked one question at a time.   _____
  4. Asked closed-ended questions when appropriate.   _____

Learning about Problem/Challenge and Situation

  Give one point for each topic adequately discussed.

Problems or Challenges

  Previous attempts to solve problem   _____
  History of the problem(s)   _____

PRACTICE EXERCISE 6 | IDENTIFYING PROBLEMS AND CHALLENGES (*continued*)

Severity or intensity of the problem(s)   _____
Feelings about having the problem(s)   _____
Effects of the problem(s) on other areas   _____
(such as health, sleeping, ability to function at school or work)

Situation

Effect of the problem on other people   _____
Available social support and strengths in environment   _____
Interactions with family   _____
Other demands and stresses in the situation/environment   _____

Developing Deeper Understanding

Skills to Enhance Understanding

Give one point for each skill used by the practitioner.

1. Explored the meaning of words and body language   _____
2. Explored the basis of conclusions drawn by client   _____
3. Allowed silence   _____
4. Identified strengths   _____
5. Asked questions about strengths.   _____

Defining the Focus

Reaching Agreement about Problems or Challenges

Give one point for each skill used by the practitioner. It rarely will be
appropriate to use all of these skills in one meeting.

1. Used rolling with resistance   _____
2. Identified discrepancies   _____
3. Advanced reflecting   _____
4. Identified a pattern or theme   _____
5. Partialized the problem   _____
6. Supported self-efficacy   _____
7. Stated agreed upon problems   _____

Common Mistakes or Inappropriate Responses (subtract one point for each)   _____

(offering advice, reassuring, offering excuses, asking leading questions, dominating
through teaching, labeling, interrogating)

Core Interpersonal Qualities

Using the scales in Appendix A, evaluate the appropriateness and effectiveness of
the practitioner's expression of empathy, warmth, and respect. On the following
lines write the scores, from 1 to 5, for warmth, empathy, respect, and genuineness.

Score for warmth   _____
Score for empathy   _____
Score for respect   _____
Score for genuineness   _____

Total Score   _____

EXPECTED COMPETENCIES

In this chapter you learned about how to use the stages of change theory and motivational interviewing techniques to help clients identify the challenges they want to work on during their sessions, how to identify client themes and patterns, how to assist clients in breaking these challenges into manageable parts, the skill of advanced reflecting, and identifying the client's key problems.

Key terms you should be able to define include: advanced reflecting, indentifying descrepancies, motivational interviewing, partializing, and rolling with resistance.

You should now be able to:

- Identify skills that can be used with clients in the pre-contemplation, contemplation, and preparation stages of change.
- Give examples of using the following skills: partializing, advanced reflecting, identifying patterns and themes, identifying discrepancies, rolling with resistance, supporting self-efficacy, and stating agreed upon problems.
- Demonstrate the skills used to reach agreement on problems.

Establishing Goals

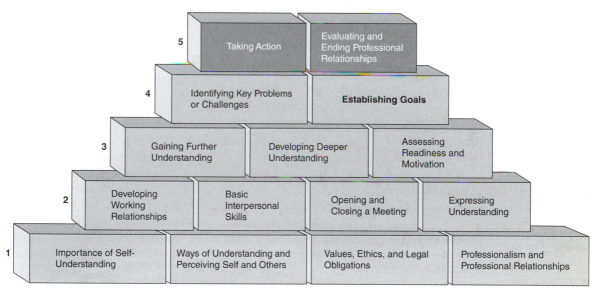

5	Taking Action	Evaluating and Ending Professional Relationships	
4	Identifying Key Problems or Challenges	**Establishing Goals**	
3	Gaining Further Understanding	Developing Deeper Understanding	Assessing Readiness and Motivation
2	Developing Working Relationships	Basic Interpersonal Skills	Opening and Closing a Meeting	Expressing Understanding
1	Importance of Self-Understanding	Ways of Understanding and Perceiving Self and Others	Values, Ethics, and Legal Obligations	Professionalism and Professional Relationships

© Cengage Learning 2013

Questions to consider as you read this chapter:

1. In what ways are goals important?
2. How do practitioners work collaboratively with clients to develop clear goals?

This chapter covers practice behaviors related to establishing mutually agreed upon goals. *You will learn the importance of*:

*   Collaborating and gaining consensus on goals
*   Developing mutually agreed-on goals that provide focus for the work and measurement criteria for outcomes
*   Establishing baselines for monitoring progress

Client Attributes

*   Willingness to think about his/her goals and to describe them clearly

After identifying the problems, practitioners help clients identify their goals. As in each previous phase of the work, the client's participation is critical to success. In this phase of the work, clients need to be willing to visualize and talk about the goal or goals they want to achieve. This chapter focuses on the process of reaching agreement about general and specific goals. Using all of the skills covered in the previous chapters, practitioners and clients come to an agreement on the primary goals for their work together.

IDENTIFYING GENERAL GOALS

Establishing goals is a crucial phase of the work done by the practitioner and client. Goals set the direction and focus of the work to be done. Clear goals are necessary in planning steps to be taken, reviewing and evaluating progress, and deciding when to end the relationship between the practitioner and client. In fact, setting goals is a task that almost all practitioners agree is essential (Curtis, 2000). Goal setting requires careful identification of the problems, thorough exploration of strengths and resources, and a focus on outcomes that fit into the client's life.

Goals are what clients hope to achieve by working with the practitioner. They are the clients' vision of what life would be like if their problems were solved. The general goal may be the opposite of the problem. For example, if the problem is defined as "turning assignments in late," then the goal might be "turning assignments in on time." With a clear understanding of the problem, clients can more easily identify their goals.

It is essential that goals be mutually established between practitioners and clients (Berg & Miller, 1992; Schauer, Everett, del Vecchio, & Anderson, 2007; Tryon & Winograd, 2011). Practitioners need to think about whether they are trying to direct clients toward certain goals or choosing goals for the clients. If the practitioner senses that he/she is working harder than the client, it is often because the practitioner has established a goal without adequate participation from the client. A satisfactory outcome to your work together depends on your ability to collaborate with clients on what will be agreeable goals for your clients (Busseri & Tyler, 2004).

Practitioners use many skills to help clients figure out their goals. Questions that seek clarification help clients figure out what goals they are motivated to achieve. In the solution-focused approach, for instance, clients are asked to describe what their life would be like if a miracle happened and the problems that led them to talk to a practitioner were solved (de Shazer & Molnar, 1984; Furman & Ahola, 1992; O'Hanlon & Weiner-Davis, 2003; Strong & Pyle, 2009; Walter & Peller, 1992). To invite clients to think about goals, practitioners use open-ended questions that are focused on the future, such as the following:

- "At the end of our work together, what do you want your life to be like?"
- "When the problems that brought you here are solved, what do you want to be doing, feeling, or thinking?"
- "When we have finished our work together, what might other people see you doing that you aren't doing now?"
- "Tell me about your picture of what you want your family to be like."
- "Let's pretend that these problems are solved. What differences will you notice in your life (or in this group, or in this organization, or in this neighborhood)?"

Exception-finding questions can also be used to establish goals (de Shazer & Molnar, 1984; O'Hanlon & Weiner-Davis, 2003; Smith & Hall, 2007; Walter & Peller, 1992). Exception-finding questions explore times when the problem was not present. For example, "Think of a time when you didn't have this problem. What were you doing, feeling, or thinking at that time?" Even if clients can only think of a short period of time when the problem did not exist, a great deal of information can be gained about what the client's life is like when the problem is not present. This description of life without the problem may be what the client wants to establish as a goal. If clients can't identify a time when the problem was not present, it sometimes helps to ask about a time when the problem was smaller or less noticeable and to encourage the clients to think about what was happening that led to that decrease in the problem.

HOMEWORK EXERCISE 13.1 | GENERAL GOALS

Review the list of examples of problem statements for individuals, families, groups, and neighborhoods in Chapter 12, pages 226–227. Write a possible general goal for each problem in the list.

IDENTIFYING MEASURABLE, ATTAINABLE, POSITIVE, AND SPECIFIC (MAPS) GOALS

In some situations, general goals are all that practitioners and clients develop. In other situations, when there is more focus on evaluation of progress or outcomes, setting specific goals is important. To assess whether goals have been achieved, clients must set goals that are measurable. Moving from general goals to Measurable, Attainable, Positive, and Specific (MAPS) goals often requires considerable work. MAPS goals need to be as clear and detailed as possible. For example, if the general goal is to use positive communication within the family, practitioners would ask a number of questions to move from the general goal to a MAPS goal. The following questions might be used:

- "Will you give me an example of what positive communication sounds like to you?"
- "When you have positive communication, what will you be doing that you aren't doing now?"
- "In what situations do you want to have more positive communication?"

As clients think about their answers to these questions, they often gain a clearer vision of their goal.

When clients face many problems, the practitioner may help them establish goals for each problem or may focus on establishing and working on one goal at a time. Working on one manageable goal can enhance the client's hope that other goals can be achieved. For example, a client may come in feeling depressed. Using the skills taught thus far, the practitioner determines that the depression began recently and is not part of a long-term pattern. The depressed mood seems to have developed in response to the death of the client's mother. Upon careful reflection, the practitioner finds that the problems leading to the depression can be partialized into worries about cleaning out and selling her mother's house, distributing the inheritance, making arrangements for the care of a dependent sibling who had resided with her mother, and grief about her mother's death. After identifying the pieces of the overall problem, the practitioner and client will determine what aspect of the problem the client wishes to address first. After experiencing success in resolving one part of a multifaceted problem, clients usually feel more confident about their ability to address the remaining issues.

Measurable and Specific Goals

The most helpful goals are those that are Measurable and Specific. Goals that are *measurable* and *specific* make it possible for clients and practitioners to evaluate whether the goals have been achieved. The client and practitioner can then acknowledge gains or changes that have been made. Setting measurable and specific goals also provides a clear direction or focus for the work. Clients and practitioners are more likely to be successful in creating solutions for problems if they have taken the time to figure out exactly what the goal is.

Some words that are commonly used in goal statements are not specific enough to be measured. Words such as "increase" and "more" are good starting points, but they are not measurable until the practitioner obtains additional specific information. If the general goal is to "get more exercise, increase the time I spend with my children, and increase the time I spend on homework," you will need to get more specific information. For example, if "getting higher grades" is the general goal, the following questions can provide the information needed to make the goal measurable and specific:

- "What are your grades now?"
- "How much do you want to raise your grades?"
- "When your grades are high enough to satisfy you, what grades will you be getting?"

General goal statements also may include vague, non-specific words with unclear meanings. For example, a beginning practitioner set the following goal with an inner-city teenager: "I will increase my self-esteem." We have already discussed problems with the word "increase," but what about "self-esteem?" That sounds like the practitioner's language, not the teenager's, and self-esteem can be defined in many ways. If a word such as "self-esteem" is used, it is best to ask the client what he/she would be doing differently if he/she had a higher level of self-esteem. Another commonly used phrase is "improved communication." Again, each person's idea of what improved communication means is different, so the practitioner should ask the client for more specifics. For example, "When you begin communicating better, what will you be doing that you are not doing now?" Or, "What will improved communication sound like?" One of the authors remembers a wife who said that she wanted her husband to show her that he loved her. When asked, "What could your husband do to show you that he loved you?" the wife said, "He would get up on some Saturday mornings and take care of the kids and let me sleep in." The practitioner and the woman's husband were quite surprised by this reply. The wife explained that getting up on Saturday mornings was something her father used to do, and she thought it was very loving. Unfortunately, she had never shared this information with her husband, who was quite willing to get up every other Saturday and take care of the kids so she could sleep later.

HOMEWORK EXERCISE 13.2 | DEVELOPING MEASURABLE AND SPECIFIC GOALS

Underline the non-specific words in each of the following statements.

1. I will get a better grade this semester than last semester.
2. In this family we are going to talk to each other more than we used to.
3. In this group we will increase the number of times that we have 100% attendance.
4. At this agency we will reduce the turnover rate by adding some new benefits.
5. In this neighborhood we will have more get-togethers this year.
6. I am going to lose some weight.
7. In this family we are going to have some quiet times for everyone to work on projects.
8. In this group we want most of our meetings to start on time.
9. In this organization we want to increase client satisfaction.

HOMEWORK EXERCISE 13.3 | VALUE OF MEASURABLE AND SPECIFIC GOALS

Suppose you are talking with three friends, and one tells you, "I sure wish I could go on a vacation." The second friend remarks, "Yes, I want to go someplace that is warm." The third friend says, "I am going to go to Florida the first week in April." Which friend do you think is most likely to achieve her goal? Why do you think that friend is most likely to achieve her goal?

Now think of goals that you have set in your life. Identify two goals that are general. "I'd like to exercise more" is an example of a general goal. Now write down two goals that are measurable and specific, such as "This week I will walk for half an hour each day." This goal is measurable and specific. To assess your progress at the end of each day, you would be able to answer "yes" or "no" to indicate whether you walked or not.

Attainable Goals

Setting goals that are *attainable* seems obvious, but it sometimes requires skillful work with the client. To be attainable, a goal needs to be something the client believes is possible to reach based on the available resources such as time, money, and people power. If the practitioner is working with a community that has very limited financial resources, an attainable goal might be to obtain a grant or to speak with a grant writer. A family who constantly fights might believe that they could achieve a goal such as having dinner together once a week to talk about topics other than their problems. Research by Bandura and Schunk (1981) found that with clients who had little success in achieving their goals, setting attainable small goals helped them sustain motivation. In our experience, establishing a series of attainable small goals helps clients experience success in goal achievement, feel more positive about their ability to achieve goals, and be motivated to continue the process of achieving goals. Many practitioners begin with a small goal that can be achieved in a reasonable period of time. After achieving that goal, the client can go on to set additional goals.

A challenge in establishing attainable goals requires helping clients identify what seems possible to them. In order to effectively motivate action, goals need to be perceived as attainable. In Chapter 11 we looked at the ways in which capacity, resources, stress, and demands affect the level of motivation. Those same factors should be considered in relation to goal attainability. Attainable goals are ones that the client can achieve with the capacity and resources available.

In our experience, a very common unattainable goal involves changing another person. Remember what you learned in Chapter 12 about seeing the problems in others. We are sure that you have experienced times when you could identify what someone else should do differently. Goals such as "You should lose 10 pounds," "You should get a job," or "You have to stop drinking" are not attainable because you can't force another person to change. However, in some situations you can use the power you have to motivate another person to change. As a practitioner, you may help clients identify what power they do have. For example, a parent can't make a child get better grades. However, the parent does have control over such things as money and the car. As a parent of a teenager, the client could say "I will not allow you to drive my car unless you have a B average." In that situation, the goal for the parent might be to consistently follow through no matter how unhappy the teenager is.

If the practitioner is working with a 9 year old child who is playing around during arithmetic and flunking arithmetic tests, the practitioner might want to help the child think of a goal that is attainable in the near future. Before setting any goals, it would be vital to determine that the child's problem did not result from skipping breakfast every day, family discord, physical problems, or a lack of basic skills. The first goal might be to get at least a C on the next quiz. If the child is not successful with this goal, further partializing of the goal may be necessary. An even smaller goal could be get a grade of satisfactory on the next assignment. After achieving the first small goal, another goal could be developed. With a young child, the practitioner would not work toward a long-term goal such as getting a B at the end of the semester. That goal is too far away to sustain motivation. When short-term, more easily attainable goals are used with children (and often with adults), the client and practitioner can celebrate each stage of the change made toward reaching a larger goal.

Clients who participate in setting goals are more likely to believe the goals are achievable. Clients who clearly visualize the goals in concrete, specific, behavioral terms improve the most (Bandura & Cervone, 1983; Berg & Miller, 1992; Cheavens, Feldman, Woodward, & Snyder, 2006; Miller, 1987; Miller & Hester, 1989). When goals are attainable, clients have an increased sense of hope about the possibility of change.

Examples the Process to Develop Attainable Goals

- "I hear that you want to weigh what you weighed when you were 30 years old. Let's consider first setting a goal that you can successfully reach in a shorter period of time. What do you think would be a reasonable, and not too hard, goal to reach in 2 months?"
- "I agree that giving up drinking and going to AA meetings every day is a terrific goal. AA is very good at celebrating each milestone in the process to lifetime sobriety. How about if one of our first goals is going to AA every day for 2 weeks? Does that sound okay to you?"
- "It sounds like your group was disappointed in your grade on the big project and you are determined to start earlier on the next big project. That sounds like a plan that will work. The next project is due 6 weeks from now. What goal would you like to achieve 3 weeks from now related to that project?"
- "So the 2 of you often argue about how to discipline the children, and think it would be better if you agreed on discipline methods. That sounds like a good goal to achieve. Since you disagree on many aspects of discipline, would it make sense to you to start with a goal of coming to an agreement about what to do when Georgiana won't spend time on her homework?"
- "In this town you have many people who are homeless and you want to develop a solution to the problem that will be acceptable to the city council and also to the people who are homeless. I wonder if the first goal might be to create a group that of people, including some people who are homeless and some of you, who are willing to work on this problem?"

HOMEWORK EXERCISE 13.4 | ATTAINABLE GOALS

Think of a goal that you (or someone else) set that you consider unattainable. For example, people sometimes set goals such as losing 25 pounds before some important event that will happen in a month. Once you have identified an unattainable goal, write down how you felt about that goal. Discuss whether you achieved the goal and, if you did achieve it, how long you maintained it.

Positive Goals

Setting goals that are *positive* keeps the focus on what the client wants to do rather than focusing on what he/she doesn't want to do. Sometimes the initial statement of goals is to stop doing something, such as stop the fighting in this family, quit drinking, get rid of the drug dealers in this neighborhood, or stop the critical interactions in this task group. The problem with negative goals is that they invite people to focus on what they don't want to do rather that what they do want to do. If you are wondering whether it is true that negative goals invite focusing on the problem, try this experiment. Right this minute, stop thinking about pink elephants. Inevitably that direction leads to thinking about pink elephants. You have to think about them before you can stop thinking about them. If a person's goal is to stop doing something, he/she tends to think about doing that thing. A goal of not drinking for the next week is measurable, attainable, and specific, but not positive. The goal not to drink doesn't give any direction about what to do. It is up to the practitioner to invite clients to think about what they want in place of whatever was negative. Practitioners use open-ended questions to invite clients to think in positive terms about what they want to start doing. The practitioner needs to ask the client, "What do you want to do instead of drinking?" This might lead to a goal such as, "When I feel like drinking, I will talk to someone that I know will be supportive," or "I will go to an AA meeting."

Examples of Questions Used to Develop Positive Goals

- "If one night at dinner you weren't fighting, what do you think you might be doing?"
- "If one day you felt the urge to drink but didn't drink, what would you do instead?"
- "What is your vision of what the neighborhood would be like without drug dealers?"
- "When you are concerned about how things are going in the group, how would you like to talk to each other about your concerns or hopes?"
- "If this agency was functioning in a way that you believe would be effective, what would people be doing that they aren't doing now?"

HOMEWORK EXERCISE 13.5 | POSITIVE GOALS

Experiment with one negative goal and one positive goal from the following list for just one day. At the end of the day write down what you learned.

1a. Today, I won't eat anything with sugar in it.
1b. Today, I will eat at least three servings of fruit.
2a. Today, I won't procrastinate on my reading assignments.
2b. Today, I will read for at least two hours.
3a. Today, I won't panic about the test.
3b. Today, I will study at least two hours for the test.
4a. Today, I won't say anything negative about anyone.
4b. Today, I will say something positive to two people.

When goals are *measurable*, *attainable*, *positive*, and *specific*, it is easier for clients to begin to create a vision of what life will be like when the goals are achieved. Having this clear vision increases their sense of hope. Sometimes it is helpful for practitioners to share their thoughts about clients' ability to achieve goals. The more strongly the clients believe in their ability to achieve the goals and in the practitioner's ability to help them, the more hope and confidence they will feel.

Example of Helping an Individual Establish a MAPS Goal

CLIENT: "I'm so upset today that I can't even think. Last night my husband went to several bars and never came home. He hadn't had a drink for almost a year and now he's starting all over again."

PRACTITIONER: "It sounds like you are really angry about him drinking again (reflecting feelings and content)."

CLIENT: "Yes, I'm angry and hurt, too, really hurt. I've given up all kinds of things. I was willing to stay at home and be with him and help him stay away from drinking and now he has blown it."

PRACTITIONER: "After making sacrifices to help him, it is particularly painful that he wasn't able to stay away from drinking (reflecting feelings and content)."

CLIENT: "Right. I've been working hard to make our life together enjoyable so he would not want to go out and drink."

PRACTITIONER: "I wonder if you are feeling resentful as well. It seems like you have put a lot effort into the relationship, and now that he went out drinking you wonder if he is willing to do his part (reflecting feelings and content)."

CLIENT: "I had made a life for myself without him because he drank so much, but when he said that if I would help him he knew that he would be able to quit drinking, I agreed. I thought we had an agreement. I have kept my end of the deal."

PRACTITIONER: "It seems like the fact that he went out drinking is particularly hurtful because you thought things were going well, and you were doing what he had asked you to do (advanced reflecting)."

CLIENT: "I've been told all alcoholics are con artists, and now I believe it."

PRACTITIONER: "I can understand how betrayed you must feel since you believe that he conned you into thinking he really would change (advanced reflecting)."

CLIENT: "I do feel conned. He seemed so sincere and so willing to be different. He even cried."

PRACTITIONER: "It seems like you are also feeling confused. His behavior was so convincing, but he wasn't able to keep his promise (reflecting feelings and content)."

CLIENT: "I am really confused. I was so sure that we were making progress."

PRACTITIONER: "It sounds like you expect people to be able to keep their promises, and the fact that your husband didn't do that is very troubling to you (advanced reflecting)."

CLIENT: "Yes, that's what I expect. I have gone out of my way to help him."

PRACTITIONER: "It seems like you feel particularly hurt because you expected that he would be able to use your help to resolve the problems he has with drinking (advanced reflecting)."

CLIENT: "Yes, that was my expectation. I was awful to him this morning. I berated him terribly. I was so angry that I just couldn't stop myself from yelling."

PRACTITIONER:	"You seem disappointed in yourself for not being able to communicate with him without yelling (identifying the problem)."
CLIENT:	"When I am angry, it is really hard for me to stop yelling. I don't want to act that way."
PRACTITIONER:	"It sounds like you want to find a way to be able to restrain yourself from attacking or berating your husband (agreement on general goal)."
CLIENT:	"Yes, I don't like myself when I act that way."
PRACTITIONER:	"How would you like to respond to him when you are disappointed in how he has acted (question to identify specific goal)?"
CLIENT:	"I want to tell him about how I feel, the anger and disappointment, in a calm way."
PRACTITIONER:	"What would you need to do in order to stay calm (question to identify positives related to goal)?"
CLIENT:	"I guess I could take a deep breath and count to 10."
PRACTITIONER:	"That sounds like an achievable goal to me. So your goal is to take a breath and count to 10 before expressing how you feel in a calm way. Do I have that right (MAPS goal)?"

Example of Helping a Family Move from a General Goal to a MAPS Goal

MOTHER:	"In this family we just don't seem to talk in a nice way to each other. I'd like us to talk together rather than doing so much yelling and criticizing."
PRACTITIONER:	"Do the rest of you agree that you would like to learn to talk to each other (question related to attainability of goal)?"
BJ (DAUGHTER):	"If Mom wasn't so mean, then we could do that."
JOHN (SON):	"She's always telling us what to do."
PRACTITIONER:	"I hear how frustrated you all have been. That's why I think it might be useful to focus on the goal of learning to talk with each other so that you might feel less frustrated and angry with each other. Are you willing to work on learning to talk differently with each other (question related to attainability and positive aspects of goal)?"
BJ:	"Yes, that would be good, but I'm not sure how to do it."
JOHN:	"I guess it's worth a try."
PRACTITIONER:	"Let's think about what it would be like if at dinner tonight nobody yelled or criticized each other. What would you be doing instead (question related to positive aspects of goal)?"
JOHN:	"Mom and Dad would ask me what I did after school rather than jumping on me about my grades, and no one would interrupt what I was trying to say."
PRACTITIONER:	"Okay, and what might you do, John (question related to positive aspects of goal)?"
JOHN:	"Maybe instead of picking on BJ, I would ask her about what she did after school."
PRACTITIONER:	"John, since you don't like people interrupting, would you be willing to listen to BJ and not interrupt her (question related to attainability and positive aspects of goal)?"
JOHN:	"Well, I guess so."
PRACTITIONER:	"BJ, if John asked you about what you did after school, what would you do (question related to specific positive aspects of goal)?"

BJ: "I'd sure be surprised, but I guess maybe I would tell him about the project I am working on."

PRACTITIONER: "Mom and Dad, when you notice John and BJ talking with each other instead of picking on each other, what might you do (question related to specific positive aspects of goal)?"

DAD: "I think I would begin to relax. I usually feel tense at dinner, like any minute I am going to have to break up a fight or send them to their rooms."

PRACTITIONER: "Okay, let me summarize what I understand you want your family dinners to be like. You want to be asking each other about what happened in your day. You want to be taking turns talking and listening to each other. It sounds to me like you would also be talking about positive things rather than about concerns. Have I got that right? (summary) Everyone agrees."

PRACTITIONER: "How many nights a week do you want to plan to all eat together (question related to measurability of goal)?"

MOM: "We have lots of things going on around dinnertime. I think three nights a week would be about all we could do."

PRACTITIONER: "I know that you have busy lives. So your goal will be eating together three nights a week, each of you will take turns talking, you will talk about positive things, and you will listen to each other. Does that sound okay to all of you? (agreement on MAPS goal) Everyone agrees."

HOMEWORK EXERCISE 13.6 | CREATING MEASUREABLE, ATTAINABLE, POSITIVE AND SPECIFIC (MAPS) GOALS

After reading each of the following general goals, write a question a practitioner could use as a step toward developing a possible MAPS goal and then write a possible MAPS goal.

1. As I understand it, your goal is to increase your self-confidence. (*Hint*: What might good self-confidence look like? What might you see in a person who had adequate self-confidence?)
2. You want to learn to appropriately discipline your children. (*Hint*: How have you seen other parents discipline in ways that you liked?)
3. You will attend AA meetings every day for 90 days. (*Hint*: What are your hunches about what this person is trying to achieve by going to AA?)
4. You will attend six family therapy meetings. (*Hint*: In order to achieve what goal?)
5. You want to stop drinking. (You can do the rest of these without any hints.)
6. You would like your family to do something together that is fun instead of working all the time.
7. You want the people in this group to stop spending so much time talking about what is going on outside of the group.
8. This task group wants to stop spending so much time complaining.

As you become more skilled as a practitioner, you may decide to approach agreement on problems and goals differently. In some situations, it makes sense to establish goals for each problem at the beginning of the work. In other situations, it is better to set the first goal and achieve it before going on to set further goals. For example, when working with a neighborhood that initially expresses the problem as, "This neighborhood is going downhill rapidly," you may come to an agreement on four problems the neighbors are most concerned about and ready to address. First, the neighbors have been unable to figure out how to influence the absentee landlords to clean up their properties. Second, the neighbors are unsure how to get the parks cleaned up and safe for their children. Third, the neighborhood doesn't have any adequate childcare services and the neighbors have been unable to come up with a way to get this gap resolved. Fourth, although the neighbors have been meeting together at the community center, they have not developed a structured organization and they believe this is important. As the practitioner, you could help them figure out which problem they wanted to work on first, move ahead to developing a general goal related to that problem, and finally develop MAPS goals related to that problem. Once you achieved that goal, you could go back and select the next most important problem on which to begin. Another way to work with the neighborhood would be to develop general goals and then develop MAPS goals for each identified problem. One of the advantages of using this approach is that you begin with an overview of the whole project. As you are focusing on one goal, your work may also be related to another goal. Sometimes establishing all the goals in the beginning helps clients more clearly visualize what they want to achieve. However, with other clients, seeing the whole scope of the work can be discouraging.

Although having measurable, attainable, positive, and specific goals allows clients to develop a clear picture of their targets and also allows clients and practitioners to measure progress toward goal achievement, some practitioners prefer to work with more general goals. As you develop more experience as a practitioner, you will be able to decide when developing MAPS goals will be most helpful and when more general goals might be adequate.

HOMEWORK EXERCISE 13.7 | ESTABLISHING SEVERAL MAPS GOALS

Think of a goal that you have such as completing your degree or completing a course. If your goal is to complete a course, would you list all the related goals such as completing each assignment with a particular grade? Or would you focus on the immediate goal of finishing the next assignment and getting a particular grade? What are the advantages and disadvantages of each way of developing goals?

AGREEMENTS FOR WORK

After the goals are defined, many practitioners establish a written or verbal agreement that serves to bring together previous understandings between the practitioner and client. These agreements are sometimes called "agreements for work" because they set the stage for the work that the client and practitioner are planning to accomplish. The agreement includes a statement of the mutually agreed-upon goals. Although agreements for work should be upheld if possible, since they are developed collaboratively between the practitioner and client, they can be modified as long as the change is acceptable (Garvin & Seabury, 1997; Street, Makoul, Arora, & Epstein, 2009).

HOMEWORK EXERCISE 13.8 | AGREEMENTS FOR WORK

Think of two agreements that you have made, such as agreements to do tasks. If the agreements were verbal, not written, did each person remember the agreement in the same way? If there were misunderstandings related to the agreement, how do you think the agreement could have been improved?

MONITORING PROGRESS AND ALLIANCE

Now that the practitioner has worked collaboratively with the client to understand the history of the problems or challenges, the people involved, and their situation, and has identified the key challenges, general goals, and MAPS goals, the stage is set for monitoring continued work together. We know from a great deal of research that a good alliance between the practitioner and client is an excellent predictor of outcome when working with individuals, families, and groups (Asay & Lambert, 1999; Hiatt & Hargrave, 1995; Shelef, Diamond, Diamond, & Liddle, 2005; Wampold, 2010; Wampold & Brown, 2005; Wampold et al., 1997). A good alliance involves a safe, trusting, comfortable, collaborative relationship. This alliance should also include an agreement between the practitioner and client about goals (Martin, Garske, & Davis, 2000; Norcross, 2010; Scott, Wampold, & Imel, 2007).

There are many valid and reliable scales for measuring alliance (Martin, Garske, & Davis, 2000). Practitioners with the best outcomes regularly seek client feedback on the alliance (Miller, Hubble, & Duncan, 2007). Without client feedback, Hiatt and Hargrave (1995) showed that ineffective counselors rated themselves as adequate. A simple to use session rating scale can be accessed on Barry Duncan's Heart and Soul website. This session rating form asks clients to rate their experience with the practitioner on a 1 to 10 scale (with 10 being the highest). The form includes four continuums: relationship (felt understood), goals and topics (worked on what was important), approach or method (was comfortable), and overall (seemed okay) (Duncan et al., 2003). If a client rates any area with a score below 8, the counselor should discuss with the client how the situation could be improved.

Miller, Hubble, and Duncan also developed an Outcome Rating Scale that they use to monitor change over time. This scale is also available on the Duncan website. The scale asks the client to assess the following areas on a scale of 1 to 10 (with 10 being the highest): personal well-being; close relationships; work, school, and friendships; and general well-being. The client rates these areas in the first appointment and regularly in following appointments. Another way to monitor progress is to ask the client to identify where they are in relation to each MAPS goal. Using this approach, the client would give each MAPS goal a score from 1 to 10, with 10 having satisfactorily reached the goal. Many practitioners ask clients to rate each goal after the goals are established. Then the practitioner and client can rate progress on goals at regular intervals. This focus on goals and progress gives direction to the client and practitioner as they think about what areas need work.

HOMEWORK EXERCISE 13.9 | MONITORING ALLIANCE AND PROGRESS

Just for practice, think of any relationship you are in and rate it from 1 to 10 (with 10 being highest) on the following areas:

- In this relationship I feel understood.
- In this relationship we focus on the goals I think are important.

- In this relationship we are comfortable with each other.
- This relationship seems okay to me.

Now think of a goal you have established for yourself. How do you rate your progress on achieving that goal? Give yourself a score from 1 to 10, with 10 meaning you are satisfied that you have achieved the goal.

Monitoring Progress Using Goal Attainment Scaling

Goal attainment scaling is another helpful way to monitor progress. Although goal attainment scaling was originally developed to monitor progress in work with patients in mental health programs (Kiresuk, Smith, & Cardillo, 1994; Turner-Stokes & Williams, 2009), it has been used effectively in many other settings (Donnelly & Carswell, 2002; Rockwell, Howlett, Stadnyk, & Carver, 2003; Turner-Stokes, 2009) and with systems of all sizes, from individuals to families and large organizations or neighborhoods (Compton, Galaway, & Cournoyer, 2005; Fisher & Hardie, 2002; Kloseck, 2007; McLaren & Rodger, 2003). Using goal attainment scaling, the client and the practitioner create a 5-point scale or continuum that ranges from the most unfavorable outcome possible to the most favorable outcome that the client believes is possible. Each level of the scale should be measurable so that the practitioner and client can determine where the client is on the scale. A scale is created for each goal. The client and practitioner can use the scale to identify the level of progress achieved during the course of the work together and/or towards the end of the work. This scale includes the MAPS goal, or the expected outcome, as the midpoint. The following example shows how to use a goal attainment scale with an individual client. Goal attainment scales are also excellent evaluation tools to use with families, groups, and organizations.

Example: Goal Attainment Scale   For a client goal of obtaining employment, the practitioner would ask the client various questions as they worked together to establish a MAPS goal:

- "What kind of job do you think you are qualified for?"
- "How many hours per week do you want to work?"
- "Is location important?"
- "What is the minimum salary you are willing to accept?"
- "Is health insurance essential?"
- "Are there any other things that are important in terms of the job?"

For this example, the MAPS goal is a full-time job that pays at least minimum wage, is no more than 45 minutes from the client's home, and provides at least minimum medical insurance. As the practitioner and client continue to work together to develop the goal attainment scale, the practitioner would ask questions such as the following:

- "What would it be like if you started moving backwards or no progress was made?" (This establishes the most unfavorable outcome thought possible.)
- "What if you almost achieved your goal, but not quite?" (This establishes the level of less than expected success.)
- "What will it be like when you are right on target for achieving your goal?" (The expected level of success is the MAPS goal.)
- "What do you think it will be like *when* you do a little better than achieving your MAPS goal?" (This establishes the greater than expected level of success. As a practitioner, it is important that you carefully choose the words you use. What message would you be sending to your client if you asked, "What would it be like *if* you were able to achieve more than your goal?" The underlying message sent by using the word "when" is much more positive than the underlying message expressed by the word "if.")
- "What do you think it will be like when you achieve the most favorable result possible in the next six months?" (This question establishes the most favorable outcome the client believes is possible. It is important to state a time frame in this question because you want the client to be thinking about a specific time frame.)

GOAL ATTAINMENT SCALE: CLIENT WHO IS UNEMPLOYED

Most unfavorable outcome	Unemployed and about ready to give up the search.
Less than expected success	A part-time, minimum wage job with no benefits.
Expected outcome	(The MAPS goal) A full-time, minimum wage job that is no more than 45 minutes from home, and has minimum medical insurance.
Greater than expected success	A full-time job that pays a dollar more than minimum wage, is no more than 45 minutes from home, has minimum medical insurance, and a few paid days off.
Most favorable outcome	A full-time job that pays two dollars more than minimum wage, is no more than 45 minutes from the client's home, has minimum medical insurance, and a few paid days off.

As practitioners work with clients, they often set more than one MAPS goal. Using goal attainment scaling, each MAPS goal would become the expected outcome. The practitioner would then work with the client to establish the most unfavorable outcome, less than expected success, greater than expected success, and most favorable outcome. As you can imagine, it takes some time to develop a full goal attainment scale for several goals. However, this tool is very helpful as practitioners and clients evaluate progress, so it is worth taking the necessary time to create it. Since the goal attainment scale clearly shows not only the MAPS goal but also possible future outcomes, it helps clients visualize and begin to believe in the possibility of achieving even the most favorable outcome.

Example: Goal Attainment Scale for Three Goals   Besides being unemployed, the client in the previous example identified two other problems.

- He was feeling so depressed that he stayed home most of the time.
- He had no contact with his friends.

As the practitioner explored with the client what his life had been like when he wasn't depressed, the client identified that he was employed, had regular contact with friends, and regularly left the house to do things that he enjoyed.

	Unemployed	Lost Contact with Friends	Stays Home Most of the Time
Most unfavorable outcome	Unemployed and about ready to give up the search.	No contact with friends.	Only goes out if absolutely necessary.
Less than expected success	A part-time, minimum wage job with no benefits.	Has re-established contact with two friends that client talks to every other week.	Leaves home for necessary errands and tasks and goes out for a walk twice a week.
Expected outcome (MAPS goal)	A full-time, minimum wage job that is no more than 45 minutes from home, and has minimum medical insurance.	Has re-established contact with two friends that client talks to at least once every other week and sees at least once a month.	Leaves home at least once a month for some pleasurable activity and goes out for a walk twice a week.
More than expected success	A full-time job that pays a dollar more than minimum wage, is no more than 45 minutes from home, has minimum medical insurance, and a few paid days off.	Has re-established contact with three friends that client talks to at least every other week and sees at least once a month.	Leaves home at least once a month for some pleasurable activity and goes out for a walk three times a week.
Most favourable outcome	A full-time job that pays two dollars more than minimum wage, is no more than 45 minutes from the client's home, has minimum medical insurance, and a few paid days off.	Has re-established contact with four friends that client talks to at least every other week and sees at least once a month.	Leaves home at least twice a month for some pleasurable activity and goes out for a walk three times a week.

HOMEWORK EXERCISE 13.10 | GOAL ATTAINMENT SCALE

Working with a partner, develop a goal attainment scale related to your life that includes three MAPS goals.

DVD Example: Establishing Goals

Watch the exploring and goal setting section of the group meeting.

- List specific statements or questions used by the practitioner that
  - Identified a general goal
  - Invited the participants to add information to make the goal measureable, attainable, positive, and specific.
- What did you like about the way the practitioner used skills related to establishing a MAPS goal?
- Give specific examples of points where the practitioner could have made a statement or asked a question to further or more specifically identify key goals.

CASE

CASE, PART 4: HIDEKO, IDENTIFYING PROBLEMS AND GOALS

With this section of the Hideko case, you will move on to working on identifying problems and goals.

(The dialogue begins several minutes into the meeting.)

HIDEKO: "I thought about the problems I want to work on, and I really want to stop feeling so stressed and tired."

VIVIANA: "I can understand that. Tell me about what would have to change for you to be less stressed and tired."

HIDEKO: "Well, I guess a lot of things might have to change. I know when I was with my boyfriend I took an afternoon on the weekend and one night off from studying and taking care of my mother. I think I need that break. Before when I wanted to see my boyfriend I would tell my mother I just had to do something with my friends sometimes and couldn't be with her all the time. She would look sad and I felt guilty but I did it anyway. Now I am either in class, studying, taking care of my mother, or helping around the house all the time. My father can afford to hire someone to clean the house, but he says that it is a waste of money. When I was going out, even though they didn't like it, he would sometimes hire someone to do the cleaning because I wasn't there all the time to do it."

VIVIANA: "Okay, so one of the problems for us to work on is that you haven't found a way to get back to going out twice a week even though your parents may object, right?"

HIDEKO: "Yes, I just haven't been able to do that. Before my boyfriend was encouraging me which helped a lot."

VIVIANA: "It sounds like another problem is that you tell yourself you should be home with your mother and so end up feeling guilty when you aren't home. Is that something you want to change?"

HIDEKO: "That is going to be tough, but I guess I should work on it. Sometimes I am pretty hard on myself. I learned "do your best," "get top grades," "work hard," and "take care of your parents." You know it's really hard because my parents are immigrants and they still believe in the values they grew up with. I want to please them, but sometimes it is just too hard. Sometimes I just don't want to do it their way."

VIVIANA: "You have very high expectations and push yourself very hard. Is that something you want to change?"

HIDEKO: "I don't know. I want to do well, but I guess I don't want to feel so driven all the time."

VIVIANA: "Being able to do well is a strength, but sometimes people push themselves too hard."

HIDEKO: "Yeah, I feel kind of like a robot. I don't get enough sleep. I get up tired and take care of my mother and go straight to studying or class. I come home and help with my mother, do the cooking, and take care of the house before I can start studying. I usually go to bed very late. I do a lot, but no one notices."

VIVIANA: "It shows a lot of strength on your part that you continue doing what you believe you are

(continued)

CASE   CASE, PART 4: HIDEKO, IDENTIFYING PROBLEMS AND GOALS *(continued)*

supposed to do even though you get so little recognition and support."

VIVIANA: "Let's take some time to talk about your goals. One of the problems you said you wanted to work on is feeling guilty when you take time for yourself. How do you want to feel about taking time for yourself?"

HIDEKO: "I want to feel okay about taking some time off. I want to get back to telling myself that I am being a good daughter and that I deserve to have some time off even if my parents don't understand that."

VIVIANA: "That sounds like an excellent goal. When you are back to feeling okay about taking time off, what will other people notice is different about you?"

HIDEKO: "Hmm. *(pause)* I will smile more. Now I hardly ever smile. Maybe I won't look so tired."

VIVIANA: "How will you look?"

HIDEKO: "I will be energetic like I used to be. I will talk more and ask questions in class. Now I hardly say anything."

VIVIANA: "Good, we have a clear goal. You will feel okay about taking time off. You will be able to see that you have achieved that goal when you are smiling more, are energetic, and talk and ask questions in class. People might even say that you are back to your old self."

HIDEKO: "Yes, picturing that makes me feel better – like I can do it."
(Later in the meeting)

VIVIANA: "We are about out of time. I think we have accomplished a lot. We have set clear goals. Will you think about steps to achieve those goals this week?"

HIDEKO: "Yes."

VIVIANA: "My suggestion is that we meet together weekly for the next 4 weeks. After 4 weeks we can evaluate where you are on each goal and decide how much longer we think we should continue meeting. Does that sound okay to you?"

HIDEKO: "Yes, I think that is a good plan."

VIVIANA: "Okay, see you next week."

Questions
1. Discuss the practitioner's use of skills related to reaching agreement on problems and goals.
2. Analyze the MAPS goal that the client and practitioner agreed on in this meeting. Discuss whether the goal is measurable, attainable, positive, and specific.
3. What did the practitioner do well in the meeting?
4. Identify any inappropriate responses used by the practitioner.

Role Play–Do a role play with one person playing Hideko and another person the practitioner. In the role play, start with one of the concerns that Hideko has discussed. The practitioner will work with Hideko to define the problem and develop a MAPS goals related to that problem. Analyze your role play:

5. What skills did the practitioner use to help the client work toward defining the problem and setting a MAPS goal?
6. Analyze the MAPS goal that the client agreed on in this role play. Is it measurable, attainable, positive, and specific?

PRACTICE EXERCISE 7 | REACHING AGREEMENT ABOUT GENERAL GOALS AND MAPS GOALS

In order to establishing MAPS goals in this practice exercise, you will use all the skills you have learned in order to reach agreement on a general goal and use questions to move to agreement on a MAPS goal.

Exercise Objectives
• To practice using skills to reach agreement about general goals and to move from a general goal to a MAPS goal.

• To practice expressing empathy, warmth, respect, and genuineness in appropriate and effective ways.

Step 1: Preparation
Form groups of three people. Each person will have the opportunity to play the roles of client, practitioner, and peer supervisor. Each meeting will last about 10 minutes.

PRACTICE EXERCISE 7 | REACHING AGREEMENT ABOUT GENERAL GOALS AND MAPS GOALS (continued)

Client Role

- Think about a problem that you encountered in the past. These exercises will be much more authentic if you talk from your own experience. You may choose to stay in the same group that you have worked with in the past and have this meeting be a continuation of a previous meeting.

Practitioner Role

- Review the behaviors introduced in this chapter and the previous chapter (see evaluation form).

Peer Supervisor Role

- Review the behaviors introduced in this chapter (see evaluation form).
- Prepare to observe and listen to the client and to keep track of the time.

Step 2: The Client Meeting

Client Role

- If the experience you plan to discuss happened more than a year ago, give the practitioner the necessary basic information, for example, "This happened when I was a junior in high school."
- Talk for a brief period, pausing to give the practitioner a chance to respond during the telling of your story. Remember that your role is to give the practitioner a client to practice with. Working on whatever problem you may be facing is not the goal.

Practitioner Role

- Open the meeting.
- Use all the previous skills.
- Focus on using the skills related to defining the focus.
- Listen to the client and observe the client's non-verbal communication.

Peer Supervisor Role

- Keep track of the time and alert the practitioner and client when 9 minutes have passed so the practitioner has time to close the meeting.
- If the practitioner isn't able to figure out what to do during the interview, it is okay for the practitioner to stop the meeting and ask for assistance.

- Write down each of the practitioner's statements. Writing out each practitioner statement is very difficult but critical in order to accurately identify statements, to give solid feedback, and to effectively evaluate the practitioner's work. You may abbreviate, use a form of shorthand, or just write the first group of words in the statement, or you can tape record the interview and transcribe or listen to the tape.

Step 3: Feedback

Purpose: Receiving immediate constructive feedback helps students enhance their practice skills. Using this evaluation system, the peer supervisor monitors the skills used by the social worker. The client, social worker, and peer supervisor identify strengths and areas for growth.

Client Role

- Share how you experienced the practitioner.
- Did you feel understood?
- Was the practitioner warm, empathic, respectful, and genuine?
- What did the practitioner do particularly well?
- In what ways could the practitioner improve?
- Did you and the practitioner agree on a MAPS goal?

Practitioner Role

- Evaluate your use of skills related to reaching agreement on problems and MAPS goals.

Peer Supervisor Role

- Give the practitioner points for opening subsequent meetings.
- Give the practitioner one point for all the skills on the evaluation form.
- Discuss with the practitioner his/her use of skills related to defining the focus. Give the practitioner 1 point for each skill used related to defining the focus.
- Discuss with the practitioner the appropriate score for warmth, empathy, respect, and genuineness.

(continued)

PRACTICE EXERCISE 7 | REACHING AGREEMENT ABOUT GENERAL GOALS AND MAPS GOALS *(continued)*

- Identify any inappropriate response made by the practitioner (see evaluation form). One minus point for every inappropriate response.
- Add all the individual points and the points on the scales to get the total score.

- *Record the feedback in the practitioner's text-book for future reference.*

OVERALL EVALUATION FORM

Name of Practitioner _____

Name of Peer Supervisor _____

Directions: Under each category (in italics) is a list of behaviors or skills. Give one point for each skill used by the practitioner.

Opening and Closing

Beginning Subsequent Meetings

Give one point for each topic covered by the practitioner.

1. Asked client where he/she would like to begin.   _____
2. Summarized previous meeting.   _____
3. Identified tasks for this meeting.   _____
4. Asked client about progress.   _____
5. Asked client about homework.   _____
6. Asked client about problems.   _____
7. Made an observation about the previous meeting.   _____
8. Did a check-in.   _____

Express Understanding

Expressing understanding is so important that for this group of skills one point should be given for each time the practitioner used one of the skills.

1. Reflected feelings   _____
2. Reflected content   _____
3. Reflected feelings and content   _____
4. Summarized   _____
5. Reflected meanings   _____

Gaining Further Understanding

Questioning Skills

Give one point for each skill used by the practitioner.

1. Expressed understanding before asking questions.   _____
2. Asked open-ended questions when appropriate.   _____
3. Asked one question at a time.   _____
4. Asked closed-ended questions when appropriate.   _____

(continued)

PRACTICE EXERCISE 7 | REACHING AGREEMENT ABOUT GENERAL GOALS AND MAPS GOALS *(continued)*

Developing Deeper Understanding

Skills to Enhance Understanding

Give one point for each skill used by the practitioner.

1. Explored the meanings of words and body language
2. Explored the basis of conclusions drawn by the client   _____
3. Allowed silence   _____
4. Identified strengths   _____
5. Asked questions about strengths   _____

Defining the Focus

Reaching Agreement about Problems or Challenges

Give one point for each skill used by the practitioner. It rarely will be appropriate to use all of these skills in one meeting.

1. Used rolling with resistance   _____
2. Identified discrepancies   _____
3. Advanced reflecting   _____
4. Identified a pattern or theme   _____
5. Partialized the problem   _____
6. Supported self-efficacy   _____
7. Stated agreed upon problems   _____

Reaching Agreement about Goals

Give one point for each skill used by the practitioner.

1. Reached agreement on a general goals   _____
2. Used questions to develop a MAPS goal   _____
3. Reached agreement on MAPS goal

Common Mistakes or Inappropriate Responses *(subtract 1 point for each)*   _____

(offering advice, reassuring, offering excuses, asking leading questions, dominating through teaching, labeling, and interrogating)

Core Interpersonal Qualities

Using the scales in Appendix A, evaluate the appropriateness and effectiveness of the practitioner's expression of warmth, empathy, respect, and genuineness. On the following lines write the scores, from 1 to 5, for warmth, empathy, respect, and genuineness.

Score for warmth   _____
Score for empathy   _____
Score for respect   _____
Score for genuineness   _____
Total score   _____

EXPECTED COMPETENCIES

In this chapter, you have learned skills to assist clients in identifying their goals and establishing measurable, attainable, positive, and specific goals (MAPS).

You should now be able to:

- Give an example of a general goal and explain how it could be developed into a MAPS goal.
- List five questions that could be used to invite a client to move from a general goal to a MAPS goal.
- Give examples of MAPS goals for an individual, family, and group.
- Explain the importance of monitoring progress and alliance.
- Explain goal attainment scaling.
- Demonstrate skills used to reach a MAPS goal.

DOING, EVALUATING, AND ENDING THE WORK

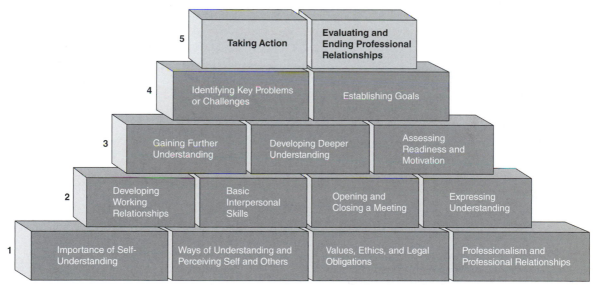

5 Taking Action | Evaluating and Ending Professional Relationships

4 Identifying Key Problems or Challenges | Establishing Goals

3 Gaining Further Understanding | Developing Deeper Understanding | Assessing Readiness and Motivation

2 Developing Working Relationships | Basic Interpersonal Skills | Opening and Closing a Meeting | Expressing Understanding

1 Importance of Self-Understanding | Ways of Understanding and Perceiving Self and Others | Values, Ethics, and Legal Obligations | Professionalism and Professional Relationships

© Cengage Learning 2013

The skills introduced in Chapters 14 and 15 build the final layer of basic practice skills. Chapter 14, Taking Action, covers how to collaboratively develop a plan of action to achieve the agreed upon MAPS goals. The chapter introduces skills to help clients move forward. As with the other phases of work, clients' strengths are an essential aspect of taking action. During this phase, clients need to use their strengths and capacities in new ways to achieve their goals. They may have to give up old mindsets and behavior patterns and learn new ways of thinking and acting. Chapter 15, Evaluation and Ending Professional Relationships, draws on the practice skills learned in previous chapters. For clients and practitioners this is a time to honestly evaluate what has worked, what was helpful, and what are the plans for maintaining progress made.

TAKING ACTION

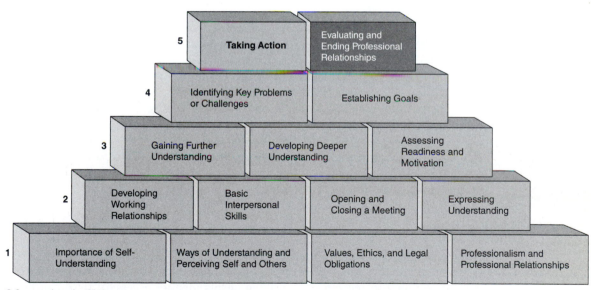

5 Taking Action | Evaluating and Ending Professional Relationships

4 Identifying Key Problems or Challenges | Establishing Goals

3 Gaining Further Understanding | Developing Deeper Understanding | Assessing Readiness and Motivation

2 Developing Working Relationships | Basic Interpersonal Skills | Opening and Closing a Meeting | Expressing Understanding

1 Importance of Self-Understanding | Ways of Understanding and Perceiving Self and Others | Values, Ethics, and Legal Obligations | Professionalism and Professional Relationships

© Cengage Learning 2013

Questions to consider as you read this chapter:

- How do you help clients move from setting goals to achieving their goals?
- How do you work with clients to develop an agreed upon plan that helps them resolve their problems?
- How do practitioners and clients evaluate progress toward goals?
- What additional skills are used during the action phase of the work?

This chapter covers practice behaviors related to taking action with clients to achieve established goals. *You will learn the importance of:*

- Developing agreed upon steps to help clients resolve their problems and achieve their goals
- Working with clients to enhance their capacities and strengths
- Using interventions that promote health and well-being

Client Attributes

- Willingness to use strengths, capacities, and resources to move toward achievement of goals

The establishment of clear goals lays the foundation for the action phase of the work by giving clients a clear picture of what they want to achieve. Generally, practitioners move from setting MAPS goals to asking clients to identify the action steps they think will be necessary to achieve a particular goal. Much of the work done by the client and the practitioner will consist of establishing and working on steps or tasks that are challenging for the client. Identifying the various steps gives clients a sense of hope as they begin to see a way to achieve their goals (Feldman, Rand, Shorey, & Snyder, 2002; Ward & Wampler, 2010).

In this chapter you will learn five more skills: teaching, directing, inviting a different perspective, giving feedback, and using self-disclosure. These skills are particularly valuable as you help clients take the steps necessary to achieve their goals. You will also learn new ways to use the skill of identifying discrepancies and a variation on identifying strengths called focusing on improvements. In the action phase of the work, you continue to use all the skills you have learned so far.

IDENTIFYING STEPS

Achieving a MAPS goal is a journey. Identifying the steps provides a road map for reaching the final destination or goal. Since many clients have not had the experience of planning to reach a goal, helping clients identify necessary steps can be an important learning experience. In addition, developing a plan for achieving a goal often enhances hope in the attainability of the goal.

Further Exploration of the Problem

Before identifying steps, further exploration about the problem may be needed to learn more specifics such as: where the problem occurs, who is involved, what are the immediate antecedents and consequences of the problem, and what meanings the client may be attributing to the problem. Practitioners explore the situation or environment to discover what precipitates and maintains the problem. Understanding the environment can require further exploration of the family, neighborhood, school, agency, significant groups and organizations, and the culture, race, and socioeconomic class of the client. For example, a practitioner was working with a mother whose goal was to learn a new way to parent her 8 year old child who was having behavior problems in school. In order to understand more about the mother's parenting style, the practitioner asked the mother to describe a typical morning with her son. The mother reported that she repeatedly told her son that it was time to get up, reminded him repeatedly to brush his teeth and get dressed, and informed him when it was time to go out to meet the bus. The son did not respond to his mother's reminders and often missed the bus. The mother excused his behavior and drove him to school. Given this start to his day, what are your hunches about how he responded in school when asked to do something? How do you think this additional information about the family's typical morning routine might help the practitioner and client identify steps to solve the problem?

Steps Identified by Clients

In the past, practitioners sometimes excluded clients from involvement in creating the action plan (Caspar, et al., 2005; Gollwitzer, 1999; Kottler, 2001; Seligman et al., 2007). If you do not include the client in developing the action plan, you are excluding them from learning valuable skills. Involving clients in every step of the process of problem-solving strengthens the working partnership between practitioner and client, and makes problem-solving and goal achievement a collaborative process. Practitioners begin the process of creating an action plan by asking what steps clients think will be necessary to reach their goals. Although clients may not possess fully formed ideas about what steps will be necessary, they do know what has worked for them in the past and what has not worked. After the client has named possible steps, the practitioner can suggest other steps that may be helpful. As in other phases of the work, collaboration is a key to success in this phase (Tryon & Winograd, 2011).

When a practitioner is working with a family or a group, every person needs to have a chance to suggest possible steps or tasks. Practitioners need to remember that at this point in the process the goal is simply to identify the steps to be taken. This is a brainstorming time. Assessing the usefulness, value, or possibility of each step will be done next. Evaluating after a possible step has been suggested limits creativity. Practitioners may need to remind clients that the plan is to identify possible steps, not to evaluate them or agree to do them.

Clients may have considerable information about what they need to do, but they need assistance in figuring out how to accomplish these tasks. Clients may generalize about the steps they have taken in the past by making comments such as, "I interviewed for a job," forgetting the many little steps that it took to get to the interview stage. It is the practitioner's job to be sure that the many discrete steps are delineated. Let's assume that your client, a mother, has the general goal of establishing a more positive relationship with her children. Her first MAPS goal is to have a clear plan that identifies at least three chores for each child, which includes consequences and rewards the mother will use consistently. Once the

MAPS goal is established, the practitioner brainstorms with the mother about possible steps to reach the goal. To increase the likelihood of success, the practitioner might ask the mother about times when she has been successful with the children in the past. Together, the practitioner and client determine the action steps the mother will take to achieve her MAPS goal. The first action step for the mother might be to develop a general list of chores the children are capable of completing. The next step might be for the mother to explain each chore to all of the children. Next, the mother could ask the children to pick three chores to complete from the list. Finally, the mother will talk with the children and identify the rewards and consequences related to each chore. Assuming the client developed these steps with the practitioner in ways that were useful to her and that she successfully accomplished them, another MAPS goal would be developed that addressed other areas that would move her toward her overall general goal of having a more positive relationship with her children.

Practitioners may also ask clients which steps they expect to find particularly difficult. If a step seems too difficult at first, it will be important to break it down into smaller steps. Sometimes when working with more than one person (a couple, a family, or a group), steps suggested by one person as reasonable may seem very challenging to another person. In this situation, the practitioner helps the clients break the step into a series of manageable smaller steps. By using this approach, clients learn the process of creating plans to achieve goals. Involving both clients and practitioners in identifying steps to achieve goals is appropriate with individual clients of all ages, as well as with families, groups, and larger systems such as organizations and communities.

Using Exception-Finding Questions to Identify Steps

In some situations, practitioners may use exception-finding questions, similar to those used in the goal-setting process (see Chapter 13), to help clients think about ways to solve problems. Using exception-finding questions, the practitioner asks the client to recall a time when the problem did not occur and to identify what he/she was doing at that time (De Jong & Berg, 1998; De Jong & Miller, 1995; Liston-Smith, 2008; McKeel, 1996). For example, in working with a family whose general goal is to have more fun together, the practitioner might ask them to think of a time when they had fun together and then ask each of them what he/she did to make that fun time possible. The family might then create a MAPS goal to plan one fun outing on a Saturday afternoon for two hours with the whole family. They could then make a list of the action steps that would make that goal happen. A teen might have a goal of getting a 3.0 grade point average (GPA) for the next semester of high school. She might be asked to think of a time when she was able to keep up with homework assignments and get a 3.0 GPA. From this answer the client and practitioner could develop action steps. Using exception-finding questions, the practitioner helps clients discover their own unique ways of solving problems. Clients can use these past successes to identify the steps they will need to take to be successful in solving their current problems and reaching their goals.

Exception-finding questions can also help clients to identify strengths that can be used in problem-solving (Kottler, 2001; Smith & Hall, 2007). For example, a female client was a successful sales person because of her flexibility and ability to quickly respond to the needs of customers. In her personal life, she tended to have relationship problems in part because she would rely on only one way of dealing with issues no matter what the circumstances were. When the practitioner asked her to think of situations in which she was more flexible, she quickly thought of her sales job. She was then able to see how she could use this flexibility to improve her personal relationships.

HOMEWORK EXERCISE 14.1 | IDENTIFYING STEPS

Think of a goal you would like to achieve (or have achieved). Next, take a few minutes to write down the steps you took to reach your goal. For example, you might use being accepted into college or graduate school or graduating from your program as the goal.

You know it took a lot of steps to achieve those goals. When listing the steps, be sure to include only those that you have control over such as "I will apply to five graduate schools" versus "I will be accepted into graduate school."

EVALUATING, ORGANIZING, AND PLANNING THE STEPS

Now that steps have been identified, the next part of the process is evaluating each step. If you truly invited brainstorming when identifying steps, you probably named some steps that will not work because they are impossible to achieve at this time or because they would be unacceptable to some person in the group. For example, when a practitioner was working with a couple who established the general goal of enhancing closeness in their relationship, one of the MAPS goals was to take a vacation together every year. The husband suggested biking to the West Coast as a possible vacation, despite the fact that this couple had not even taken a bike ride around the block recently. When evaluating this step, they agreed that someday they would like to bike to the West Coast, but for now, a more realistic step might be to bike together at least three times a week, weather permitting. Another client was discussing a power struggle between herself and her husband. The practitioner asked what small step might move her toward her general goal of a positive relationship with her husband. She said, "He could always agree with me." She and the practitioner both laughed and then went on to identify steps that were more realistic and possible for her to accomplish by herself.

After evaluating each possible step, the client and practitioner will need to organize the list of steps by prioritizing the steps to work on first, second, and so on. Sometimes clients want to start with the step that seems easiest to accomplish. Other clients prefer to begin by working on a step that seems most important or perhaps is causing the most discomfort. Some practitioners create a plan with the client that involves identifying all the steps and organizing them in order of which ones will be worked on first. When working with a task group or organization, this method of creating an overall plan is particularly useful. When working with an individual, couple, or family, the practitioner may choose to use a more general approach of identifying some steps and/or asking clients at the beginning of each meeting what they want to work on or what their goal is for that meeting.

When planning for achieving steps, it is important that clients see the value of each step, have a solid plan for completing each step, and understand and agree to complete each step. This is easier when working with an individual than when working with more than one person. Even if you are just working with a couple, or a parent and one child, a step may be acceptable to one person but not to another person. It is up to the practitioner to work with each person to find a step that will be acceptable to all. Sometimes this process may take considerable time, but it is important for all of the people involved to come to an agreement. Sometimes it is advisable to agree on a possible step and then wait until the next session to decide to implement it, so that each person involved can really think through if it fits for him or her. In the process of discussing which step is acceptable to everyone in the couple, family, or group, they are learning how to work together collaboratively. As the practitioner, it will be important for you to emphasize points of agreement (similar to noticing a theme), to reflect your understanding of what is important to each person, and to ask questions to invite each person to clearly identify what he/she wants or is willing to do.

It is essential to discuss with clients how they can use their strengths, capacities, and resources to complete each step. Practitioners might ask clients to think about other times when they faced new tasks. What did they do or tell themselves to help with accomplishing the task? If clients can't think of a new task or skill that they learned, the practitioner can suggest one, such as learning to ride a two-wheel bike, to drive a car, to read, to clean house, to cook, or to accomplish some other task.

Working together, the client and practitioner may identify additional incremental steps to achieve the more difficult or larger action steps. Creating small steps that can be successfully achieved helps clients gain a sense of confidence. For example, with a client whose goal was to effectively lead a group, the practitioner worked with the client to identify the various steps necessary to successfully conduct a group, and talked about which tasks the client felt comfortable doing and what strengths the client had that could be used in leading a group. The practitioner and client then picked the first task to be accomplished. They selected a small task that the client felt ready to begin doing. This task was to be active in a group by identifying when the group seemed to have come to a decision or was ready to move on to the next task. The practitioner and client discussed the value of this step in achieving the client's goal. In making a plan to complete the step, the practitioner asked the client what actions he thought would be necessary to achieve this step. Organizing and creating incremental steps helps ensure successful achievement of the MAPS goal. In addition, clients learn something about the process of creating plans to achieve goals—a skill that can be applied to many other situations in their lives.

HOMEWORK EXERCISE 14.2 | PLANNING AND ORGANIZING STEPS

For this homework assignment, put the steps from Homework Exercise 14.1 in order. Remember the various ways to order steps and select the one that you think would work best for you.

MONITORING PROGRESS AND FOCUSING ON IMPROVEMENT

Now that a specific plan has been developed, it is important to monitor progress and focus on improvement. Monitoring progress involves evaluating whether the client is satisfied with their progress (Lambert & Shimokawa, 2011). It makes sense to reuse whatever monitoring system you introduced when you established goals. If you had the client identify a 1 to 10 score related to each goal after the goals were identified, you can ask the client to rate the goals again using the same 1 to 10 scale. If in your first or second interview you used a form that asked clients to rate their satisfaction from 1 to 10 on several areas such as: satisfaction with work or school, satisfaction with close relationships, satisfaction with social relationships, and satisfaction with life in general, you can ask them to complete that form again.

If little progress has been made, the problem may be related to the established goal or goals. Reconsidering whether the goals are attainable and highly valued is a useful practice. The practitioner and client could explore whether the client is really motivated and able to achieve the goals at this time. Maybe the goals are not attainable because they involve someone else changing. Some clients want to achieve the goals they set, but they do not have enough energy to move ahead because of the many stresses and demands in their lives. For example, a couple stated a general goal of improving their marriage, but in reality, neither partner was committed to doing anything except attending weekly meetings with the practitioner. They always gave the practitioner many reasons for not focusing on their marriage between meetings. In the fifth meeting, the practitioner talked with the couple about whether they were ready to invest the time and energy required to improve their marriage or whether the many stresses they were facing made working on their marriage impossible at that time.

Sometimes progress is being made, but it seems slow to the practitioner. In this situation, the practitioner may not understand all of the challenges the client experiences. Working with the client to create smaller steps or devoting more time to helping the client get ready to successfully complete tasks may be useful.

Part of the monitoring process should be focusing on progress or improvement that has been made. Focusing on improvement is similar to identifying strengths and helps clients see what they are doing well. Any progress should be noticed, reinforced, and fully explored. For example, at the beginning of a meeting the practitioner might ask, "What steps have you taken since our last meeting to move toward your goals?" A practitioner might ask a family or a group, "In the last week, what did each of you do to help make your time together go well?" These questions imply that the practitioner believes the clients will be moving forward. Whatever the client says about positive movement, the practitioner can ask the client to elaborate. Practitioners might ask about the details related to the accomplishment.

It is important to emphasize any positive steps, particularly those that the client might not be valuing. Clients sometimes criticize themselves for not doing enough instead of complimenting themselves for every small change. Practitioners, realizing how difficult change can be, should invite clients to celebrate each step in the process.

Clients can be asked to focus on positives: "Between now and the next time we meet, I want you to find one aspect of your behavior that went well and that you'd like to continue doing." Research has demonstrated that using this type of assignment correlates positively with improvement (Kazantzis & Ronan, 2006; Neimeyer & Feixas, 1990).

Examples of Focusing on Improvement

- With an individual: "After talking to your boss, how did you feel about yourself?"
- With a family: "Will each of you tell one person in the family about one thing he or she did last week that you liked?"
- With a family: "Will you tell us about what you did that made things go a little bit better for the family this week?"
- With a group: "Let's go around the circle and share one positive thing we noticed when we first met each other."
- With a team: "We have been working together for a while now. How about if we take a minute to review what we have accomplished?"

HOMEWORK EXERCISE 14.3 | FOCUSING ON IMPROVEMENT

In a conversation with a fellow student, friend, or family member, spend 10 minutes listening, expressing understanding, and focusing on improvement. Of course, you will have to think about what the person is doing right. Remember that each small step in the direction of the person's goals is an improvement that deserves recognition.

SKILLS TO ENHANCE ACHIEVEMENT OF STEPS

As with previous phases of work, there are new skills that are particularly helpful in the action phase. Each of these skills can be used to help clients master a step in their plan. The new skills are: teaching, directing, inviting a different perspective, giving feedback, and using self-disclosure. A somewhat different use of identifying discrepancies is also useful, as is focusing on improvements. Besides these new skills, you will find that in the action phase you will continue to rely on the skills related to expressing understanding and exploring. At the end of this chapter, there is a summary of the skills useful in the action phase, their purposes, examples of when they might be used, and methods of using the skills.

Teaching

As practitioners help clients to learn new behaviors through taking action steps, they may assume an educator role. We discussed teaching in Chapter 5 with the warning that it could imply there is only one correct way of doing things, or that the practitioner knew the "right way" of doing things. This way of teaching could lead the client to seeing the practitioner as dominating. However, at some points in the process, teaching can be used as a way of conveying information the clients may not have. In the role of educator, the practitioner is facilitating change by helping individuals, families, and groups learn new methods, ways of thinking, behaviors, and ways of acting (Fryer-Edwards, et al., 2006; Minuchin, Colapinto, & Minuchin, 1998). Clients may need instruction or guidance in any number of areas, such as appropriate ways to encourage their children, to contact potential employers, to approach community leaders, to communicate their needs effectively, or to conduct a meeting using parliamentary procedure. In groups with a focus on topics such as parenting skills, social skills, assertiveness skills, appropriately expressing feelings, making friends, or recovering from some difficult experience such as major illness, divorce, or death, the practitioner often provides information and instruction (Barker, Cook, & Borrego, 2010; Sexton & Alexander, 2002). Teaching may occur in an organized class, such as a class for parents who want to learn better ways to discipline their children, for teams who want to learn to work together more effectively, or for children who want to learn to make friends. Teaching is appropriate when the practitioner realizes that new information might help clients achieve their goals.

Sometimes new information is essential to help clients take necessary steps. For example, while working with the client who wanted to be an effective leader, the practitioner taught the client about effective leadership, suggested a class for the client to attend, and suggested reading a book on leadership. Working with families, practitioners often teach about problem-solving skills, communication skills, effective discipline methods, and/or parenting methods (Alexander, Robbins, & Sexton, 2000; Magill-Evans, Harrison, Benzies, Gierl, & Kimak, 2007). Working with groups, practitioners might teach ways of accepting diversity, resolving conflicts, making decisions, and/or leading a group.

In the role of educator, the practitioner might help clients understand what is considered normal in various contexts. For example, parents might need to learn what to expect from children at different ages. Patients with newly diagnosed diabetes or cardiovascular disease might need to learn about how to manage their illness. People in a grief group might need to learn the predictable stages of the grieving process. Participants in a neighborhood group might need to learn what to expect from government officials.

As a practitioner who may know how to accomplish a particular step, it is easy to forget that the client may not know the necessary behaviors and may need to work with the practitioner to be ready to accomplish the step. In the case of the client who wanted to learn to lead a group, the client was hesitant about what to say to indicate that the group had come to a decision (action step). The practitioner suggested practicing in their session what he might say in a group to identify when a decision was made. This kind of practice is called *rehearsing* or *role playing*. In the role of educator, practitioners sometimes help clients with difficult tasks by modeling new ways of acting, and by inviting clients to rehearse or practice the behaviors that are challenging for them (Burlingame, MacKenzie, & Strauss, 2004; Mueser, Wallace, & Liberman, 1995; Packard & Conway, 2006). Rehearsing helps the client experience the action step so he/she will be more comfortable when it is time to actually take the step. By practicing the action step, clients reduce their anxiety and are more likely to experience success. Role playing with the practitioner and other group members is a common way to practice skills such as being assertive, or being clear and direct about wants and needs with a boss, teenager, partner, or spouse. In the role play, the practitioner can play the role of the client and model a way of behaving, or can play the role of the other person as clients try alternative ways of relating and communicating. For example, in a women's support group, one of the women was working on being assertive at work. After discussing the situation, the practitioner suggested that the woman role play the boss and pick a group member or the practitioner to act in an assertive way. After seeing appropriate assertive behavior modeled, another group member played the role of the boss while the woman tried acting in an assertive way. Whenever people are considering using a new behavior, practicing that behavior in a safe situation helps build their sense of confidence. With a neighborhood group that wants to talk to the mayor about improving the street lights in their neighborhood, the practitioner could decide to invite the participants to practice what they want to say before actually going to talk with the mayor.

Once clients have learned about and practiced the new behavior, it is important to explore their readiness to actually do the task. Using scaling questions, the practitioner might ask the client, "On a scale of 1 to 10, with 10 being absolute certainty that you can and will complete this task before our next appointment, what score would you give yourself right now?" If the score is below 8, the client probably needs more support or some other directions to feel more confident about successfully completing the action step. The practitioner and the client together will need to identify any obstacles and decide what additional steps are needed before they attempt the previously defined step.

It will also be essential to discuss with clients how they can use their strengths, capacities, and resources to complete each task. Practitioners can help clients list strengths and resources they can use to accomplish the task. If clients have trouble thinking of strengths, the practitioner can ask them to think about strengths they used to complete some other task, such as learning to read or write, to garden, to repair a leaky faucet, and so on.

HOMEWORK EXERCISE 14.4 | TEACHING

Think of a time when you needed to learn something from another person in order to achieve one of your goals. In what ways did the other person's teaching help you achieve your goal?

Directing

In the action phase of work, there are times when it is appropriate for practitioners to be directive. Being directive involves asking clients to do something new or to go in a different direction. For example, in a meeting the practitioner may ask the client to go back to something that was said earlier, to talk more about a particular topic, or to try saying something differently (maybe using stronger words or a gentler tone). Directing is often used in role plays or during rehearsing. In a task group the practitioner might direct the members to go back and focus on a topic that needed further exploration.

Directing may be used when inviting clients to engage in new behavior. The practitioner may encourage clients to do certain things, such as explore an area of interest or further explore thoughts or feelings. When directing, the practitioner suggests that the client complete a specific action. Following the practitioner's direction, clients practice behaviors before having to use them in real-life situations.

Examples of Directing
- With an individual: "Imagine you are talking to your supervisor now. Tell her what you want her to know."
- With a neighborhood group: "Will you take turns practicing what you are going to say to the police chief about the lack of patrol persons in this neighborhood?"
  - "Tonight several folks have expressed their frustration with how slowly this process is moving. Will some of the rest of you share your thoughts and feelings about the process we are using?"
- With a family: "During these meetings, I'd like you to talk about your own thoughts and feelings, so will you begin your sentences with 'I' rather than 'you'?"
- With a group: "I noticed you directing your comments to me. Would you be willing to talk directly to Herbert about your feelings?"
  - "I'd like go back to the problem of some members not feeling heard."
  - "Let's stop for a minute and talk about how what each of you thinks about how this group is doing."
  - (Tyrone is a group member who has been looking at the floor and not talking during a group meeting.) "I would like the group to give Tyrone feedback about what they have seen him doing in this meeting."
  - "LinLee, how did you feel about telling the group about your experiences in working with management? I imagine others have had similar experiences. Will someone else tell us about your experiences working with people who are in powerful positions?"

Giving homework is another way of directing that involves asking clients to complete an activity between meetings (Allen, 2006; Kazantzis & Ronan, 2006; Kazantzis, Whittington, & Dattilio, 2010). These directions usually involve completing a series of agreed-upon steps. When asking the client to respond to a specific direction, the practitioner should ask about the client's willingness and readiness to engage in the activity (Brodley, 2006). Scaling questions work well here to assess willingness and readiness. For example, "On a scale of 1 to 10, with 10 being 'I am definitely willing and feel ready to do this activity' and 1 being not at all ready to do this activity, what number would you give yourself?"

Examples of Using Homework Assignments
- With an individual: "Between now and our next appointment, will you make a list of all of the jobs that you think might interest you?"
- With a community group: "Between now and our next meeting, will each of you talk to two people in your neighborhood or church about this project?"
- With a family: "Between now and our next meeting, will each of you pay attention to something you like or appreciate about your family?"

HOMEWORK EXERCISE 14.5 | DIRECTING

In the next couple of days pay attention to ways that people direct others. Describe ways of directing that you think are effective and appropriate and ways of directing that you think are ineffective or inappropriate. Make a list of qualities and behaviors that are important when directing appropriately and effectively.

Inviting a Different Perspective

Sometimes clients have trouble taking action because their view of themselves, the world, situations, or other people is limiting their progress. Remember what you learned in Chapter 2 about constructs. Many times people have decided upon constructs that may have been appropriate when they were developed, but which now inhibit their current growth and development. Sharing another perspective invites clients to view experiences, feelings, thoughts, behaviors, or situations in a new way. This skill is also referred to as reframing (Goldenthal, 1996; Van Wormer, 2007). Clients see their life from their own perspective, but the practitioner or others may see things differently. A new perspective invites clients to see things differently, to change their behaviors or thoughts, and increase their success in achieving their action steps and goals.

When practitioners offer a different perspective, clients may not accept the new perspective. For example, one of the authors worked with a woman who had problems trusting people. One night the man she was dating was not able to drive to her town to see her. A few days later he told her that he needed more time to decide if he wanted to move into a committed relationship. She reported that these two incidents meant that he was definitely seeing another woman. Offering a different perspective, the practitioner said, "He might have been telling you the truth about being busy one night and not being quite ready to make a commitment to you." In this case, the client did not want to change her view of the situation, so the practitioner moved on to expressing understanding.

Examples of Offering Different Perspectives
- About a decision: "I hear that you consider this decision of whether to leave your job and go to graduate school to be scary. Maybe it is also an exciting opportunity to make a change."
- About a feeling: "You said that you feel scared about talking to the mayor about the lighting in the neighborhood. I wonder if maybe part of that feeling is excitement about this new challenge."
- About an experience: "You said that you haven't learned anything from this group experience, but think about whether you have learned some important lessons about how to be a more effective group member."
- About a behavior: "Maybe his disruptive behavior in class is an indication that he is bored."
- About group dynamics: "Maybe the other members of the team are not resisting change, but rather wanting more time to explore all the options before making a decision."

- About a conflict: "Another way of looking at this conflict is that it gives us an opportunity to practice accepting and understanding our differences."
- About self-concept: "I hear that you feel angry at yourself for being impatient with your daughter. Do you also feel good about the fact that now you are sometimes more patient with her?"
- About another person's behavior: "I understand that you see your wife as wanting to start a fight with you. Another way of looking at what she is doing is that she wants you to hear her position."
- About group performance: "It is disappointing that we didn't complete several of our goals. Maybe instead of criticizing ourselves for ending this project without completing all of our goals, we should be celebrating everything that we did accomplish."
- About a new experience: "It sounds like you feel kind of scared about going to Spain for a semester and are worried about whether you will be safe there. For a minute, let's talk about what you think will be exciting and fun about being in Spain."

Practitioners sometimes use questions to invite clients to see things differently. Practitioners may challenge clients to evaluate whether their behaviors, thoughts, or feelings are effective in getting them what they want. Asking "how" questions often evokes responses in which the client is invited to reflect upon new or existing information. Questions can be used to invite clients to think about something they have avoided or to look at something from a different perspective.

Examples of Using Questions to Invite a New Perspective

- Individual client: "How do you think he felt when you refused to talk to him?"
  - "Is there another way of explaining his behavior?"
- Family: "How do the rest of you feel about your mother's decision to go back to work?"
  - "Just for a minute, would you think about this from your dad's point of view?"
- Task group: "How do the rest of you feel about Tom's wish to do this part of the project by himself?"
  - "What else might be going on that would explain Tom's need to do this part of the project alone?"
- A counseling group: "When Jose expressed his disappointment at thinking that Andrea got more attention from me than he did, did that feeling remind anyone else of how you have felt in other group situations or in your family?"
- An organization or community: "How does the group feel about Simone wanting to drop out of this project?"

HOMEWORK EXERCISE 14.6 | INVITING A DIFFERENT PERSPECTIVE

Tell a partner about your thoughts or views about a particular situation. Ask your partner to suggest a different way of looking at the situation. Now change roles and have your partner tell you about his/her thoughts about a particular situation. When he/she is finished, suggest another way of looking at the experience.

Identifying Discrepancies

We first discussed the skill of identifying discrepancies in Chapter 12. Identifying discrepancies is similar to confrontation and is used during the action phase of work as a way to invite clients to see or think about something differently. The discrepancy usually involves a behavior that seems to be moving the client away from the stated goal and/or is preventing successful completion of an action step. Practitioners base these statements on discrepancies they have observed, heard, or surmised from the work with the client. Since the practitioner's intent is to invite the client to think about the discrepancy, it is important to allow some time for the client to consider what has been said or to ask about the client's thoughts about what has been said. In the following examples you will see how this skill can be used with individuals, families, and groups.

Discrepancies can include differences between:

What a client is saying or doing and what the practitioner is noticing.

- With a group: "I hear most of the members of the group saying that you agree with this plan, but I noticed that some of you are looking at the floor and seem uncomfortable. I wonder if maybe you are hesitant to express how you feel about this plan."
- With an individual: "You're talking about being scared, but you're smiling."
- With a family: "I hear you saying that you want everyone in the family to have time to talk, but I noticed that twice when Susie started to speak, someone else talked for her."

What the client is saying and what the practitioner heard the client say at another time.

- With an organization: "During this week's meeting, folks are indicating that cars driving too fast through the neighborhood isn't the problem, but in our last meeting several folks seemed ready to do something about cars speeding in areas near where your children often play. Help me understand what changed since last week."
- With an individual: "I've heard you mention before that teaching is something that you really enjoy, but now you are talking about giving up your teaching job."
- With a task group: "Last week I thought we had come to consensus about approaching the teacher, and now I hear that several of you are not willing to do that."
- With a family: "Last week at our family meeting you all agreed to set aside 2 hours every Saturday to work together cleaning up the house. Now a couple of you are saying that you're not willing to do this."

What the client is saying in the meeting and the client's actions outside the meeting.

- With an individual: "In our last session you said you were determined to get medical treatment, but you still haven't made an appointment with a doctor."

- With an organization: "All of you agreed that the problems in this neighborhood need to be solved. I understood that you were willing to talk to two neighbors about their view of the problems, but at this meeting only one person told us about talking to her neighbors."
- With a couple: "At our last session, you decided that it was important to be positive with each other, but when I just asked you about positive statements, neither of you remembered doing that."

What the client says is important or is the goal and his/her behavior.

- With an individual: "When you said that you wanted your son to live at home, I noticed that you were shaking your head 'no'. I wonder if maybe you aren't really sure about having him at home."
- With a task group: "Last week the group said that they felt prepared to move ahead with plans to contact the absentee landlords, but now everyone seems hesitant to talk about moving ahead."
- With a couple: "You have said you want your husband to express his feelings, but I notice that whenever he does you shrug your shoulders and turn away."
- With an individual: "You said that you wanted to talk more openly with your wife, and now I hear you saying that you are not willing to tell her about your concern over losing your job. Will you help me understand that?"

HOMEWORK EXERCISE 14.7 | IDENTIFYING DISCREPANCIES

Think about a discrepancy in your life, such as a discrepancy between a goal and your actions. Write down what you might say as a practitioner noticing this discrepancy. Think about other discrepancies that you know about, maybe in your family or in a group. If you were a practitioner noticing this discrepancy, write down what you might say.

GIVING FEEDBACK

Upon reaching the action phase, a solid working relationship has been established and goals agreed upon, so the additional skills of giving feedback, self-disclosure, and immediacy can be used. Giving feedback involves stating what the practitioner sees and hears. It is important to differentiate giving feedback from giving your opinion of what the client has said.

When giving feedback, practitioners share an awareness of what clients are showing nonverbally or expressing in their tone of voice. Since practitioners cannot be sure how clients will receive feedback, it is important to follow up with a question such as, "What are your thoughts about that?" This is a time when it is particularly important to use your observation skills and notice how the client reacts to the feedback. Feedback about feelings often gives clients permission to express more of how they are feeling. For example, if the practitioner says, "you look very sad," the client may start to cry. As a practitioner, it is important for you to be willing to be with clients as they express how they feel. This is often a good time to allow silence.

Examples of Giving Feedback

- "I notice that you are smiling."
- "I heard your voice crack when you said the word 'daughter.'"
- "I notice that your hands are clenched."
- "You look like you are about to cry."
- To the husband: "As you are talking, I noticed that your wife looks like she is about to cry."
- "Your voice got quiet when you said that your dad is quite ill."
- To a team, task group, or family: "I've noticed that Maria and Thuy are the only people who have voiced an opinion."
    - "All of you seem very quiet today."
    - "I notice that several people in the group look at me frequently, even when they are talking to someone else."
    - "I think our team is beginning to agree; I see heads nodding."
    - "As I look around the room, I am noticing that many folks are beginning to look tired. Maybe we should finish our meeting soon."

Giving feedback in a group or family is important. Rather than the practitioner giving feedback, he/she might ask members of the family or group to share their feedback. For example, the practitioner might say, "What have you noticed about Manuel's behavior during this discussion?" Since we so rarely receive truthful feedback, hearing this honest information is very valuable (Kottler, 1994; Sparks & Muro, 2009).

HOMEWORK EXERCISE 14.8 | Giving Feedback

Giving feedback is another skill that might feel awkward at first because it is probably something you have not done before. On three different occasions, think about what you might say if you were going to give feedback. Write down your ideas about what you could say to give feedback.

SELF-DISCLOSURE

Practitioners use self-disclosure to share personal information, observations, and opinions with the client in order to give the client a different perspective or offer an illustration or example. The information may be about the practitioner's personal experience or his/her experience of the client. As with giving feedback, it is important that self-disclosures occur in relationships that are strong and well-developed (Myers & Hayes, 2006). The use of self-disclosing statements by practitioners needs to be employed sparingly, and the focus should be kept on the client (Callaghan, 2006; Meier & Davis, 2004). There are three suggested guidelines to consider prior to using self-disclosure (Anderson & Mandell, 1989; Henretty & Levitt, 2010; Mahalik, VanOrmer, & Simi, 2000).

- First, the goal of any disclosure should be to enhance or preserve the relationship. For example, the practitioner might say, "I have been feeling concerned because it seems like you have been less open in discussing your problems in the last couple of sessions. I wonder if there is a problem between us that you are willing to discuss." (Practitioner is sharing his/her feelings.)

- Second, practitioners need to ensure that their personal needs do not take precedence over those of the client. The practitioner should not share anything about his/her personal life or problems that might invite the client to feel like he/she should take care of the practitioner.
- Third, disclosure must be for the benefit of the client and be designed to keep the focus on the client. The practitioner might briefly say, "I have some understanding of the challenges you are facing dealing with your mother's illness because I faced something similar several years ago."

Ethical concerns should be considered when using self-disclosure. Beginning practitioners may feel uncomfortable because the client is sharing a great deal of personal information and they are not sharing anything about themselves. In such a case, the beginning practitioner may choose to tell the client something about his/her personal life in the same way that he/she might share with a friend. Talking about your personal life can easily lead to blurred professionalism, and the client's perceptions of the practitioner may be irrevocably damaged (Curtis, 1982; Henretty & Levitt, 2010). If the purpose of the self-disclosure is to gain sympathy or support from the client, the practitioner has crossed the line from professional to personal.

Self-disclosure can be a way of subtly including personal values in interactions with clients. When practitioners disclose decisions they have made or life experiences they have had, clients may think they should follow the practitioner's example. Examples might be a practitioner disclosing that she had an abortion, got a divorce, returned to work and put her young children into daycare, or had an affair. Each of these disclosures could imply that the practitioner is recommending similar behavior to a client whose values, life situation, and needs might be quite different than the practitioner's.

Another challenging aspect of self-disclosure is how to respond when asked direct and often personal questions, particularly if these questions are asked early in the relationship with the client. Practitioners need to consider what led the client to ask the question. If the client, a middle-aged mother of four children who is living in poverty, asks the young, well-dressed female practitioner, "Do you have children?" what are your hunches about the client's reasons for asking this question? In our experience, this kind of question is often an indication that the client is afraid that the practitioner doesn't have enough life experience to understand his/her situation. Although there are different opinions about how to respond to such a question, we recommend that you keep the focus on the client and say something like, "I wonder if maybe you are concerned about whether I will be able to understand your situation. Will you tell me more about what it is like for you to be caring for four children?" Many personal questions are veiled concerns about not being understood.

Some personal questions a client might ask may be efforts to change the relationship from a professional relationship to a personal relationship. These are the kinds of questions you might ask a friend over coffee, such as, "Who are you going to vote for?" "What is your favorite type of music?" or "What do you think about (some sports team)?" Rather than answering the question, the practitioner needs to talk with the client about the nature of their relationship. The practitioner might say, "I am glad that you want to talk with someone about music. That is a great topic to introduce with someone you would like to make friends with, but it is important for us to stay focused on the goals we established. Since one of those goals involves making more friends, perhaps you would be willing to ask someone you would like to get to know better about his or her favorite type of music."

Another kind of personal question is actually a request for advice, such as, "How do you think teenagers should be disciplined?" or "I notice you are married. What do you do when you are angry with your husband?" Once again, the best policy is to explore the client's underlying concern. The practitioner might say, "Figuring out the most effective way to discipline teenagers is challenging. What have you tried that has worked?" or "What do you think might be worth a try?"

Self-disclosure can enhance genuineness in the relationship. As we discussed in Chapters 5 and 10, being genuine is important in practitioner-client relationships. Practitioners may share their thoughts, feelings, and/or opinions about the immediate situation. For example, a practitioner might say, "I am having trouble paying attention to what you are saying because it seems like you are repeating the same things." In a team meeting, the practitioner might state, "I am feeling frustrated because it seems like only a few of us are doing most of the work." To a family, the practitioner could say, "I am amazed at how much you have accomplished in a short period of time." These statements share something about the practitioner's thoughts and feelings. This willingness to share is experienced by clients as being genuine.

HOMEWORK EXERCISE 14.9 | SELF-DISCLOSURE

Think about how you might feel in a professional relationship with a doctor, dentist, lawyer, or professor if after talking about your challenge, the professional told you about a similar challenge he/she faced. You might feel reassured, thinking that if the professional had a similar challenge he/she could understand you, or you might feel uncomfortable, thinking "This is more than I wanted to know about this person" or maybe "Am I supposed to do something to help him/her?" Do you think the self-disclosure would change your relationship with the professional person, or maybe invite you to think the professional person was inviting you to be a friend?

Immediacy

Immediacy is a particular type of feedback that involves the practitioner commenting on what seems to be happening currently in the relationship between the practitioner and the client (Egan, 2007). Using the skill of immediacy, the practitioner focuses on what is happening in the moment. Giving the client feedback about how the practitioner is experiencing their relationship may help the client understand other relationships. For example, with a client who reports many problems maintaining relationships, the practitioner might say, "When you talk rapidly and don't identify what you want to focus on, I feel excluded, almost as if you do not want to maintain a connection with me." In a situation with a client who has been involved and focused, and who suddenly seems distant and withdrawn, the practitioner might say, "I noticed that you are looking away and aren't saying much (giving feedback)," or "I wonder if I said or did something that is troubling to you (immediacy)."

Immediacy is like self-disclosure because it involves the practitioner sharing his/her feelings or thoughts. It is sometimes appropriate for practitioners to disclose their current feelings, but *only* if they are relevant to the immediate tasks or goals of the client. Self-disclosure of what the practitioner is experiencing in the present has a greater impact than reporting on experiences from the past. For example, a group practitioner might say, "I am feeling frustrated about what is going on in the group right now. It seems to me like we are avoiding dealing with the real problem. I wonder how other group members are feeling about what just happened."

| HOMEWORK EXERCISE 14.10 | IMMEDIACY |

In a relationship, think about what you might say if you were to comment on what you thought was happening between the two of you. For example, "I notice that as I am talking to you, you are glancing at the football game on television. I wonder if you are too distracted to talk with me." Write down what you might say.

TABLE 14.1 | SKILLS TO ENHANCE ACHIEVEMENT OF STEPS

Skill	Purpose	Examples	Specific Methods
Teaching	To help clients learn new methods, new ways of thinking, new behaviors, and new ways of acting.	• Ways to communicate needs in an appropriate way. • Better ways to discipline children.	• Providing information or explaining. • Demonstrating. • Rehearsing or role playing.
Directing	To invite clients to try something new or to go in a different direction.	• Asking a client to say something using "I" instead of "you" statements. • Suggesting a different approach to disciplining children.	• Making a suggestion. • Giving homework. • Giving direction in a role play.
Inviting a different perspective	To help clients view their experiences, feelings, thoughts, behaviors, or situation in a new way by sharing another perspective with them.	• Asking a client to consider her husband's inability to share his feelings as a lack of communication skills rather than a demonstration of his indifference to her.	• Offering an alternate view. • Asking questions to help clients consider another perspective.
Identifying discrepancies	To invite clients to see or think about something differently.	• "One of the goals we identified is that you will spend time with your AA friends who support the way you want to live. Help me understand what happened that led you to go to a bar and eventually get drunk."	• Pointing out an incongruity between the client's present behavior and his or her broader goals and values.

(continued)

TABLE 14.1 | SKILLS TO ENHANCE ACHIEVEMENT OF STEPS (*CONTINUED*)

Skill	Purpose	Examples	Specific Methods
Giving feedback	To give the client information he/she may not be aware of.	• "I noticed that when you started talking about seeing your father you clenched your jaw and made a fist."	• Describing to the client what the practitioner sees and hears (verbal and nonverbal).
Immediacy	To help the client understand his/her patterns of interpersonal behavior problems by examining the client's responses to the practitioner, the work process, or the client/ practitioner relationship.	• Change in client behavior towards the practitioner. • Client pattern of avoiding eye contact with the practitioner.	• Discussing client reactions to the practitioner. • Statements about client behavior toward the practitioner.
Self-disclosure	To share personal information, observations, and opinions with the client in order to give another perspective.	• Practitioner comments on what he/she is experiencing with a group at the time.	• Statements about the practitioner's current thoughts or feelings or one of the practitioner's past experiences that is directly relevant to the client.

 DVD Example: Taking Action

Watch the taking action meetings with the individual, family, and/or the group.
- List specific statements or questions used by the practitioners that
  - Identified steps
  - Organized steps
  - Evaluated or monitored progress
  - Focused on progress
  - Taught
  - Directed
  - Invited a different perspective
  - Identified a discrepancy
  - Gave feedback
- Identify any points where the practitioners used self-disclosure. In what ways do you think the use of self-disclosure was appropriate or inappropriate?
- Identify any points where the practitioners used immediacy or could have used immediacy.
- What did you like about the way the practitioners used skills related to taking action?
- Give specific examples of points where the practitioners could have done more to invite specific action.

CASE	CASE, PART 5: HIDEKO, TAKING ACTION

You are now ready to move into the action phase of work with Hideko.

1. Think about the case from the perspectives discussed in Chapter 2: constructivism, resilience, ecological, family systems, dual perspective, strengths, and empowerment. Discuss how each perspective might be used to help you understand and work with Hideko.

2. Select one goal from the work with Hideko in Part 4 in Chapter 11. Write a basic plan for the beginning of the action phase of the work. Your plan should identify at least five steps and discuss three action phase skills that could be used.
   Role Play–Do a role play with one person playing the role of Hideko and one person in the role of practitioner. In your role play you will be moving from a MAPS goal into the action phase.

3. Evaluate the practitioner's work in the role play.

4. What did the practitioner say to invite Hideko to identify steps she might take to reach the goal? In what ways did it invite her to work further to identify steps?

5. In what ways did the practitioner focus on improvements? List specific statements made by the practitioner. If the practitioner did not use this skill, write two statements that the practitioner could have used.

6. Did the practitioner use teaching? If so, what topics were covered? In what ways did the use of this skill seem helpful? If not, give an example of how teaching could be used.

7. Did the practitioner use inviting a different perspective? If so, what did the practitioner say? In what ways did the use of this skill seem helpful? If not, give an example of how this skill could have been used.

8. Did you notice any discrepancies between the client's statements and her reported behavior? If so, did the practitioner identify the discrepancies? In what ways did the use of this skill seem helpful? If not, how might this skill have been used?

9. Did the practitioner use self-disclosure? If not, how might self-disclosure have been used?

PRACTICE EXERCISE 8 | TAKING ACTION

Because these skills require considerable practice to master, you will be using and evaluating the use of identifying key problems and MAPS goals as well as the skills introduced in this chapter. In the practice exercises each set of skills will be included at least twice.

Exercise Objectives
- To practice skills related to taking action (see the evaluation form).
- To practice expressing warmth, empathy, respect, and genuineness in appropriate and effective ways.

Step 1: Preparation
Form groups of three people. Each person will have the opportunity to play the roles of client, practitioner,

and peer supervisor. Each meeting will last about 10 minutes. For this exercise it will be easier to work with the same group of people that you have worked with in the previous two practice exercises. If you work with the same group of people, you will be able to start after the beginning and exploration parts of the meeting.

Client Role
- Think about the problem you discussed in the previous meetings.

Practitioner Role
- Think about important things to observe in the client and to do in the interview.
- Review the behaviors introduced in this chapter and the previous chapter (see evaluation form).

(continued)

PRACTICE EXERCISE 8 | TAKING ACTION *(continued)*

Peer Supervisor Role
- Review the behaviors introduced in this chapter (see evaluation form).
- Prepare to observe and listen to the client, to keep track of the time, and to write down what the practitioner says.

Step 2: The Client Meeting

Client Role
- If the experience you plan to discuss happened more than a year ago, give the practitioner the necessary basic information, e.g., "This happened when I was a junior in high school."
- Talk for a brief period, pausing to give the practitioner a chance to respond during the telling of your story. Remember that your role is to provide the practitioner a client to practice with. Working on whatever problem you may be facing is not the goal.

Practitioner Role
- Use the skills related to taking action.
- You can stop the meeting at any time to get suggestions from the persons in the role of the client or peer supervisor.
- Listen to the client and observe the client's nonverbal communication.

Peer Supervisor Role
- Keep track of the time and alert the practitioner and client when 9 minutes have passed so the practitioner has time to close the meeting.
- *Write down each of the practitioner's statements.* Writing out each practitioner statement is very difficult but critical in order to accurately identify statements, to give solid feedback, and to effectively evaluate the practitioner's work. You may abbreviate, use a form of shorthand, or just write the first group of words in the statement, or you can tape record the interview and transcribe or listen to the tape.

Step 3: Feedback

Purpose: Receiving immediate constructive feedback helps students enhance their practice skills. Using this evaluation system, the peer supervisor monitors the skills used by the social worker. The client, social worker, and peer supervisor identify strengths and areas for growth.

Client Role
- Share how you experienced the practitioner.
  - Did you feel understood?
  - Was the practitioner warm, empathic, respectful, and genuine?
  - What did the practitioner do particularly well?
  - In what ways could the practitioner improve?

Practitioner Role
- Evaluate your use of skills related to taking action.

Peer Supervisor Role
- Based on your notes, give feedback to the practitioner on the use of skills that express understanding, gain further understanding, and define the focus. Give the practitioner one point for each skill used.
- Discuss with the practitioner the use of skills related to taking action. Give the practitioner 1 point for each taking action skill used.
- Discuss with the practitioner the appropriate score for warmth, empathy, respect, and genuineness.
- Identify any inappropriate response made by the practitioner (see evaluation form). One minus point for every inappropriate response.
- Add all the individual points and the points on the scales to get the total score.
- *Record the feedback in the practitioner's textbook* for future reference.

PRACTICE EXERCISE 8 | Taking Action *(continued)*

Evaluation Form

Name of Practitioner_____

Name of Peer Supervisor_____

Directions: Under each category (in italics) is a list of behaviors or skills.
Give one point for each skill used by the practitioner.

Express Understanding
Expressing understanding is so important that for this group of skills
one point should be given for each time the practitioner used one of the skills.

1. Reflected feelings   _____
2. Reflected content   _____
3. Reflected feelings and content   _____
4. Summarized   _____
5. Reflected meanings   _____

Gaining Further Understanding

Questioning Skills

Give one point for each skill used by the practitioner.

1. Expressed understanding before asking questions.   _____
2. Asked open-ended questions when appropriate.   _____
3. Asked one question at a time.   _____
4. Asked closed-ended questions when appropriate.   _____

Developing Deeper Understanding

Skills to Enhance Understanding

Give one point for each skill used by the practitioner.

1. Explored the meanings of words and body language   _____
2. Explored the basis of conclusions drawn by the client   _____
3. Allowed silence   _____
4. Identified strengths   _____
5. Asked questions about strengths   _____

Defining the Focus

Reaching Agreement about Problems or Challenges

Give one point for each skill used by the practitioner. It rarely will
be appropriate to use all of these skills in one meeting.

1. Used rolling with resistance   _____
2. Identified discrepancies   _____
3. Advanced reflecting   _____
4. Identified a pattern or theme   _____
5. Partialized the problem   _____
6. Supported self-efficacy   _____
7. Stated agreed upon problems   _____

(continued)

PRACTICE EXERCISE 8 | TAKING ACTION *(continued)*

Reaching Agreement about Goals
   Give one point for each skill used by the practitioner.

   1. Reached agreement on a general goals   _____
   2. Used questions to develop a MAPS goal   _____
   3. Reached agreement on MAPS goal   _____

Taking Action
Give one point for each skill used by the practitioner. It rarely will be
appropriate to use all of these skills in one meeting.

   1. Identified steps   _____
   2. Focused on improvement   _____
   3. Taught   _____
   4. Directed   _____
   5. Invited a different perspective   _____
   6. Gave feedback   _____
   7. Used self-disclosure   _____

Common Mistakes or Inappropriate Responses *(subtract 1 point for each)*   _____
(offering advice, reassuring, offering excuses, asking leading questions,
dominating through teaching, labeling, and interrogating)

Core Interpersonal Qualities
Using the scales in Appendix A, evaluate the appropriateness and
effectiveness of the practitioner's expression of warmth, empathy, respect,
and genuineness. On the following lines write the scores, from 1 to 5,
for warmth, empathy, respect, and genuineness.

   Score for warmth   _____
   Score for empathy   _____
   Score for respect   _____
   Score for genuineness   _____
Total score   _____

EXPECTED COMPETENCIES

In this chapter you have learned about working with clients to create and monitor an action plan to achieve their identified goals. You have also learned the following skills that are useful in the action phase of your work with clients: identifying steps, focusing on improvements, teaching, directing, inviting a different perspective, identifying discrepancies, giving feedback, using self-disclosure, and immediacy.

You should be able to define the following word: immediacy.

You should now be able to:

- Give an example of using exception-finding questions to help identify a step.
- Identify several reasons for focusing on improvement.
- Explain when and why practitioners might instruct their clients.

- Describe how a practitioner might invite clients to consider taking a new perspective on their experiences, behaviors, thoughts, feelings, or situations.
- Give an example of a statement identifying a discrepancy.
- Give an example of how a practitioner might direct a client.
- Give an example of giving feedback to a client.
- Explain appropriate and inappropriate uses of self-disclosure.
- Demonstrate the skills related to taking action.

EVALUATING AND ENDING PROFESSIONAL RELATIONSHIPS

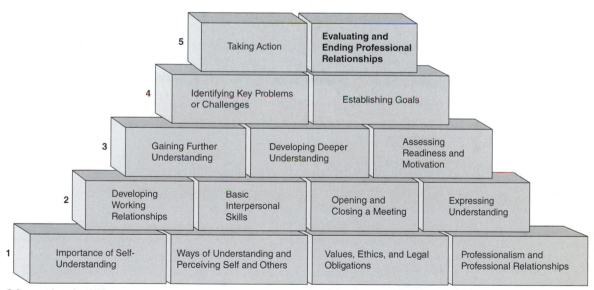

5 Taking Action | **Evaluating and Ending Professional Relationships**

4 Identifying Key Problems or Challenges | Establishing Goals

3 Gaining Further Understanding | Developing Deeper Understanding | Assessing Readiness and Motivation

2 Developing Working Relationships | Basic Interpersonal Skills | Opening and Closing a Meeting | Expressing Understanding

1 Importance of Self-Understanding | Ways of Understanding and Perceiving Self and Others | Values, Ethics, and Legal Obligations | Professionalism and Professional Relationships

© Cengage Learning 2013

Questions to consider as you read this chapter:

- What do you need to do as you end a professional relationship?
- What will you do to continue your professional development?

This chapter covers practice behaviors related to evaluating and ending professional relationships and evaluating and planning for professional development. *You will learn the importance of*:

- Critically analyzing, monitoring, and evaluating all of your work interventions
- Appropriately facilitating transitions and endings
- Planning for career-long professional development

Client Attributes
- Willingness to share perceptions about changes made and their thoughts and feelings related to ending the relationship

This final chapter covers important aspects of evaluating client progress and ending the relationship between clients and the practitioner. Once the practitioner and client have established clear goals, these goals provide a basis for evaluating progress and deciding when to end the relationship. Clients play a key role in evaluating progress. They are usually the main reporters of progress or lack of progress. Since professional relationships are purposeful, once the purpose or goal has been achieved, the relationship should end. The process of ending a relationship with a client includes preparing the client for ending, reviewing your work together, sharing feelings about ending, evaluating overall client progress, and supporting plans for continued growth. In keeping with the topic of evaluation, the chapter ends with a discussion of self-evaluation and on-going future professional development.

EVALUATING PROGRESS
Evaluation as an Ongoing Process

Since evaluation should be continuous, throughout this book we have discussed evaluation in relation to each phase of work, from beginning work with clients to expressing understanding, exploring, setting goals, and taking action. In this section we will review how evaluation fits into the earlier phases of work with clients.

Before the first meeting with a client, the practitioner should evaluate if additional information is needed about the client and what level of expertise is likely to be necessary to help the client effectively. During the exploration stage of the work, practitioners must evaluate whether they are obtaining the necessary information, if other people need to be involved, and if additional information about resources or challenges must be collected. Practitioners also need to evaluate whether they have the skills and abilities needed to work with a specific client. Some clients pose special challenges with which the practitioner may not be qualified to work. In this case, a referral should be made. Practitioners need to determine as early as possible whether they are qualified, willing, and able to work with a particular client. Sometimes this determination can be made based on the intake process, when preliminary information is provided before the practitioner begins meeting with the client.

Ongoing evaluation can be conducted after each session to identify how well the clients think they are being heard and to determine the strength of the relationship between the practitioner and the client. Some of this evaluation may be completed with paper-and-pencil questions. The evaluation can also be accomplished during the meeting by asking the client how he/she has experienced the session, how he/she feels about what has been discussed so far, or what has been most helpful in today's meeting. For example, the practitioner might ask any or all of the following questions, "How did you feel about our work today?" (pause) "What was most helpful?" (pause) "How would you evaluate what we have discussed so far in our sessions together?" Remember that a positive relationship between the practitioner and client will make it much easier for the client to work toward goal achievement.

During the exploring phase, the practitioner evaluates whether he/she fully understands the problems, situation, and client. During the goal-setting phase of the work, practitioners evaluate whether they accurately perceive the goals and the clients' level of motivation. Also during goal setting, practitioners monitor the quality of the alliance between the practitioner and client and do a baseline assessment on goals. In the action phase, the practitioner and client develop a plan for goal achievement that will provide a blueprint to evaluate progress. They also regularly monitor progress on goals.

After each meeting the practitioner should consider whether the work is leading to achievement of the identified goals (Lambert & Shimokawa, 2011). If the skills being used are not helping the client move forward, it is up to the practitioner to decide what changes are needed. Maybe the practitioner has not fully understood the client's situation or has chosen an inappropriate approach or method for working on the problem. The practitioner is obligated to evaluate and make a change (Bannink, 2007; Kottler, 2001; O'Connell, 2005; Tohn & Oshlag, 2000). If progress is being made, it is important to highlight successes and focus on improvement. An evaluation that emphasizes progress is supportive to clients and gratifying to practitioners. Research has shown that self-efficacy is enhanced as clients succeed in solving the problems they have identified (Bodenheimer et al., 2002; Chang, 2010). As self-efficacy increases, so does the client's sense of empowerment. Taking time to evaluate and celebrate each success is crucial to clients' growth.

One of the most important times for evaluation occurs during the ending process. During the ending phase of the work, the practitioner evaluates the entire process and identifies what was most helpful, what did not work as effectively, what was learned, and what are additional areas for growth. Involving or partnering with clients in this overall evaluation is essential. The practitioner and client might begin this evaluation by talking about what problems the client had at the beginning of the helping process, followed by reviewing what has been accomplished. The practitioner may share his/her assessment of progress and ask the client for a similar assessment. It is important that the practitioner share thoughts and feelings about the positive changes the client has made and recognize the client's efforts. The practitioner may also help the client identify areas for additional work and affirm his/her ability to solve these problems by using the skills developed in their work together.

As you remember, scaling questions are an excellent tool to use for evaluating progress (De Jong & Hopwood, 1996; Strong, Pyle, & Sutherland, 2009; Zalter & Fiske, 2005). They can be used in your final evaluation with clients. If the client has high scores on achievement of goals, he/she may feel ready to end the relationship with the practitioner. If the scores are lower, the practitioner might discuss with the client what additional work is needed to improve the scores.

Goal attainment scaling, which you learned about in Chapter 13, is an excellent way to monitor and evaluate progress. Practitioners who create goal attainment scales with their clients regularly ask clients where they are on each continuum. When clients reach the expected outcomes on the continuum, they are ready to end the work with the practitioner. The goal attainment scales can also be used by the practitioner and client to discuss steps the client may take on his/her own to reach the most favorable outcome.

Examples of Ending Evaluation
- "Let's review our goal attainment continuum again to see if you believe you've reached the expected outcome."
- "When we began working on reviewing the agency's policies on providing services to elderly clients, we identified several goals. In our next meeting, let's review what we have accomplished in relation to each goal."
- "As you know, our final meeting will be three weeks from today (reminding the client of when the relationship will end). Before our next meeting, will you think about what has been most helpful to you?"
- "Early on in this project we established clear goals. I think we should talk together about whether those goals have been achieved and decide if further work is necessary. Is that okay with you?"
- "On a scale of 1 to 10, with 10 being that you are completely satisfied with where you are in relation to this goal that we set, what number would you give yourself?"
- "I remember that when we started working together you told me that folks in the family yelled at each other at almost every meal. You have come a long way since then. Let's spend a few minutes reviewing what you have accomplished since we began working together."

HOMEWORK EXERCISE 15.1 | ONGOING EVALUATION AND MEASURING PROGRESS

Write down at least three ways that you do ongoing evaluation on your progress toward goals. How is ongoing evaluation helpful to you?

Identify two goals that you set for yourself in the past: one goal that you achieved and one that you did not achieve. For each goal, think about what you did to keep yourself focused on achieving your goal. How did you measure your progress toward achieving the goal? Can you identify specific differences between the two goals in terms of the ways you stayed focused on each goal and monitored your progress?

It may be that you are so good at achieving goals that you move toward goals almost without consciously realizing what you are doing, but we often work with clients who are incapable of achieving their goals. Helping clients monitor their progress will increase their confidence in their ability to achieve their goals and increase their motivation to take the action needed to achieve their goals.

Evaluation for Professional Development

Good practitioners are continually involved in evaluation of their work. As they work with clients, practitioners may elicit feedback about the things they said or did that were helpful as well as those that were not. As part of the final evaluation process, practitioners may invite clients to complete an evaluation form that asks about satisfaction with services, and/or the practitioner. The practitioner may decide to discuss satisfaction with the client face-to-face (Novick & Novick, 2006). Asking clients for feedback about their level of satisfaction with the work and what they identify as being most helpful gives practitioners important information for helping future clients.

ENDING PROFESSIONAL RELATIONSHIPS

Professional relationships end for a number of reasons. Sometimes clients know from the beginning of the process that their managed care provider or insurance has approved only a limited number of meetings, or that they have only a certain amount of money for the service. Sometimes the practitioner and client decide that they have achieved their goals, and now the client is ready to go on to a different kind of work. Sometimes clients achieve the results they want quickly and drop out of the helping process (Frank & Frank, 1991; Jakobsons, Brown, Gordon, & Joiner, 2007; Kazdin, 1995; Talmon, 1990). The client may choose not to continue the work for any number of other reasons: more pressing demands, illness, dissatisfaction with services, or moving to a different area (Gager, 2004; Pinto et al., 2007). Some clients do not continue because they feel uncomfortable and believe that the practitioner did not understand them (Barrett, Chua, Crits-Christoph, Gibbons, Casiano, & Thompson, 2008; Lever & Gmeiner, 2000).

It is good practice to follow up when clients leave unexpectedly. Following up gives a practitioner the opportunity to ask about the client's decision to leave; to acknowledge the rights of clients to withdraw at any time; to offer to continue working with the client in the future; and to possibly gain some closure on the relationship. Ending because goals have been achieved or because clients are ready to move ahead on their own is a rewarding outcome for both clients and practitioners.

The Ending Process

In many ways, ending a professional relationship is similar to ending a meeting. As you remember from Chapter 6, there are six tasks for ending a meeting. The first task is for the practitioner to indicate that the meeting is about to end. In the ending process for a professional relationship, if there are a limited number of meetings available, the practitioner identifies how many more meetings are remaining.

Otherwise the client and practitioner will decide together how many more meetings are needed. Sometimes if the client and practitioner have been meeting weekly, they will decide to move from weekly meetings to less frequent meetings until they are ready to end the relationship.

Second, at the end of a meeting the practitioner provides a summary of the meeting. In the ending process for a professional relationship, the practitioner and client summarize such things as what has been most important, what changes have been made, and what was most difficult. Reviewing and remembering both the good and the difficult times in the process is important, even in brief professional relationships. During this review process, the client may thank the practitioner for his/her help.

Third, at the end of a meeting the practitioner reviews any tasks that the client agreed to complete before the next meeting. In the ending process for a professional relationship, the practitioner and the client identify what tasks remain to be completed after the relationship has ended.

Fourth, at the end of a meeting the practitioner discusses plans for future meetings. In the ending process for a professional relationship, the practitioner tells the client that he/she can return for future meetings if needed.

Fifth, at the end of a meeting the practitioner invites client feedback about the meeting. In the ending process for a professional relationship, the practitioner invites feedback about the entirety of their work together.

Sixth, at the end of a meeting the practitioner asks the client about any final questions. This task is similar at the end of a professional relationship.

In talking to clients about ending the professional relationship, it is important to ask about their plans for maintaining the gains they have made, for pursuing continued growth, and for obtaining ongoing support. There are many ways that clients may continue to obtain support and to work on growth. The client may have friends, family, neighbors, church members, colleagues, and members of groups who have been supportive and encouraging. Some clients move to other ways of sustaining their growth such as taking courses, becoming politically active, getting a new job, or joining a health club.

Feelings about Ending

In long-term relationships, the client and practitioner need to allow time to talk about their feelings about ending the relationship. They may be feeling happy and pleased about their achievements and ready to move on (Fortune, 1987; Horowitz, 2010). As you remember, focusing on improvement is important during the helping process. At the end of the helping relationship, practitioners allow time to celebrate what has been achieved and to recognize the strengths of the client. Fortune, Pearlingi, and Rochelle (1992) found that positive reactions about the work which was accomplished were common. Clients reported feeling proud of their accomplishments and pleased to be ready to continue on their own. Practitioners were also positive about their clients' success and their own ability to be effective in helping clients (Mitchell et al., 2007).

The ending of a practitioner–client relationship is a significant event, and some clients feel a sense of loss, sadness, fear, and even anger about the relationship ending. Practitioners should encourage clients to express their feelings. The practitioner might say, "We've spent a lot of time during this last meeting talking about your progress during our time together, but we haven't talked about our feelings about ending our relationship. What feelings do you have at this time?"

Clients who have limited supportive relationships or are hesitant about their ability to continue on their own are more likely to express painful feelings. When the ending is not within a client's control, but mandated by financial or insurance limitations, he/she may feel angry. Sometimes the process of ending brings up old feelings of abandonment or loss for clients. They may suddenly say they are not ready to end the relationship with the practitioner after all. It is important to explore these feelings and to help clients realize that they have new skills to deal with their problems and that they can receive support from other relationships. Often clients can be encouraged to see this ending as an opportunity to prove to themselves that they can manage independently. With clients who are feeling hesitant about continuing on their own, it is particularly important to discuss available resources. Of course, clients always have the possibility of returning to the practitioner at some point in the future.

Endings with groups can bring up similar feelings to endings with individuals, couples, and families. In a study on effects of ending support groups, Kacen (1999) found that when participants experienced the group as cohesive and supportive, they felt temporary anxiety when the group ended. It is important to discuss normal feelings about ending supportive relationships. Often clients are pleased that they are ready to leave the group but are also ambivalent or scared about the prospect of no longer having the support of the group (Latner, Stunkard, Wilson, & Jackson, 2006).

Practitioners also experience emotions as relationships end. Spending time together listening to feelings, thoughts, and experiences; talking about problems; setting goals; and evaluating progress often creates a strong bond that practitioners are also reluctant to end. When appropriate, a practitioner might also share feelings about ending the relationship. When practitioners share their feelings, the client may respond with additional feelings. Having the opportunity to share these feelings provides a sense of closure or completeness and opens the door to ending the relationship and saying goodbye.

Examples of Practitioner Statements that Share Feelings about Ending

- "I'm going to miss seeing you and hearing about your progress. I am happy that you have achieved your goals."
- "I am going to miss our time together. I feel sad when I think about not seeing you, but I am glad that you are satisfied with the progress you have made."
- "This will be the last time that I see you. I am glad to have been part of your journey as you figured out the best way to help your aging father. I hope the nursing home works out well for your father."
- "I am glad that in our work together you were able to mend your relationship with your brother. I hope that over time you will become close friends and support each other."
- "I can see that you are really excited about the opportunities that your new job is going to provide for you. I'm so glad that you achieved your goal of getting a new job that offers you new opportunities."

Endings with Task Groups and Larger Groups

Ending professional relationships with task groups, neighborhoods, organizations, and communities involves the same process as ending with individuals and families. First, it is important for the practitioner to talk about when the work will be completed or when the community or organization plans to continue the work without the assistance of the practitioner. Second, the practitioner needs to work with the organization or group to develop a thorough summary of what has been accomplished, as this will help to stabilize future changes. This discussion should lead to a review of agreed-upon tasks and future plans. Third, with large groups such as neighborhoods, organizations, and communities, it is essential that the practitioner work with the group to make plans for sustaining and building on the accomplishments. Scheduling a follow-up meeting is particularly helpful, as it gives the practitioner and the group an opportunity to review the plans and discuss continued development. Fourth, as part of any ending with a large group, there should be a system for evaluating the work accomplished and for giving feedback to the practitioner and each other. Fifth, and finally, celebrating the successes that have been achieved and recognizing individual and group efforts should be included in any ending.

Examples of Practitioner Statements for Ending Relationships with Groups

- "Since this is our last meeting, let's talk about what you remember about our work together in this group."
- "I have enjoyed working with each of you and will miss seeing you. I am confident that you folks will continue to use the parenting methods you learned in this group."
- "I have enjoyed working with your neighborhood group. I am pleased to see that many of you have moved into leadership positions in the group and are supporting each other as you move ahead with your plans."
- "Since next week will be our last meeting together, I think we should make a plan for how we will celebrate everything that you have achieved."
- "Let's take a few minutes to talk about resources that might be helpful to your group in the future."

HOMEWORK EXERCISE 15.2 | ENDINGS

Think of a time when you ended an important relationship. How did you feel? What were some of the things that you needed to talk about before saying goodbye? Did you discuss the ending or changing of the relationship (for example, if your friend was moving a long distance away) or did you avoid talking about the possibly painful ending? What did you do that made the process easier or harder? Write down your ideas about how you can use what you know about ending relationships in your work as a practitioner.

Examples of the Overall Process from Evaluating to Ending

- Discuss readiness to complete work together:
    - "Let's go over your goals and identify what we have completed and what we still need to work on." (You could use a scaling question related to each goal.)

- Evaluate progress:
  - "Let's review where you are in relationship to your goals. On a scale of 1 to 10, with 10 being accomplishment of the goal we are working on, what score would you give yourself?" (Using goal attainment scaling would also be appropriate.)
- Evaluate the client's satisfaction with work completed:
  - "What are some of the things you liked about our work together?"
  - "Are there things that you were not satisfied with?"
  - "I'd like to hear any suggestions you have for improving our services."
- Identify when the meetings will end:
  - "We have decided to have two more meetings."
  - "As you remember, I will be leaving the agency at the end of next month."
- Share feelings about the work and the relationship:
  - "Would you tell me about when you were most uncomfortable in our work together?"
  - "I have enjoyed working with you."
  - "How are you feeling about the fact that our work together will be ending?"
  - "Sometimes ending a relationship like this one brings up memories of other relationships that ended. Is that happening for you?"
- Summarize accomplishments and review strengths:
  - "Let's talk about the challenges that brought you here and what you have accomplished."
  - "I am really pleased with all you were able to achieve. What are some of the things that you are most proud of accomplishing?"
  - "Some of your strengths that I have noticed in our work together are ..."
  - "What are your ideas about how you can use your strengths in the future?"
- Discuss plans for the future:
  - "Who are some of the people you might turn to for help if the going gets rough?"
  - "What are your ideas about things you can do to maintain the progress you have achieved? Let's review the tasks you are going to continue to work on."

 DVD Example: Evaluating and Ending Professional Relationships

Watch the evaluation/ending meetings of the individual, group, and/or family.

- Identify specific ways that any one of the practitioners invited evaluation of the professional relationship or progress.
- What did you like about the way the practitioners used skills to invite evaluation?
- Give specific examples of points where any one of the practitioners could have done more to invite evaluation of the professional relationship and/or progress.

- Identify specific ways any one of the practitioners handled the following tasks related to ending:
    o Identified how many meetings were left
    o Summarized or invited clients to summarize important aspects of the process and/or important changes made
    o Identified tasks to continue working on
    o Discussed process for clients to return if necessary
    o Sought feedback about the process
    o Asked about final questions
    o Discussed feelings about ending
    o Discussed ways clients could maintain progress made
- What did you like about the way the practitioners used skills related to ending?
- Give specific examples of points where the practitioners could have done more to invite appropriate closure.

PLANNING FOR CAREER-LONG PROFESSIONAL DEVELOPMENT

As you evaluate and end your work with clients, you should also reflect on the next steps in your career development. Remember that in Chapter 4 we identified that engaging in career-long learning is part of being a helping professional. Practitioners need to be involved in evaluation and growth throughout their career. Besides self-evaluation and evaluation from clients, getting feedback from peers and supervisors is very helpful. One way to get feedback is to assess your work using the same practice evaluation system that you used in this book and to share with your supervisor your self-assessment as well as your goals for improvement. To assist you with that process we have included a complete evaluation form in Appendix B.

The best practitioners pursue ongoing professional development through several methods. They develop self-knowledge by participating in personal counseling, reflecting on their own values and ethics in their work with diverse clients, and/or participating in lifelong learning to constantly keep abreast of new ideas, programs, and resources. They also develop professionally through effective training in their formal education, through high-quality supervision at training sites and from peer consultation. At different times in your professional career, you may find yourself focusing on one of these areas more than another, but each is important to your ultimate success.

There are many ways to create a career development plan. As you are in the beginning of your career, you probably have quite a long list of areas to learn about. These areas will include such things as practice skills and knowledge related to different types of client challenges, different cultural groups, different system sizes, etc. Some practitioners choose to specialize in working with particular types of clients such as: first generation Mexican-American immigrants, people with alcohol addictions, men in prison, neighborhoods with high violence rates, couples, families, groups, etc. These practitioners may choose to subscribe to professional journals, read the latest literature, attend continuing education workshops, and get additional training and supervision related to their particular area of interest. Other practitioners are less specialized and may tend to focus on learning that they identify as necessary for them to gain more expertise in their current field of practice.

STAYING CURRENT ON EVIDENCE-BASED PRACTICE

In recent years there has been increasing interest in empirically based or evidence-based practice, or practice methods based on research studies conducted to determine the most effective ways to respond to the various problems clients present (Norcross & Wampold, 2011). Although learning specific empirically based treatment approaches is beyond the scope of this book, keeping current with this research is an expected part of being a professional and should be a key element in your professional development. After mastering the foundational skills in this book, you will learn specific approaches for working with individuals, families, groups, and organizations. Most of the evidence-based practice studies have focused on work with individuals (Castonguay & Beutler, 2006; Fonagy, Target, Cottrell, Phillips, & Kurtz, 2002). There are fewer research studies involving work with couples (Sexton, Alexander, & Mease, 2003; Thyer, 2006), and even fewer on work with families (Edmond, Megivern, Williams, Rochman, & Howard, 2006; Roberts, Vernberg, & Jackson, 2000; Sexton, Alexander, & Mease, 2003). Little has been done to determine the most effective way to intervene when addressing the problems larger groups may present (Aarons & Palinkas, 2007; Burlingame, Mackenzie, & Strauss, 2004). As you learn about and evaluate possible approaches, it will be important for you to determine which approaches have been empirically shown to be effective with specific types of client problems and situations.

Besides research related to effective methods for working with children and adults, individuals, families and groups, understanding the rapidly growing body of research on brain development is essential for anyone in the counseling field. Our knowledge of brain functioning is being translated into new counseling practices (Badenoch, 2008; Cozolino, 2010; Ecker, 2010; Fosha, Siegel, & Solomon, 2009; Schore, 2009; Siegel, 2010; Toomey & Ecker, 2009). Many of the skills you learned (being fully present, attending, observing, and empathizing) are crucial to integrating information about brain functioning into your practice.

You are entering a fascinating field that requires continued learning and development. We hope this new learning will keep your career exciting and stimulating.

CASE | ## CASE PART 6: HIDEKO, EVALUATION AND ENDING

After all your work with Hideko, you are now going to evaluate your progress and end your relationship with her.

Put yourself in the role of practitioner and answer the following questions.

1. What are your plans for monitoring progress with the client?
2. What will you say to invite the client to give you feedback?
3. How will you and the client decide when to end your time together?
4. How might you prepare the client for the end of the professional relationship?
5. What could you do to help the client express her feelings about ending the relationship?
6. Write at least five things that you might say as part of ending the relationship.
7. What issues and concerns in your own life arose as you worked with this client?

Role Play–Do a role play with one person playing the client and another person playing the practitioner. Role play evaluating the goals, evaluating progress, and ending the work together. Use Practice Exercise Evaluation Form 9 to evaluate this final meeting.

PRACTICE EXERCISE 9 | EVALUATION AND ENDING

Exercise Objectives
- To practice ending the professional relationship with a client.

Step 1: Preparation
Form groups of three people. Each person will have the opportunity to play the roles of client, practitioner, and peer supervisor. Each meeting will last 15 minutes.

Client Role
- Prepare to discuss a problem. Since the focus of this meeting is evaluating and ending, work with someone in the role of practitioner that you have worked with before. Consider starting the meeting by listing the MAPS goals that were previously established.

Practitioner Role
- Review the skills of evaluating and ending with clients (see evaluation form).

Peer Supervisor Role
- Review the skills of evaluating and ending with clients (see evaluation form).
    Prepare to observe and listen to the client, to keep track of the time, and to write down what the practitioner says.

Step 2: The Client Meeting
Client Role
- Respond to practitioner. For this role play you may have to invent some responses.

Practitioner Role
- Use previously learned skills and skills that are designed specifically for evaluating and ending with clients.
- You can stop the meeting at any time to get suggestions from the persons in the role of the client or peer supervisor.
- Listen to the client and observe the client's nonverbal communication.

Peer Supervisor Role
- Keep track of the time and alert the practitioner and client when 13 minutes have passed so the practitioner has time to close the meeting.
- Write down each practitioner statement and question. You may abbreviate, use a form of shorthand, or just write the first group of words in the statement, or you can tape record the interview and transcribe or listen to the tape.

Step 3: Feedback
Purpose: Receiving immediate constructive feedback helps students enhance their practice skills. Using this evaluation system, the peer supervisor monitors the skills used by the social worker. The client, social worker, and peer supervisor identify strengths and areas for growth.

Client Role
- Share how you experienced the practitioner.
    - Did you feel understood?
    - Was the practitioner warm, empathic, respectful, and genuine?
    - What did the practitioner do particularly well?
    - In what ways could the practitioner improve?

Practitioner Role
- Evaluate how well you worked with your client to evaluate his or her satisfaction and progress toward goal achievement.
- Evaluate how well you covered all the important topics related to ending a professional relationship (identified when the meetings will end, shared feelings about the relationship and work, summarized strengths and accomplishments, and discussed future plans).

Peer Supervisor Role
- Give feedback to the practitioner from your notes on the skills for evaluating and ending with clients.
- Although the focus of this meeting is on evaluating and ending, the practitioner may use other skills. Give feedback on the use of skills other than those related to evaluating and ending.
- Evaluate the practitioner's use of the core interpersonal qualities of warmth, empathy, respect, and genuineness. (All of the scales are in Appendix A.)
- Identify any inappropriate response made by the practitioner (see evaluation form). One minus point for every inappropriate response.
- Add all the individual points and the points on the scales to get the total score.
- Record the feedback in the practitioner's textbook for future reference.

PRACTICE EXERCISE 9 | EVALUATION AND ENDING *(continued)*

EVALUATION FORM: EVALUATING AND ENDING

Name of Practitioner_____

Name of Peer Supervisor_____

Directions: Under each category (in italics) is a list of behaviors or skills.
Give one check mark, worth one point, for each skill used by the practitioner.

Express Understanding
Expressing understanding is so important that for this group of skills one
point should be given for each time the practitioner used one of the skills.

1. Reflected feelings
2. Reflected content
3. Reflected feelings and content
4. Summarized
5. Reflected meanings

Gaining Further Understanding

Questioning Skills
Give one point for each skill used by the practitioner.

1. Expressed understanding before asking questions.
2. Asked open-ended questions when appropriate.
3. Asked one question at a time.
4. Asked closed-ended questions when appropriate.

Developing Deeper Understanding

Skills to Enhance Understanding
Give one point for each skill used by the practitioner.

1. Explored the meanings of words and body language
2. Explored the basis of conclusions drawn by the client
3. Allowed silence
4. Identified strengths
5. Asked questions about strengths

Taking Action
Give one point for each skill used by the practitioner. It rarely will be
appropriate to use all of these skills in one meeting.

1. Identified steps
2. Focused on improvement
3. Taught
4. Directed
5. Invited a different perspective
6. Gave feedback
7. Used self-disclosure

(continued)

PRACTICE EXERCISE 9 | EVALUATION AND ENDING *(continued)*

Evaluating and Ending

Give one point for each skill used by the practitioner.

1. Discussed readiness to complete work together.
2. Evaluated progress.   _____
3. Evaluated client's satisfaction with work completed.   _____
4. Identified when the meetings would end.   _____
5. Shared feelings about the work and the relationship.   _____
6. Summarized accomplishments and strengths.   _____
7. Discussed plans for the future.   _____

Common Mistakes or Inappropriate Responses *(subtract 1 point for each)*   _____

(offering advice, reassuring, offering excuses, asking leading questions,
dominating through teaching, labeling, and interrogating)

Core Interpersonal Qualities

Using the scales in Appendix A, evaluate the appropriateness and effectiveness of
the practitioner's expression of warmth, empathy, respect, and genuineness. On
the following lines write the scores, from 1 to 5, for warmth, empathy, respect,
and genuineness.

Score for warmth
Score for empathy   _____
Score for respect   _____
Score for genuineness   _____
Total score   _____

CASE | **CASE PART 7: HIDEKO'S REVIEW OF PROGRESS**

After working with the practitioner for several months, Hideko reported that she was taking time to be with her friends twice a week. She had given herself permission to take some time off without feeling guilty. She reported that she was smiling more, talking and asking questions, and feeling more energetic. She has to keep reminding herself that it is okay to take time for herself. She still isn't getting recognition from her parents. However, she was working on giving recognition to others and finding that they responded by recognizing some of the good things that she did. Although she didn't want to just accept her parents' rules about who she should date, she had met a Japanese man who was a new medical resident at the hospital. They had gone out twice and she liked him. She knew that even though her parents might accept him, it would still be a challenge to maintain a relationship while being a graduate student and helping her mother. She thought that if this relationship continued she would probably have to talk to her parents and her brother about getting someone to come in regularly to help her mother.

Discussion–After reading how the real case ended, discuss your thoughts and feelings about the case as a whole.

EXPECTED COMPETENCIES

In this chapter, you have learned about evaluating progress and ending the professional relationship in an effective and supportive way.

You should now be able to:

- Give two examples of appropriate evaluation comments.

- Describe the six steps in the ending process.
- Explain at least four things you plan to do to continue your professional development.
- Demonstrate evaluating and ending a professional relationship.

PRACTICE EVALUATION SCALES

Listening: Content and Process Evaluation Scale

Level 1:   The practitioner did not summarize any of the major elements of content or describe anything about the client's way of speaking.

Level 3:   The practitioner summarized four elements of content but did not describe anything about the client's way of speaking.

Level 5:   The practitioner summarized all the major elements of content and accurately and fully described the client's way of speaking, including: communication style, volume, and speed of delivery.

Warmth Evaluation Scale

Level l: The practitioner communicated *little or no concern* for the client and appeared cold, detached, stiff, and/or mechanical.

Level 3:   *At least half the time*, the practitioner verbally and nonverbally communicated concern and caring appropriate to the unique needs of the client.

Level 5:   The practitioner *consistently* communicated verbal and nonverbal expressions of concern and caring appropriate to the unique needs of the client.

Empathy Evaluation Scales

Level 1:   *Once during the meeting* the practitioner communicated an understanding of the client's experience and feelings with enough clarity that the client indicated agreement.

Level 3:   *Three times during the meeting* the practitioner communicated an understanding of the client's experience with enough clarity that the client indicated agreement.

Level 5:   *Five times during the meeting* the practitioner communicated an understanding of the client's experience with enough clarity that the client indicated agreement.

Genuineness Evaluation Scales

Level 1:   The practitioner appeared *stiff, tense, distracted, and/or detached* from the process most of the time, and *responses were obviously not connected* to the client's *feelings*, flat affect.

Level 3:   The practitioner appeared *sincere and relaxed, but* not clearly connected to or focused on the process.

Level 5:   The practitioner appeared *sincere, relaxed, and focused* on the client, and *selectively shared personal reactions* to the client's feelings, comments, and behavior.

Respect Evaluation Scale

Level 1:   The practitioner did not invite discussion of and/or recognize the client's strengths, resources, and/or capacities, and/or showed a lack of respect for the client's abilities, such as helping or providing answers that the client did not ask for.

Level 3:   *Once during the meeting*, the practitioner invited discussion of and/or recognized the client's strengths, resources, and/or capacities, and the practitioner did nothing that showed a lack of respect for the client's abilities, such as helping or providing answers that the client did not ask for.

Level 5:   *Three times during the meeting*, the practitioner invited discussion of and/or recognized the client's strengths, resources, and/or capacities, and the practitioner did nothing that showed a lack of respect for the client's abilities, such as helping or providing answers that the client did not ask for.

OVERALL PRACTICE EVALUATION FORM

Name of Practitioner_____

Name of Peer Supervisor_____

Directions: Under each category (in italics) is a list of behaviors or skills. Give one point, for each skill used by the practitioner.

Building Relationships

Attending

Give one point for each behavior used by the practitioner.

1. Open and accessible body posture _____
2. Congruent facial expression _____
3. Slightly inclined toward the client _____
4. Regular eye contact unless inappropriate _____
5. No distracting behavior _____
6. Minimal encouragement _____

Observing

Give one point for each item accurately described by the practitioner.

1. Facial expression _____
2. Eye movement and eye contact _____
3. Body position and movement _____
4. Breathing patterns _____
5. Muscle tone _____
6. Gestures _____
7. Skin tone changes _____

Active Listening Skills Content and Process

Using the listening scale in Appendix A, evaluate the accuracy and completeness of the practitioner's ability to summarize what the client said and describe the client's way of speaking, including such things as speaking style, vocal tone and volume, and speed of delivery.

On the following line write the score, from 1 to 5, for listening.   _____

Opening and Closing

Beginning Skills (for a meeting)

 Give one point for each topic covered by the practitioner.

 1. Introduced yourself and your role.   _____
 2. Sought introductions.   _____
 3. Identified where the meeting will be held.   _____
 4. Identified how long the meeting will last.   _____
 5. Described the initial purpose of the meeting.   _____
 6. Explained some of the things you will do.   _____
 7. Outlined the client's role.   _____
 8. Discussed ethical and agency policies.   _____
 9. Sought feedback from the client.   _____

Beginning Subsequent Meetings

 Give one point for each topic covered by the practitioner.

 1. Asked client where he/she would like to begin.   _____
 2. Summarized previous meeting.   _____
 3. Identified tasks for this meeting.   _____
 4. Asked client about progress.   _____
 5. Asked client about homework.   _____
 6. Asked client about problems.   _____
 7. Made an observation about the previous meeting.   _____
 8. Did a check-in.   _____

Closing Skills (for a meeting)

 Give one point for each topic covered by the practitioner.

 1. Identified that the meeting was about to end.   _____
 2. Provided a summary of the meeting.   _____
 3. Reviewed any tasks that the client agreed to complete.   _____
 4. Discussed plans for future meetings.   _____
 5. Invited client feedback about the work.   _____
 6. Asked client about any final questions.   _____

Expressing Understanding

 Expressing understanding is so important that for this group of skills one point should be given for each time the practitioner used one of the skills.

 1. Reflected feelings   _____
 2. Reflected content   _____
 3. Reflected feelings and content   _____
 4. Summarized   _____
 5. Reflected meanings   _____

Gaining Further Understanding

Questioning Skills

Give one point for each skill used by the practitioner.

1. Expressed understanding before asking questions.   _____
2. Asked open-ended questions when appropriate.   _____
3. Asked one question at a time.   _____
4. Asked closed-ended questions when appropriate.   _____

Learning about Problem/Challenge and Situation

Give one point for each topic adequately discussed.

Problems or Challenges

Previous attempts to solve problem   _____
History of the problem(s)   _____
Severity or intensity of the problem(s)   _____
Feelings about having the problem(s)   _____
Effects of the problem(s) on other areas   _____
(such as health, sleeping, and ability to function at school or work)

Situation

Effects of the problem on other people   _____
Available social support and strengths in environment   _____
Interactions with family   _____
Other demands and stresses in the situation/environment   _____

Developing Deeper Understanding

Skills to Enhance Understanding

Give one point for each skill used by the practitioner.

1. Explored the meanings of words and body language   _____
2. Explored the basis of conclusions drawn by client   _____
3. Allowed silence   _____
4. Identified strengths   _____
5. Asked questions about strengths   _____

Defining the Focus

Reaching Agreement about Problems or Challenges

Give one point for each skill used by the practitioner. It rarely will be appropriate to use all of these skills in one meeting.

1. Used rolling with resistance   _____
2. Identified discrepancies   _____
3. Advanced reflecting   _____
4. Identified a pattern or theme   _____
5. Partialized the problem   _____
6. Supported self-efficacy   _____
7. Stated agreed upon problems   _____

Reaching Agreement about Goals

Give one point for each skill used by the practitioner.

1. Reached agreement on a general goal _____
2. Used questions to develop a MAPS goal _____
3. Reached agreement on MAPS goal _____

Taking Action

Give one point for each skill used by the practitioner. It rarely will be appropriate to use all of these skills in one meeting.

1. Identified steps _____
2. Focused on improvement _____
3. Taught _____
4. Directed _____
5. Invited a different perspective _____
6. Gave feedback _____
7. Used self-disclosure _____

Evaluating and Ending

Give one point for each skill used by the practitioner.

1. Discussed readiness to complete work together. _____
2. Evaluated progress. _____
3. Evaluated client's satisfaction with work completed. _____
4. Identified when the meetings would end. _____
5. Shared feelings about the work and the relationship. _____
6. Summarized accomplishments and strengths. _____
7. Discussed plans for the future. _____

Common Mistakes or Inappropriate Responses *(subtract one point for each)* _____

(offering advice, reassuring, offering excuses, asking leading questions, dominating through teaching, labeling, and interrogating)

Core Interpersonal Qualities

Using the scales in Appendix A, evaluate the appropriateness and effectiveness of the practitioner's expression of warmth, empathy, respect, and genuineness. On the following lines write the scores, from 1 to 5, for warmth, empathy, respect, and genuineness.

Score for warmth _____
Score for empathy _____
Score for respect _____
Score for genuineness _____

Total score _____

REFERENCES

Aarons, G. A., & Palinkas, L. A. (2007). Implementation of evidence-based practice in child welfare service provider perspectives. *Administration and Policy in Mental Health and Mental Health Services Research, 34*(4), 411–419. doi:10.1007/s10488-007-0121-3

Abrams, L. S., & Moio, J. A. (2009). Critical race theory and the cultural competence dilemma in social work education. *Journal of Social Work Education, 45*(2), 245–261.

Ackerman, A. J., & Hilsenroth, M. J. (2001). A review of therapist characteristics and techniques negatively impacting the therapeutic alliance. *Psychotherapy, 38,* 171–185.

Adams, R. (2003). *Social work and empowerment* (3rd ed.). Basingstoke, England: Palgrave Macmillan.

Aisenberg, E., & Herrenkohl, T. (2008). Community violence in context: Risk and resilience in children and families. *Journal of Interpersonal Violence, 23*(3), 296–315.

Albanese, M., & Mitchell, S. (1993). Problem-based learning: A review of the literature on its outcomes and implementation issues. *Academic Medicine, 68*(1), 52–81.

Alexander, J. J., Robbins, M. S., & Sexton, T. L. (2000). Family-based interventions with older at-risk youths: From promise to proof to practice. *Journal of Primary Prevention, 42,* 185–205.

Alexander, P. C., & Morris, E. (2008). Stages of change in batterers and their response to treatment. *Violence and Victims, 23*(4), 476–492. doi:10.1891/0886-6708.23.4.476

Allen, D. M. (2006). Use of between session homework in systems-oriented individual psychotherapy. *Journal of Psychotherapy Integration, 16,* 238–253.

American Association on Intellectual and Developmental Disabilities. (2010). Definition of intellectual disability. Retrieved September 7, 2010, from http://www.aaidd.org/content_100.cfm?navID=21

Anderson, S. C., & Mandell, D. L. (1989). The use of self-disclosure by professional social workers. *Social Casework: The Journal of Contemporary Social Casework, 70,* 259–267.

Anderson, S. K., & Handelsman, M. M. (2010). *Ethics for psychotherapists and counselors: A proactive approach.* Chichester, U.K.: Wiley-Blackwell.

Anderson, T., Ogles, B. M., Patterson, C. L., Lambert, M. J., & Vermeersch, D. A. (2009). Therapist effects: Facilitative interpersonal skills as a predictor of therapist success. *Journal of Clinical Psychology, 65*(7), 755–768. doi:10.1002/jclp.20583

Anderson, T., Ogles, B., & Weiss, A. (1999). Creative use of interpersonal skills in building a therapeutic alliance. *Journal of Constructivist Psychology, 12,* 313–330.

Ansfield, M. E. (2007). Smiling when distressed: When a smile is a frown turned upside down. *Personality and Social Psychology Bulletin, 33*(6), 763–775. doi:10.1177/0146167206297398

Asay, T. P., & Lambert, M. J. (1999). The empirical case for the common factors in therapy: Quantitative findings. In M. A. Hubble, B. L. Duncan, & S. D. Miller (Eds.), *The heart & soul of change: What works in therapy?* (pp. 23–55). Washington, DC: American Psychological Association.

Ayonrinde, O. (2003). Importance of cultural sensitivity in therapeutic transactions: Considerations for healthcare providers. *Disease Management and Health Outcomes, 11*(4), 233–248.

Bachelor, A., & Horvath, A. (1999). The therapeutic relationship. In M. A. Hubble, B. L. Duncan, & S. D. Miller (Eds.), *The heart and soul of change: What works in therapy* (pp. 133–178). Washington, DC: American Psychological Association.

Badenoch, B. (2008). *Being a brain-wise therapist: A practical guide to interpersonal neurobiology.* New York: W. W. Norton.

Baez, R. (2003). *Teaching basic clinical skills: Assessment of a manual based training program.* Unpublished dissertation, Azusa Pacific University, Azusa, CA.

Baldwin, S. A., Wampold, B. E., & Imel, Z. E. (2007). Untangling the alliance-outcome correlation: Exploring the relative importance of therapist and patient variability in the alliance. *Journal of Consulting and Clinical Psychology, 75*(6), 842–852.

Balmford, J., Borland, R., & Burney, S. (2008). Is contemplation a separate stage of change to precontemplation? *International Journal of Behavioral Medicine, 15*(2), 141–148. doi:10.1080/10705500801929791

Bandura, A. (1977). Self-Efficacy: Toward a unifying theory of behavioral change. *Psychology Review* (84), 191–215.

Bandura, A. (1989). Human agency in social cognitive theory. *American Psychologist, 44*(9), 1175–1184.

Bandura, A. (1994). Self-efficacy. In V. S. Ramachaudran (Ed.), *Encyclopedia of human behavior* (Vol. 4, pp. 71–81). New York: Academic Press.

Bandura, A., & Cervone, D. (1983). Self-evaluative and self-efficacy mechanisms governing the motivational effects of goals systems. *Journal of Personality and Social Psychology, 45,* 1017–1028.

Bandura, A., & Schunk, D. H. (1981). Cultivating competence, self efficacy, and intrinsic interest through proximal self-motivation. *Journal of Personality and Social Psychology, 41,* 586–598.

Bannink, F. P. (2007). Solution-focused brief therapy. *Journal of Contemporary Psychotherapy, 37*(2), 87–94. doi:10.1007/s10879-006-9040-y

Barker, C. H., Cook, K. L., & Borrego, Jr., J. (2010). Addressing cultural variables in parent training programs with latino families. *Cognitive and Behavioral Practice,* 17(2), 157–166. doi:10.1016/jcbpra.2010.01.002

Barker, R. L., & Branson, D. M. (2000). *Forensic social work,* (2nd ed.) Binghamton, NY: Haworth Press.

Barnett, J. (2007). Whose boundaries are they anyway? *Professional Psychology: Research and Practice, 38*(4), 401–405.

Barrett, M. S., Chua, W., Crits-Christoph, P., Gibbons, M. B., Casiano, D., & Thompson, D. (2008). Early withdrawal from mental health treatment: Implications for psychotherapy practice. *Psychotherapy (Chic), 45*(2), 247–267.

Barrows, H. S., & Tamblyn, R. M. (1980). *Problem-based learning: An approach to medical education.* New York: Springer Series on Medical Education (p. 224).

Baum, B. E., & Gray, J. J. (1992). Expert modeling, self-observation using videotape, and acquisition of basic therapy skills. *Professional Psychology: Research and Practice, 23,* 220–225.

Baxter, J. S., Boon, J. C. W., & Marley, C. (2006). Interrogative pressure and responses to minimally leading questions. *Personality and Individual Differences, 40*(1), 87–98. doi:10.1016/j.paid.2005.06.017

Beahrs, J. O., & Gutheil, T. G. (2001). Informed consent in psychotherapy. *The American Journal of Psychiatry, 158,* 4–10.

Becvar, D. S., & Becvar, R. J. (2006). *Family therapy: A systemic integration* (6th ed.). Boston: Allyn & Bacon.

Bedi, R. P. (2006). Concept mapping the client's perspective on counseling alliance formation. *Journal of Counseling Psychology, 53,* 26.

Belkin, G. S. (1984). *Introduction to counseling.* Dubuque, IA: Brown.

Benjamin, L. S. (2003). *Interpersonal reconstructive therapy: Promoting change in nonresponders.* New York: Guilford.

Bennet, L. A., Wolin, S. J., & Reiss, D. (1987). Couples at risk for transmission of alcoholism: Protective influences. *Family Process, 26,* 111–129.

Bennett-Levy, J. (2006). Therapist skills: A cognitive model of their acquisition and refinement. *Behavioural and Cognitive Psychotherapy, 34,* 57–78.

Bennett-Levy, J., & Beedie, A. (2007). The ups and downs of cognitive therapy training: What happens to trainees' perception of their competence during a cognitive therapy training course? *Behavioural and Cognitive Psychotherapy, 35,* 61–75. doi:10.1017/S1352465806003110

Beresford, P., Croft, S., & Adshead, L. (2008). 'We don't see her as a social worker': A service user case study of the importance of the social worker's relationship and humanity. *The British Journal of Social Work, 38*(7), 1388–1407. doi:10.1093/bjsw/bcm043

Berg, I. K., & Miller, S. D. (1992). *Working with the problem drinker: A solution-focused approach.* New York: Norton.

Bernotavicz, F. (1994). A new paradigm for competency-based training. *Journal of Continuing Social Work Education, 6,* 3–9.

Bernstein, P., Tipping, J., Bercovitz, K., & Skinner, H. A. (1995). Shifting students and faculty to a PBL curriculum: Attitudes changed and lessons learned. *Academic Medicine, 70*(3), 245–7.

Beutler, L., Machado, P., & Allstetter-Neufelt, A. (1994). Therapist variables. In A. Bergin & S. Garfield (Eds.), *Handbook of psychotherapy and behavior change* (4th ed., pp. 229–269). Toronto: Wiley.

Beutow, S. A., (2009). Something in nothing: Negative space in the clinician-patient relationship. *Annals of Family Medicine, 7,* 80–83. doi:10.1370/afm.914

Beyeback, M., Morejon, A. R., Palenzuela, D. L., & Rodriguez-Arias, J. L. (1996). Research on the process of solution-focused therapy. In S. D. Miller, M. A. Hubbles, & B. L. K. Duncan (Eds.), *Handbook of solution-focused brief therapy* (pp. 251–271). San Francisco: Jossey-Bass.

Blitz, L. V. (2006). Owning whiteness: The reinvention of self and practice. *Journal of Emotional Abuse, 6*(2/3), 241–263.

Boardman, T., Catley, D., Grobe, J. E., Little, T. D., Ahluwalia, J. S., (2006). Using motivational interviewing with smokers: Do therapist behaviors relate to engagement and therapeutic alliance? *Journal of Substance*

Abuse Treatment, 31(4), 329–339. doi:10.1016/j.jsat.2006.05.006

Bodenheimer, T., Lorig, K., Holman, H., & Grumbach, K. (2002). Patient self-management of chronic disease in primary care. *JAMA 288,* 2469–2475.

Boland-Prom, K. W. (2009). Results from a national study of social workers sanctioned by state licensing boards. *Social Work, 54*(4), 351–360.

Branscombe, N. R., Schmitt, M. T., & Schiffhauer, K. (2007). Racial attitudes in response to thoughts of White privilege. *European Journal of Social Psychology, 37*(2), 203–215.

Breunlin, D. C., Schwartz, R. C., & MacKune-Karrer, B. (1997). *Metaframeworks: Transcending the Models of Family Therapy, Revised and Updated.* New York: Jossey-Bass.

Brill, N., & Levine, J. (2005). *Working with people: The helping process.* Retrieved from http://www.ablongman.com/samplechapter/0205401848.pdf

Britton, P. C., Williams, G. C., & Conner, K. R. (2008). Self-determination theory, motivational interviewing, and the treatment of clients with acute suicidal ideation. *Journal of Clinical Psychology, 64,* 52–66. doi:10.1002/jclp.20430

Brodley, B. T. (2006). Client-initiated homework in client-centered therapy. *Journal of Psychotherapy Integration, 16,* 140–161.

Brooks, E., Harris, C. R., & Clayton, P. H. (2010). Deepening applied learning: An enhanced case study approach using critical reflection. *Journal of Applied Learning in Higher Education, 2,* 55–76. Retrieved from http://www.missouriwestern.edu/appliedlearning/journalvol2/jalhe_vol_2.pdf#page=54

Brower, A. M. (1988). Can the ecological model guide social work practice? *Social Service Review, 62,* 411–429.

Brueggemann, W. G. (2001). *The practice of macro social work* (2nd ed.). Belmont, CA: Brooks/Cole.

Bucky, S. F., Callan, J. E., & Stricker, G. (Eds.). (2005). *Ethical and legal issues for mental health professionals: A comprehensive handbook of principles and standards.* Binghamton, NY: Haworth Press.

Bullis, R. K. (1990). Cold comfort from the supreme court: Limited liability protection for social workers. *Social Work, 35*(4), 364–366.

Burdge, B. (2007). Bending gender, ending gender: Theoretical foundations for social work practice with the transgender community. *Social Work, 52*(3), 243–250. Retrieved from http://web.ebscohost.com.proxy.ulib.iupui.edu

Burlingame, G. M., MacKenzie, K. R., & Strauss, B. (2004). Small-group treatment: Evidence for effectiveness and mechanisms of change. In M. J. Lambert (Ed.), *Bergin and Garfield's handbook of psychotherapy and behavior change* (pp. 647–696). New York: Wiley.

Burlingame, G. M., McClendon, D. T., & Alonso, J. (2011). Cohesion in group therapy. *Psychotherapy, 48*(1), 34–42.

Burr, V. (1995). *An introduction to social constructivism.* London: Routledge.

Busseri, M. A., & Tyler, J. D. (2004). Client-therapist agreement on target problems, working alliance, and counseling effectiveness. *Psychotherapy Research, 14,* 77–88.

Butler, W., & Powers, K. (1996). Solution-focused grief therapy. In S. D. Miller, M. A. Hubble, & B. L. Duncan (Eds.), *Handbook of solution-focused brief therapy* (pp. 228–250). San Francisco: Jossey-Bass.

Callaghan, G. M. (2006). Functional assessment of skills for interpersonal therapists: The FASIT system. *The Behavior Analyst Today, 7*(3), 399–433.

Campbell, J. (2006). *Essentials of clinical supervision.* Hoboken, NJ: Wiley.

Canda, E. R., & Furman, L. D. (1999). Spiritual diversity in social work practice. New York: Free Press.

Carlson, T. D., Kirkpatrick, D., & Hecker, L. (2002). Religion, spirituality, and marriage and family therapy: A study of family therapists' beliefs about the appropriateness of addressing religious and spiritual issues in therapy. *American Journal of Family Therapy, 30,* 157–171.

Carter, B. (2003). Gender and child protection. *International Social Work, 46,* 555–557.

Carter, B., & McGoldrick, M. (Eds.). (1999). *The expanded family life cycle: Individual, family, and social*

perspectives (3rd ed.). Boston: Allyn & Bacon.

Cartwright, B. Y., Daniels, J., Zhang, S. (2008). Assessing multicultural competence: Perceived versus demonstrated performance. *Journal of Counseling & Development, 86*(3), 318–322.

Caspar, F., Grossman, C., Unmussig, C., & Schramm, E. (2005). Complementary therapeutic relationship: Therapist behavior, interpersonal patterns, and therapeutic effects. *Psychotherapy Research, 15,* 91–102. doi:10.1080/10503300512331327074

Castonguay, L. G., & Beutler, L. E. (Eds.) (2006). *Principles of therapeutic change that work.* New York: Oxford University Press.

Chang, D. F., & Berk, A. (2009). Making cross-racial therapy work: A phenomenological study of clients' experiences of cross-racial therapy. *Journal of Counseling Psychology, 56*(4), 521–536.

Chang, J., (2010). The reflecting team: A training method for family counselors. *The Family Journal, 18*(1), 36–44. doi:10.1177/1066480709357731

Chang, V. N. (1996). *I just lost myself: Psychological abuse of women in marriage.* Westport, CT: Praeger.

Chang, V. N., & Scott, S. T. (1999). *Basic interviewing skills: A workbook for practitioners.* Chicago: Nelson-Hall.

Chang, V. N., & Sullenberger, S. W. (2009). Enhancing the success of SOTL research: A case study using modified problem-based learning in social work education. *Journal of the Scholarship of Teaching and Learning, 9*(2), 1–9.

Cheavens, J. S., Feldman, D. B., Woodward, J. T., & Snyder, C. R. (2006). Hope in cognitive psychotherapies: On working with client strengths. *Journal of Cognitive Psychotherapy, 20,* 135–145.

Cheney, B., McMenamin, D., & Shorter, D. I. (2010). Relapse. In P. Levounis & B. Arnaout (Eds.), *Handbook of motivation and change: A practical guide for clinicians* (ch 8). Arlington, VA: American Psychiatric Publishing, Inc.

Chestang, L. (1972). *Character development in a hostile environment.* Occasional Paper

No. 3. Chicago: University of Chicago.

Cheung, Y. W., Mok, B. H., & Cheung, T.-S. (2005). Personal empowerment and life satisfaction among self-help group members in Hong Kong. *Small Group Research*, 36, 354–377.

Cho, H. J. (2005). Reviving the old sermon of medicine with the placebo effect. *Revista Brasileira de Psiquiatria*, 27, 336–340.

Clark, C. C. (2003). *Group leadership skills*. New York: Springer.

Clauss-Ehlers, C. S. (2004). Reinventing resilience: A model of culturally focused resilient adaptation. *Community Diversity and Ethnic Minority Psychology*, 5, 65–75.

Collins, D. (1990). Identifying dysfunctional counseling skill behaviors. *The Clinical Supervisor*, 8(1), 67–79.

Compton, B., Galaway, B., & Cournoyer, B. (2005). *Social work processes* (7th ed.). Belmont, CA: Thomson Learning.

Congress, E. (2008). Individual and family development theory. In P. Lehman & N. Coady (Eds.), *Theoretical perspectives for direct social work practice: A generalist-eclectic approach* (2nd ed.). New York: Springer Publishing Company.

Congress, E. P. (2000). What social workers should know about ethics: Understanding and resolving practice dilemmas. *Advances in Social Work*, 1(1), 1–22.

Congress, E. P. (2002). Using the culturagram with culturally diverse families. In A. R. Roberts & G. J. Greene (Eds.), *Social work desk reference* (pp. 57–61). Oxford, England: Oxford University Press, Inc.

Congress, E. P. (2009). Access and advocacy with immigrants and refugees: Legal, ethical, and practice issues. Presented at BPD conference, Arizona, March 20.

Conley, D. & Glauber, R. (2008). All in the family?: Family composition, resources, and sibling similarity in socioeconomic status. *Research in Social Stratification and Mobility*, 26(4), 297–306. doi: 10.1016/j.rssm.2008.08.003

Constantine, M. G., Lewis, E. L., Conner, L. C., & Sanchez, D. (2000). Addressing spiritual and religious issues in counseling African Americans: Implications for counselor training and practice. *Counseling and Values*, 45(1), 28–38.

Contarello, A. (2003). Body to body: Copresence in communication. In L. Fortunati, J. E. Katz, & R. Riccini (Eds.), *Mediating the human body: Technology, communication, and fashion* (pp. 123–131). Mahwah, NJ: Lawrence Erlbaum Associates.

Conyne, R. K., & Bemak, F. (2004). Teaching group work from an ecological perspective. *The Journal for Specialists in Group Work*, 29, 7–18.

Cooper, M. (2007). Humanizing psychotherapy. *Journal of Contemporary Psychotherapy*, 37(1), 11–16. doi: 10.1007/s10879-006-9029-6

Corey, G. (2009). The counselor: Person and professional (pp. 16-35). *Theory and practice of counseling and psychotherapy*. Belmont, CA: Thomson Brooks/Cole.

Cottone, R. R., & Tarvydas, V. M. (2003). *Ethical and professional issues in counseling* (2nd ed.). Upper Saddle River, NJ: Prentice Hall.

Cozolino, L. (2004). *The making of a therapist: A practical guide for the inner journey*. New York: Norton.

Cozolino, L. (2010). *The neuroscience of psychotherapy: Healing the social brain* (2nd ed.). New York: W. W. Norton.

Cuellar, I., & Paniagua, F. A. (2000). *Handbook of multicultural mental health: Assessment and treatment of diverse populations*. New York: Academic Press.

Cunha, F., Heckman, J. J., Lochner, L., & Masterov, D. V. (2005). Interpreting the evidence on life cycle skill formation. In E. Hanushek & F. Welch (Eds.), *Handbook of the economics of education*.

Curtis, J. M. (1982). The effect of therapist self-disclosure on patients' perceptions of empathy, competence, and trust in an analogue psycho-therapeutic interaction. *Psychotherapy: Theory, Research, Practice, Training*, 19, 54–62.

Curtis, R. C. (2000). Using goal-setting strategies to enrich the practicum and internship experiences of beginning counselors. *Journal of Humanistic Counseling Education and Development*, 38(4), 194–216.

Daniel, J. H., Roysircar, G., & Abeles, N. (2004). Individual and cultural diversity competency: Focus on the therapist. *Journal of Clinical Psychology*, 60, 755–770.

Davis, B. (2001). The restorative power of emotions in child protection services. *Child & Adolescent Social Work Journal*, 18, 437–454.

Decety, J. & Lamm, C. (2006). Human empathy through the lens of social neuroscience. *The Scientific World JOURNAL*, 6, 1146–1163. doi: 10.1100/tsw.2006.221

Decety, J., & Moriguchi, Y. (2007). The empathic brain and its dysfunction in psychiatric populations: Implications for intervention across different clinical conditions. *BioPsychoSocial Medicine*, 1, 22–65.

De Jong, P., & Berg, I. K. (1998). *Interviewing for solutions*. Pacific Grove, CA: Brooks/Cole.

De Jong, P., & Hopwood, L. E. (1996). Outcome research on treatment conducted at the brief family therapy center, 1992–1993. In S. D. Miller, M. A. Hubbles, & B. L. Duncan (Eds.), *Handbook of solution-focused brief therapy* (pp. 272–298). San Francisco: Jossey-Bass.

De Jong, P., & Miller, S. D. (1995). How to interview for client strengths. *Social Work*, 40, 729–736.

De Longis, A., & Holtzman, S. (2005). Coping in context: The role of stress, social support, and personality in coping. *Journal of Personality*, 73, 1633–1656.

de Shazer, S., & Molnar, A. (1984). Four useful interventions in family therapy. *Journal of Marital and Family Therapy*, 10, 297–304.

Dewees, C. H. (2006). An investigation of bereaved parents: Coping strategies and effects on the marital relationship. (Doctoral dissertation, St. Mary's University, 2006). *Dissertation Abstracts International*, 66, 12-A.

Dietz, L. J., Jacobs. A., Levin, J., Martin, L., Mary Babb Morris, M. B., & Zakolski, L. A. (2010). Privileged communications: Communications to social workers. *American Jurisprudence* (2nd ed.)

Dishion, T. J., & Stormshak, E. A. (2007). *Intervening in children's lives: An ecological, family centered approach to mental health care.* Washington, DC: American Psychological Association.

Dodd, P., & Gutierrez, L. (1990). Preparing students for the future: A power perspective on community practice. *Administration in Social Work, 14,* 63–78.

Dodge, K. A., Pettit, G. S., & Bates, J. E. (1994). Socialization mediators of the relation between socioeconomic status and child conduct problems. *Child Development, 65,* 649–665.

Dolgoff, R., Loewenberg, F. M., & Harrington, D. (2005). *Ethical decisions for social work* (p. 262). Belmont, CA: Thomson Brooks/ Cole.

Donovan, K., & Regehr, C. (2010). Elder abuse: Clinical, ethical, and legal considerations in social work practice. *Clinical Social Work Journal, 38*(2), 174–182.

Dore, M. M., & Alexander, L. B. (1996). Preserving families at risk of child abuse and neglect: The role of the helping alliance. *Child Abuse and Neglect, 20,* 349–361.

Dowden, C., & Andrews, D. A. (2000). Effective correctional treatment and violent reoffending: A meta-analysis. *Canadian Journal of Criminology, 42,* 449–467.

Doyle, C. (2001). Surviving and coping with emotional abuse in childhood. *Clinical Child Psychology and Psychiatry, 6,* 387–402.

Dudley-Grant, G. R., Mendez, G. I., & Zinn, J. (2000). Strategies for anticipating and preventing psychological trauma of hurricanes through community education. *Professional Psychology: Research and Practice, 31,* 387–392.

Duggan, A. (2006). Understanding interpersonal communication processes across health contexts: Advances in the last decade and challenges for the next decade. *Journal of Health Communication, 11*(1), 93–108. doi:10.1080/ 10810730500461125

Duncan, B. L., Miller, S. D., Sparks, J. A., Claud, D. A., Reynolds, L. R., Brown, J., & Johnson, L. D. (2003). The session rating scale: Preliminary psychometric properties of a "working" alliance measure. *Journal of Brief Therapy, 3*(1), 3–12.

Eagle, M. N., Migone, P., & Gallese, V. (2007). Intentional attunement: Mirror neurons and the neural underpinnings of interpersonal relations. *Journal of the American Psychoanalytic Association, 55,* 131–176.

Early, T., & GlenMaye, L. F. (2000). Valuing families: Social work practice with families from a strengths perspective. *Social Work, 45,* 118–130.

Ecker, B. (2010). The brain's rules for change: Translating cutting-edge neuroscience into practice. *Psychotherapy Networker, 34*(1), 43–45.

Edmond, T., Megivern, D., Williams, C., Rochman, E., & Howard, M. (2006). Integrating evidence-based practice and social work field education. *Journal of Social Work Education, 42*(2), 377–396. doi: 10.5175/JSWE.2006.200404115

Egan, G. (2002). *The skilled helper: A problem-management approach to helping* (7th ed.). Pacific Grove, CA: Brooks/Cole.

Egan, G. (2007). *The skilled helper: A problem-management and opportunity-development approach to helping* (8th ed.). Belmont, CA: Brooks/Cole, Thomson Higher Education.

Elliott, R., Bohart, A. C.; Watson, J. C.; & Greenberg, L. S. (2011). Empathy. *Psychotherapy, 48*(1), 43–49.

Ellis, J., (2006). Researching children's experience hermeneutically and holistically. *Alberta Journal of Educational Research, 52*(3), 111–126.

Elman, N. S. (2005). Professional development: Training for professionalism as a foundation for competent practice in psychology. *Professional Psychology: Research and Practice, 36,* 367–375. doi: 10.1037/0735-7028.36.4.367

Everson, S. A., Maty, S. C., Lynch, J. W., & Kaplan, G.A. (2002). Epidemiologic evidence for the relation between socioeconomic status and depression, obesity, and diabetes. *Journal of Psychosomatic Research, 53,* 891–895.

Farber, B. A., Berano, K. C., & Capobianco, J. A. (2004). Clients' perceptions of the process and consequences of self-disclosure in psychotherapy. *Journal of Counseling Psychology, 51*(3), 340–346.

Farber, B. A., & Doolin, E. M. (2011). Positive regard. *Psychotherapy, 48*(1), 58–64.

Farber, B. A., & Lane, J. S. (2002). Positive regard. In J. C. Norcross (Ed.), *Psychotherapy relationships that work: Therapist contributions and responsiveness to patients* (pp. 175–194). New York: Oxford University Press.

Feldman, D., Rand, K., Shorey, H., & Snyder, C. (2002). Hopeful choices: A school counselor's guide to Hope Theory. *Professional School Counseling, 5,* 298–308.

Fisher, C. B. (2003). *Decoding the ethics code.* Thousand Oaks, CA: Sage Publications.

Fisher, K., & Hardie, R. J. (2002). Goal attainment scaling in evaluating a multidisciplinary pain management program. *Clinical Rehabilitation, 16,* 871–877.

Fishman, P., Taplin, S., Meyer, D., & Barlow, W. (2000). Cost-effectiveness of strategies to enhance mammography use. *Effective Clinical Practice, 4,* 213–220.

Fivush, R. (2004). Voice and silence: A feminist model of autobiographical memory. In J. M. Lucariello, J. A. Hudson, R. Fivush, & P. J. Bauer (Eds.), *The development of the mediated mind: Sociocultural context and cognitive development* (pp. 79–99). Mahwah, NJ: Lawrence Erlbaum Associates.

Flaskas, C. (2004). Thinking about the therapeutic relationship: Emerging themes in family therapy. *The Australian and New Zealand Journal of Family Therapy, 25,* 13–20.

Fonagy, P., Target, M., Cottrell, D., Phillips, J., & Kurtz, Z. (2002). *What works for whom? A critical review of treatments for children and adolescents.* New York: Guilford.

Forbes, C. E., Schmader, T., & Allen, J. J. B. (2007). The role of devaluing and discounting in performance monitoring: A neurophysiological study of minorities under threat. *Social Cognitive and Affective Neuroscience, 3,* 253–261. doi: 10.1093/scan/nsn012

Ford, G. G. (2006). *Ethical reasoning for mental health professionals.* Thousand Oaks, CA: Sage.

Fortune, A. E. (1987). Grief only? Client and social worker reactions to termination. *Clinical Social Work Journal, 15,* 159–171.

Fortune, A. E., Pearlingi, B., & Rochelle, C. D. (1992). Reactions to termination of individual treatment. *Social Work, 37,* 171–178.

Fosha, D., Siegel, D. J., & Solomon, M. F. (2009). *The healing power of emotion: Affective neuroscience, development & clinical practice.* New York: W. W. Norton & Co.

Fox, K. (2005). Coming of age in the eBay generation: Life-shopping and the new life skills in the age of eBay. *Social Issues Research Center.* Retrieved from: http://www.sirc.org/publik/Yeppies.pdf

Frank, J. D., & Frank, J. B. (1991). Persuasion and healing: A comparative study of psychotherapy (3rd ed.). Baltimore: Johns Hopkins University Press.

Friedlander, M. L., Escudero, V., Heatherington, L., Diamond, G. M. (2011). Alliance in couple and family therapy. *Psychotherapy, 48*(1), 25–33.

Friedman, N. (2005). Experiential listening. *Journal of Humanistic Psychology, 45,* 217–238.

Friedman, R. C., Downey, J. I. (2008). Sexual differentiation of behavior: The foundation of a developmental model of psychosexuality. *Journal of the Psychoanalytic Association, 56*(1), 147–175. doi:10.1177/0003065108315690

Fryer, R. G., & Levitt, S. D. (2004). Understanding the black-white test score gap in the first two years of school. *The Review of Economics and Statistics, 86,* 447–464.

Fryer-Edwards, K., Arnold, R. M., Baile, W., Tulsky, J. A., Petracca, F., & Back, A. (2006). Reflective teaching practices: An approach to teaching communication skills in a small-group setting. *Academic Medicine, 81*(7), 638–644. doi:10.1097/01.ACM.0000232414.43142.45

Fuertes, J. N., Stracuzzi, T. I., Bennett, J., Scheinholtz, J., Mislowack, A., Hersh, M., & Cheng, D. (2006). Therapist multicultural competency: A study of therapy dyads. *Psychotherapy: Theory, Research, Practice, Training, 43*(4), 480–490.

Furman, B., & Ahola, T. (1992). *Solution talk: Hosting the therapeutic conversations.* New York: Norton.

Gager, F. P. (2004). Exploring relationships among termination status, therapy outcome, and client outcome. *Dissertation Abstracts International, 64,* 3522.

Garvin, C., & Seabury, B. (1997). *Interpersonal practice in social work: Promoting competence and social justice.* Boston: Allyn & Bacon.

Gelso, C. J., & Carter, J. A. (1994). Components of the psychotherapy relationship: Their interaction and unfolding during treatment. *Journal of Counseling Psychology, 41,* 296–306.

Gelso, C. J., & Hayes, J. A. (1998). *The psychotherapy relationship: Theory, research, and practice.* New York: Wiley.

Gerdes, K. E., & Segal, E. A. (2009). A social work model of empathy. *Advances in Social Work, 10*(2), 114–127.

Gergen, K. J. (2006). Social construction as an ethics of infinitude: Reply to Brinkmann. *Journal of Humanistic Psychology, 46,* 119.

Germain, C. B., & Gitterman, A. (1995). Ecological perspective. In L. Beebe et al. (Eds.), *Encyclopedia of social work: Vol. 1* (19th ed., pp. 816–824). Washington, DC: NASW Press.

Gibson, L. (2006). Mirrored emotions. *University of Chicago Magazine, 98*(4), 34–39.

Gilbert, L. A., & Scher, M. (1999). *Gender and sex in counseling and psychotherapy.* Boston: Allyn & Bacon.

Gilligan, R. (2004). Promoting resilience in child and family social work: Issues for social work practice, education and policy. *Social Work Education, 23*(1), 93–104.

Gilligan, P., & Furness, S. (2006). The role of religion and spirituality in social work practice: Views and experiences of social workers and students. *The British Journal of Social Work, 36*(4), 617–637. doi: 10.1093/bjsw/bch252

Glosoff, H. L., Herlihy, B., & Spence, E. B. (2000). Privileged communication in the counselor-client relationship. *Journal of Counseling and Development, 78,* 454–462.

Goldenberg, H., & Goldenberg, I. (1998). *Counseling today's families.* Pacific Grove, CA: Brooks/Cole.

Goldenthal, P. (1996). *Doing contextual therapy: An integrated model for working with individuals,* couples, and families. New York: Norton.

Gollwitzer, P. M. (1999). Implementation intentions: Strong effects of simple plans. *American Psychologist, 54,* 493–503.

Goodman, E. (1999). The role of socioeconomic status gradients in explaining differences in U.S. adolescents' health. *American Journal of Public Health, 89,* 1522–1528.

Gordon, K. A. (1995). Self-concept and motivational patterns of resilient African American high school students. *Journal of Black Psychology, 21,* 239–256.

Gordon, R. A., Druckman, D., Rozelle, R. M., & Baxter, J. C. (2006). Non-verbal behavior as communication: Approaches, issues, and research. In O. Hargie (Ed.), *The handbook of communication skills* (pp. 73–119). New York: Rutlege.

Gorske, T. T., & Smith, S. R. (2009). The initial interview: Collaborative information gathering. *Collaborative Therapeutic Neuropsychological Assessment* (pp. 45–55). doi:10.1007/978-0-387-75426-0_4

Greeff, A., & Merwe, V. (2003). Variables associated with resilience in divorced families. *Social Indicators Research, 68,* 59–75.

Green, R. K., & Cox, G. (1978). Social work and malpractice: A converging course. *Social Work, 23*(2), 100.

Gutheil, T. G., & Brodsky, A. (2008). Definitions and dilemmas. In T. Gutheil & A. Brodsky (Eds.), *Preventing boundary violations in clinical practice* (pp. 15–30). New York: The Guilford Press.

Hagedorn, W. B. (2005). Counselor self-awareness and self-exploration of religious and spiritual beliefs: Know thyself. In C. S. Cashwell & Y. J. Scott, *Integrating spirituality and religion into counseling: A guide to competent practice* (pp. 63–84). Alexandria, VA: American Counseling Association.

Hammond, S. A. (1998). *The thin book of appreciative inquiry.* Bend, OR: Thin Book Publishing.

Hanna, F. J. (2002). Building hope for change. In F. J. Hanna (Ed.), *Therapy with difficult clients: Using the precursors model to awaken change*. Washington, DC: American Psychological Association.

Hanner, J. (2010). Maintenance. In P. Levounis & B. Arnaout (Eds.), *Handbook of motivation and change: A practical guide for clinicians* (ch 8). Arlington, VA: American Psychiatric Publishing, Inc.

Hardina, D. (2005). Ten characteristics of empowerment-oriented social service organizations. *Administration in Social Work, 29*, 23–42.

Harris, L. (2010). Unwritten rules: What women need to know about leading in today's organizations. Charleston, SC: BookSurge Publishing.

Harvey, J. (2007). Moral solidarity and empathetic understanding: The moral value and scope of the relationship. *Journal of Social Philosophy, 38*(1), 22–37. doi: 10.1111/j.1467-9833.2007.00364.x

Haslam, D. R., & Harris, S. M. (2004). Informed consent documents of marriage and family therapists in private practice: A qualitative analysis. *American Journal of Family Therapy, 32*, 359–374.

Hayes, J., Gelso, C., & Hummel, A. (2011). Managing counter-transference. In J. C. Norcross (Ed.), *Psychotherapy relationships that work* (2nd ed.). New York: Oxford University Press.

Hayes, A. M., Laurenceau, J., Feldman, G., Straus, J. L., & Cardaciotto, L. (2007). Change is not always linear: The study of nonlinear and discontinuous patterns of change in psychotherapy. *Clinical Psychology Review, 27*(6), 715–723. doi: 10.1016/j.cpr.2007.01.008

Hedges, L. E. (2000). *Facing the challenge of liability in psychotherapy*. Northvale, NJ: Jason Aronson, Inc.

Henig, R. M. (2010). *What is it about 20-somethings?* New York Times.com. Retrieved from: http://www.nytimes.com/2010/8/11/magazine/22-Adulthood-t-html

Henretty, J. R., & Levitt, H. M. (2010). The role of therapist self-disclosure in psychotherapy: A qualitative review. *Clinical Psychology Review, 30*(1), 63–77. doi:10.1016/j.cpr.2009.09.004

Herring, R. D. (1996). Synergetic counseling and Native American Indian students. *Journal of Counseling and Development, 74,* 542–547.

Heyman, J. C., Buchanan, R., Marlowe, D., & Sealy, Y. (2006). Social workers' attitudes toward the role of religion and spirituality in social work practice. *Journal of Pastoral Counseling, 41,* 3–19.

Hiatt, D., & Hargrave, G. (1995). The characteristics of highly effective therapists in managed behavioral provider networks. *Behavioral Healthcare Tomorrow, 4,* 19–22.

Hill, C. E., (2006). Therapist techniques, client involvement, and the therapeutic relationship: Inextricably intertwined in the therapy process. *Psychotherapy: Theory/Research/Practice/Training, 42*(4), 431–442. doi: 10.1037/0033-3204.42.4.431

Hill, C. E., & Lent, R. W. (2006). A narrative and meta-analytic review of helping skills training: Time to revive a dormant area of inquiry. *Psychotherapy: Theory, Research, Practice, Training, 43,* 154–172.

Hillbrand, M., & Young, J. L., (2008). Instilling hope into forensic treatment: The antidote to despair and depression. *Journal of the American Academy of Psychiatry and the Law, 36*(1), 90–94.

Hodge, D. R. (2005a). Spiritual life maps: A client-centered pictorial instrument for spiritual assessment, planning, and intervention. *Social Work, 50,* 197–206.

Hodge, D. (2005b). Social workers and the house of Islam: Orienting practitioners to the beliefs and values of Muslims in the United States. *Social Work, 50*(2), 162–173.

Hoff, E. (2003). The specificity of environmental influence: Socioeconomic status affects early vocabulary development via maternal speech. *Child Development, 74*(5), 1368–1378.

Holroyd, J. C., & Brodsky, A. M. (1977). Psychologists' attitudes and practices regarding erotic and nonerotic physical contact with patients. *American Psychologist, 32,* 843–849.

Home, A. (1999). Group empowerment. In W. Shera & L. Wells (Eds.), *Empowerment practice in social work: Developing richer conceptual foundations* (pp. 234–245). Toronto: Canadian Scholars' Press.

Hopps, J. G., Pinderhughes, E., & Shankar, R. (1995). *The power to care: Clinical practice effectiveness with overwhelmed clients.* New York: Free Press.

Horowitz, R. (2010). The complexities of change in the psychotherapy of serious mental illness: A practitioner's reflections. *Clinical Social Work Journal, 37*(2), 104–111. doi:0.1007/s10615-008-0181-1

Horvath, A. O., & Bedi, R. P. (2002). The alliance. In J. C. Norcross (Ed.), *Psychotherapy relationships that work: Therapist contributions and responsiveness to patients* (pp. 37–69). New York: Oxford University Press.

Horvarth, A. O., Del Re, A. C., Fluckiger, C., & Symonds, D. (2011). Alliance in individual psychotherapy. *Psychotherapy, 48*(1), 9–16. doi:10.1037/a0022186

Hosking, D. M. (2005). Bounded entities, constructive revisions, and radical re-constructions. *Cognition, Brain, Behavior, 9,* 609–622.

Houston-Vega, M. K., & Nuehring, E. M. (1996). *Prudent practice: A guide for managing malpractice risks.* Annapolis Junction, MD: National Association of Social Workers.

Hubble, M. A., & Miller, S. D. (2004). The client: Psychotherapy's missing link for promoting a positive psychology. In P. A. Linley & S. Joseph (Eds.), *Positive psychology in practice.* Hoboken, NJ: Wiley.

Humphreys, J. (2003). Resilience in sheltered battered women. *Issues in Mental Health Nursing, 23,* 137–152.

Hyman, B., & Williams, L. (2001). Resilience among women survivors of child sexual abuse. *Affilia, 16*(2), 198–219.

Iacoboni, M. (2009). Imitation, empathy, and mirror neurons. *Annual Review of Psychology, 60,* 653–670.

Ivey, A. E., & Ivey, M. B. (2003). *Intentional interviewing and counseling: Facilitating client development in a multicultural society* (5th ed.). Pacific Grove, CA: Brooks/Cole.

Jacobs, E. E., Masson, R. L., & Harvill, R. L. (1998). *Group counseling: Strategies and skills* (3rd ed.). Pacific Grove, CA: Brooks/Cole.

Jacobs, E. E., Masson, R. L., & Harvill, R. L. (2009a). Basic skills for group leaders. *Group counseling: Strategies and skills* (pp. 121–140). Belmont, CA: Thomson Brooks/Cole.

Jacobs, E. E., Masson, R. L., & Harvill, R. L. (2009b). Closing a session or group. *Group counseling: Strategies and skills* (pp. 349–376). Belmont, CA: Thomson Brooks/Cole.

Jacobs, E. E., Masson, R. L., & Harvill, R. L. (2009c). Getting started: The beginning stage and beginning phase. *Group counseling: Strategies and skills* (pp. 85–119). Belmont, CA: Thomson Brooks/Cole.

Jakobsons, L. J., Brown, J. S., Gordon, K. H., & Joiner, T. E. (2007). When are clients ready to terminate? *Cognitive and Behavioral Practice*, 14(2), 218–230. doi:10.1016/j.cbpra.2006.09.005

Jenson, J. (2007). Research, advocacy, and social policy: Lessons from the risk and resilience model. *Social Work Research*, 31(1), 3–5.

Jernigan, M. M., Green, C. E., Helms, J. E., Perez-Gualdron, L., & Henze, K. (2010). An examination of people of color supervision dyads: Racial identity matters as much as race. *Training and Education in Professional Psychology*, 4(1), 62–73.

Johnson, L. R., Bastien, G., & Hirschel, M. J. (2009). Psychotherapy in a culturally diverse world. In S. Eshun & R. A. R. Gurung (Eds.), *Culture and mental health: Sociocultural influences, theory, and practice.* Oxford, UK: Wiley-Blackwell. doi:10.1002/9781444305807

Jones, A. C. (2003). Reconstructing the stepfamily: Old myths, new stories. *Social Work*, 48, 228–236.

Kacen, L. (1999). Anxiety levels, group characteristics, and members' behaviors in the termination stage of support groups for patients recovering from heart attacks. *Research on Social Work Practice*, 9, 656–672.

Katsavdakis, K. A., Gabbard, G. O., & Athey, G. I. (2004). Profiles of impaired health professionals. *Bulletin of the Menninger Clinic*, 68, 60–72.

Katzman, G. P. (2010). Action. In P. Levounis & B. Arnaout (Eds.), *Handbook of motivation and change: A practical guide for clinicians* (ch 6). Arlington, VA: American Psychiatric Publishing, Inc.

Kazantzis, N., & Ronan, K. R. (2006). Can between-session (homework) activities be considered a common factor in psychotherapy? *Journal of Psychotherapy Integration*, 16, 115–127.

Kazantzis, N., Whittington, C., & Dattilio, F. (2010). Meta-analysis of homework effects in cognitive and behavioral therapy: A replication and extension. *Clinical Psychology: Science and Practice*, 17(2), 144–156. doi:10.1111/j.1468-2850.2010.01204.x

Kazdin, A. E. (1995). Scope of child and adolescent psychotherapy research: Limited sampling of dysfunctions, treatments, and client characteristics. *Journal of Child Clinical Psychology*, 24, 125–140.

Keijsers, G. P. J., Schaap, C. P., & Hoogduin, C. A. L. (2000). The impact of interpersonal patient and therapist behavior on outcome in cognitive-behavior therapy. *Behavior Modification*, 24, 264–297.

Kelch, B. P. (2010). Incorporating the stages of change model in solution focused brief therapy with non-substance abusing families: A novel and integrative approach. *The Family Journal*, 18(2), 184–188. doi:10.1177/1066480710364325

Kelly, G. A. (1991). *The psychology of personal constructs: Vol. 1. A theory of personality.* London: Routledge. (Original work published 1955).

Kendall, F. E. (2001). *Understanding white privilege.* Retrieved May 4, 2007, from http://www.cwsworkshop.org/resources/WhitePrivilege.html

Kim, B. S. K., Hill, C. E., Gelso, C. J., Goates, M. K., Asay, P. A., & Harbin, J. M. (2003). Counselor self-disclosure, East Asian American adherence to Asian cultural values, and counseling process. *Journal of Counseling Psychology*, 50(3), 324–332. doi:10.1037/0022-0167.50.3.324

Kim, B. S. K., Ng, G. F., & Ahn, A. J. (2005). Effects of client expectations for counseling success, client counselor worldview match, and client strengths. *Journal of Counseling Psychology*, 52, 67–76.

Kington, R. S., & Smith, J. P. (1997). Socioeconomic status and racial and ethnic differences in functional status associated with chronic diseases. *American Journal of Public Health*, 87(5), 805–810.

Kiresuk, T. J., Smith, A. & Cardillo, J. E. (1994). *Goal attainment scaling: Applications, theory, and measurement.* Mahwah, NJ: Erlbaum.

Klosek, M. (2007). The use of goal attainment scaling in a community health promotion initiative with seniors. *BMC. Geriatrics*, 7:16.

Knapp, S., Gottlieb, M., Berman, J., & Handelsman, M. M. (2007). When laws and ethics collide: What should psychologists do? *Professional Psychology: Research and Practice*, 38(1), 54–59.

Knight, C. (2006). Integrating solution-focused principles and techniques into clinical practice and supervision. *The Clinical Supervisor*, 23(2), 153–173. doi:10.1300/J001v23n02_10

Koerin, B. B., Harrigan, M. P., & Reeves, J. W. (1990). Facilitating the transition from student to social worker: Challenges of the younger student. *Journal of Social Work Education*, 26(2), 199–208.

Kolden, G. G., Klein, M. H., Wang, C-C., & Austin, S. B. (2011). Congruence/genuineness. *Psychotherapy*, 48(1), 65–71.

Kottler, J. A. (1994). *Advanced group leadership.* Pacific Grove, CA: Brooks/Cole.

Kottler, J. A. (2001). *Making changes last.* Philadelphia: Brunner-Routledge.

Kottler, J. A. (2003). *On being a therapist* (3rd ed.). San Francisco: Jossey-Bass.

Kraemer, S. (2006). Something happens: Elements of therapeutic change. *Clinical Child Psychology and Psychiatry*, 11(2), 239–248. doi:10.1177/1359104506061415

Kruger, J., & Dunning, D. (1999). Unskilled and unaware of it: How difficulties in recognizing one's own incompetence lead to inflated self-assessments. *Journal of Personality and Social Psychology*, 77, 1121–1134.

Krupnick, J. L., Sotsky, S. M., Elkin, I., Simmens, S., Moyer, J., Watkins, J., & Pilkonis, P. A. (2006). The role of the therapeutic alliance in psychotherapy and pharmacotherapy outcome: Findings in the National Institute of

Mental Health Treatment of Depression Collaborative Research Program. *Focus, 4,* 269–277.

Krupnick, J. L., Sotsky, S. M., Simmens, S., Moyer, J., Elkin, I., Watkins, J., & Pilkonis, P. A. (1996). The role of the therapeutic alliance in psychotherapy and pharma-cotherapy outcome: Findings in the National Institute of Mental Health Treatment of Depression Collaborative Research Program. *Journal of Consulting and Clinical Psychology, 64,* 532–539.

Kuntze, J., van der Molen, H. T., & Born, M. P. (2009). Increase in counseling communication skills after basic and advanced microskills training. *British Journal of Educational Psychology, 79,* 175–188. doi:10.1348/000709908X313758

Lam, J., & Grossman, F. (1997). Resilience and adult adaption in women with and without self-reported histories of childhood sexual abuse. *Journal of Traumatic Stress, 10*(2), 175–196.

Lamb, D. H., Catanzaro, S. J., & Moorman, A. S. (2004). Sexual and nonsexual boundary violations involving psychologists, clients, supervisees, and students: Implications for professional practice. *Professional Psychology: Research and Practice, 29,* 498–503.

Lambert, M. J., & Barley, D. E. (2002). Research summary on the therapeutic relationship and psychotherapy outcome. In J. C. Norcross (Ed.), *Psychotherapy relationships that work: Therapist contributions and responsiveness to patients* (pp. 17–35). New York: Oxford University Press.

Lambert, M., & Bergin, A. (1994). The effectiveness of psychotherapy. In A. Bergin & S. Garfield (Eds.), *Handbook of psychotherapy and behavior change* (4th ed., pp. 143–189). Toronto: Wiley.

Lambert, M. J., & Shimokawa, K. (2011). Collecting client feedback. *Psychotherapy, 48,* 72–79.

Lamond, A., Depp, C., Allison, M., Langer, R., Reichstadt, J., Moore, D., et al. (2009). Measurement and predictors of resilience among community-dwelling older women. *Journal of Psychiatric Research, 43,* 148–154.

Latner, J. D., Stunkard, A. J., Wilson, G. T., & Jackson, M. L. (2006). The perceived effectiveness of continuing care and group support in the long-term self-help treatment of obesity. *Obesity: A Research Journal, 14,* 464–471. doi:10.1038/oby.2006.61

Lazarus, A. A. (2003). Boundary crossing vs. boundary violations. *Annals of the American Psychotherapy Association, 6*(1), 25–26.

Lazarus, R. S., & Folkman, S. (1984). *Stress, appraisal, and coping.* New York: Springer.

Leadbeater, B., Dodgen, D., & Solarz, A. (2005). The resilience revolution: A paradigm shift for research and policy? In R. Peters, B. Leadbeater, & R. McMahon (Eds.), *Resilience in children, families, and communities: Linking context to practice and policy.* New York: Kluwer Academic/Plenum.

Lee, J. A. (2001). *An empowerment approach to social work practice: Building the beloved community* (2nd ed.). New York: Columbia University Press.

Lever, H., & Gmeiner, A. (2000). Families leaving family therapy after one or two sessions: A multiple descriptive case study. *Contemporary Family Therapy, 22,* 39–65.

Levy, C. S. (1973). The value base of social work. *Journal of Education for Social Work, 9*(1), 34–42.

Levy, A., & Wall, J. (2000). Children who have witnessed community homicide. Incorporating risk and resilience in clinical work. *The Journal of Contemporary Human Services, 81*(4), 402–411.

Lewin, K. (1952). Group decision and social change. In G. E. Swanson, T. N. Nowcomb, & E. L. Hartley (Eds.), *Readings in social psychology* (pp. 168–185). New York: Holt, Rinehart, and Winston.

Lietz, C. (2006). Uncovering stories of family resilience: A mixed method study of resilient families, part 1. *Families in Society: The Journal of Contemporary Social Services, 87*(4), 557–582.

Lietz, C. (2007). Uncovering stories of family resilience: A mixed method study of resilient families, part 2. *Families in Society: The Journal of*

Contemporary Social Services, 88(1), 147–155.

Liston-Smith, J. (2008). Appreciative Inquiry and solution-focused coaching: Applications of positive psychology in the practice of coaching. *The Coaching Psychologist, 4*(2), 1748–1104.

Littauer, H., Sexton, H. & Wynn, R. (2005). Qualities clients wish for in their therapists. *Sand J Caring Sci, 19,* 28–31.

Littrell, J., & Beck, E. (1999). Perceiving oppression: Relationships with resilience, self esteem, depressive symptoms, and reliance on God in African American homeless men. *Journal of Sociology and Social Welfare, 26,* 137.

Liu, W. M., Pickett, T., & Ivey, A. E. (2007). White middle-class privilege: Social class bias and implications for training and practice. *Journal of Multicultural Counseling and Development, 35,* 194–206.

Lombardi, M. M. (2007). Authentic learning for the 21st century: An overview. *EDUCAUSE Learning Initiative.* Retrieved January 26, 2011, from http://connect.educause .edu/library/abstract/ AuthenticLearningfor/39343

Longshore, D., & Teruya, C. (2006). Treatment motivation in drug users: A theory-based analysis. *Drug and Alcohol Dependence, 81*(2), 179–188. doi:10.1016/j.drugalcdep.2005.06.011

Lopez, S. J., & Magyar-Moe, J. L. (2006). A positive psychology that matters. *Counseling Psychologist, 34,* 323–330.

Lyons, M., Smuts, C., & Stephens, A. (2001). Participation, empowerment and sustainability: (How) do the links work? *Urban Studies, 38,* 1233.

Mackelprang, R. W, & Salsgiver, R. O. (2009). *Disability: A diversity model approach in human services.* Chicago: Lyceum Books, Inc.

Madureira, A. F. (2007). The psychological basis of homophobia: Cultural construction of a barrier. *Integrative Pyschological and Behavioral Science, 4,* 225–247. doi:10.1007/s12124-007-9024-9

Magill-Evans, J., Harrison, M. J., Benzies, K., Gierl, M., & Kimak, C. (2007). Effects of parenting education on first-time fathers' skills in interactions with their infants. *Fathering: A Journal of Theory, Research, and Practice About Men as Fathers*, 5(1), 42–57. doi:10.3149/fth.0501.42

Mahalik, J. R., VanOrmer, E. A., & Simi, N. L. (2000). Ethical issues in using self-disclosure in feminist therapy. In M. Brabeck (Ed.), *Practicing feminist ethics in psychology. Psychology of women book series* (pp. 189–201). Washington, DC: American Psychological Association.

Mahoney, M. J. (1986). The tyranny of techniques. *Counseling and Values*, 30, 169–174.

Mahoney, M. J. (2003). *Constructivist psychotherapy: A practical guide*. New York: Guilford.

Mahoney, M. R. (2003). Class and Status in American Law: Race, interest, and the anti-transformation cases. *Southern California Law Review*, 77, 799–891.

Marterella, M. K., & Brock, L. J. (2008). Religion and spirituality as a resource in marital and family therapy. *Journal of Family Psychotherapy*, 19(4), 330–344.

Martin, D. J., Garske, J. P., & Davis, M. K. (2000). Relation of the therapeutic alliance with outcome and other variables: A meta-analytic review. *Journal of Consulting and Clinical Psychology*, 68(3). Retrieved February 12, 2010, from http://web.ebscohost.com/ehost/

Mathiak, K., & Weber, R. (2006). Toward brain correlates of natural behavior: fMRI during violent video games. *Human Brain Mapping*, 27(12), 948–956. doi:10.1002/hbm.20234

McClure, F., Chavez, D., Agars, M., Peacock, M., & Matosian, A. (2008). Resilience in sexually abused women: Risk and protective factors. *Journal of Family Violence*, 23, 81–88.

McCullough, M. E., & Snyder, C. K. (2000). Classical sources of human strength: Revisiting an old home and building a new one. *Journal of Social and Clinical Psychology*, 19, 1–10.

McDonald, P., & Coleman, M. (1999). Deconstructing the hierarchies of oppression and adopting an a-multiple modela approach to anti-oppression practice. *Social Work Education*, 18, 19–33.

McKeel, A. J. (1996). A clinician's guide to research on solution focused brief therapy. In S. D. Miller, M. A. Hubbles, & B. L. Duncan (Eds.), *Handbook of solution-focused brief therapy* (pp. 251–271). San Francisco: Jossey-Bass.

McLaren, C., & Rodger, S. (2003). Goal attainment scaling: Clinical implications for paediatric occupational therapy practice. *Australian Occupational Therapy Journal*, 50:216–224. doi:10.1046/j.1440-1630.2003.00379.x

Medvene, L. J., Base, M., Patrick, R., & Wescott, J. (2007). Advance directives: Assessing stage of change and decisional balance in a community-based educational program. *Journal of Applied Social Psychology*, 37(10), 2298–2318. doi:10.1111/j.1559-1816.2007.00259.x

Meier, P. S., Barrowclough, C., & Donmall, M. C. (2005). The role of the therapeutic alliance in the treatment of substance misuse: A critical review of the literature. *Addiction*, 100(3), 304–316. doi:10.1111/j.1360-0443.2004. 00935.x

Meier, W. M., & Davis, S. R. (2004). *The elements of counseling*. Belmont, CA: Brooks/Cole.

Menen, S. (2004). *Manual-based clinical skills training: Developing relationship-centered clinical proficiency*. Unpublished dissertation, Azusa Pacific University, Azusa, CA.

Melor, K., & Sigmund, E. (1975). Discounting. *Transactional Analysis Journal*, 5, 295–302.

Metcalf, L., Thomas, F., Duncan, B. L., Miller, S. D., & Hubble, M. A. (1996). What works in solution-focused brief therapy: A qualitative analysis of client and therapist perceptions. In S. D. Miller, M. A. Hubble, & B. L. Duncan (Eds.), *Handbook of solution-focused brief therapy* (pp. 335–350). San Francisco: Jossey-Bass.

Meyer, B., Pilkonis, P. A., Krupnick, J. L., Egan, M. K., Simmens, S. J., & Sotsky, S. M. (2002). Treatment expectancies, patient alliance, and outcome: Further analyses from the national institute of mental health treatment of depression collaborative research program. *Journal of Consulting and Clinical Psychology*, 70, 1051–1055.

Middendorf, J., & Pace, D. (2005). Decoding the disciplines: A model for helping students learn disciplinary ways of thinking. *New Directions for Teaching and Learning*, 98, 1–12.

Miley, K., O'Melia, M., & DuBois, B. (2004). *Generalist social work practice: An empowering approach* (4th ed.). Boston: Pearson.

Miller, B. (2004). Feminist family therapy: Empowerment in social context. *Journal of Marital & Family Therapy*, 30, 391.

Miller, S. D., Hubble, M., & Duncan, B. (2007). Supershrinks: What is the secret of their success? Retrieved February 12, 2010, from www .pechchotherapynetworker.org/ compenent/content/article/85-2007-novemberdecember/176-supershrinks

Miller, W. R. (1987). Motivation and treatment goals. *Drugs and Society*, 1, 131–151.

Miller, W. R., & Hester, R. K. (1989). Treating alcohol problems: Toward an informed eclecticism. In R. K. Hester & W. R. Miller (Eds.), *Handbook of alcoholism treatment approaches*. Elmsford, NY: Pergamon Press.

Miller, W. R., & Moyers, T. B. (2006). Eight stages in learning motivational interviewing. *Journal of Teaching in the addictions*, 5(1), 1–15. doi:10.1300/J188v05n01_02

Miller, W. R., & Rollnick, S. (2002). *Motivational interviewing: Preparing people for change* (2nd ed.). New York: Guilford.

Minuchin, P., Colapinto, J., & Minuchin, S. (1998). *Working with families of the poor*. New York: Guilford.

Mitchell, A. M., Wesner, S., Garand, L., Gale, D. D., Havill, A., & Brownson, L. (2007). A support group intervention for children bereaved by parental suicide. *Journal of Child and Adolescent Psychiatric Nursing*, 20(1), 3–13. doi:10.1111/j.1744-6171.2007.00073.x

Mizrahi, T., Mayden, R. W., Starks, S. H., Fong, L., Montero, E., et al. (2001). NASW standards for cultural competence in social work practice [Electronic Version]. *National Committee on Racial and Ethnic Diversity*, 19. Retrieved September 6, 2010 from http://www.naswdc.org/ practice/standards/ NASWCulturalStandards.pdf

Mohr, W. K. (2003). The substance of a support group. *Western Journal of Nursing Research, 25,* 676–692.

Morrow, D. F., & Messinger, L. (2006). *Sexual orientation and gender expression in social work practice: Working with gay, lesbian, bisexual, and transgender people.* New York: Columbia University Press.

Moursund, J. (1993). *The process of counseling and therapy.* Pacific Grove, CA: Brooks/Cole.

Mueser, K. T., Wallace, C. J., & Liberman, R. P. (1995). New developments in social skills training. *Behavior Change, 12,* 31–40.

Murphy, B. C., & Dillon, C. (2003). *Interviewing in action: Relationship, process, and change.* Pacific Grove, CA: Brooks/Cole.

Murphy, P. M., Cramer, D., & Lillie, F. J. (1984). The relationship between curative factors perceived by patients in psychotherapy of depression: An exploratory study. *British Journal of Medical Psychology, 57,* 187–192.

Myers, D., & Hayes, J. A. (2006). Effects of therapist general self-disclosure and counter transference disclosure on ratings of the therapist and the session. *Psychotherapy: Theory, Research, Practice, Training, 43,* 173–185.

Nash, J. (2005). Women in between: Globalization and the new enlightenment. *Signs, 31,* 145.

Nash, S. (2006). The changing of the Gods: Abused Christian wives and their hermeneutic revision of gender, power, and spousal conduct. *Qualitative Sociology, 29*(2), 195–209.

National Association of Social Workers (2009). People with disabilities. *Social work speaks, eighth edition: NASW policy statements, 2009-2012* (pp. 247–51). Washington, DC: NASW Press.

Neimeyer, R. A., & Feixas, G. (1990). The role of homework and skill acquisition in the outcome of group cognitive therapy for depression. *Behavior Therapy, 21,* 281–292.

Neitzke, G. (2007). Confidentiality, secrecy, and privacy in ethics consultation. *HEC Forum, 19*(4), 293–302. doi:10.1007/s10730-007-9049-y

Newton, T. (2006). Script, psychological life plans, and the learning cycle.

Transactional Analysis Journal, 36, 186–195.

Ng, T. W. H., Sorensen, K. L., & Eby, L. T. (2006). Locus of control at work: A meta-analysis. *Journal of Organizational Behavior, 27*(8), 1057–1087. doi:10.1002/job.416

Nichols, M. P., & Schwartz, R. C. (2006). *Family therapy: Concepts and methods.* Boston: Allyn & Bacon.

Norcross, J. C. (2010). The therapeutic relationship. In Duncan, B. L., Miller, S. D., Wampold, B. E. & Hubble, M. A. (Eds.), *The heart & soul of change: Delivering what works in therapy?* (pp. 113–143). Washington, DC: American Psychological Association

Norcross, J. C., Ratzin, A. C., & Payne, D. (1989). Ringing in the New Year: The change process and reported outcomes of resolutions. *Addictive Behaviors, 14,* 205–212.

Norcross, J. C., & Wampold, B. E. (2011) Evidence-based therapy relationships: Research conclusions and clinical practices. *Psychotherapy, 48*(1), 98–102.

Northhouse, P. G. (2010). *Leadership: Theory and practice.* Thousand Oaks, CA: Sage.

Norton, D. (1978). *The dual perspective: Inclusion of ethnic minority content in the social work curriculum.* New York: CSWE.

Novick, J., & Novick, K. K. (2006). *Good goodbyes: Knowing how to end in psychotherapy and psychoanalysis.* Lanham, MD: Jason Aronson.

O'Brien, M. (2005). Studying individual and family development: Linking theory and research. *Journal of Marriage and Family, 67,* 880–890.

O'Connell, B. (2005). *Solution-focused therapy.* London: Sage Publications.

O'Hanlon, B., & Weiner-Davis, M. (2003). *In search of solutions: A new direction in psychotherapy.* New York: Norton.

Olsson, C., Bond, L., Burns, J., Vella-Brodrick, D., & Sawyer, S. (2003). Adolescent resilience: A concept analysis. *Journal of Adolescence, 26,* 1–11.

Orlinsky, D. E., Ronnestad, M. H., Gerin, P., Davis, J. D., Ambühl, H., Davis, M. L., … Schröder, T. A. (2005). The development of psychotherapists. In D. E. Orlinsky

& M. H. Ronnestad (Eds.), *How psychotherapists develop: A study of therapeutic work and professional growth* (pp. 3–13). Washington, DC: American Psychological Association.

Orlinsky, D., Grawe, K., & Parks, B. (1994). Process and outcome in psychotherapy: A review of reviews. *Psychotherapy, 21,* 431–438.

Packard, B. W., & Conway, P. F., (2006). Methodological choice and its consequences for possible selves research. *Identity: An International Journal of Theory and Research, 6*(3), 251–271.

Passalacqua, S., & Cervantes, J. M. (2008). Understanding gender and culture within the context of spirituality: Implications for counselors. *Counseling and Values, 52*(3), 224.

Patel, E. (2007). *Acts of faith: The story of an American Muslim, the struggle for the soul of a generation.* Boston: Beacon press.

Patterson, J., Williams, L., Edwards, T., Chamow, L., & Grauf-Grounds, C. (2009). *Essential skills in family therapy: From the first interview to termination.* New York: Guilford Press.

Perkins, D. D., Crim, B., Silberman, P., & Brown, B. B. (2004). Community development as a response to community-level adversity: Ecological theory and research and strengths-based policy. In K. I. Maton, C. J. Schellenbach, B. J. Leadbeater, & A. L. Solarz (Eds.), *Investing in children, youth, families, and communities: Strengths-based research and policy.* Washington, DC: American Psychological Association.

Peters, R., Leadbeater, B., & McMahon, R. (2005). *Resilience in children, families and communities: Linking context to practice and policy.* New York: Kluwer Academic/Plenum

Peterson, C., & Seligman, M. E. P. (2004). *Character strengths and virtues: A handbook and classification.* New York: Oxford.

Pewewardy, N. (2004). The political is personal: The essential obligation of white feminist family therapists to deconstruct white privilege. *Journal of Feminist Family Therapy, 16*(1), 53–67.

Pfeifer, J., Iacoboni, M., Mazziotta, J. C., & Depretto, M. (2008).

Mirroring others' emotions relates to empathy and interpersonal competence in children. *NeuroImage, 39,* 2076–2085.

Pike, C., Bennett, R., & Chang, V. N. (2004). Measuring competency in the use of basic social work interviewing skills. *Advances in Social Work, 5,* 61–76.

Pinto, R. M., McKay, M. M., Baptiste, D., Bell, C. C., Madison-Boyd, S., Paikoff, R., … Phillips, D. (2007). Motivators and barriers to participation of ethnic minority families in a family-based HIV prevention program. *Social Work Mental Health, 5*(1), 187–201. doi:10.1300/J200v05n01_09

Pipes, R. B., Holstein, J., & Aguiree, M. G. (2005). Examining the personal-professional distinction: Ethics codes and the difficulty of drawing a boundary. *American Psychologist, 60*(4), 325–335.

Plant, E. A., Hyde, J. S., Keltner, D., & Devine, P. G. (2000). The gender stereotyping of emotions. *Psychology of Women Quarterly, 24,* 81–92.

Ponterotto, J. G., Casas, J. M., Suzuki, L. A., & Alexander, C. M. (Eds.) (2010). *Handbook of multicultural counseling.* Thousand Oaks, CA: Sage Publications, Inc.

Pope, K. S., & Keith-Spiegel, P. (2008). A practical approach to boundaries in psychotherapy: Making decisions, bypassing blunders, and mending fences. *Journal of Clinical Psychology, 64*(5), 638–652. doi:10:1002/clp20477

Pope, K. S., Keith-Spiegel, P., & Tabachnick, B. G. (2006). Sexual attraction to clients: The human therapist and the (sometimes) inhuman training system. *Training and Education in Professional Psychology, S*(2), 96–111.

Pope, K. S., Levenson, H., & Schover, L. (1979). Sexual intimacy in psychology training: Results and implications of a national survey. *American Psychologist, 11,* 157–162.

Pope, K. S., & Vasquez, M. J. T. (1998). *Ethics in psychotherapy and counseling: A practical guide* (2nd ed.). San Francisco: Jossey-Bass.

Pope, K. S., & Vetter, V. A. (1992). Ethical dilemmas encountered by members of the American Psychological Association. *American Psychologist, 47,* 429–438.

Powell, J. (2005). 'Value talk' in social work research: Reflection, rhetoric and reality. *European Journal of Social Work, 8*(1), 23–39.

Prest, L. A., & Keller, J. F. (2007). Spirituality and family therapy: Spiritual beliefs, myths, and metaphors. *Journal of Marital & Family Therapy, 19*(2), 137–148. doi:10.1111/j.1752-0606.1993. tb00973.x

Prest, L. A., Russel, R., & D'souza, H. (1999). Spirituality and religion in training, practice and person development. *Journal of Family Therapy, 21,* 60–77.

Principe, J. M., Marci, C. D., Glick, D. M., & Ablon, J. S. (2006). The relationship among patient contemplation, early alliance, and continuation in psychotherapy. *Psychotherapy: Theory/Research/ Practice/Training, 43*(2), 238–243. doi:10.1037/0033-3204.43.2.238

Prochaska, J. O. (1999). How do people change, and how can we help many more people? In M. A. Hubble, B. L. Duncan, & S. D. Miller (Eds.), *The heart and soul of change.* Washington, DC: American Psychological Association.

Prochaska, J. O., Norcross, J. C., & DiClemente, C. C. (1994). *Changing for good.* New York: Morrow.

Proctor, E. K., & Davis, L. E. (1994). The challenge of racial difference: Skills for clinical practice. *Social Work, 39*(3), 314–323.

Rahman, Q., & Wilson, G. D. (2003). Born gay? The psychobiology of human sexual orientation. *Personality and Individual Differences, 38,* 1337–1382.

Rapp, R. C., Siegal, H. A., Li, L., & Saha, P. (1998). Predicting post-primary treatment service and drug use outcome: A multivariate analysis. *American Journal of Drug and Alcohol Abuse, 24,* 603–615.

Rappaport, J. (1981). Studies in empowerment: Introduction to the issue. *Prevention in Human Services, 3,* 1–7.

Rappaport, J. (1985). The power of empowerment language. *Social Policy, 24*(2), 2–3.

Raskin, J. D. (2001). On relativism in constructivist psychology. *Journal of Constructivist Psychology, 14,* 285–313.

Reamer, F. G. (1994). *The foundation of social work knowledge.* New York: Columbia University Press.

Reamer, F. G. (1995). Malpractice claims against social workers: First facts. *Social Work, 40*(5), 595–601.

Reamer, F. G. (2001). How to practice ethically: Part 1. *The New Social Worker, 8*(4), 4–7.

Reamer, F. G., & Siegel, D. H. (2007). Ethical issues in open adoption: Implications for practice. *Families in Society: The Journal of Contemporary Social Services, 88*(1), 11–18.

Remley, T. P., & Herlihy, B. (2001). *Ethical, legal, and professional issues in counseling.* Upper Saddle River, NJ: Prentice Hall.

Riley, J., & Masten, A. (2005). Resilience in context. In R. Peters, B. Leadbeater, & R. McMahon (Eds.), *Resilience in children, families, and communities. Linking context to practice and policy.* New York: Kluwer Academic/Plenum.

Rink, E., & Tricker, R. (2005). Promoting healthy behaviors among adolescents: A review of the resiliency literature. *American Journal of Health Studies, 20*(1), 39–46.

Roberts, M. C., Vernberg, E. M., & Jackson, Y. (2000). Psychotherapy with children and families. In C. R. Snyder & R. E. Ingram (Eds.), *Handbook of psychological change: Psychotherapy processes and practices for the 21st century* (pp. 500–519). Hoboken, NJ: Wiley.

Rockwell, K., Howlett, S., Stadnyk, K., & Carver, D. (2003). Responsiveness of goal attainment scaling in a randomized controlled trial of comprehensive geriatric assessment. *Journal of Clinical Epidemiology, 56,* 736–743

Roe, D., Dekel, R., Harel, G., Fennig, S., & Fennig, S. (2006). Clients' feelings during termination of psychodynamically oriented psychotherapy. *Bulletin of the Menninger Clinic, 70*(1), 68–81.

Rogers, C. R. (1951). *Client centered therapy: Its current practice, theory, and implications.* Chicago: Houghton Mifflin.

Rogers, C. R. (1957). The necessary and sufficient conditions of therapeutic personality change. *Journal of Consulting Psychology, 21,* 95–103.

Rogers, C. R. (1958). The characteristics of a helping relationship. *Personnel and Guidance Journal, 37,* 6–16.

Rogers, C. R. (1961a). *On becoming a person.* Boston: Houghton-Mifflin.

Rose, S. M. (2005). Empowerment: The foundation for social work practice in mental health. In S. A. Kirk (Ed.), *Mental disorders in the social environment: Critical perspectives* (pp. 190–200). New York: Columbia University Press.

Rosenbaum, M., & Ronen, T. (1998). Clinical supervision from the standpoint of cognitive behavior therapy. *Psychotherapy: Theory, Research and Practice, 35,* 220–230.

Roysircar, G. (2004). Cultural self-awareness assessment: Practice examples from psychology training. *Professional Psychology: Research and Practice, 35,* 658–666.

Rupert, P. A., & Morgan, D. J. (2005). Work setting and burnout among professional psychologists. *Professional Psychology: Research and Practice, 36,* 544–550.

Rutan, J. S., & Stone, W. N. (2001). Psychodynamic group psychotherapy (3rd ed.). New York: Guilford Press.

Safran, S. A., Heimberg, R. G., & Juster, H. R. (1997). Clients' expectancies and their relationship to pretreatment symptomatology and outcome of cognitive-behavioral group treatment for social phobia. *Journal of Consulting and Clinical Psychology, 65,* 694–698.

Saiger, G. M., Rubenfeld, S., & Dluhy, M. D. (2008). Some thoughts on the existential lens in group psychotherapy. In *Windows into today's group therapy: The National Group Psychotherapy Institute of the Washington School of Psychiatry* (pp. 153–168). New York: Routledge/Taylor & Francis Group.

Saleebey D. (1992). The strengths perspective in social work. New York: Longman.

Saleebey, D. (2002a). The strengths perspective: Possibilities and problems. In D. Saleebey (Ed.), *The strengths perspective in social work practice* (3rd ed., pp. 264–283). Boston: Allyn & Bacon.

Saleebey, D. (2002b). Introduction: Power to the people. In D. Saleebey (Ed.), *The strengths perspective in social work practice* (3rd ed., pp. 1–22). Boston: Allyn & Bacon.

Saleebey, D. (2002c). The strengths approach to practice. In D. Saleebey (Ed.), *The strengths perspective in social work practice* (3rd ed., pp. 80–94). Boston: Allyn & Bacon.

Saltzburg, S. (2008). Mentoring beyond homophobia: Reauthoring for cultural competence. *The Journal of Baccalaureate Social Work, 13*(2), 35–53.

Sassaroli, S., & Ruggiero, G. M. (2005). The role of stress in the association between low self-esteem, perfectionism, worry, and eating disorders. *International Journal of Eating Disorders, 37,* 135–141.

Schauer, C., Everett, A., del Vecchio, P., & Anderson, L. (2007). Promoting the value and practice of shared decision-making in mental health care. *Psychiatric Rehabilitation Journal, 31*(1), 54–61. doi:10.2975/31.1.2007.54.61

Schoon, I., & Bynner, J. (2003). Risk and resilience in the life course: Implications for interventions and social policies. *Journal of Youth Studies, 6*(1), 21–31.

Schore, A. N. (2009). Right brain affect regulation: An essential mechanism of development, trauma, dissociation, and psychotherapy. In D. Fosha, D. Siegel, & M. Solomon (Eds.), *The healing power of emotion: Affective neuroscience, development, & clinical practice* (pp. 112–144). New York: W.W. Norton.

Schriver, J. M. (2010). *Human behavior and the social environment: Shifting paradigms in essential knowledge for social work practice* (5th ed.). Boston: Allyn & Bacon.

Scott, B. A., Wampold, B. E., & Imel, Z. E. (2007). Untangling the alliance-outcome correlation: Exploring the relative importance of therapist and patient variable in the alliance. *Journal of Consulting and Clinical Psychology, 75* (6), 842–852.

Searight, H. R., & Searight, B. K. (2009). Implementing problem-based learning in an undergraduate psychology course. *InSight: A Journal of Scholarly Teaching, 4,* 69–76.

Seccombe, K. (2002). "Beating the odds versus changing the odds": Poverty, resilience and family policy. *Journal of Marriage and Family, 64,* 384–394.

Seelau, S. M., & Seelau, E. P. (2005). Gender-role stereotypes and perceptions of heterosexual, gay, and lesbian domestic violence. *Journal of Family Violence, 20,* 363–371.

Seligman, H. K., Wallace, A. S., DeWalt, D. A., Schillinger, D., Arnold, C. L., Shilliday, B. B., Delgadillo, A., Bengal, N., & Davis, C. T. (2007). Facilitating behavior change with low-literacy education materials. *American Journal of Health Behavior, 31,* S69–S78.

Seligman, L. (2004). *Technical and conceptual skills for mental health professionals.* Upper Saddle River, NJ: Pearson.

Sexton, T. L., & Alexander, J. F. (2002). Family-based empirically supported interventions. *The Counseling Psychologist, 30,* 238–261.

Sexton, T. L., Alexander, J. F., & Mease, A. C. (2003). Levels of evidence for the models and mechanisms of therapeutic change in family and couple therapy. In M. J. Lambert (Ed.), *Handbook of psychotherapy and behavior change* (5th ed., pp. 590–646). New York: Wiley.

Sexton, T. L., & Griffin, B. L. (1997). *Constructivist thinking in counseling practice, research, and training.* New York: Teachers College Press.

Shapiro, S. L., Biegel, G. M., & Warren, K. (2007). Teaching self-care to caregivers: Effects of mindfullness-based stress reduction on the mental health of therapists in training. *Training and Education in Professional Psychology, 1*(2), 105–115. doi:10.1037/1931-3918.1.2.105

Shavers, V. L. (2007). Measurement of socioeconomic status in health disparities research. *Journal of National Medical Association, 99*(9), 1013–1023.

Shelef, K., Diamond, G. M., Diamond, G. S., & Liddle. H. A. (2005). Adolescent and parent alliance and treatment outcome in MDFT. *Journal of Consulting and Clinical Psychology, 73*(4), 689–698.

Shepard, D., & Morrow, G. (2003). Critical self monitoring. In J. A. Kottler & W. P. Jones (Eds.), *Doing better*. New York: Brunner/Routledge.

Sherman, M. D., & Thelan, H. M. (1998). Distress and professional impairment among psychologists in clinical practice. *Professional Psychology: Research and Practice, 29*, 79–85.

Shirk, S. R., Karver, M. S., & Brown, R. (2011). The alliance in child and adolescent psychotherapy, *Psychotherapy, 48*, 17–24.

Shulman, L. (1992). *The skills of helping individuals, families, and groups*. Itasca, IL: F. E. Peacock.

Siegall, M., & Gardner, S. (2000). Contextual factors of psychological empowerment. *Personnel Review, 29*, 703–722.

Siegel, D. J. (2010). *The mindful therapist: A clinician's guide to mindsight and neural integration*. New York: W. W. Norton.

Siegel, D. J., & Hartzell, M. (2003). *Parenting from the inside out: How a deeper self-understanding can help you raise children who thrive*. New York: Penguin.

Simi, N. L., & Mahalik, J. R. (1997). Comparison of feminist versus psychoanalytic/dynamic and other therapists on self-disclosure. *Psychology of Women Quarterly, 21*, 465–483.

Simon, B. (1994). *The empowerment tradition in American social work: A history*. New York: Columbia University Press.

Sirin, S. R. (2005). Socioeconomic status and academic achievement: A meta-analytic review of research. *Review of Educational Research, 75*(3), 417–453.

Skovholt, T. M. (2001). *The resilient practitioner: Burnout prevention and self-care strategies for counselors, therapists, teachers, and health professionals*. Needham Heights, MA: Allyn & Bacon.

Smith, D. C., & Hall, J. A. (2007). Strength—oriented referrals for teens (SORT): Giving balanced feedback to teens and families. *Health & Social Work, 32*(1), 69–72. Retrieved from http://www.abct.org/sccap/docs/pro_POP_Smith_2007.pdf

Smith, Deborah (2003). 10 ways practitioners can avoid frequent ethical pitfalls. *Monitor on Psychology, 34*(1), 50.

Smith, S. A., Thomas, S. A., & Jackson, A. C. (2004). An exploration of the therapeutic relationship and counseling outcomes in a problem gambling counseling service. *Journal of Social Work Practice, 18*, 99–112.

Snyder, C. R., & Lopez, S. J. (2001). *Handbook of positive change*. New York: Wiley.

Sommers-Flanagan, R., & Sommers-Flanagan, J. (2007). *Becoming an ethical helping professional: Cultural and philosophical foundations*. Hoboken, New Jersey: John Wiley & Sons.

Souvignier, E., & Mokhlesgerami, J. (2006). Using self-regulation as a framework for implementing strategy instruction to foster reading comprehension. *Learning and Instruction, 16*(1), 57–71. doi:10.1016/j.learninstruc.2005.12.006

Sparks, J. A., & Muro, M. L. (2009). Client-directed wraparound: The client as connector in community collaboration. *Journal of Systematic Therapies, 28*(3), 63–76. doi:10.1521/jsyt.2009.28.3.63

Stam, H. J. (1998). Personal-construct theory and social constructivism: Difference and dialogue. *Journal of Constructivist Psychology, 11*, 187–203.

Starfield, B. (2006). State of the art in research of equity in health. *Journal of Health Politics, Policy, & Law, 31*(1), 11–32.

Steinglass, P., Bennet, L. A., & Wolin, J. (1987). *The alcoholic family*. New York: Basic Books.

Stoltz, K. B., & Kern, R. M. (2007). Integrating lifestyle, the therapeutic process, and the stages of change. *Journal of Individual Psychology, 63*(1), 32–47.

Stone, G. L., & Vance, A. (1976). Instructions, modeling, and rehearsal: Implications for training. *Journal of Counseling Psychology, 23*, 272–279.

Strachan, D. (2007). Questions for closing a session. *Making Questions Work* (pp. 209–211). San Francisco, CA: Jossey-Bass.

Street, R. L., Makoul G., Arora, N. K., & Epstein, R. M. (2009). How does communication heal? Pathways linking clinician-patient communication to health outcomes. *Patient Education and Counseling, 74*(3), 295–301. doi:10.1016/j.pec.2008.11.015

Strom-Gottfried, D. (1999). Professional boundaries: An analysis of violations by social workers. *Families in Society: The Journal of Contemporary Social Services, 80*, 439–449.

Strong, T., Pyle, N. R. (2009). Constructing a conversational "miracle": Examining the "miracle question" as it is used in therapeutic dialogue. *Journal of Constructivist Psychology, 22*(4), 328–353. doi:10.1080/10720530903114001

Strong, T., Pyle, N. R., & Sutherland, O. (2009). Scaling questions: Asking and answering them in counseling. *Counseling Psychology Quarterly, 22*(2), 171–185.

Stular, S. (1998). Social construction of gender identity. *Druzbena konstrukcija spolne identitete, 35*, 441–454.

Sue, D. W., & Sue, D. (1990). *Counseling the culturally different: Theory and practice*. New York: Wiley.

Talmon, M. (1990). *Single session therapy*. San Francisco: Jossey-Bass.

Tambling, R., & Johnson, L. (2008). The relationship between stages of change and outcome in couple therapy. *American Journal of Family Therapy, 36*(3), 229–241. doi:10.1080/01926180701290941

Tanner, J. L., & Arnett, J. J. (2009). The emergence of 'emerging adulthood': the new life stage between adolescence and young adulthood. In Andy Furlong (Ed.), *Handbook of youth and young adulthood: New perspective and agendas* (pp. 39–45). NY: Routledge Taylor & Francis Group.

Thomas, S. E. G., Werner-Wilson, R. J., & Murphy, M. J. (2005). Influence of therapist and client behaviors on therapy alliance. *Contemporary Family Therapy: An International Journal, 27*(1), 19–35.

Thompson, R. A. (2006). The development of the person: Social understanding, relationships, conscience, self. In N. Eisenberg, W. Damon, & R. M. Lerner (Eds.), *Handbook of child psychology: Social, emotional, and personality development* (6th ed., pp. 24–98). Hoboken, NJ: Wiley.

Thwaites, R., & Bennett-Levy, J. (2007). Conceptualizing empathy in cognitive behaviour therapy: Making the implicit explicit. *Behavioural and Cognitive Psychotherapy, 35*, 591–612. doi:10.1017/S1352465807003785

Thyer, B. A. (2006). Social work education and clinical learning: Towards evidence-based practice? *Clinical Social Work Journal, 35*(1), 25–32. doi:10.1007/s10615-006-0064-2

Tohn, S. L., & Oshlag, J. A. (2000). *Crossing the bridge: Integrating solution focused therapy into clinical practice.* Sudbury, MA: Solutions Press.

Tomsen, S. (2006). Homophobic violence, cultural essentialism and shifting sexual identities. *Social Legal Studies, 15*(3), 389–407. doi:10.1177/0964663906066616

Toomey, B., & Ecker, B. (2009). Of neurons and knowing: Constructivism, coherence psychology, and their neurodynamic substrates. *Journal of Constructivist Psychology, 20*, 201–245.

Tremblay, R. (2005). Disruptive behaviors: Should we foster or prevent resiliency? In R. Peters, B. Leadbeater, & R. McMahon (Eds.), *Disruptive behaviors: Should we foster or prevent resiliency?* New York: Kluwer Academic/Plenum.

Trevos, A. K., Quick, R. E., & Yanduli, V. (2000). Application of motivational interviewing to the adoption of water disinfection practices in Zambia. *Health Promotion International, 15*, 207–214.

Tronick, E. (2009). Multilevel meaning making and dyadic expansion of consciousness theory. In D. Fosha, D. J. Siegel, & M. F. Solomon (Eds.), *The healing power of emotion.* New York, NY: Norton.

Tryon, G. S., & Winograd, G. (2011). Goal consensus and collaboration. *Psychotherapy, 48*, 50–57.

Tsai, M., Callaghan, G. M., Kohlenberg, R. J., Follette, W. C., & Darrow, S. M. (2009). Supervision and therapist self-development. *A Guide to Functional Analytic Psychotherapy*, 1–32. doi:10.1007/978-0-387-09787-9_8

Tseng, W. S. (2001). Culture and psychotherapy: An overview. In W. S. Tseng & J. Streltzer (Eds.), *Culture and psychotherapy: A guide to clinical practice* (pp. 3–12). Washington, DC: American Psychiatric Press.

Tully, C. T. (2000). *Lesbians, gays, and the empowerment perspective.* New York: Columbia University Press.

Tummala-Narra, P. (2010). Review of the book *Dialogues on difference: Studies of diversity in the therapeutic relationship*, edited by J. C. Muran. *Psychoanalytic Psychology, 27*(3), 389–394.

Turner-Stokes, L., & Williams, H. (2009). Goal attainment scaling: A direct comparison of alternative rating methods. *Clinical Rehabilitation, 24*(1), 70–72.

Tuvblad, C., Grann, M., & Lichtenstein, P. (2006). Heritability for adolescent antisocial behavior differs with socioeconomic status: Gene-environment interaction. *The Journal of Child Psychology and Psychiatry, 47*(7), 734–743. doi:10.1111/j.1469-7610.2005.01552.x

Ungar, M. (2002). A deeper, more social ecological social work practice. *Social Service Review, 76*, 480.

U.S. Census Bureau (2008). 2008 National Populations Projections. Retrieved from http://www.census .gov/population/www/projections/analytical-document08

U.S. Census Bureau (2009). 2009 National Population Projections (Supplemental). Retrieved from http://www.census.gov/population/www/projections/analytical-document09

Valle, M. F., Huebner, E. S., & Suldo, S. M. (2006). An analysis of hope as a psychological strength. *Journal of School Psychology, 44*(5), 393–406. doi:10.1016/j.jsp.2006.03.005

Van Buren, A. (2002). The relationship of verbal-nonverbal incongruence to communication mismatches in married couples. *North American Journal of Psychology, 4*, 21–36.

Van Wormer, K. (2007). Motivational interviewing: A theoretical framework for the study of human behavior and the social environment. *Advances in Social Work, 8*(1), 19–29.

Vasconez, H. C., Donnelly, M. B., Mayo, P., & Schwartz, R. W. (1993). Student perceptions of the effectiveness of a problem-based surgery curriculum. *Academic Medicine, 10*(Suppl), S28–30.

Vayda, E., & Bogo, M. (1991). A teaching model to unite classroom and field. *Journal of Social Work Education, 27*, 271–278.

Vernon, D. T., & Blake, R. L. (1993). Does problem-based learning work: A meta-analysis. *Academic Medicine 68*(7), 550–563.

Viederman, M. (1999). Presence and enactment as a vehicle of psychotherapeutic change. *Journal of Psychotherapy Practice and Research, 8*, 274–283.

Vinton, L., & Harrington, P. (1994). An evolution of the use of videotape in teaching empathy. *Journal of Teaching in Social Work, 9*, 71–84.

Vito, J. P. (2010). Preparation. In P. Levounis & B. Arnaout (Eds.), *Handbook of motivation and change: A practical guide for clinicians* (ch 5). Arlington, VA: American Psychiatric Publishing, Inc.

Vodde, R., & Gallant, J. P. (1995). Skill training as a place for self-exploration: A qualitative study of teaching social work methods from a postmodern perspective. *Journal of Teaching in Social Work, 11*, 119–137.

Waller, M. (2001). Resilience in ecosystemic context: Evolution of the concept. *American Journal of Orthopsychiatry, 73*(3), 290–297.

Walsh, F. (2002). A family resilience framework: Innovative practice applications. *Family Relations, 51*(2), 130–137.

Walsh, F. (2006). *Strengthening family resilience* (2nd Ed.). New York: Guilford.

Walsh, F. (2010). Spiritual diversity: Multifaith perspectives in family therapy. *Family Process, 49*(3), 330–348.

Walsh, Z., & Kosson, D. S. (2007). Psychopathy and violent crime: A prospective study of the influence of socioeconomic status and ethnicity. *Law Human Behavior, 31*, 209–229.

Walter, J. L., & Peller, J. E. (1992). *Becoming solution-focused in brief therapy.* Philadelphia: Brunner/Mazel.

Wampold, B. E., (2001). *The great psychotherapy debate: Models, methods, and findings.* Mahwah, NJ: Lawrence Erlbaum Associates.

Wampold, B. E. (2010). The research evidence for common factors models: A historically situated perspective. In Duncan, B. L., Miller, S. D., Wampold, B. E., & Hubble, M. A. (Eds.), *The heart & soul of change: Delivering what works in therapy?* (pp. 49–82). Washington, DC: American Psychological Assoc.

Wampold, B. E., & Brown, G. S. (2005). Estimating variability in outcomes attributable to therapists: A naturalistic study of outcomes in managed care. *Journal of Consulting and Clinical Psychology, 73*(5), 914–923.

Wampold, B. E., Mondin, G. W., Moody, M., Stich, F., Benson, K., & Ahn, H. (1997). A meta-analysis of outcome studies comparing bona fide psychotherapies: Empirically, 'all must have prizes.' *Psychological Bulletin, 122,* 203–215.

Wang De-hua, L. H. (2007). Nonverbal language in cross-cultural communication. *Sino-US English Teaching, 4*(10), 66–70.

Ward, D. B., & Wampler, K. S. (2010). Moving up the continuum of hope: Developing a theory of hope and understanding its influence in couples therapy. *Journal of Marital and Family Therapy, 36,* 212–228. doi:10.1111/j.1752-0606.2009.00173.x

Weick, A. (1993). Reconstructing social work education. *Journal of Teaching in Social Work, 8,* 11–30.

Weick, A., & Chamberlain, R. (1996). Putting problems in their place: Further explorations in the strengths perspective. In D. Saleeby (Ed.), *The strengths perspective in social work practice* (2nd ed., pp. 39–48). White Plains, NY: Longman.

Weick, A., Rapp, C., Sullivan, W. P., & Kisthardt, W. (1989). A strengths perspective for social work practice. *Social Work, 34,* 350–354.

Welfel, E. R. (2006). Ethics in counseling and psychotherapy (3rd ed). Belmont, CA: Brooks/Cole.

Werner, E. (2005). Resilience research: Past, present, and future. In R. Peters, B. Leadbeater, & R. McMahon (Eds.), *Resilience in children, families, and communities: Linking context to practice and policy.* New York: Kluwer Academic/Plenum.

Westra, M. (1996). *Active communication.* Belmont, CA: Brooks/Cole.

Whitney, S. D., Tajima, E. A., Herrenkohl, T. I., & Huang, B. (2006). Defining child abuse: Exploring variations in ratings of discipline severity among child welfare practitioners. *Child & Adolescent Social Work Journal, 23*(3), 316–342

Wiebe, L. M. (2002). Connection in the therapeutic relationship: Sharing a subjective world. *Dissertation Abstracts International, 62,* 5398.

Wilkerson, K. (2006). Peer supervision for the professional development of school counselors: Toward an understanding of terms and findings. *Counselor Education and Supervision, 46*(1), 59–67.

Williams, D. R. (2004). Race, socioeconomic status, and health: The added effects of racism and discrimination. *Annals New York Academy of Sciences,* 173–188.

Williams, E. N., Hurley, K., O'Brien, K., & de Gregorio, A. (2003). Development and validation of the Self-Awareness and Management Strategies (SAMS) scales for therapists. *Psychotherapy: Theory, Research, Practice, Training, 40,* 278–288.

Williams, S., & Mickelson, K. (2004). The nexus of domestic violence and poverty: Resilience in women's anxiety. *Violence Against Women, 10*(3), 283–293.

Williams, T. K., & Thornton, M. C. (1998). Social construction of ethnicity versus personal experience: The case of Afro-Amerasians. *Journal of Comparative Family Studies, 29,* 255.

Witty, M. (2007). Client-centered Therapy. In N. Kazantzis & L. Llabate (Eds.), *Handbook of homework assignments in psychotherapy research, practice, and prevention* (pp. 35–50). Boston, MA: Springer Science + Business Media, LLC. doi:10.1007/978-0-387-29681-4_3

Wolfer, T. A., & Scales, T. L. (2005). *Decision cases for advanced social work practice: Thinking like a social worker.* Belmont, CA: Thomson.

Wolin, S. (1999). A mindset of hope: Reaching today's youth. *The Community Circle of Caring Journal, 3*(3), 38–42.

Wolin, S. (2003). What is a strength? *Reclaiming Children and Youth, 12*(1), 18.

Wolkow, K. E., & Ferguson, H. B. (2001). Community factors in the development of resiliency: Considerations and future directions. *Community Mental Health Journal, 37,* 489–498.

Wolski, R. S. (2004). Reconceptualizing the individual: An ecological approach. *Dissertation Abstracts International, 64,* 2419.

Wong, Y. (2006). Strength-centered therapy: A social constructionist, virtues-based psychotherapy. *Psychotherapy, 43,* 133–146.

Woods, H. (2004). *The truth about women and power* (6th ed.). New York: McGraw Hill.

Worthington, E., Jr., & Scherer, M. (2007). Forgiveness is an emotion-focused coping strategy that can reduce health risks and promote health resilience: Theory, review and hypotheses. *Psychology and Health, 19*(3), 385–405.

Wylie, M. S. (1996). Going for the cure. *The Family Therapy Networker, 20*(4), 21–37.

Yalom, I. D. (1995). *The theory and practice of group psychotherapy* (4th ed.). New York: Basic Books.

Younggren, J. N., & Gottlieb, M. (2004). Managing risk when contemplating multiple relationships. *Professional Psychology: Research and Practice, 35*(3), 255–260.

Zalter, B., & Fiske, H. (2005). Scaling in action. *Journal of Family Psychotherapy, 16,* 107–109.

Zimmerman, M. A. (1990). Toward a theory of learned hopefulness: A structural modal analysis of participation and empowerment. *Journal of Research in Personality, 24,* 71–86.

Zimmerman, M. A., & Rappaport, J. (1988). Citizen participation, perceived control, and psychological empowerment. *American Journal of Community Psychology, 16,* 725–750.

Zur, O., Bloomgarden, A., & Mennuti, R. B. (2009). Therapist self-disclosure: Standard of care, ethical considerations, and therapeutic context. In *Psychotherapist revealed: Therapists speak about self-disclosure in psychotherapy* (pp. 31–51). New York: Routledge/Taylor & Francis Group.

GLOSSARY

Action stage when clients are ready to take specific steps, and may take steps with little or no support from the practitioner.

Adaptations the processes people use to sustain or raise the level of fit between themselves and their environment.

Advanced reflecting expressing empathic understanding by identifying the values, meanings, feelings, and expectations beneath or behind the expressed message.

Advocate a role involving working to obtain services for clients and/or to improve political, social, or environmental conditions.

Advocating the process of working to influence or change the policies of institutions, governments, and/or economic, political, and social systems.

Attending behavior involved with completely focusing on the client.

Beneficence a guiding principle for professionals describing the need for action to help or benefit others.

Bisexual attracted to both sexes.

Boundaries borders that surround some type of entity (parents, children, systems, client, service providers, healthcare workers).

Boundary violation a behavior involving the practitioner doing something that exploits, harms, or violates the client in some way.

Broker a role involving informing and linking clients with the services and resources needed.

Burnout a syndrome involving "increasing discouragement and emotional and physical exhaustion" (Dewees, 2006, p. 316).

Case management or coordination a process involves providing interagency coordination and monitoring of services.

Closed-ended questions questions that can be answered with one word, such as yes or no.

Closed family system a family system that tends to exist in relative isolation, with communication taking place primarily between members.

Compelling forces the advantages or benefits of taking action including an increased quantity and quality of services and greater effectiveness in meeting the group's needs.

Confidentiality information shared by the client with the therapist in the course of treatment, which is not to be shared with others.

Constructivism a perspective that identifies how individuals describe their experience in terms of personal constructs.

Consultation the process of getting advice, guidance, and information from an expert in a particular area.

Contemplation the transtheoretical stage of change that involves ambivalence or conflict between the pros and cons related to making a change.

Culture the customary beliefs, social forms, and behavior patterns of a racial, religious, or social group.

Cultural competence the application of the cultural knowledge about individuals and groups of people to the standards, policies, practices, and attitudes in the helping process to result in better outcomes (Mizrahi et al., 2001)

Developmental disability a severe, chronic disability of an individual that: 1) is attributable to a mental or physical impairment or combination of mental and physical impairments; 2) is manifested before the individual attains age 22; 3) is likely to continue indefinitely; and 4) results in substantial functional limitations in self-care, language, learning, mobility, self-direction, independent living, and/or economic self-sufficiency; and 5) reflects the individual's need for a combination and sequence of special, interdisciplinary, or generic services, individualized supports, and/or other forms of assistance that are of lifelong or extended duration and are individually planned and coordinated (114 STAT. 1684 PUBLIC LAW 106-402-OCT. 30, 2000).

Disability to not be able, or to be without ability (Mackelprang & Salsgiver, 2009).

321

Discounting a cognitive distortion that allows individuals to avoid dealing with a problem by denying its existence or minimizing its significance (Forbes, Schmader, & Allen, 2007; Melor & Sigmund, 1975).

Dual perspective a perspective that views an individual as interacting and adapting to two surrounding systems, nurturing and sustaining.

Ecological perspective a perspective that views human beings as evolving and adaptive in a continuous transaction with their environment, with both the humans and the environment constantly changing due to these interactions.

Empathy the ability to understand another person's feelings, thoughts, and behavior from the other person's viewpoint.

Empowerment a process in which individuals, groups, and/or communities become able to take control of their circumstances and achieve their own goals.

Ethical codes codes that provide an explanation of what can be expected in the interactions between both professionals and clients, and professionals and other professionals and contain statements about what the professionals must and must not do.

External locus of control the belief that there is no connection between a person's behavior and their desired outcome.

Ethical dilemma a choice involving "two or more relevant but contradictory ethical directives: when every alternative results in an undesirable outcome for one or more persons" (Dolgoff, Loewenberg, & Harrington, 2005, p. 258).

Ethnicity a group of people distinguished by a shared history, culture, beliefs, values, and behaviors (Tseng, 2001).

Family two or more people who define themselves as a family based on ties of affection, co-residence, biology, or tradition.

Family system the family within which an individual interacts, where the interactions are seen to be as important as the individuals that comprise the family.

Fiduciary relationship A relationship where the confidence is based on the particular expertise or superior knowledge and education of the practitioner.

Force field the total psychological environment existing for an individual or group at a certain point in time.

Gender stereotypes what our culture teaches us to assume is true or will be true of someone who is biologically female or male.

Genuine behavior behavior that is sincere and authentic.

Helping relationships relationships in which the attitudes, thoughts, and feelings expressed by the practitioner are intended to be helpful to the client.

Heterosexism a belief that male-female sexuality is the only natural, normal, and moral mode of sexual behavior (Mohr, 2003).

Homophobia an individualized fear and hatred of homosexuals (Madureira, 2007).

Identity achievement the commitment to one identity after an exploration of different identities.

Identifying discrepancies a motivational interviewing strategy that involves pointing out an incongruity between the client's present behavior and something he/she values or wants.

Immediacy feedback that involves the practitioner commenting on what seems to be happening currently in the relationship between the practitioner and the client (Egan, 2007).

Informed consent full disclosure of the purposes, goals, techniques, and procedure rules for assessment and work with the client, stated in language that is understandable to the client.

Intellectual disability a disability characterized by significant limitations both in intellectual functioning and in adaptive behavior, which covers many everyday social and practical skills. This disability originates before the age of 18 (American Association on Intellectual and Developmental Disabilities, 2010).

Internal locus of control the belief that a person's behavior will produce desired changes.

Life stressors issues that are perceived as exceeding the personal and environmental resources available to manage them.

Listening fully focusing on understanding what the other person is attempting to communicate.

Malpractice professional negligence in which a professional fails to follow the generally accepted standards of their profession, resulting in injury to a client.

Maintenance in this transtheoretical stage, clients develop ways to cope with temptations and to reward day-to-day successes.

Mediation the process of providing an impartial forum for disputing parties (individuals, groups, communities, or organizations) to discuss areas of disagreement or misunderstanding and hopefully reach an acceptable resolution.

Motivational interviewing client-centered counseling that helps clients increase motivation by assisting them in exploring and resolving ambivalence about making changes.

Multiple roles relationships an individual having two or more types of relationships (either simultaneously or sequentially) in another person's life.

Non-maleficence a guiding principle for professionals to act without malice in order to do no harm.

Non-verbal communication communication that includes such things as facial expressions, breathing patterns like sighing, gestures, movement, and posture.

Nurturing environment the environment composed of family, friends, and close associates at school or work.

Observing noticing all the behaviors that accompany communication.

Open-ended questions questions that are broad and require more than one or two word answers.

Open family system a system characterized by the willingness to assimilate new information and to engage in ongoing interactions with their environment.

Partializing a skill that involves breaking a complex problem into manageable parts.

People first language a form of politically correct linguistic prescriptivism aiming to avoid perceived and subconscious dehumanization when discussing people with disabilities.

Personality a socially constructed idea that includes the qualities, traits, characteristics, and behavior patterns that distinguish each individual.

Person-environment fit assesses how well a person's (or group's) needs, goals, and rights mesh with the traits and functioning of the physical and social environment.

Personal constructs explanations of an event or series of events that eventually become the lens through which the individual sees the world.

Placebo effect a positive effect based on a person's belief in the intervention.

Pre-contemplation when a person denies the problem and/or lacks understanding that the behavior is problematic (the first transtheoretical stage of change).

Preparation stage clients are preparing to change by getting information about making changes, by taking small steps related to change, and by thinking about possible goals.

Protective factors factors found within the individual (spirituality, internal locus of control, sense of humor) and outside sources of support in the family and society.

Professional a person who has specialized training for a particular career and who acts in conscientious, appropriate ways in the workplace.

Professional identity the way a professional describes his or her role and area of expertise.

Race a group of people characterized by specific physical characteristics that differentiate them from other groups of people (Tseng, 2001).

Reflecting content a skill involving restating in your own words what a client has said.

Reflecting feelings a skill involving attuning to the client in order to understand how the client feels, and then communicating that understanding.

Reflecting feelings and content a skill involving attuning to the client to understand both what they are saying and how they are feeling, and then communicating that understanding.

Reflecting meaning a skill in which the practitioner expresses his/her understanding of the underlying meaning of what the client is discussing.

Religion the communal behaviors (prayer, fasting, celebration of certain holy days, etc.) that are the result of people of similar beliefs coming together to practice these beliefs in a shared setting, such as a church, synagogue, or mosque (Heyman, Buchanan, Marlowe, & Sealy, 2006; Hodge, 2005a).

Relapse the stage of change that involves going back to the problematic behavior, and not maintaining the goals.

Resilience the ability to overcome, recover from trauma, and thrive in the face of overwhelming life conditions or risk factors.

Relationship boundaries the limits set in relationships that may include legal and moral standards.

Respect practitioners express respect by affirming and appreciating clients without condoning their harmful behaviors, by acknowledging clients' strengths, and by communicating their regard for clients' thoughts, feelings, and abilities.

Restraining forces the disadvantages and costs involved with each action taken to fulfill the identified need including such things as limited time, money, and manpower.

Risk factors influences existing within and outside of an individual that can pose a significant threat to the healthy development of the individual.

Rolling with resistance a motivational interviewing strategy in which the practitioner expresses understanding the client's viewpoints or ambivalence about change and avoids arguments for change.

Scope of practice the identified activities that licensing boards and other organizations allow qualified professionals to engage in.

Seeking clarification a skill that involves using questions to invite clients to thoroughly explain their thoughts and feelings with more specific details.

Self-efficacy a person's belief in his/her ability to successfully handle or deal with a situation.

Sexual orientation the direction or directions of one's sexual, affectionate, or loving attraction on a continuum from only same-sex attraction to only opposite sex attraction.

Social cognitive theory the theory that considers the impact of environmental, personal, and behavioral factors on readiness to change.

Social constructivism a perspective that focuses on how relationships, language, and context influence an individual's or a group's interpretation of self, others, and the world.

Socioeconomic status the position in the social hierarchy that is attributed to individuals, families, and groups.

Spirituality an individual's relationship with God or any Ultimate Power (including nature, sacred texts, etc.) that influences his or her mission or purpose in life (Hodge, 2005a).

Strengths perspective a perspective that views all people as having strengths.

Summarizing a skill involving attuning to considerable information provided by the client and communicating understanding of all of this information.

Supervision the process of working with a more experienced professional who teaches, directs, oversees, and assists.

Sustaining environment an environment consisting of the people encountered in the wider community and broader society.

System a complex entity within which interactions are as important as the individuals. Any group of people can be a system as long as they have some relation to one another and are contained by a boundary or understanding of which people are part of the system.

Systems theory a theory takes into account the entire system with which an individual interacts.

Termination the point in time when there is no temptation to return to the problematic behavior (Roe, Dekel, Harel, Fennig, & Fennig, 2006).

Transgender refers to individuals who do not identify with or conform to the gender roles assigned to their sex.

Transsexual transgendered individuals who choose to change their body surgically and/or with hormones in order align their body with their gender.

Values preferred conceptions of people, preferred outcomes for people, and also preferred ways of dealing with people.

Warmth conveying caring and interest to clients through the practitioner's demeanor.

White privilege an institutionalized set of benefits granted to those who resemble the people in power in a culture's institutions (Kendall, 2001) where the majority of the population is Caucasian.

INDEX